Party Funding and Campaign Financing in International Perspective

Columbia-London Law Series

General Editors:

George A Bermann
Walter Gellhorn Professor of Law and Jean Monnet
Professor of European Union Law, Columbia Law School
and
Terence Daintith
Emeritus Professor of Law, University of London,
formerly Director, Institute of Advanced Legal Studies

Volume 1: Party Funding and Campaign Financing in International Perspective

Party Funding and Campaign Financing in International Perspective

Edited by

K D EWING AND SAMUEL ISSACHAROFF

·HART·
PUBLISHING

OXFORD AND PORTLAND, OREGON
2006

Published in North America (US and Canada) by
Hart Publishing
c/o International Specialized Book Services
5804 NE Hassalo Street
Portland, Oregon
97213-3644
USA

Hart Publishing, Salters Boatyard, Folly Bridge, Abingdon Rd,
Oxford, OX1 4LB
Telephone: +44 (0) 1865 245533 Fax: +44 (0) 1865 794882
email: mail@hartpub.co.uk
WEBSITE: http//:www.hartpub.co.uk

British Library Cataloguing in Publication Data
Data Available

ISBN 10: 1-84113-570-4 (hardback)
ISBN 13: 978-1-84113-570-0 (hardback)

Typeset by Compuscript Ltd, Shannon
Printed and bound in Great Britain by
TJ International Ltd, Padstow, Cornwall

Introduction to the Columbia-London Law Series

Several years ago we conceived the notion that the remarkable depth and range of the intellectual interests of our colleagues in the Columbia University School of Law and the law schools of the different colleges of the University of London might from time to time be applied collectively to address legal problems of common and pressing concern to both the United States and the United Kingdom. In furtherance of this idea, and in the spirit of close international professional collaboration between universities that the world in which we live requires—the Columbia University School of Law and the Institute of Advanced Legal Studies—(which provides research services and organisation across the UK and the University of London in particular)—embarked on a long-term programme of joint research workshops and publication. We are proud to present here, as the inaugural volume of the Columbia-London Law Series, the first published fruits of this initiative.

Our role as series editors has been to identify, in consultation with our respective colleagues, the most promising common legal themes, and to invite faculty from Columbia, and from the Law Schools of the colleges of the University of London to develop a research agenda and organise a joint workshop in which other leading American and British scholars (and indeed scholars from elsewhere) have been encouraged to participate. Each project is thus developed and guided jointly by leading specialists from Columbia and London respectively.

We are deeply indebted to the relevant institutions—Columbia Law School, the Institute of Advanced Legal Studies, and the Law Schools of the colleges of the University of London—for the intellectual and material support they have committed to this programme. Needless to add, we are also indebted to Richard Hart and Hart Publishing of Oxford for undertaking publication of the Columbia-London Law Series.

The subject of this initial volume and the underlying workshop—Election Law—was and is a natural for this style of collaboration. As debates surrounding the fairness, in both the United States and the United Kingdom—countries which present themselves as democratic models to other, more troubled parts of the world—the importance of the subject cannot be exaggerated. We are delighted to have been able to recruit, as leaders of this first project, two such distinguished specialists in the field as Professors Keith Ewing of King's College London and Sam Issacharoff of Columbia Law School. They have ensured that the Columbia-London Law Series has been appropriately launched in the spirit of joint study, reflection and problem-solving that is the impetus for the entire Series.

George A Bermann
Walter Gellhorn Professor of Law and Jean
Monnet Professor of European Union Law
Columbia University School of Law

Terence Daintith
Emeritus Professor of Law,
University of London; formerly Director,
Institute ofAdvanced Legal Studies

Preface

This volume emerges from a two-day workshop held in July 2002 at the Institute for Advanced Legal Studies (IALS) in the University of London. That workshop marked the inaugural effort of the joint undertaking between the IALS and Columbia Law School to explore the international dimensions of contemporary legal problems. This particular volume deals with the questions of party funding and campaign financing—issues of controversy in most parts of the world. They are also issues that have given rise to a range of different forms of intervention in response, these providing a fertile base for our deliberations. The topicality of the issues considered in this volume is reflected not only in the constant concerns about party funding and campaign financing; but also in the fact that since our meeting in July 2002, we have witnessed major decisions of the US Supreme Court and the Supreme Court of Canada, as well as an investigation and report by the Electoral Commission in the United Kingdom. Indeed, it was these impending court cases which led us to delay publishing this volume, and which explains the abnormally long gestation between conception and delivery of the manuscript. This undertaking simply would not have occurred, nor would this volume exist, without the painstaking efforts, support and encouragement of George Bermann of Columbia Law School and Terence Daintith of the IALS. Through their efforts we were able to draw two dozen scholars from three continents to begin our common undertaking. We were also able to draw representatives from the political parties in the United Kingdom: their contribution was particularly valued. As in all endeavours, expanding the scope of inquiry requires greater effort, but hopefully rewards with more ample results.

Samuel Issacharoff
K D Ewing
31 December 2004

Table of Contents

List of Contributors

Richard Briffault is Vice-Dean and Joseph P Chamberlain Professor of Legislation, Columbia Law School, New York.

Stephen Day is an Associate Professor of European Politics, in the Faculty of Economics, Oita University, Japan.

Akiko Ejima is a Professor at the Law School, Meiji University, Tokyo, Japan.

K D Ewing is Professor of Public Law at King's College London, England.

Colin Feasby is a practising lawyer with Osler, Hoskin & Harcourt LLP, Calgary, Alberta, Canada and JSD Candidate, Columbia University, New York.

Andrew Geddis is a Senior Lecturer, Faculty of Law, Otago University, Dunedin, New Zealand.

Navraj Singh Ghaleigh is a Lecturer in Public Law at the University of Edinburgh, Scotland.

Janet L Hiebert is a Professor in the Department of Political Studies, Queen's University, Kingston, Ontario, Canada.

Samuel Issacharoff is Harold R Medina Professor in Procedural Jurisprudence, Columbia Law School, New York.

Louis Massicotte is an Associate Professor of Political Science at the University of Montréal, Québec, Canada.

Graeme Orr is a Senior Lecturer in the Law School, Griffith University, Brisbane, Queensland, Australia.

Nathaniel Persily is an Assistant Professor of Law and Political Science, University of Pennsylvania Law School, Philadelphia.

Jacob Rowbottom is a Fellow of King's College, Cambridge, England.

Jo Shaw is Salvesen Professor of European Institutions at the University of Edinburgh, Scotland.

1

Introduction

KD EWING AND SAMUEL ISSACHAROFF

ELECTIONS ARE BY their nature a difficult undertaking. Partisans must be mobilised, ideas communicated, materials distributed, and often across ample territories under terrible constraints of time. Much political theory addresses the forms of democratic selection. We can learn much about presidential and parliamentary systems, or the tension between direct and representative democracy, or the conflicting virtues of proportional and districted or geographical systems of representation. We can learn as well of the importance of communicating ideas free from the repressive hand of the State and of the critical role of intermediary institutions, notably political parties, in making effective political speech. Yet there remains a critical shortcoming in the attention to democratic theory. All the undertakings necessary to bring democracy to life, certainly a most noble ambition of human society, turn indispensably on the most base of commodities: money. Representative democracy is the system of governance of mass societies, by their nature those that exist beyond the easy negotiation of the family discussion or a small town gathering. No matter how lofty the political ambition, democracy in mass societies requires resources. And not just resources in the abstract, but the ability to raise money and spend it to further political aims.

The Core Dilemmas

Turning our attention away from the higher planes of democratic theory and toward the institutional pathways by which political parties and political campaigns are funded illuminates two constant problems in all democratic societies. How are the central actors in the political arena supposed to gather the funds necessary to operate effectively on behalf of their chosen political ends? And, how may they spend money in furtherance of their political objectives? The aim of this volume is to explore these issues in the specific context of a number of national settings. We come to this undertaking sceptical of any easy one-size-fits-all solutions. By giving thick descriptive accounts of the struggles over political financing in discrete national debates, we aim to show that the financing questions cannot be addressed independently of the constitutional conventions of the country, the nature of the political parties in the country, and the means of access to publication and the media in any given nation. There are in fact a number of different factors that determine the form and content of the law relating to party funding and campaign financing in different countries.

Because of the intensity of debate on political financing in many countries, and because of the reflective glare of the frequent scandals that attach to money in politics, there is an easy tendency to focus narrowly from within a particular national setting and not recognise the range of international mechanisms that have developed. Even as great a political philosopher as John Rawls succumbed to viewing financing exclusively within the liberty framework of American debates and seeing government regulation of contributions as dependent on deeper philosophical attachments to liberty.[1] But surely the regulation of contributions must depend on the nature of political parties. It may be one matter in the United States, where the political parties do not have a mass institutional base, to restrict contributions from any particular source to a few thousand dollars, or even to prohibit union contributions to political parties altogether. But in a country with a Labour Party built upon the union structure, that same rule would be an invitation to state assault upon a central political actor. Similarly, the high role of constitutional oversight in the United States and Canada yields surprisingly divergent results in terms of whether contributions or expenditures may be curtailed.

Laissez Faire and Transparency

The national studies in this volume reveal a rich diversity in the approach to regulation. But regulation is one of only three options available to policy makers. The first is to leave political money alone by adopting—consciously or otherwise—a strategy of *laissez faire* and self regulation. But certainly in the jurisdictions examined in this volume—Australia, Canada, the European Union, Japan, New Zealand, Quebec, the United Kingdom and the United States—that is no longer seen to be an option. Laissez faire and self regulation may be the most desirable approach, but it is now the least viable. This is because laissez faire and self regulation can operate only when the political actors accept to be bound by a core set of values which place a premium on transparency, the avoidance of improper influence or dependence, and fair electoral competition. Although some systems operated a largely voluntary system for the best part of the twentieth century, it has largely broken down and is no longer seen to be acceptable in any major jurisdiction in the world. Paradoxically, the intensity of regulation in more recent years has coincided with the end of ideological politics in most western democracies. Parties and candidates are competing more aggressively to manage national political systems which in many cases have less control over national policy than

[1] J Rawls, *Political Liberalism* (New York, Columbia University Press, 1993).

perhaps at any time since the industrial revolution. The strategies of privatisation and deregulation pursued by all countries in an increasingly globalised world have nevertheless provided great opportunities for corporations and individuals seeking to benefit from the delegation of state service provision.

A step beyond laissez faire and self regulation is what might be referred to as *non-regulatory intervention*. This takes the form of intervention designed to require actors to disclose information about their finances. Specifically it may require information about donors and spending. As such transparency may have a number of objectives: it may be designed to prevent electoral corruption, reflecting the famous aphorism that sunlight is the best disinfectant. Experience shows, however, that there are areas of political giving and spending into which the sun does not shine without a great deal of help. A more realistic objective may be to equip voters with information about the interests and individuals backing a candidate or party, to help the voter have a clearer idea of the interests that the candidate or party is likely to identify with or support. But we should not overlook the ambition that transparency may help to moderate conduct by candidates and parties. Transparency may be said to be a hybrid between laissez faire and State regulation—a form of coercive laissez faire and self regulation—in the sense that it requires information to be placed in the public domain. Once in the public domain, the media, rival political groups, and ultimately the electors may choose how to use that information. By requiring transparency the State may indirectly compel the parties to adapt their practices to a standard of behaviour that has community approval. In this way political actors may be induced to moderate their behaviour for fear of adverse electoral consequences. The requirement of transparency may, however, require a State apparatus to ensure that reporting obligations are enforced: it may even involve the use of civil, electoral or criminal sanctions to enforce compliance.

Supply Side and Demand Side Options

Just as few countries now place their faith exclusively in laissez faire, so few countries place faith in transparency alone. The problem with transparency is that it reveals problems that then need to be addressed by *regulatory measures*. Most of the jurisdictions considered in this volume have moved some way beyond transparency, and have embraced one of a number of regulatory tools. But these regulatory tools essentially approach from one of two directions. The first is from the supply side by regulating the flow of money to the candidates and the political parties. This may be done by restricting the source of funding on the one hand and the amount of funding on the other. The aim here is to ensure that parties and candidates are not seen to be dependent on inappropriate sources of funding and not dependent on appropriate sources of funding to an inappropriate extent. Inappropriate sources of funding will vary. For some it may be legal as opposed to natural persons, for others it may be foreign governments, corporations or individuals, and for others still it may be government contractors or licencees—whether donations are induced by way of tollgating or kickbacks. An appropriate source of funding may become inappropriate if it places a party or candidate in a position of vulnerability to such an extent that it may compromise the obligation to promote a public rather than a personal private interest. But as already pointed out this is an option that is fraught with difficulty in some jurisdictions because of the nature and structure of their political parties.

The second regulatory approach is from the demand side with initiatives designed to reduce the need for unlimited sources of funding. This can be done in a number of ways. The most direct is to limit the amount that parties and candidates may lawfully spend in an election. If this route is chosen, it may be necessary also to limit the spending of third parties—such as corporations, trade unions and interest groups. This is an option which has been adopted by a number of countries which are dealt with in this volume, notably Canada and the United Kingdom. The model was pioneered in the United Kingdom in 1883 with spending limits by candidates and developed in Canada with the introduction of national campaign spending limits by the political parties. But this too is a tool fraught with difficulty, though for different reasons than those relating to contribution limits. If the latter are a threat to freedom of association, spending limits will be seen by others as a threat to freedom of expression and perhaps as a bar to the entry of new players on the political scene. Demand side steps may, however, also be taken indirectly by the use of State funding of various kinds to help the parties and candidates meet core needs of a wide and varied kind. State funding for these purposes may take various forms. The practice in many jurisdictions is to make funds available to the political parties to assist with their operational costs as well as their election costs. Indeed in the case of South Africa, this practice finds expression in the constitutional obligation that:

> To enhance multi-party democracy, national legislation must provide for the funding of political parties participating in national and provincial legislatures on an equitable and proportional basis.[2]

In other jurisdictions—such as US presidential elections—public money will be available to those candidates who agree to accept a voluntary ceiling on their campaign expenditure and who agree not to accept private donations for their campaigns.

Public or Private Funding?

The growing interest in State funding is in some respects very paradoxical. Although various forms of State aid can be identified from the early years of

[2] The Constitution of the Republic of South Africa, Article 235.

democratic government, the idea that political parties should be funded by the State is one associated with the north European social democracies which pioneered it in the 1950s and 1960s. This was a period of the expanding State, in terms of budgets and functions, and the idea was widely adopted in all continents of the world where elections in the liberal tradition take place. But the position is now very different, with the hollowing out of the State, which is now in retreat in many parts of the world. If not in retreat, its role is changing—now much less a provider and increasingly an enabler, if that. How paradoxical it is then that as the State is in retreat so the organisations managing that retreat should themselves seek its support. It is all the more paradoxical that the State is being asked to provide for organisations that are losing members and voters, with recent general elections in Canada and the United Kingdom producing the lowest turnouts since 1918. Is the State being asked to provide life support for organisations in terminal decline? Are taxpayers being conscripted to fund organisations which electors have chosen to desert? It is nevertheless an inescapable fact that in many countries the State is being asked to provide more and more of the resources of the candidates and parties, whether directly in the form of cash grants or indirectly in the form of aid in kind.

One compelling reason why the State may feel obliged to step in to fill the funding gap is simply that the alternative is worse. With a declining membership base and growing financial demands, political parties are easy prey for the rich and powerful for whom the political parties offer opportunities for greater wealth and power. Although there may be resentment about the taxpayer subsidising the political parties, given the alternative, is this not the least worst option? While there may be genuine concern about political parties becoming fossilised parts of the State apparatus, it may also be that political parties are changing throughout the world, and that we have transcended the mass membership party. The circle may be turning so that what we see in embryo is the recreation of what Duverger classified as elitist or traditional parties:

> These parties do not aim at recruiting the largest possible membership, but at enlisting the support of notable individuals: they are more concerned with quality than quantity. These prominent citizens are sought out either because of their prestige, which endows them with a certain moral influence, or because of their wealth, which enables them to underwrite the expenditures of election campaigns.[3]

One way of resolving these dilemmas is to use State funding strategically to encourage the parties to recruit members and engage people in the political process. But there is no country that has ensured that its parties are adequately funded as a result of tax breaks. By the same token electoral turnout at the last Canadian federal election suggests that money for votes may not be the recipe for a secure funding base.

[3] M Duverger, *Party Politics and Pressure Groups* (New York, Thomas Y Crowell, 1972).

Shaping Regulatory Choices

As already indicated, in this study we have contributions from Australia, Canada (including a separate contribution from Quebec), Japan, New Zealand, the United Kingdom, and the United States, as well as the European Union. A striking feature of all of these systems is that none has chosen the path of laissez faire completely, and all have felt impelled to regulate and legislate. However, this is not to exaggerate the nature and scale of regulation in some countries at least: some countries (such as New Zealand) are distinguished as 'light touch', some countries (such as Australia) as 'stalled', some countries (such as the United Kingdom) as 'big bang', some countries (such as the United States and Japan) as 'gradualist', and others still (such as Canada and Quebec) as 'saturated', such being the nature and extent of regulation. Although there is some evidence of regulatory stalling in Australia, the national studies reveal generally that regulation is a dynamic and continuing process. Regulation creates an appetite for more regulation, with the appetite appearing near insatiable. Our study reveals that there is no escape in modern democracies from the regulator's embrace, which offers a number of seductions. The real issue which tests our understanding is thus, not why countries regulate political money but why regulation takes the form that it does in different countries and jurisdictions? What are the factors that explain the rich diversity of regulatory approach that we encounter in the chapters that follow?

From the material in the chapters that follow, we tentatively suggest that the choice of regulatory method will depend on a number of factors, not least the history and political tradition of the jurisdiction in question. It is important to emphasise that these are influential not determinative factors and also that the nature of the influence and its weight may vary from country to country. Among the more important factors are the following:

- Geographical: the size of the country, in terms of its area and population. Larger jurisdictions are likely to generate more political money, and present greater regulatory challenges.
- Historical: the legacy of political development and the consequences of earlier regulatory initiatives and regulatory failures. In truth most systems have evolved and bear the legacies of their pasts.
- Financial: the distribution of money and wealth, and the way in which the monied classes seek to secure political influence, including the way in which they seek to influence political parties and candidates.
- Sociological: the distribution of scarce resources—such as media of communication—needed for electoral purposes, which may invite some intervention to ensure fair access and to avoid abuse.
- Constitutional: the nature of constitution (written or unwritten), the contents of the constitution, and the distribution of legally sovereign power under the constitution—who is the guardian of the constitution?

- Judicial: the role of the courts to restrain or influence the content of regulation, the values developed by the courts, and the willingness of the courts to constrain the autonomy of the rule makers.
- Ideological: the weight attached in a particular jurisdiction to the sometimes conflicting values of political liberty and political equality. Where is the ideological centre of gravity in the event of conflict?
- Structural: the nature of the political system, whether it be a parliamentary democracy or one based upon a strict separation of powers, and the nature of the electoral system, whether it be proportional representation or first past the post.
- Organisational: the nature of the party system and the composition, organisation and structure of political parties. Are parties direct parties of individuals or indirect parties of other organisations, or both?
- Political: the nature of the problems that arise—although they may be common across different systems, the symptoms may vary and the regulators may be responding to different variants on common themes.

The Importance of Supervision and Enforcement

Although these different factors may help to determine regulatory outcomes, it is clear that they operate in different ways to produce different solutions in different jurisdictions. But apart from regulatory methods, also important is regulatory effectiveness. It is one thing to regulate, but something else to ensure that regulation is effective. The key to effectiveness is supervision and enforcement, a matter which is also addressed in radically different ways in different jurisdictions, again reflecting different constitutional and political traditions. Most regulatory systems addressed in this volume have established a separate supervisory body such as the Australian Electoral Commission or the Federal Election Commission in the United States. But the composition and powers of these bodies vary enormously. The main difference is between the American approach of a weak bi partisan agency with limited function and the broader ranging Australian, British and Canadian approach based on the principle of an independent and non partisan agency. It may be argued that in some respects the principle of a bi partisan agency is a hangover from a laissez faire regime, with the operation of the rules being left to the parties themselves to determine. It is a form of self regulation of the enforcement regime if not self-regulation of the substance of the regime.

But it is not only the composition of regulatory agencies that is important. So too are their powers and the sanctions which the law provides for the violation of regulatory standards. The need for powers will depend to a large extent on function and the nature of the regulation the agency has been created to supervise. A body established in part to administer public funds will need fewer powers than a body whose duties include ensuring that campaign spending limits have not been violated. Here we encounter a real irony in the sense that effective regulation of party funding and campaign financing depends on the initiative of elected officials to create and empower an autonomous institutional structure to supervise and investigate the very people who have created the scheme. The sceptic might well question the likelihood of such a step being taken, and it is clear that not all systems have risen to the challenge. Certainly there are temptations for elected officials to mould finance rules to cushion themselves from challenge, both financially and electorally. It is also clear that an agency with powers over elected officials running for office is likely only to be created at a time of political crisis or as a result of powerful external pressure, and that it will require cross-party support to implement. General appeals to fair electoral competition and the need to constrain the appearance of improper influence are unlikely to be effective. But even then the obstacles to efficiency may be considerable, with constitutional constraints in some countries preventing the adoption of the remarkable powers of the Electoral Commission in the United Kingdom, which at least formally exceed those of the police investigating a murder.

The Regulatory Trajectory

The underlying theme uniting this book is the idea of a regulatory trajectory. We set up three different models of party funding and campaign financing, the effectiveness of each being considered by the authors of the different national studies. It is important to emphasise that our categories are not watertight, and that there is considerable leakage between them. Our judgments are therefore relative: relative to Canada or the United Kingdom, New Zealand has a system of laissez faire, though not a system wholly without regulation; relative to Australia, Japan or Quebec, the United Kingdom has a system of private funding; and relative to the United States (with the possible exception of presidential elections and a few States), these three jurisdictions have moved to varying degrees in the direction of public funding for political parties or election campaigns, as indeed most recently has Canada. But in developing this trajectory from laissez faire or self regulation, to the regulation of private funding, and to the growing role of the State in the funding of parties, we anticipate the possibility that obstacles will be encountered. These have arisen most spectacularly in the United States, where the Supreme Court gutted a major part of the campaign finance legislation of the 1970s made in the aftermath of the Watergate scandal. Problems have been encountered in the courts in Australia and Canada where *Buckley v Valeo*[4] was initially persuasive. But as already pointed out the Canadians have broken free with the result that spending limits remain part and parcel of the Canadian regulatory model, which is now the most highly developed of all the systems considered here.

[4] 424 US 1 (1976).

In developing our regulatory trajectory, we begin with what is currently the most primitive regulatory model, which is that now found in New Zealand, also the smallest jurisdiction dealt with. Here the regulatory load is carried mainly by imperfect transparency rules, though there are control mechanisms in place which help indirectly to contain the costs of campaigning. From New Zealand we move to a form of intense direct regulation of a largely private funding system, namely the United Kingdom where 'big bang', reforms saw the introduction of a number of controls on donations, as well as party spending. It was thus an attempt to address the problem with both supply side (by controlling donations) and demand side initiatives (by controlling spending). But as we will also see, a conscious gap in the regulatory framework (no contribution cap) has been ruthlessly exploited by the party that authored the legislation, highlighting the failure of the legislation to deal with the problem that led to its introduction. From the United Kingdom, we move to three systems that have adopted various forms of public funding, these being Australia, Japan, and Quebec, all hybrid public/private systems. The nature of the support varies from system to system, as does the extent to which it operates in conjunction with different forms of regulation. But in all cases—and to varying degrees—they provide examples of State intervention to relieve the financial pressure on the parties. This takes the form of election funding (Australia), annual cash subventions (Japan) and large scale funding of annual running costs and election campaigns (Quebec).

Of considerable interest are the countries in which strong constitutional oversight frames the forms of regulatory intervention. The key example is no doubt the United States, where the analytic divide between the expressive interests in expenditures and the regulatory interest in controlling contributions rose to constitutional prominence in *Buckley v Valeo*. While the *Buckley v Valeo* divide largely framed the issue for constitutional debate in the United States, constitutional issues were slower to evolve in Canada which approached regulation with greater emphasis on the need to regulate expenditures rather than contributions. But with the adoption of the Charter of Rights and Freedoms in Canada, these constitutional concerns have assumed a prominence in that jurisdiction as well, with considerable problems encountered not by spending limits generally but by third-party spending limits particularly. We focus several chapters on the United States and Canada precisely because their constitutionally-based regulatory models are in a process of swift overhaul. In Canada, the most recent decision of the Supreme Court in *Harper v Canada*[5] found in the Charter a commitment to political equality that allowed government regulation aimed at levelling the political playing field. In the United States, the Supreme Court upheld most of the newly minted Bipartisan Campaign Reform Act of 2002 on an expansive view that campaigns may be regulated to thwart not just corruption, but a weakly defined public perception of the corruption of politics by wealth. The likely effect of both *Harper v Canada* and the American *McConnell v FEC*[6] is to move the regimes of strong constitutional oversight more closely onto the regulatory trajectory as well.

[5] [2004] SCC 33.

[6] McConnell v Federal Election Commission, 540 US 93 (2003).

Conclusion

We do not attempt to catalogue the rules governing party funding and campaign finance in all countries in the world. Rather we focus on extended analytic assessments of these divergent regulatory regimes. We intend to show the range of regulatory possibilities and the surprisingly high level of discontent with each. The regulatory regimes may be distinct, but they seem, per Tolstoy, each to be unhappy in its own unique way.

Part I

'Light Touch' Regulation and its Discontents

2

The Regulation of Campaign Funding in New Zealand: Practices, Problems and Prospects for Change

ANDREW GEDDIS*

Introduction

THE REGULATION OF campaign funding has proven a less fraught topic in New Zealand than in many other jurisdictions. This fact largely is attributable to a more general truth; election campaigns in New Zealand remain comparatively cheap events. The country's Electoral Commission reports, for example, that political parties and individual candidates declared spending a total of $10,123,977 on the 2002 general election campaign. A little over two million ballots were cast in that election, meaning that about NZ$5 (then equivalent to US$3) was spent by the primary electoral contestants for every voter who participated. While comparisons are complicated by the different time periods and types of expenses covered by disclosure rules in particular countries, this figure appears lower than the amounts spent on campaigning in many other developed Western democracies.

A number of structural factors might explain why spending on New Zealand's election campaigns has not risen to the levels experienced elsewhere. Its relatively sparse population reduces the amount of money required for electoral contestants to communicate with the voters, and may help foster a more direct, less cost-intensive style of campaigning. Equally, the smaller size of the country's economy not only means there are fewer resources available to fund election campaigns, but also lessens the incentive for large-scale spending aimed at achieving electoral victory by reducing the potential 'rent seeking' rewards for gaining public power. Government decision-makers are also easily accessed, diminishing the need to try to 'buy' access through campaign donations. Finally, election campaigns are

* My thanks to Amy Annan for her invaluable research help. Elements of this chapter have previously appeared in A Geddis, 'Regulating the Funding of Election Campaigns in New Zealand: A Critical Overview' (2004) 10 *Otago Law Review* 575.

short—lasting a matter of weeks rather than months—and occur with comparative frequency due to a triennial election cycle.

Alongside these structural features, the Electoral Act 1993 explicitly seeks to restrict election expenditures by candidates and political parties through imposing a fixed spending cap on their campaigns. Furthermore, strict restrictions on using the broadcast media for political advertising limit the electoral participants' spending on this most expensive means of communicating with voters. This regulatory approach has as its primary focus the creation of a relatively level playing-field amongst electoral participants. New Zealand has therefore chosen to respond to the concern that disparities in economic power may undermine the presumptive equality of participants in its democratic processes by attempting to restrict the electoral contestants' demand for money, rather than by seeking to control the supply of funds to the electoral contestants via limits on the donations that they may receive. This regulatory choice helps contain the overall influence of campaign spending in New Zealand by preventing the kind of 'arms race' in electoral expenditures observed in countries without such limits.

Aside from these general structural and regulatory factors, another reason why the issue of campaign funding has provoked relatively little discussion in New Zealand is the subsidiary role played by the judiciary when viewed alongside such countries as Australia,[1] Canada,[2] and the USA.[3] The absence of a written constitution, and especially of an entrenched Bill of Rights, means New Zealand's courts have no constitutional, or 'higher law', power to review the impact of campaign funding regulation on individual rights.[4] Therefore, decisions about how to regulate the funding of elections remain the sole preserve of Parliament,[5] meaning that the country has escaped the confusion that arises when the legislature and courts disagree over whether some regulatory measure is constitutionally permissible.

However, notwithstanding the above comments, it is inconceivable that any democracy could remain *completely* untroubled by the role that money ought to play in its electoral processes.[6] Despite the relative quietude of New Zealand's experience, the issue of campaign funding has arisen in a number of different ways. In particular, the adoption in the mid-1990s of a Mixed Member Proportional (MMP) voting system forced a reconsideration of how campaign funding ought to be regulated in this new electoral environment. This move to MMP is discussed below,[7] so for now

[1] See eg, *Australia Capital Television v Commonwealth* (1992) 177 CLR 166.

[2] See eg, *Libman v Quebec* [1997] 151 DLR (4th) 385; *Figueroa v Canada (A–G)* [2003] 1 SCR 912; *Harper v Canada (A–G)* [2004] SCC 33.

[3] See eg, *Buckley v Valeo* 424 US 1 (1976); *Nixon v Shrink Missouri Government PAC* 528 US 377 (2000); *McConnell v FEC* 124 SCt 619 (2003).

[4] New Zealand Bill of Rights Act 1990, s 4.

[5] This is not to say that the courts have played *no* role in shaping New Zealand's electoral process; see J Boston *et al*, 'Courting Change: The Role of the Judiciary in Altering and Electoral System' (1997) 8 *Public Law Review* 229.

[6] See A Geddis, 'Three Conceptions of the Electoral Moment' (2003) 27 *Australian Journal of Legal Philosophy* 53.

[7] See below nn 17–22 and accompanying text. See also A Geddis, 'Gang Aft A-Gley: New Zealand's Attempt to Combat "Party Hopping" By Elected Representatives' (2002) 1 *Election Law Journal* 557, 559–61.

it is sufficient to note that reform of the voting system ushered in a general change in New Zealand's electoral processes. Prior to this watershed event, New Zealand's electoral system (and the laws governing it) continued to display the imprint of the nation's colonial heritage. The system of electoral representation used in the United Kingdom was adopted wholesale when local representation was first introduced in 1852,[8] and even after New Zealand gained full political independence in 1947,[9] its regulatory approach to most electoral issues (including that of campaign funding) continued to closely mirror that country's system. Debate about the appropriateness of this situation gained traction in 1986, when a Royal Commission on the Electoral Process reported on the issue.[10] Another decade then passed before the adoption of MMP fully moved New Zealand's electoral processes out of the United Kingdom's shadow, and gave the country its own 'home-grown' form of representation.

This chapter examines the main features of New Zealand's system of government and campaign funding regulation. It then considers in greater depth some particular problems with this system that have come to the fore in recent years, and critically evaluates a number of proposals that have been made to deal with these problems.

New Zealand's System of Government and Campaign Funding Regulation

Before turning to look in detail at how New Zealand's legal system regulates campaign funding, a quick summary of its system of governance and its electoral processes may prove useful for the uninitiated. New Zealand has a Westminster style government, with a unicameral Parliament (the House of Representatives) consisting of 120 members. Of these, 69 are directly elected from individual constituencies, while 51 are selected from political party lists according to the MMP voting system, in the manner outlined below. A general parliamentary election must be held at least every three years, but may be held earlier if the current government so chooses. The members of the party—or, as has proven to be the case since the introduction of MMP, the members of the coalition of parties—that control a majority of the parliamentary seats following such an election then form the government (or executive).

With this background sketch of New Zealand's processes of representative government in place, this section first reviews the general restrictions on electoral spending in New Zealand designed to prevent the overt corruption of the political process. It then examines restrictions placed on the campaign spending of the political parties, individual candidates, and 'third parties' who may wish to be involved in the electoral process. Finally, this section considers the special restrictions placed on the use of the broadcasting media for electoral purposes.

[8] New Zealand Constitution Act 1852 (Imp).
[9] Statute of Westminster Adoption Act 1947 (NZ).
[10] Report of the Royal Commission on the Electoral System, *Towards A Better Democracy* (December, 1986) 5–6, para 1.6–1.7 (hereafter RCES).

General Restrictions on Electoral Spending

Since the passage of the Corrupt Practices Prevention Act 1881, various forms of electoral spending—such as bribing or 'treating' voters—have been prohibited so as to preserve the integrity of the electoral process. These offences still exist, and it is a 'corrupt practice' for anyone to 'buy' votes directly from electors through bribery,[11] or to pay for 'food, drink, entertainment or provision' for the purpose of swaying an elector's vote.[12] It is also an 'illegal practice' knowingly to provide money 'for any purpose which is contrary to the provisions of [the Electoral Act 1993].'[13] In addition, a rather odd prohibition on paying an elector to exhibit an election notice on their house or land remains on the statute books,[14] the rationale for which is unclear. However, these provisions are rarely invoked,[15] reflecting the overall fact that New Zealand appears to be relatively free of overt corruption, both in its electoral system and its general processes of governance.[16]

Regulation of the Funding of Political Party Campaigns

Right up until the 1990s, virtually no restrictions existed with regards to the funding of, or spending on, a political party's election campaign. This laissez faire attitude towards the electoral activities of political parties was the product of two interlinked, but progressively illusory, assumptions. The first was that the individual candidate, rather than the political party he or she represented, was the primary campaigner in the electoral contest. Consequently, political parties were treated as private unincorporated associations which only incidentally involved themselves in the public political life of the community.[17] There was no requirement for them to register, or to file public accounts; and few legal controls were placed on the parties' financial activities.

This approach became increasingly untenable as nationwide political parties developed into the primary actors on the political stage. By the time that the Royal Commission on the Electoral System issued its wide-ranging report in 1986, it was able confidently to state that:

> It is the political parties inside and outside Parliament that in reality present the electorate with a choice of Government. They provide the candidates and prepare the policies between which the voters choose. . . . All these changes mean that the

[11] Electoral Act 1993, s 216.
[12] *Ibid* s 217.
[13] *Ibid* s 220.
[14] *Ibid* s 219.
[15] The last case in which bribery of a voter was alleged was the *Bay of Islands Election Petition* (1915) 34 New Zealand LR 578.
[16] Transparency International's Corruption Perceptions Index 2004 ranks New Zealand the third-equal least corrupt country of all those surveyed; see <http://www.transparency.org/cpi/2004/cpi 2004.en.html#cpi2004>.
[17] *Peters v Collinge* [1993] 2 New Zealand LR 554, 575. See also M Wilson, 'Political Parties and Participation' in A Simpson (ed), *The Constitutional Implications of MMP* (Wellington, VUW Press, 1998) 169.

> principal purpose of elections is now in fact to enable the people to decide in accordance with the electoral law which of the competing political parties will provide the Government.[18]

Building on this acknowledgement of the political parties' central role in the electoral system, the Royal Commission recommended the adoption of the MMP voting system, based on the (then) West German model.[19] Under MMP, each voter has two votes: one for a local constituency candidate; the other for the voter's preferred political party. However, the latter 'Party Vote' is crucial, as the overall composition of Parliament is (in the final analysis) determined by the share of the Party Vote received by each political party *qua* political party.[20] The Royal Commission's recommendation thus represented a conscious decision to institutionalise the political parties' role as the primary vehicles through which the public's representatives are selected.[21]

The Royal Commission's recommendations were endorsed by the public through a referendum held in 1993.[22] This vote in favour of MMP led to the enactment of the Electoral Act 1993, which in turn requires political parties wishing to contest the Party Vote to register with a newly created Electoral Commission.[23] In 1995, amendments to the Electoral Act 1993 made three further important changes to the regulatory framework governing political parties. First, a cap was placed on how much a registered political party can spend on advertising at an election. Second, each registered political party was required to make a public return setting out its expenditure on the election contest. Finally, the disclosure of the identity of some (but as shall be seen, not all) sizeable donors to each political party was mandated. These reforms enacted recommendations made by the Royal Commission, on the grounds that 'if elections are to be fair and our democracy is to prosper, it is important that the effects of [economic] inequalities are minimised.'[24]

The 1995 measures continue to govern the funding of the political parties' election campaigns. Under them, the total 'election expenses' of a registered political party are limited to $1 million, plus an additional $20,000 for each individual constituency seat contested.[25] The definition of election expenses incorporates any expenditure made on an 'election activity'-defined as all advertising of any kind, radio or television broadcasting, or published material, which encourages (or appears to encourage) voters to vote for the party (or not to vote for any other

[18] RCES, n 10 at 6.

[19] RCES, n 10 at 63–4.

[20] The New Zealand Electoral Commission provides a description of how MMP operates at <http://www.elections.govt.nz/elections/esyst/govt_elect.html>. See also G Palmer and M Palmer, *Bridled Power: New Zealand Government Under MMP* (Auckland, Oxford University Press, 2004 (4th ed)) 22–38.

[21] RCES, n 10 at 61–2.

[22] See generally, K Jackson and A McRobie *New Zealand Adopts Proportional Representation* (Aldershot, Ashgate Publishing, 1998).

[23] Electoral Act 1993, s 62(1). In order to register, a political party must show it has at least 500 current financial members, and state that it intends contesting future elections; *Ibid*, ss 63, 71A.

[24] RCES, n 10 at 190.

[25] Electoral Act 1993, s 214B(2)(a).

party).[26] The activity must occur in the three months preceding an election, although if the activity is paid for outside of these three months, it still falls within the spending limits.[27] In theory, therefore, a political party contesting all 69 electorates is restricted to spending a maximum of $2.38 million on advertising its campaign in the three month period leading up to polling day. However, there are no restrictions on how much a party can spend on advertising outside of this three month pre-election period. The limits also exclude spending on travel or conducting opinion polls within the three months.[28] What is more, the cost of activities such as convening focus groups to test reactions to policy positions, or hiring campaign consultants, will also fall outside this limit so long as these activities are kept separate from the development or conduct of the party's advertising campaign.

Following an election, the secretary of each registered political party is required to file a return of the party's election expenses with the Electoral Commission.[29] Although the Electoral Act 1993 does not specify the form this return must take, the Court of Appeal has ruled that the Electoral Commission can require parties to provide a breakdown of their election expenses in terms of the various areas in which these are made.[30] Thus, a registered party must publicly reveal how much it has spent on each of the following categories: advertising; broadcasting; and general publication of notices, posters, billboards, etc. In addition, it must list each of the persons to whom payment was made in respect of each of these categories, as well as how much was paid to them. This return must also be accompanied by an independent auditor's report, stating whether (in the auditor's opinion) the party's return is an accurate reflection of the actual expenses incurred.[31]

Political parties are also required to disclose the identity of some of the donors who fund their activities. The secretary of a registered party is required to make an annual return to the Electoral Commission listing every donation received by a person or body involved with the administration of the party's affairs that by itself, or in the aggregate, exceeds $10,000.[32] The return must include the total value of any such donation and, where the identity of the donor is known, the name and address of the donor.[33] However, where the donor's identity is not known to any candidate of the party, or any person involved with the administration of the party,[34] the contribution need only be listed as coming from an anonymous source.[35] The party's auditor must also submit a report on the party's annual return.[36]

[26] *Ibid* s 214B(1). The definition excludes spending on advertising which relates exclusively to the election of any of the party's individual candidates, *Ibid.*
[27] Electoral Act 1993, s 214B(1) (definition of 'election activity').
[28] *Ibid* s 214B(1)(e) (definition of 'election expense').
[29] Electoral Act 1993, s 214C(1).
[30] *Electoral Commission v Tate* [1999] 3 New Zealand LR 174.
[31] Electoral Act 1993, s 214C(1).
[32] *Ibid,* ss 214G(1) 214F.
[33] *Ibid,* s 214G(1)(a)(i).
[34] *Ibid,* s 3(1) (definition of 'anonymous'); see below nn 79–82 and accompanying text.
[35] Electoral Act 1993, s 214G(1)(a)(ii).
[36] *Ibid* s 214H(1) and (2).

The shortcomings of these disclosure provisions are discussed in the following section. But aside from problems with this aspect of the controls on party fund raising, the rules governing party spending only place an as yet theoretical limit on the political parties' activities, for no party has ever reported expending the full amount allowed under the legislation.[37] Therefore, the $2.38 million cap on election expenses is apparently more than any party is able to raise to pay for its campaign—or, at the very least, has chosen to spend on its campaign. Here the structural constraints on campaign spending in New Zealand, discussed in the introduction to this chapter, seem relevant. Because New Zealand is not a 'high cost' campaigning environment, parties are able to gain electoral success without necessarily having to spend excessive amounts of money.[38] In turn, this may somewhat reduce the perceived need for parties to try to raise and spend sums in excess of the amount mandated by the Electoral Act 1993.

Regulation of the Funding of Individual Candidate Campaigns

In contrast to the relaxed attitude historically displayed toward political parties, controls on the campaign funding of individual candidates have existed since 1895. In that year, limits were placed on the amount candidates could spend on seeking election, and they also were required to file a post-election return setting out these election expenditures, as well as the sources of their funding.[39] These restrictions have remained in place throughout New Zealand's subsequent electoral history, and have been carried over into the Election Act 1993.[40]

A candidate may incur no more than $20,000 in 'election expenses', defined as expenses incurred by or on behalf of a candidate for an 'election activity'. In relation to an individual candidate, an 'election activity' is defined as any kind of advertising, any radio or television broadcasting, or any publication or distribution of any notice, poster, or billboard, which is carried out by the candidate's campaign.[41] In addition, the activity must relate solely to the candidate in his or her capacity as a candidate, must relate exclusively to his or her campaign, and must take place in the three months before the election is held.[42] Therefore, as with the political parties, the Electoral Act 1993 restricts only the amount a candidate may spend on advertising his or her candidacy during the three months preceding an election.[43]

[37] The most spent by any registered party in the 2002 general election campaign was $1.6 million.

[38] For example, the National Party's declared spending at the 1999 election was almost twice as great as was the Labour Party's, yet Labour out-polled National by 38.74 per cent to 30.50 per cent. Similarly, the ACT Party spent more than five times as much on its campaign in 2002 than did the New Zealand First Party, only for the latter to receive 10.4% of the vote to ACT's 7.1%, Electoral Commission, *New Zealand Electoral Compendium*, (2nd ed, 2000).

[39] See Corrupt Practices Prevention Amendment Act 1895, ss 8, 12.

[40] Electoral Act 1993, s 213(1).

[41] *Ibid* (definition of 'election activity').

[42] *Ibid.*

[43] As with the political parties, the definition of 'election expense' is in terms of when the 'election activity' occurs, not when the payment for it is made. See Electoral Act 1993, s 213(1)(b). An amendment to the Electoral Act in 2002 has also slightly broadened the definition to include spending by a candidate on 'negative' or 'attack' advertising aimed against a rival candidate. See, *ibid,* s 213(1)(c)(ii).

However, by contrast with the provisions governing political party spending, the limits only apply to expenditures on advertising which 'relates exclusively' to the election campaign, rather than to all advertising which broadly 'encourages' voters to vote in a particular way.[44]

The requirement that spending 'relate exclusively to the campaign for the return of the candidate' before qualifying as an 'election expenditure' has provoked some confusion.[45] The Electoral Act 1993 tries to clarify the issue by apportioning election expenses incurred on election activity relating to the campaigns of two or more candidates between all of the candidates concerned.[46] However, the status of activities which have the effect of both encouraging voters to vote for a candidate, and which also serve some other purpose—such as promoting an issue in a referendum held concurrently with an election—is still unclear. There is some suggestion from the courts that the portion of the spending connected with advertising the candidate's campaign ought to be counted as an election expenditure,[47] but this conclusion is necessarily speculative as the issue has yet to be addressed head on.

The uncertainty over the sorts of spending that constitute an 'election expense' also affects the requirement that candidates file a post-election return listing their election expenses.[48] Because it is often debatable how some spending on a particular activity should be characterised, candidates have room to be somewhat creative in the returns that they file so as to ensure that their reported spending falls beneath the $20,000 maximum. Candidates are also required to list in this post-election return any 'election donations' that they may have received.[49] An election donation is defined as any donation, or series of donations, made to the candidate's campaign that in the aggregate exceeds $1,000.[50] Where the identity of the source of an election donation is known, the return must list the name and address of the donor, as well as the amount donated.[51] However, where this information is not known by the candidate, the amount of the election donation need only be listed as an 'anonymous donation'.[52]

While gaps undoubtedly exist in the controls that apply to candidate spending, overall the rules have worked to restrain candidate spending. The limited amount of such spending in New Zealand is also attributable to the fact that candidate advertising does not really have that great an impact on the election outcome. Most voters endorse an individual candidate based on his or her party affiliation, so the campaign spending by political parties has long been of greater importance in the electoral race. The centrality of the party vote under MMP merely cements

[44] Compare the provisions for political parties, above n 26.
[45] See *Re Wairarapa Election Petition* [1988] 2 New Zealand LR 74, 107–9.
[46] Electoral Act 1993, s 214(1) and (2).
[47] See *Re Wairarapa Election Petition* [1988] 2 New Zealand LR 74, 108.
[48] Electoral Act 1993, s 210(1).
[49] *Ibid*, s 210(1)(b), s 210(9).
[50] *Ibid*, s 210(9)(a).
[51] *Ibid*, s 210(1)(b).
[52] *Ibid*, s 210(1)(c).

this fact into place. Also, while determined candidates can (and sometimes undoubtedly do) exceed the $20,000 limit on their election expenses, they run a real risk if caught. Any candidate found to have knowingly exceeded the spending limit on his or her campaign commits a 'corrupt practice',[53] which carries a punishment of up to one year in prison. In addition, committing a corrupt practice automatically enters the malefactor into the 'corrupt practices list',[54] disqualifying him or her from voting or holding public office for three years.[55] This is a heavy sanction, and makes candidates cautious about too obviously flouting the rules.

Regulation of Campaign Spending by 'Third Parties'

In addition to individual candidates and political parties, any developed democratic system also contains a plethora of 'third parties' with an interest in the outcome of the election, who want to take some part in the campaign battle.[56] Participation of such third parties in New Zealand's electoral processes is regulated by sections 221 and 221A of the Electoral Act 1993. Section 221 prohibits the publication of any advertisement which 'is used or appears to be used to promote or procure the election of a constituency candidate',[57] or 'encourages or persuades or appears to encourage or persuade voters to vote for a party',[58] unless it is authorised in writing by the candidate or party concerned, and contains a statement setting out the 'true name' and address of the person for whom, or at whose direction, it is published.[59] Section 221A covers any advertisement 'relating to an election.' The publication of the latter type of advertisement also requires a statement identifying the 'true name' of the person for whom, or at whose direction, it is published[60]; but unlike advertisements advocating support for a particular candidate or party, it does not require any formal authorisation.

Section 221 prevents third parties from undertaking unilaterally any advertising which has the effect of advocating support for a particular primary participant contesting the election. It also limits such third party spending, even if the way in which it does so is not immediately apparent. Because the definition of a candidate or political party's 'election expenses' covers activities carried out with the party or candidate's authority, the authorisation of a third party's expenditure by a primary participant causes that spending to become a part of the participant's election expenses. Third party advertising which advocates support for a candidate or party can therefore never extend, at least in theory, beyond the expenditure limits imposed on the primary participants in the electoral contest.

[53] *Ibid*, s 213(3)(a).

[54] *Ibid*, s 100.

[55] *Ibid*, s 80(e). This was the fate of the Labour Party MP, Reg Boorman, following the case of *Re Wairarapa Election Petition* [1988] 2 New Zealand LR 74.

[56] See A Geddis, 'Democratic Visions and Third-Party Independent Expenditures' (2001) 9 *Tulane Journal of International and Comparative Law* 5, 22.

[57] Electoral Act 1993, s 221(1)(a).

[58] *Ibid*, s 221(1)(b).

[59] *Ibid*, s 221(2)(a) and (b).

[60] *Ibid*, s 221A(1).

This authorisation requirement effectively precludes third parties from running 'parallel campaigns' promoting candidates and parties they wish to see in office. However, authorisation is only required where an advertisement is 'used to promote or procure the election of a constituency candidate', or 'encourages or persuades or appears to encourage or persuade voters to vote for a party'. Clearly, advertisements which 'expressly advocate' the election of a particular candidate or party—by saying something like 'Vote for X'—fall within these terms. However, beyond easy cases such as these, it is very difficult to define in advance the kind of message that will 'appear[] to encourage or persuade' voters to support some party. In particular, the status of 'issue advocacy' advertisements, which do not refer specifically to any candidate or party but rather promote a position in respect of a public policy issue which also features in some primary participant's election campaign, is problematic.[61] Section 221 is generally regarded as excluding such communications from its ambit, which obviously leaves a wide loophole in the limits on third party spending. Any third party wishing to influence an election can evade the restrictions imposed by section 221 simply by casting its message in terms of the 'issues' involved, rather than directly exhorting voters to vote for a particular party or candidate.

However, such advertising will still fall under the ambit of section 221A. This provision was enacted in 1995 following a recommendation by Parliament's Electoral Law Committee that 'negative' advertising—advertising which attacks rather than promotes a party or candidate—should be regulated.[62] Previously, it was assumed that as negative advertising fell outside section 221, it could be published anonymously.[63] Given this lacunae in the law, the Committee was concerned that voters should be able to evaluate the credibility of such advertisements in light of who is paying for them. The Committee also recognised the problems involved in requiring those wishing to advertise against a candidate or party to gain the consent of all competing participants, not to mention the difficulty in apportioning the costs between them. It also considered a less burdensome procedure in respect of negative advertising would help compensate for the limits that section 221 placed on expressive rights in respect of 'positive' express advocacy. The term 'relating to an election' was correspondingly enacted by section 221A to cover not only negative advertising, but also issue advocacy aimed at influencing an election.

Because third parties are under no obligation to disclose the amount spent on election related advertising, it is difficult to gauge just how much of this type of expenditure occurs during an election campaign. Certainly, each election has seen some advertising by third parties—in particular, employer and union groups—on issues that one or another political party has been closely aligned with, and which

[61] See generally, A Geddis, 'Confronting The "Problem" of Third Party Expenditures in United Kingdom Election Law' (2001) 27 *Brooklyn Journal of International Law* 103.

[62] Electoral Law Committee, *Inquiry into the 1993 General Election: Report of the Electoral Law Committee* (1994) AJHR I.21A.

[63] Compare *DPP v Luft* [1977] AC 962.

may therefore help to promote that party's election campaign. But that said, such spending has not appeared to have had any appreciable impact on any recent election result. This fact may also be due to the lack of any real controls on the making of donations to political parties, which allows third parties seeking to influence the electoral process to funnel direct financial aid to the parties, rather than having to spend their resources independently.

However, if this situation should change-for instance, were the donation process to be made more transparent (as is discussed in the next section)-the issue of third party spending might become more pressing. The loopholes in the limits on these types of expenditure (in particular, the failure of the limits to cover 'issue advocacy') means that, should some electoral participant wish to do so, it could completely evade the existing limits on campaign spending. That said, it is debatable whether the present veto granted to the political parties and individual candidates over advertising that appears to support their campaign can be justified. Requiring authorisation before advertising on behalf of a party or candidate, and then carving the cost of that advertising out of the party or candidate's own expenses, means that the form of the advertisement is likely to be largely dictated by the party or candidate. Therefore, the existing limits on third party spending are both too loose (in that they may be easily evaded in their entirety), and too rigid (in that, where they do apply, they give the primary participants too much control over the content of a third party's message).

Broadcasting Regulation[64]

New Zealand's regulatory schema places heavy restrictions on the use of the broadcast media—both radio and television—for political ends. All broadcast media, whether privately owned or State run, are regulated by the Broadcasting Act 1989. This legislation prohibits any broadcaster from permitting the broadcast of any 'election programme' at any time. An election programme is defined as one which encourages or persuades (or appears to encourage or persuade) the voters to vote for (or not to vote for) some individual candidate or political party, or which advocates support for or opposes a candidate or political party, or which notifies that a meeting is to be held in conjunction with an election.[65] There are only a few specific exceptions to this blanket ban on using the broadcast media to campaign,[66] of which the most important for current purposes are those allowing the political parties and individual candidates limited usage of the broadcast media during an election campaign.

The State distributes limited access to the broadcasting resource to qualifying political parties in the period prior to an election, in the form of a grant of money

[64] See generally, A Geddis, 'Reforming New Zealand's Election Broadcasting Regime' (2003) 14 *Public Law Review* 164.

[65] Broadcasting Act 1989, s 69(1).

[66] The ban does not apply to 'the broadcasting, in relation to an election, of news or comment or of current affairs programmes'; *Ibid* s 70(3). The official bodies charged with overseeing New Zealand's electoral process may place an election programme 'for the purposes of the Electoral Act 1993', and broadcasters may carry 'non-partisan advertisements' as a community service; see *Ibid* s 70(2)(b).

for the sole purpose of allowing the broadcast of election advertisements.[67] Since 1990, this 'broadcasting allocation' has amounted to a total of a little over $2 million. The Electoral Commission is charged with distributing the broadcasting allocation between all qualifying political parties requesting a share.[68] The allocation criteria involves such factors as: the number of votes the party attracted at the last election; the number of votes gained by the party in any by-election held since the last general election; any other indications of public support for that political party (such as results of public opinion polls and the number of persons who are members of that political party); as well as the general 'need to provide a fair opportunity for each political party . . . to convey its policies to the public . . .'[69] Clearly, the application of such a complex formula will generate disputes, and following every allocation decision there are complaints that some of the parties have been unfairly treated.[70] The fact that the Electoral Act 1993 requires a representative of each of the two largest political parties to take part in the allocation decision,[71] while the minor political parties are given no direct voice in the process,[72] only sharpens these complaints.

Irrespective of the fairness of this allocation process (a question considered in the final part of this chapter), it provides the political parties with virtually their only means of direct access to the broadcast media.[73] A political party may only broadcast an election programme in the time purchased with money allocated to it by the Commission. While the costs of producing an election programme may be paid for from the broadcasting allocation, they do not have to be. Instead, parties may spend their own funds on such production costs, although this expenditure will still count as an 'election expense' to be counted towards the total that party may spend on its general election advertising.[74]

An additional exception to the blanket ban on using the broadcast media for electioneering is made for individual candidates. A candidate may purchase time to broadcast an election programme, so long as it relates solely to the promotion of their candidacy, and is broadcast in the three months prior to the election. However, any such spending by a candidate will count as an 'election expense', and must therefore be counted towards the maximum of $20,000 that she may spend on advertising her campaign.

[67] Money provided as a part of the broadcasting allocation may *only* be used for the purpose of making and screening an election program; *Ibid* s 74(1)(a).

[68] *Ibid* ss 73, 74A. In order to qualify for a share of the allocation, a party must either be registered, or be deemed to be prepared to run candidates in at least 5 constituency seats, when Parliament is dissolved for an election; *Ibid* s 75(1)(a).

[69] *Ibid* s 75(2).

[70] See generally, S Corban, 'Funding Political Party Broadcasting' (1997) *Auckland University Law Review* 265, 272–82.

[71] Electoral Act 1993, s 8(4).

[72] Although all qualifying parties have the right to be heard by the Commission before it makes the allocation decision; Broadcasting Act 1989, s 76.

[73] *Ibid* s 70(2)(a). In addition, the State-owned television and radio network is required to screen the opening and closing addresses of qualifying political parties; *Ibid* s 77A(3).

[74] However, the value of any broadcasting resources received by a party does not count towards that party's maximum election expenses. *Ibid* s 214B(1).

These rules radically restrict the electoral participants' direct access to the broadcast media. A political party only may use the sums allocated to it by the Electoral Commission to purchase air time. While individual candidates remain free to use the broadcast media to advertise their candidacy (albeit subject to strict conditions), the $20,000 spending cap on their campaigns effectively limits access to the purchase of a few spots on local radio stations. Third parties may only use the broadcast media to run general, issue-focussed ads which do not expressly advocate support for or opposition to any party, or even appear to encourage voters to support or not to support a particular party or candidate.[75]

Problems with New Zealand's System of Campaign Funding Regulation—and Proposed Solutions

It should be noted at the outset of this section that the overall regulation of campaign *expenditures* in New Zealand appears to be operating satisfactorily. Those competing for election mostly abide by the spending limits, although a few accusations of over-spending by individual candidates arise after each election. It would be wrong to attribute this success entirely to some intrinsic superiority of the regulatory scheme, as there are several loopholes in the law that could be taken advantage of by an electoral participant wishing to avoid the controls on spending. However, because New Zealand is a 'low-cost' campaign environment, and because the use of the most expensive communication medium largely is put off limits, there is no great incentive to spend amounts in excess of that allowed by the legislation.

That being so, the issues of greatest concern centre around how electoral contestants gain their election funds, rather than how those funds subsequently are used. Any person or organisation may give as much money as he, she or it wishes to any electoral contestant. Contributors need not be citizens, or even residents, of New Zealand. In this context, concerns have been expressed about the ease with which large scale donors can fund the campaigns of election participants without disclosing their identity to the voting public. I term this the problem of 'faceless' donations.[76] Additionally, there have been complaints that the State does not do enough to support the political parties' election campaigns, thus leaving them overly reliant on private funding sources. These arguments have been raised

[75] That said, the enforcement of this ban is not strict. On several occasions before the 2002 election, for example, the 'Sensible Sentencing Trust' broadcast an advertisement highlighting law and order as an election issue. The screening of this advertisement followed a series of public meetings, jointly organised by the Trust and the ACT Party, 'to promote the message of Zero Tolerance for Crime and Truth-in-Sentencing . . ., As such, it is strongly arguable that even though the Trust's advertisement did not explicitly mention the ACT Party, its message on crime had become so connected with that of the ACT Party that the advertisement did 'appear[] to encourage or persuade voters to vote for a party' as per s 69(1). However, in the event no complaint was laid against the Trust.

[76] See generally, A Geddis, 'Hide Behind the Targets, In Front of All the People We Serve: New Zealand Election Law and the Problem of "Faceless" Donations' (2001) 12 *Public Law Review* 51.

specifically in relation to the broadcasting allocation, as well as in the wider context of taxpayer funding for political parties.[77]

This section considers each of these problems in turn. It also examines a number of contemporary proposals to deal with the problems outlined. However, whether these suggestions will be translated into actual reforms is unclear, as Parliament's Justice and Electoral Committee recently has recommended a 'fundamental review of the law relating to parliamentary elections and that this review be completed and any changes be in place for the 2008 general election.'[78] Given this fact, only an overview and evaluation of the different reform proposals is possible, rather than definite predictions about the shape of future changes.

Donation Disclosure and the Problem of 'Faceless' Contributions

The rules requiring the public disclosure of the identity of large-scale donors to the political parties (and, to a lesser extent, individual candidates) suffer from two major flaws.[79] First of all, the disclosure regime is retroactive in its operation. While a political party is required annually to file a report detailing all the reportable donations received in the previous year, it does not have to make any special disclosure of its funding sources prior to an election. Therefore, voters are left in the dark during an election campaign as to who is supporting each party financially in its bid to win public power. Indeed, the public may not learn of the identities of a party's donors for some considerable time after the election, as a political party's annual financial report is not due until the end of April in the following year. Thus, some nine months had elapsed after the 2002 general election before the public discovered who the parties' major financial supporters were. A more frequent disclosure of the identity of major donors to a political party, especially in the immediate run-up to an election, would be more desirable.

The second shortcoming of the public disclosure regime is the loophole created by allowing candidates and political parties to continue to accept donations that come from 'faceless' sources. The disclosure requirements incorporated into the Electoral Act 1993 were intended to allay any concerns that political parties might exchange favourable policy outcomes for political donations. However, the political parties have taken advantage of gaps in this legislative framework. First of all, the parties' continuing ability to receive 'anonymous' donations has been exploited widely, as the return of party donations filed with the Electoral Commission for the 2002 election year bears out.[80] Although the sources of such donations are not meant to be 'known' to the party, the definition calls for *actual*

[77] See generally, A Geddis, 'Towards a System of Taxpayer Funding for New Zealand Elections?' (2002) 10 *Otago Law Review* 181.

[78] Justice and Electoral Committee, *Inquiry into the 2002 General Election*, (March, 2004) AJHR I.7c, 9.

[79] These disclosure requirements are discussed above nn 32–6 and accompanying text. For a more complete discussion of the issue, see Geddis, n 76, at 54–6.

[80] The Labour Party reported receiving $380,000 in 'anonymous' donations (out of its total of $671,719 in reported donations), the National Party $200,050 (out of $529,167.71), the ACT party $50,000 (out of $88,971), and the Progressive Coalition $40,000 (out of $105,000).

knowledge rather than constructive knowledge. Hence, as long as donors takes steps to disguise their contributions—for instance, by paying it over via a bank check—the recipient can legitimately list the source as 'anonymous', even if well aware of its likely origin.

In addition, nothing in the legislation prevents the funnelling of donations through conduit bodies, such as trusts. Thus, for example, the National Party reported receiving $205,167.71 from three trust entities in 2002,[81] while the Progressive Coalition also reported a donation of $26,000 from the 'Progressive Members Fund'. In such a case the law only requires that the party list the conduit body as the source of the donation, even if the recipient fully knows the trust has been used to pass along another person's donation. Finally, the splitting of a donation amongst several 'straw donors', each of whom individually give less than the reportable amount, remains legal. It has been revealed that some donors have made use of this stratagem in the past, and there is at least circumstantial evidence that the practice continues today.[82]

These forms of faceless donation would not be troubling if the candidates and political parties genuinely had no idea who was funding their campaigns, as there would then be no danger that they would feel any resulting obligation to any particular individual or interest group.[83] It is clear, however, that the donations received generally are not faceless in this sense. Rather, as media reports have revealed, fundraisers for the parties actively advise potential donors how to avoid being publicly identified. In so doing the parties and their financial supporters may trample on the spirit of the law, but they remain within its technical bounds. Therefore, there is abundant evidence that the donor disclosure regime contained in the Electoral Act 1993 is hopelessly flawed. It allows any donor who wishes to avoid publicly disclosing her identity to do so, and even permits the intended recipient of a political donation to advise a donor on how to achieve this result—a state of affairs that makes something of a mockery of having any sort of public disclosure regime for political donations.

It seems likely that any test intended to distinguish between genuinely faceless donations and faux-anonymous contributions to a candidate or political party would prove impractical in application, as well as carrying unacceptable costs in terms of enforcement.[84] In light of these problems, New Zealand ought to follow Australia, Canada, the United States, and (lately) the United Kingdom, and ban political parties from receiving anonymous donations greater than a certain, nominal amount. This was the approach recommended in the Royal Commission's 1986 report, which also called for preventing the use of 'front'

[81] In 1999, this party reported receiving over $500,000 from a single trust.

[82] In 2002, the ACT Party reported spending the most of any political party on 'election expenses' (some $1.6 million). However, its financial report for that year showed it received only $89,000 in reportable donations. This discrepancy creates a strong inference that the remaining $1.5 million in funding was contributed in ways that kept each donation below the $10,000 disclosure threshold.

[83] See I Ayres and J Bulow, 'The Donation Booth: Mandating Donor Anonymity to Disrupt the Market for Political Influence' (1998) 50 *Stanford Law Review* 837.

[84] Geddis, n 76 at 55–6.

organisations to avoid the disclosure requirements.[85] A majority of the members of Parliament's Justice and Electoral Committee also have indicated their 'support [for] significant changes to the law governing donations to political parties',[86] while preferring to subject the matter to further study before making concrete recommendations for reform. It therefore remains to be seen if these words will be translated into practice in time for the 2008 general election.

The 'Fairness' of the Allocation of Broadcasting Resources

A second, and perennial, problem with the supply of campaign funds to New Zealand's political parties is the perceived unfairness of the distribution of broadcasting allocation amongst the political parties.[87] While complaints have been made ever since the present allocation system was introduced in 1990,[88] allegations that the distribution is inequitable have been sharpened by the move to a more diverse electoral climate under MMP. Two separate, inconsistent complaints have been raised. First of all, the smaller political parties argue that the major parties (Labour and National) receive a disproportionate amount of the allocation, given that they already enjoy greater attention from the 'free' news media.[89] Reinforcing this charge is the fact that representatives of these two parties take an active decision-making rolc in the allocation process,[90] while other parties only have a right to be 'consulted' on the allocation.[91]

While the smaller political parties are united in calling for the major party representatives to be removed from the allocation process,[92] it comes as no shock that these two parties oppose such a move, on the grounds that it is 'important for there to be political input in the process in order to ensure that the allocation procedures are fair and to allow the views of the political parties (which are the "prime users") to be taken into account.'[93] However, the fact that section 76 of the Broadcasting Act 1989 already requires the Commission to hear from all qualifying political parties before making any allocation decision makes it hard to see the continuing presence of major party representatives on the allocation committee as anything but an entrenchment of their dominant electoral position. Nevertheless, as Labour and National control 79 of the 120

[85] RCES, n 10 at 189–90.

[86] Justice and Electoral Committee, *Inquiry into the 1999 General Election*, (December, 2001) AJHR I.7C, 104.

[87] *Ibid* at 116–22.

[88] Corban, n 70, at 272–82.

[89] Corban, n 70 at 273. For the 2002 election, the Labour and National parties were each allocated $615,000—a combined total of almost 60 per cent of the $2.081 million distributed Electoral Commission, a Written Decision on Allocation of Time and Money to Political Parties for Broadcasting of Election Programmes' 25 July 2002, p 11.

[90] Broadcasting Act 1989, s 8(4).

[91] *Ibid* s 76.

[92] Report of the MMP Review Committee, *Inquiry into the Review of MMP* (August, 2001) AJHR I.3A, 55. The Electoral Commission has also recommended repeatedly to Parliamentary select committees that the political party representatives be removed from the allocation process.

[93] *Ibid* at 57.

seats in Parliament, the minor parties face an uphill battle in their bid to change the status quo.

In contrast, established political parties complain that the ease with which a party may qualify for a share of the broadcasting allocation enables fringe organisations to siphon it away from more 'serious' electoral contenders. Presently, all that is required for a party to gain a share of the allocation is that it either be registered, or deemed to be running candidates in 5 or more seats, at the time Parliament is dissolved for an election.[94] In the wake of the introduction of MMP, the number of parties meeting this threshold has increased markedly—rising from 7 in 1993, to 22 in 1999, before falling back to 14 in 2002. Yet in this period the amount of the broadcasting resource to be distributed has remained static,[95] even as the costs of accessing it have increased due to rising advertising rates. Therefore, 'serious' electoral contenders have had to share a progressively shrinking pie with an increased number of fringe parties, whose chance of actual electoral success is negligible.

The call to tighten the qualifying criteria for access to the resource is met with a claim that the current allocation formula provides a means by which emerging political movements can have some chance of attracting public support. Therefore, the underlying problem would seem to be that the current allocation criteria contained in section 75 of the Broadcasting Act 1989 tries to be all things to all people. It rewards larger parties for their greater levels of public support, whilst also seeking to 'provide a fair opportunity for each political party . . . to convey its policies to the public'. Any distributive decision is thus forced to serve two contradictory goals. While complaints about the division of the broadcasting allocation will probably never be completely eliminated, they probably could be reduced if the criteria were more clearly designed to serve one or the other goal, rather than both simultaneously.

In terms of proposals to increase the overall amount of the parties' access to the broadcasting resource, three main ideas have been floated.[96] One is to retain the current restrictions on the parties purchasing broadcast time, with a concomitant increase in the amount of the broadcasting allocation granted to the parties to buy this time. The second is to continue with the present levels of allocation, but also allow the parties to spend their own financial resources on buying air time, up to a set cap.[97] The third proposal is to remove the present restrictions on the purchase of broadcasting time by the political parties, and instead allow this as another 'election expense' within the general spending limit on such activities. The money currently allocated for purchasing broadcasting time would then be distributed amongst the political parties as a part of a more general system of taxpayer funding, to be spent by the parties on whatever election activities they desire.

[94] Broadcasting Act 1989, s 75(1)(a).

[95] The Broadcasting Act 1989, s 74(2) requires that the same amount of money be appropriated for the Broadcasting Allocation as was appropriated at the previous election, unless Parliament expressly legislates for an increase. Parliament has not done so in the past decade.

[96] These ideas were considered in greater depth by the MMP Review Committee, n 92 at 61.

[97] This model was included in two legislative proposals in the 1990s, neither of which gained final passage. See Broadcasting Amendment Bill (No 2) 1993; Broadcasting Amendment Bill 1995.

The present situation is that the broadcasting allocation is the subject of near universal condemnation. Even the Electoral Commission, charged with conducting the allocation process, has stated that it 'considers the current system of allocating time and funds to the political parties for election broadcasting is unfair and unsatisfactory, and that the procedures required by the [Broadcasting] Act are very time-consuming, cumbersome, and expensive.'[98] What should be done about the issue is, of course, a different question, on which there is much less agreement. Not surprisingly, each party tends to support the proposal most propitious to their own electoral needs, and so no consensus (or even majority support) has coalesced behind any one approach. As such, it is difficult to predict with any great certainty what steps might be taken to fix a system that is widely agreed to be broken, without any real concordance on what the real problem with the system is, and therefore how it should be fixed.[99]

Increased Taxpayer Funding for Election Campaigns

In addition to problems that have emerged with the broadcasting allocation, there have been more general claims that the State fails to give adequate support to the election campaigns of the political parties, thereby leaving the parties too reliant on sources of private funding. It has also been suggested that any move to ban faceless donations will necessitate the introduction of some form of public (or taxpayer) funding for the parties' election campaigns. If donors are forced to disclose their identities, this argument goes; they will no longer be prepared to give substantial political contributions, thus harming the democratic process by depriving the political parties of the funds they need to run their election campaigns.[100]

Whether such an outcome would eventuate in New Zealand is not entirely certain.[101] As a prediction, it is belied by the experience of various other countries—such as Australia, Canada, and the United States—which require the public disclosure of the identity of donors to political parties, yet have found that donors are still prepared to give parties significant sums as 'money contributes to and flows to power and the monied have learned to live with disclosure.'[102] However, even if the predicted decline in donations in a post-disclosure environment did not eventuate, there are several other arguments that might support a move towards the provision of greater taxpayer funding for election campaigns in New Zealand. The broadcasting allocation provides a precedent, so the introduction of further taxpayer funding for election campaigns simply would involve the expansion of an existing feature of New Zealand's election law, rather than the importation of a completely exogenous concept. Additionally, most of the

[98] See MMP Review Committee, n 92 at 60.
[99] My own suggestions are canvassed in Geddis, n 64 at 180–2.
[100] RCES, n 10 at 217.
[101] Geddis n 77 at 182–3.
[102] KZ Paltiel, 'Canadian Election Expense Legislation 1963–1985', in HE Alexander (ed), *Comparative Political Finance In The 1980s* (New York, Cambridge University Press, 1989) 67.

Western democracies with which New Zealand compares itself provide some form of taxpayer assistance to their political parties' election campaigns. So perhaps the taxpayer funding of election campaigns forms some kind of international democratic 'best practice' to which New Zealand also should conform.

This position was adopted by the Royal Commission in its 1986 report, where it supported the introduction of taxpayer funding on the grounds that it would help to offset any fundraising advantage that 'rich' (or established) parties enjoy over 'poor' (or newly emerging) parties.[103] To put the point another way, the Royal Commission believed taxpayer funding would ensure all the parties had access to adequate resources with which to communicate their policy positions to the electorate, thus helping to create an electoral environment in which voters were able to cast their ballots in a fully informed manner.[104] However, it is debatable whether this is a problem that really exists in New Zealand. There is little evidence that the political parties cannot raise enough money to run campaigns that adequately communicate their messages to the voters. Even though the amounts spent in each election campaign are quite divergent, there is no indication that this fact has had any negative impact on the overall competitiveness of the electoral process.[105]

In addition, any potential benefits to be gained from a taxpayer funding scheme must be balanced against the risk that such a move will reduce the opportunities for the supporters or members of a political party to become involved in the operations of that party. Rather than having to deal with ideologically motivated (and often troublesome and demanding) supporters or party members, a political party's hierarchy might prefer to use taxpayer funding to hire others to accomplish the tasks volunteer participants would usually perform. The possibly alienating effects of funding the political parties with taxpayer money may pose a particular risk in New Zealand, where the levels of membership in the political parties are already reported to be in steep decline.[106] Also, public concerns already have been expressed that the MMP voting system, with its closed 'party lists', puts too much control over the political parties in the hands of the party hierarchy. These are reasons to be cautious about instituting a form of taxpayer funding that does not encourage the direct, voluntary participation of party members and supporters, lest such a move exacerbate the perception that the political parties are becoming increasingly isolated from their grassroots supporters.[107]

As a matter of public policy, therefore, the issue of wider taxpayer funding for the political parties' election campaigns is even more contested than is the issue of allocating the broadcasting resource.[108] To begin with, there is a sharp ideological

[103] Above, n 10 at 216–17. The Commission's recommendation was not included in the Electoral Act 1993. For an account of why this was so see Jackson & McRobie, n 22 at 138–56.

[104] D Oliver, 'Fairness and Political Finance: The Case of Election Campaigns', in R Blackburn (ed), *Constitutional Studies* (London, Mansell, 1992) 132.

[105] See Geddis, n 77 at 191–3.

[106] R Mulgan, *Politics in New Zealand* (Auckland, Auckland University Press, 2nd ed, 1997) 248–9.

[107] Compare RCES, n 10 at 216–17.

[108] Although the two issues fall to be considered together, given that the $2 million already made available to the political parties through the broadcasting allocation forms a potential 'seed amount' for any extended public funding scheme. See Geddis, n 64 at 182.

division between the parties as to whether such a step is either necessary or desirable. The parties on the 'right' all oppose any additional state funding beyond that currently provided for the purchase of broadcast time.[109] Those parties on the 'left' support some sort of taxpayer funding for election campaigns, but there is little consensus on the exact structure of such a scheme.[110] About all that seems agreed upon is that the funding should be distributed in a bulk grant after an election has been held, with the amount to be given to each party assessed in line with some dollars-per-vote formula.[111]

As indicated above, there are reasons in the New Zealand context to be cautious about too great an extension of the amount of taxpayer funding given to the political parties. Certainly, any such funding should be structured so as to ensure it does not obviate the need for parties to reach out to as wide a base of individual supporters as possible. One alternative means of achieving this end is through an indirect system of taxpayer funding via tax rebates on small, individual donations,[112] rather than through relying upon direct funding provided by the central government. However, the point may be a moot one given the current lack of agreement amongst the parties as to whether any sort of further taxpayer funding is a good idea. Further developments must wait for Parliament's Justice and Electoral Committee to complete its review of the issue, and for the Government's response to any recommendations made by that body.

[109] Report of the MMP Review Committee, *Inquiry into the Review of MMP* (August, 2001) AJHR I. 3A at 62.

[110] *Ibid.*

[111] This was also the recommendation of the Royal Commission on the Electoral System. See RCES, n 10 at 226–8.

[112] Geddis, n 77 at 191–3.

Part II

'Big Bang' Regulation of a Private Funding Regime

3

Expenditure, Donations and Public Funding under the United Kingdom's *Political Parties, Elections and Referendums Act 2000*—And Beyond?

NAVRAJ SINGH GHALEIGH

Introduction

IT IS NO exaggeration to say that the regulatory environment for electoral campaigning and political parties in the UK has been radically transformed. With the enactment of the *Political Parties, Elections and Referendums Act 2000* (hereinafter, 'the Act' or '*PPERA*'), practically every aspect of the giving to, spending by and accountability of, political actors has undergone (often significant) revision. Whilst other contributions to this volume address questions of disclosure[1] and political advertising,[2] the focus here is on the impact the Act has had on expenditure and donation capping, and the intimately related question of public funding. In these areas, whether actively or passively, the presence of the Act looms large. However, it would be incomplete to stop there. The time of radical reform may be over, but processes of revision are still in motion.

From the first, it should be recognised that reasons were not wanting for the enactment of the *Political Parties, Elections and Referendums Act*, the UK's first comprehensive legal intervention into the regulation of party and electoral funding since the *Corrupt and Illegal Practices Act 1883*.[3] Public confidence in the political system had reached a nadir in the mid- and late-1990s, in no small part due to the perception and actuality of political sleaze which arguably contributed to the

[1] See ch 4 by KD Ewing.

[2] See ch 5 by J Rowbottom.

[3] With the *Election Petitions and Corrupt Practices Act 1868* and the *Ballot Act 1872*, this Act establishes the statutory foundations (scarcely built upon thereafter) of the pre-2000 regime of party political funding and campaign finance in the UK.

ongoing collapse of voter turnout in the UK.[4] The parties themselves complained (with a degree of credibility) that they operated under such constraints of debt and uncertainty of income as scarcely to be able to perform their constitutional functions.[5] Among some political commentators was the persistent complaint that those legal rules that did apply to the funding of political parties were regularly flouted.[6] Further, constitutional innovations from within (Scottish and Welsh Devolution and the *Human Rights Act 1998*) and political developments from outwith (European Monetary Union and the prospects of an attendant referendum) placed new demands on a venerable regime. Given also the European Court of Human Rights' finding that the UK's law relating to third party expenditure limits fell foul of Article 10's commitment to freedom of expression,[7] the time for reform of a regime rooted in the political configurations of the late Victorian period was not so much ripe, as very nearly spoiled.

The Case for Reform

When Justice White characterised his own country's system of campaign finance as a 'nonsensical, loophole ridden patchwork',[8] he could as well have been referring to the pre-*PPERA* system of party funding. The UK's approach to the regulation of money and politics has long been both partial and fragmented. Some key issues of party funding have been subjected to detailed regulation whilst others have only been constrained by the mores of the relevant actors. The *Corrupt and Illegal Practices Act 1883*[9]—which tightly constrained parliamentary candidates' expenditure after the notorious election of 1880[10]—is a case in point.

In order to combat massive constituency level spending (which had in the 1880 general election approximated to bribery), the 1883 Act placed a severe cap on constituency level 'election expenditures'.[11] Compliance on the part of candidates

[4] Popular 'trust' in British political parties nearly halved from 1987 to 1997 and (connectedly?) the turnout in general elections fell from 77.7% to 59.4% from 1992 to 2001. See respectively, 'British Social Attitudes/British Election Surveys and Electoral Commission' *The General Election 2001* (London, Politicos, 2001).

[5] See P Webb, *The Modern British Party System* (Thousand Oaks, Sage, 2000) 238–9.

[6] Michael Crick, Committee on Standards in Public Life (CSPL), *The Funding of Political Parties in the United Kingdom* (Cm 4057-I, 1998) 184 ('Opening Statement').

[7] *Bowman v United Kingdom* (1998) EHRR 1.

[8] *FEC v National Conservative Political Action Committee* 470 US 480, 518 (1985).

[9] The relevant provisions of that Act had been repeatedly re-enacted, most recently in the *Representation of the People Act 1983*. The fullest account of the pre-*PPERA* regime is to be found in KD Ewing, *The Funding of Political Parties in Britain* (Cambridge, Cambridge University Press, 1987).

[10] Spending in that election was generally agreed to be 'excessive [and] contrary to the public interest', see HC Deb, col 597 (16 August 1883). For an account of the background to the 1883 Act, see C O'Leary, *Elimination of Corrupt Practices in British Elections 1868–1911* (Oxford, Oxford University Press, 1961).

[11] Latterly reproduced in the *Representation of the People Act 1983*, ss 76(1) and 118. Based on the number of electors in a constituency and whether it was a county or borough seat (that is, a rural or urban seat), the level of these caps averaged about £8,300 in the 1997 general election.

(and their agents) was ensured by the requirement that parliamentary candidates submit, to the Returning Officer, returns of all campaign expenditures. The failure to make a valid return and evidence of overspending could prompt the voiding of a result by an election court.[12] Such tight controls on candidate expenditure would of course be rendered nugatory if third parties could incur expenses for or against a particular candidate, party or position with impunity.[13] That loophole was closed by section 34 of the *Representation of the People Act 1918* which effectively prohibited non-candidates from incurring expenditure 'with a view to promoting or procuring the election of a candidate at an election' above the level of £5 (at 1983 prices) without the consent of a candidate or her agent.[14] The failure to comply invited criminal sanctions.[15]

Superficially, the foregoing amounts to an effective control on constituency level spending during general elections. Election expenditure was tightly controlled and the participatory primacy of political parties assured. This regime sprang of course from the experience of high, distortive, expenditure in the late Victorian electoral process. But it was this very rootedness in the political experience of the 1880s that also served to undermine the effectiveness of the regulatory regime.

A particularly damaging loophole arose from the fact that although the amount that candidates could expend during the campaigning period at general elections was closely regulated and constrained at the *constituency level*, there were no spending limits at the *national level*. In a sense, such an absence is hardly surprising given that in the 1880s the primary locus of electoral competition was very much the local, not the national, stage—in the general election of 1880 a mere 2 per cent of total expenditure was incurred by the central parties.[16] But the shift to national campaigning has long since been a feature of political campaigns, such that the constituency level campaigns are only exceptionally something other than 'sideshows'.[17] Accordingly, constituency limits not operating in tandem with national spending limits were substantially meaningless. The death knell for the effectiveness of constituency limits was marked by the decision in *R v Tronoh Mines Ltd*[18] which revolved around the question of whether campaign

[12] *Ibid*, ss 120–6. However, such outcomes were extremely rare—see Ewing at n 9 above, 73ff.

[13] As the Canadian Supreme Court noted in the case of *Libman v Quebec* (1997) 151 DLR. (4th) 385 at 413.

[14] Successively re-enacted, most recently in s 75, *Representation of the People Act 1983*.

[15] These provisions were challenged successfully in *Bowman v United Kingdom* (1998) EHRR 1.

[16] £2,500,000 – £106m at 1997 prices. See, Committee on Standards in Public Life, *The Funding of Political Parties in the United Kingdom* (Cm 4057-I, 1998), para 2.3.

[17] The phrase is David Butler's, as quoted in M Linton, '*The Funding of Political Parties*', in R Blackburn(ed), *The Electoral System in Britain* (London, Longmans, 1999) at 55–6. Further, in the 1997 general election, 90% of the £60 million spent by the Conservative and Labour Parties collectively was expended at the national level, see D Butler and D Kavanagh, *The Election of 1997* (Basingstoke, Macmillan, 1997) at 205, 223. This is not to deny however the high levels of political energy (and cash) directed at a small number of marginal seats at all general elections.

[18] [1951] 1 All ER 697.

expenditures of parties and interest groups at the national level were constrained by the limits discussed above. The court held that the *Representation of the People Act 1918* simply did not extend to the prohibition of expenditure for 'general propaganda, even though the general political propaganda does incidentally assist a particular candidate amongst others.'[19] Accordingly, expenditure incurred on advertisements designed to support one party generally in all constituencies but not specifically supporting any particular candidate in any particular constituency was not contrary to limits on constituency spending, thereby allowing for expenditure at the national level without legal constraint and opening the way for national election campaigns.[20]

If the controls on what political parties could expend were partial, in the sense of incompleteness, those concerning the sources of their income were transparently so in the sense of bias. Both major British political parties have traditionally been overwhelmingly dependent on institutional donations—corporations and affiliated trade unions bankrolling the Conservative Party and Labour Party respectively[21]—but the regulatory impositions upon those donors have differed greatly in their degree of burdensomeness.

The financial relationship between trade unions and the Labour Party has long been the subject of interest for judicial and parliamentary legislators and indeed one of the seminal cases in the early history of the British labour movement—*Amalgamated Society of Railway Servants v Osborne*[22]—was intimately bound up with the concerns of party funding. In that case, the House of Lords enjoined trade unions from engaging in political activities by invalidating their political funds, on the basis that it was,

> unjust and oppressive [and] illegal to compel . . . a member of a trade union . . . either to contribute to the promotion of a political policy of which he might possibly disapprove, or be expelled from the union to which he belonged for so many years and forfeit all benefits from the money he had subscribed.[23]

The *Trade Union Act 1913* substantially reversed the effect of *Osborne*, establishing a framework that has been the basis for successive regimes of trade union governance. Unions have since been required to ballot their members on a resolution for the adoption of political objects, which if successful allows the establishment of separate political funds from which donations to parties could be made.[24]

[19] *Ibid*, at 700, per McNair J.

[20] See DE Butler, 'Elections: Legislation and Litigation', in DE Butler (ed), *The Law, Politics and the Constitution* (Oxford, Oxford University Press, 1999) 175–7, and also CR Munro, 'Elections and Expenditure' [1976] *Public Law* 300, commenting on *DPP v Luft* [1976] 2 All ER 569.

[21] It is however noteworthy that in the course of the 1990s both major parties succeeded in weaning themselves off their reliance on institutional benefactors. See P Webb, *The Modern British Party System* (Thousand Oaks, Sage, 2000) 236–7.

[22] [1910] AC 87.

[23] *Ibid*, at 105, per Lord Atkinson.

[24] *Trade Union Act 1913*, s 3.

Individual members must be entitled to seek exemption from paying into the fund without prejudice (denial of benefits etc).[25] The *Trade Union Act 1984* further required that ballots be undertaken every 10 years for the continuance of the political fund.[26]

There is no suggestion that this is anything other than appropriate—on the contrary, the requirements of consulting members, obtaining their (majority) support and allowing exemptions seems to be a fine model for donor accountability and transparency. But what was objectionable was the absence of comparable burdens regarding donations by companies which were in fact free to donate as much as they wished, subject only to the *de minimis* requirement of having to declare the fact of a contribution in their director's annual report and the identity of the recipient, where that largess exceeded £200.[27] In addition to the principled objection to such an absence of accountability and transparency, the risk of conflicts of interest on the part of directors also arises, as does that of shareholder opposition. The murky link between corporate donations and political parties was described as 'unsatisfactory' by the important report of the Committee on Standards in Public Life in 1998.[28] Likewise unsatisfactory was the absence of any prohibition on donations from foreign individuals or corporations—a matter which arose in various party funding scandals in the 1990s.[29]

Turning to the question of public or state funding for political parties, the approach taken in the UK has very much been of the 'lonely furrow' variety. Granting state aid to parties based on electoral success, whether based on votes or seats gained, has never in the UK garnered the support it has in France, Sweden and Norway (and elsewhere), despite advocacy by the Houghton Committee.[30] A second approach, operating through the fiscal system and giving tax relief or tax credits to donors (subject to limits), with the goal encouraging donations to

[25] *Ibid*, s 5. The question of members' participation in the 'political levy' subsequently became a favourite political football, revolving around the question of whether members should be required to 'contract in' or 'contract out'.

[26] *Trade Union Act 1984*, s 12.

[27] Introduced by *Companies Act 1967*, updated by *Companies Act 1985*, sch 7, paras 3–5. The figure of £200 was last updated in 1980. Searches at Companies House only revealed a list of donating companies, not how much they gave for which details, laborious cross-referencing to companies' annual reports was required. Finally, the declaration requirement extended only to monetary gifts, not to 'in kind' donations (such as staffing or know-how) or soft loans.

[28] Committee on Standards in Public Life, *The Funding of Political Parties in the United Kingdom* (Cm 4057-I, 1998), paras 6.24–6.37, recommending prior authorisation by shareholders.

[29] See Ewing at ch 4 in this volume.

[30] Houghton Committee on *Financial Aid to Political Parties* (Cmhd 6601, 1976), recommended state subventions to political parties on the basis of specified sums per vote gained at the previous election, in three forms: (1) annual grants to political parties nationally which passed a low threshold of electoral support; (2) support to candidates at the constituency level (so as to counterbalance the extra power that (1) may give to the national party through reimbursement of election expenses and; (3) a scheme similar to (2) but to candidates for local government elections.

political parties has remained similarly unpopular, despite its widespread usage in the USA (at Federal[31] and State[32] level) and Canada.[33] Nor has a system combining both of those methods ever caught on, as it has in Germany. Rather, the provision of public funding in Britain has been patchy but wide reaching, ranging from the humdrum—granting free access to public building for meetings during campaigning periods[34] and providing one free postal election address to candidates in general election campaigns[35]—to the highly strategic—the Short/Cranborne schemes[36] which fund the parliamentary work of the opposition parties[37] and the provision of free broadcasting time.[38]

From the perspective of transparency however, the pre-*PPERA* system was not so much curious as straightforwardly neglectful in its complete absence of any legal requirements for parties to disclose publicly their finances, whether expenditures or receipts. Although since its formation in 1906, the Labour Party has always voluntarily published its accounts annually, such records have been short on detail. For instance, it was not until 1983 that breakdowns of the donations from each affiliated trade union to the party's general election fund were given. Having said that, this position was significantly more defensible than that of the Conservative Party which remained hostile to transparency until as recently as 1998 when its Treasurer, Cecil Parkinson, giving evidence to the Committee on

[31] Presidential Campaign Election Fund.

[32] See generally, MJ Malbin and TL Gais, *The Day After Reform:Sobering Campaign Finance Lessons From the American States* (Albany, NY; Rockefeller Institute Press, 1998).

[33] A scheme of tax relief on donations was favoured by the Neill Committee's report, *The Funding of Political Parties in Britain* (Cm 4057, 1998) recommendations 38 and 39.

[34] *Representation of the People Act 1983*, s 95.

[35] *Ibid*, s 91. Not to be underestimated, 134 million such mailings were delivered during the 2001 general election—amounting in global terms to a significant free facility. See Report of the Electoral Commission, *Election 2001:Official Results*, (2002), ((http://www.electoralcommission.gov.uk/about-us/election01results.cfm (last accessed 23 April 2005) at 44.

[36] The former scheme, pertaining to the funding of opposition work in the House of Commons was introduced in 1975, see HC Deb col 1869, 20 March 1975. The extension to like work in the House of Lords came about by Resolution on 27 November 1996.

[37] Including research assistance to front bench spokespersons and the leaders' offices. The quantum of 'Short money' was nearly tripled by government with effect from 1 April 1999—see Secretary of State for the Home Department, 'The Funding of Political Parties in the UK: the Goverment's Proposals for Legislation in Response to the Fifth Report of the Committee on Standards in Public Life', July 1999. Cm 4413, para 6.8.—and has almost certainly been misused by the Conservative Party, see *Fourth Report of the Public Administration Select Committee* (HC (2000–1) No 264) para 40ff, esp para 50.

[38] The purchase of broadcast political advertising has traditionally been prohibited by the *Broadcasting Act 1981*, sch 2 ('Rules as to Advertisements'). From 1947 until 1997 (when it was disbanded), the allocation of free party political broadcasts ('PPB') and party election broadcasts ('PEB') was determined by the Committee on Political Party Broadcasting which consisted of representatives from the political parties and broadcasters. Although an efficient procedure from the perspective of major parties, the potential unfairness to minor or new parties has caused concern—see *R v BBC* [1997] EMLR 605. See also J Rowbottom in chp 5 this volume.

Standards in Public Life, manfully argued the case for de facto anonymity in donations.[39]

Given this ragbag of rules, of disparate provenance and varying degrees of utility and partiality, it is unsurprising that enforcement was not the responsibility of a single, dedicated body but left to the collective alertness of returning officers, the police and the ordinary courts. It has been suggested that together they proved to be a less than effective monitor.[40] But it is nonetheless striking that the 'traditional' approach to party funding in UK had been strangely effective for a very long time, at least in the sense of there being an absence of large scale corruption[41] and public disgruntlement with political process.[42] A particular political culture, a certain 'way of doing things' is clearly at play. But whilst this long immunised the United Kingdom from the major party funding scandals that dogged comparable democracies, towards the end of the Major era (1992–97) a telling series of apparent quid pro quos revealed the fragility of the system and its reliance on social norms. And once those previously solid social norms had melted into air, there was precious little law to take their place. An 'arms race' had emerged between the major parties involving an unseemly dash for cash followed by the regular campaigning binges which not only disproportionately disadvantaged the less well financed parties, but also created the impression (however inaccurate) of parties and governments being in hock to their wealthy benefactors (whether trade unions or off-shore potentates). As it stood, legal regulation could supply scant remedy. The need for reform was well appreciated by the Labour Party in opposition[43] and upon taking office it referred the matter of party funding to the independent investigatory Committee on Standards in Public Life, which delivered a series of comprehensive recommendations in November 1998.[44] Preceded

[39] Committee on Standards in Public Life, *The Funding of Political Parties in the United Kingdom* (Cm 4057, 1998) para 1375. For an (in)famous variant of this argument from Alastair McAlpine, see Ewing at ch 4 in this volume. It should be noted that there are sophisticated and democracy promotive arguments in favour of secrecy in political donations—see I Ayres and J Bulow, 'The Donation Booth: Mandating Donor Anonymity to Disrupt the Market for Political Influence' (1998) *50 Stanford Law Review*, 837–891—but they remain nonetheless perfectly politically unacceptable.

[40] Committee on Standards in Public Life, *The Funding of Political Parties in the United Kingdom* (Cm 4057, 1998) para 1908–85 (oral evidence); 184–5 (written evidence). See also KD Ewing, *The Funding of Political Parties in Britain* (Cambridge, Cambridge University Press, 1987) 77–80.

[41] Compare the scale and impact of party funding/campaign finance scandals in the USA ('Watergate'), Germany ('Kohlgate'), Italy ('Tangentopoli'), Japan ('Recruit') or France (the 'Dumas affair').

[42] As disappointing as the turnout at the 2001 general election was, it is unlikely that a turnout of only 60.7% will ever be hailed as a triumphant result, as in the recent US election.

[43] See the Labour Party's evidence to the Home Affairs Committee of 1993, *Report on Funding of Political Parties*, (HC (1993–94) 301) and the Election Manifesto of 1997, Labour Party, *Because Britain Deserves Better* (London, Labour Party, 1997) which promised to ban 'foreign funding', oblige parties 'to declare the source of all donations above a minimum figure' and 'ask the Nolan Committee [Committee on Standards in Public Life] to consider how the funding of political parties should be regulated and reformed'. See also Ewing in chp 4 this volume.

[44] *The Funding of Political Parties in the United Kingdom* (Cm 4057, 1998); for my comments, see NS Ghaleigh, 'The Funding of Political Parties in the United Kingdom: the Case for Cherry Picking' (1999) *Public Law* 43–50. Lord Neill's own account of the Committee's work was given during the Lords debates on *PPERA*, at HL Deb, vol 403, col 1124 (3 April 2000).

by a White Paper which closely tracked the Committee's recommendations,[45] the government's Bill was introduced to the House of Commons on 10 January 2000.

Pressure Points and *PPERA*

'The conduct of elections will never be quite the same again'[46]

This claim from the (then) Home Secretary's introduction of the *Political Parties, Elections and Referendums Bill* to Parliament was likely as aspirational as predictive. And given the Act's engagement with almost all the pressure points discussed above, it is unlikely to be a mere boast. That being said, it is inevitably the case that given the charged and critical arena that it seeks to regulate, the successes of *PPERA* have not been regarded as complete and there remain numerous questions regarding the architecture of the regime. This may be merely an inevitable consequence of attempting a novel and ambitious structure. Alternatively, the flaws may be such that mere 'snagging' will not suffice. A new round of construction may be necessary.

The Electoral Commission

It will be clear from the discussion below that the Electoral Commission is the keystone in the new Act's architecture.[47] From the distribution of state aid,[48] to maintaining that political parties are financially accountable,[49] the Commission's tasks are diverse. And, the responsibilities conferred by the Act go even further to include reporting on elections and referendums,[50] keeping electoral matters under review[51] and even limited legislative powers.[52]

Nonetheless, enforcement is the Electoral Commission's primary task—according to section 145, the Commission will have the 'general function of monitoring compliance' with the provisions pertaining to accounting requirements, contributions, expenditure (of political parties and third parties), disclosure and

[45] CSPL *The Funding of Political Parties in the United Kingdom* (Cm 4413, 1999).

[46] 'The conduct of elections will never be quite the same again … The time has come to get down to the business of restoring public confidence in our political institutions.' HC Deb vol 343, col 45 (10 Jan 2000) (Straw).

[47] Calls for such a body are not especially new and were frequent in 1990s—C Chataway, *Agenda for Change: Report of the Hansard Society Commission on Electoral Campaigns* (London, Hansard Society, 1991); P Nairn, *Report of the Commission on the Conduct of Referendums* (London, Constitution Unit, 1996); Constitutional Commission, *Establishing an Electoral Commission* (London, Constitution Unit, 1997); DE Butler, *Keeping Election Law Up-to-Date: The Case for an Electoral Commission* (London, Hansard Society, 1998).

[48] Political Parties, Elections and Referendums Act (*PPERA*), s 12—policy development grants; *Ibid* s 11—broadcasting allocation.

[49] Through the disclosure/reporting processes—see generally parts III and IV of the Act.

[50] *PPERA*, s 5. For the Electoral Commission's first report on the general election 2001, see http://www.electoralcommission.gov.uk/ last accessed 23 April 2005.

[51] *PPERA*, s 6.

[52] *PPERA*, sch 8(3).

reporting and the conduct of referendums. The broad range of duties can only be meaningfully undertaken if the Commission is provided with a similarly full range of supervisory powers, which are duly conferred.[53] Given this range of responsibilities, it would not be unreasonable to fear the risk of overburdening—not least because any future problem in the field will elicit demands for the Electoral Commission to 'look at it'.[54] Indeed, a key aspect of the 'revision process' referred to above is the Commission's review of 2003/4, 'The Funding of Political Parties',[55] which revisited many of the issues that so concerned the Neill Committee's 1998 report, including expenditure and donation limits, and the question of public funding.

What is perhaps most notable about the Electoral Commission is its composition. Modelled on the National Audit Office, the Act seeks not to regulate the political valency of the Commission, but rather to ensure that it has none whatsoever. Unlike the bipartisan Federal Election Commission (USA) or the 'neutral' Bundestag President (Germany), the members of the Commission are selected on the basis of their near total absence of political experience. In order to be seen to be above the party political fray, appointees to the Commission should be non-political figures who have not previously been involved in a substantial way in the party political process. Individuals who have within the past 10 years held senior office in a party, been elected or been a major donor to a political party are viewed as partial. Naturally therefore, once appointed, electoral commissioners are excluded from such activity.[56] Thus, the current Chair of the Electoral Commission was previously the Chief Executive of British Red Cross, and other current commissioners include senior figures in local and city administration and a former BBC journalist and executive. This absence of direct political know-how potentially raises the problem of appointees having insufficient experience of and insight into their regulated community to undertake their responsibilities successfully—although one may perhaps overestimate the sophistication of contemporary party politics.

Disclosure

The shortcomings of the pre-*PPERA* regime as regards the disclosure of donations and expenditure is alluded to above.[56a] For present purposes, suffice it to say that

[53] These powers—including that to compel production of records, demand explanations of the same and even the power to authorise the entering of the premises of a 'supervised organisation or individual', *PPERA*, s 146(3)—are arguably over-full from the perspectives of Arts 6 and 8 ECHR.

[54] An early occurrence of this was with regard to 'e-campaigning'—see '2001: Cyber Space Odyssey. The internet in the UK election', edited by S Coleman at http://www.hansard–society.org.uk/cyberodyssey.pdf, last accessed 23 April 2005. For a treatment of the demands created by the internet on (US) campaign finance law, see T Potter, *The Internet and Federal Election Law*, http://www.brook.edu/gs/cf/headlines/internet.htm last accessed 23 April 2005.

[55] Available at: http://www.electoralcommission.gov.uk/templates/search/document.cfm/11394 last accessed 23 April 2005.

[56] *PPERA*, s 3. For extended discussion of the merits of absolute impartiality, see Lord Goodhart, HL Deb, vol 511, col 1760–1 (11 May 2000).

[56a] For a full account of these insufficiencies and of the solutions offered by *PPERA*, see Ewing, chapter four in this collection.

the measures adopted in the Act are certainly comprehensive in their response to the questions of principle raised, and pay no shortage of attention to practical problems of loopholing and circumvention. To the extent that inadequacies are nonetheless perceived, it may not be unreasonable to await the conclusion of a full electoral cycle, at the very least, before drawing strongly critical conclusions.

Expenditure Limits

Although expenditure limits have long been a feature of British party political funding, their stunted scope—that is, their restriction to constituency level expenditure only—has been problematic. The absence of national expenditure limits has contributed to the oft-remarked upon 'arms race' between the major parties in which each seeks to trump the electoral expenditure of the other, inexorably driving up the cost of campaigns. Quite apart from the opportunity costs incurred by accumulating such war chests,[57] and the certainty that parties less attractive to moneyed interests will be left at the starting gates in this contest, the chase for unlimited funds leaves open the very real possibility of parties gravitating not to their broader membership or support base for funding, but towards a small number of large donors. If our model of democracy includes a notion of participatory, inclusive politics in which the grassroots has a meaningful input, this is an unsavoury outcome. Moreover, not unreasonably, reliance on substantial donors raises questions of parties' independence from their paymasters—the Labour Party's former reliance on trade union funding, and the Tories' on corporate donations being only the best known examples. After all, what is the purpose of the democratic process if expressed electoral preferences are to be trumped by the debts accumulated by political parties to discrete, insular and wealthy minorities? Responding to these concerns,[58] *PPERA* has squarely addressed these issues by introducing two key innovations—national expenditure limits for direct participants and third parties—and retaining two key features of the previous regime—local expenditure limits, for both candidates and third parties.

National expenditure limits were perhaps the single most necessary reform identified by the Neill Committee,[59] and *PPERA* responds straightforwardly. Schedule 9 of the Act establishes a cap of roughly £20m on the 'campaign expenditure' of political parties, based on the number of candidates they field in a general

[57] For an American perspective, see D Morris, *Behind the Oval Office: Winning the Presidency in the Nineties* (New York, Random House, 1997), who reports Clinton to have anguished, 'I can't think. I can't act. I can't do anything but go to fund-raisers and shake hands. You want me to issue executive orders; I can't focus on a thing but the next fund-raiser. Hilary can't, Al can't, we're all getting sick and crazy because of it.' At 100–1.

[58] Many of which found articulation in the Labour Party's submission to Home Affairs Committee of 1993, *Report on Funding of Political Parties*, (HC (1993–94) 301), and the CSPL.

[59] Committee on Standards in Public Life, *The Funding of Political Parties in the United Kingdom* (Cm 4057-I, 1998) ch 10.

election.[60] 'Campaign expenditure' is defined to mean those items which are (a) included in schedule 8 of the Act[61] and, (b) are incurred 'with a view to promoting or procuring the electoral success' of the party.[62] Indicative of the scrupulousness which characterises much of the Act, a series of potential loopholes in relation to these limits have been foreclosed. Soft loans, the free or discounted use of property, services or facilities are to count as campaign expenditures at their market, not given, rate.[63] And this applies equally to local as to national party expenditure (where it is directed towards promoting the success of the party, not a candidate)[64]—so long as it is incurred with the authorisation of the treasurer of the relevant accounting unit.[65] Finally, the failure to comply with these limits attracts a criminal sanction.[66] As noted above, local expenditure limits are futile without like support at the national level, and vice versa. Accordingly, the traditional tight constraints on constituency spending have been retained by *PPERA* and updated somewhat—encompassing 'in kind' support for candidates within the definition of election expenses[67] and taking a realistic approach to the limits on by-election expenditure and increasing them.[68]

The second innovation of the Act in respect of expenditure limits also relates to spending at the national level, but not by parties or candidates, but rather by non-participants, or third parties. The importance of the need to regulate their activity was pointedly noted in the important Canadian case, *Libman v Quebec (AG)*,[69] in which the Supreme Court stated that 'the spending limit system would lose all its effectiveness if independent spending were not also limited.'[70]

Similarly challenging issues of third party spending were posed in the case of *Bowman v UK*[71] in which the severe constraint on third parties' spending imposed by section 75 of *Representation of the People Act 1983* was successfully challenged in Strasbourg. *PPERA*'s response to this challenge is an interesting microcosm of many of the battles in constitutional law that lie ahead, in its attempt to render compatible a traditionally British approach to the substance of constitutional regulation and the exogenous demands of the ECHR system.

[60] The number of seats contested by a party is multiplied by £30,000. There are 641 contestable constituencies at a general election, assuming that the British parties do not contest the Northern Irish seats.

[61] Such as advertising, market research, the costs of rallies and meetings etc. The schedule also notes items which are not to be counted for these purposes, such as staff salaries and certain overhead costs.

[62] *PPERA*, s 72.

[63] *PPERA*, s 73. The section does apply to seconded staff, but not to volunteers.

[64] *PPERA*, s 72(8).

[65] *PPERA*, s 75. The act of incurring expenditure on behalf of a political parties without the authority of its treasurer is an offence pursuant to s 75(2).

[66] *PPERA*, s 79(2).

[67] *PPERA*, s 134.

[68] *PPERA*, s 132.

[69] (1997) 151 DLR (4th) 385.

[70] *Ibid*, 413. Although this case dealt with referendum, not ordinary electoral, expenditure limits, it was accepted that for present purposes, identical issues arise, *Ibid*, 409.

[71] 26 EHRR 1 (1998).

The Court's primary concern in *Bowman* was that the £5 restriction on third parties expenditure imposed by the *Representation of the People Act 1983* amounted to a complete barrier to such parties publishing information with a view to influencing the electorate in favour of a particular view. This was adjudged contrary to Article 10 ECHR, which when read together with Article 3 of the First Protocol to the Convention, amounts to an understanding that 'free elections and freedom of expression, particularly freedom of political debate, together form the bedrock of any democratic system.' And this was notwithstanding the permissible state interest of legislating for the promotion of candidate equality.

PPERA's introduction of third parties expenditure limits will work in harness with those already in existence at the local level. In respect of the latter, the Act has closely followed the recommendations of the Neill Committee and extended the old limit imposed by section 75 of £5 to £500.[72] Given the Court's sympathy with the old provision's purpose, but objecting to its stifling of practically all speech, this threshold (which would facilitate, say, a full page advertisement in a local newspaper) would appear to satisfy the *Bowman* judgment's strictures. But it is at the national level that the innovation has occurred, with the Act creating a new category of political participants—'recognised third parties'[73]—which must notify the Electoral Commission of their intention to spend substantial sums in a general election.[74] These actors are restricted ('controlled', in the language of the Act)[75] in their expenditures which are 'incurred by or on behalf of the third party in connection with the production or publication of election material ¼ which can reasonably be regarded as intended to (a) promote or procure electoral success' for a candidate or party, or 'otherwise enhance the standing' of such a party or candidate.[76] Third parties' 'controlled expenditure' is limited to £793,500 for those expenses incurred in relation to England, £108,000, £60,000 and £27,000 for Scotland, Wales and N Ireland respectively.[77]

The *Bowman* judgment required that third parties have a greater freedom to disseminate materials during an election. An initial reluctance to permit such an extension of authority issues perhaps from the American experience which demonstrates that unless these activities are carefully and effectively regulated, electoral campaigns will be hijacked by formally non-contesting organisations, either on behalf of political parties or single interest groups. The impact of such an experience is negative in that the electorate's attention is diverted from common

[72] *PPERA*, s 131. See Lord Bassam, HL Deb, vol 403, col 1124 (3 April 2000) and Lord Bach, HL Deb, vol 1024, col 220 (24 October 2000).

[73] *PPERA*, s 88.

[74] It is an offence for third parties not to notify the Electoral Commission if they knew, or ought to know, that they would spend £10,000 at a general election in England, or £5,000 each for Scotland, Wales or N Ireland—*PPERA*, s 94(4), (5).

[75] *PPERA*, s 85(2).

[76] *PPERA*, ss 85(2), (3).

[77] *PPERA*, sch 10(3)(2).

issues to those of sectarian, monied interests.[78] Given the Strasbourg Court's judgment, a balance will have to be struck between the candidates to an election whilst allowing for a wider debate on issues considered important by the public, or sections thereof. The legislative judgment evidenced by *PPERA* is of a clear hierarchy of participatory rights, with third parties assuming a lowly position.

A feature of the expenditure limit scheme unmentioned so far, is that notion of the 'regulated period'—the 12 months prior to the calling to the general election within which all expenses must be incurred.[79] The curiousness of this provision is immediately apparent in a regime where elections occur not on fixed dates but are announced a mere four to six weeks prior to polling day.[80] It is impossible for those intending to incur expenditure to accurately 'time their run'. A possible exception to that dilemma is of course, the party in government. Since it effectively determines that date of polling day, it alone will be able to manage its electoral expenditure in the knowledge of the quantative and temporal constraints imposed by the Act and although it may be the case that expenditure by parties is invariably end-loaded, that justification is premised upon a particular strategy of electoral campaigning and militates against parties adopting other approaches. An alternative technique—equally unappealing—is for participants to accept the formula for what they can spend in the year before the election campaign and spend it every year. Alternatively they may take a risk in the hope that the courts will find in their favour when they plead that they acted in good faith and spent in the normal way, not knowing when the election would be.

Ultimately, the question is, given the retrospective character of the provision, whether it is appropriate to put people who may incur substantial liabilities in the position of not knowing when they embark on a particular course of action whether it will be within the framework of the law. Political parties and also third party campaigners cannot know when elections will occur. That is scarcely a fair footing on which to set up a system given that the last two years of a Parliament can often be regarded as an election period. At such times, there is a constant awareness that there might be an election and it would be difficult for an organisation to plan its expenditure when it is so uncertain as to what period the 365-day-rule refers. Thus the rule gives the incumbent party singular tactical advantage because it does at least have an idea of when the election campaign will start. It can time its spending to maximum effect in advance of announcement of general election, whereas all others must wait until announcement. Given such hesitations, criticisms are not best directed at the notion of expenditure limits themselves, or of the 'regulated period', but rather the absence of fixed parliamentary terms. A better embedded constitutional arrangement one could scarcely imagine, but its

[78] For one such critique, see R Dworkin, *The Curse of American Politics*, The New York Review of Books, 17 October 1996.

[79] The regulated period for 'registered parties' is at *PPERA*, sch 9(3)(7); *Ibid*, at sch 10(3)(3)(b) for third parties. Essentially, the clock runs retrospectively from the date of the general election.

[80] *Representation of the People Act 1983* sets a minimum period of 17 working days between the calling of a general election and the poll taking place.

principled defences are limited, and the manifest unfairness that it introduces when combined with the eminently sensible provisions of *PPERA* ought to put pressure on an antiquated and largely purposeless constitutional anomaly.

In its inquiry into the Funding of Political Parties of 2003/4, and subsequent Report,[81] the Electoral Commission has recently revisited the question of expenditure caps. Like the CSPL in 1998, the Electoral Commission has moved off from the recognition that political parties perform a vital role in democratic life and require adequate funding in order to undertake that task. Adequacy in this respect refers not only to the proper funding of electoral campaigning, but also to the full range of inter-election activities, such as party building and developing policy. Notwithstanding these facts, and the newness of the *PPERA* structure, the EC has recommended significant changes to the scheme of expenditure limits as they currently stand. In its evidence taking processes, the Commission was clearly much impressed by claims that the electorate found local campaigning significantly more informative and engaging than the centrally run campaigns of the national parties—even to the extent of expressing outright hostility to the omnipresent billboard campaigns which are run at such great cost by the parties. Accordingly, their approach is to revisit the relationship between national and local expenditure limits, recommending a doubling of candidate expenditure limits (to approximately £16,000) and a simultaneous lowering of national expenditure limits to around £15m. These findings are somewhat tentative, couched as they are in the caveat that they ought to be subject to an analysis of the 2005 general election.

The question of national spending caps, and their level, was dealt with at length by the Neill Commission. The levels of expenditure therein recommended were subsequently adopted in *PPERA*. The current figure of national expenditure of £20m for a party contesting all UK seats balances out to about 50p spent per party per elector in the 12 months prior to a general election. And that 50p is to cover all communications (whether electronic, paper or personal), all administration and other costs. It scarcely seems extravagant and might be argued that that the real distaste from the public comes from the irregular announcements that this or that potentate has donated £*X*m to such and such party. It is that the engenders disquiet and attempts to constrain what are, by international standards, relatively modest levels of expenditure may be misplaced. Attempts to lower spending caps will severely constrain the capacity of parties to effectively campaign. Given that the UK's is not a regime of paid broadcasting which swallows vast sums from party coffers, it will not be that aspect of campaigning (possibly the least popular) that will be cut, but the meet-and-greets, and other costly activities.[82] In such circumstances it is likely not only that such spending limits will severely impinge upon the quality of political communication between parties and the electorate, but that it will generate challenges to the slashed expenditure ceilings under the free speech provision of the *Human Rights Act*.

[81] Above n 55. See that Report at 1.8 ff for the Commission's process and methods in this enquiry.

[82] See M Pinto-Duschinsky, 'Financing Politics: A Global View' (2002)13:4 *Journal of Democracy* 69–86.

As regards the recommendation that constituency level expenditure limits be doubled, this too is somewhat vulnerable to criticism. Whatever else the failings of the pre-*PPERA* scheme, its jewel in the crown was the tight expenditure constraints under which local campaigns operated. Low limits ensured that no one party could substantially out-gun its opponents, that most candidates could actually raise such an amount and above all that local candidates were able to adequately fund their campaigns without being beholden to either local grandees or the national party. And these virtues have persisted through to the present day. A local expenditure limit of circa £8,000 (which, like a speed limit, is best viewed as a maximum, not a target) is within the fundraising capacities of most major party candidates, without resort to mechanisms beyond raffles and dinners. The Electoral Commission's suggestion that such a limit should be doubled will place a degree of stress on each of the desirable features. The elevated fund raising capacities of major parties and incumbents will be significantly more telling when local campaigns will actually be entitled to spend all (or at least, much more) that they can raise. The threat is not so much of 'arms races' as of unipolar local campaigns.

Yet, even for those campaigns that are better able to exploit the new higher limits, the risk is that a culture of dependence, hitherto absent at the local level, will creep into existence. Being responsible for their own funding has given individual candidates a considerable degree of freedom so far as the conduct of their campaigning is concerned. Of course, central parties insist on a degree of 'singing from the same hymn sheet', but this is substantially of mutual benefit in that local campaigns are able to purchase and utilise centrally produced campaigning materials, the themes of which are reinforced by the national campaigns. But once candidates are required to seek funds from wealthy individuals in the area or redistributed funds via the central party, that degree of autonomy would be rapidly eroded. The marginal cost of raising an additional £8,000 or so should not be underestimated in the context of most British constituencies and candidates will have only limited options when seeking to fill their coffers. Optimistic forecasting may take the view that central parties would benevolently fund local campaigns on a no-strings-attached basis, especially if lowered national expenditure limits were to leave them with an additional £5m swilling about. It is doubtful whether a similar approach could be applied to local benefactors. The idea that donors within constituencies would be willing to part with thousands of pounds and seek no assurances is fanciful. This is not so much a criticism of such persons, but of a (proposed) system that would give them undue leverage over the campaigning process.

Donation Limits

Regulating the supply side of party funding has two main aspects: controlling how much comes into a party's coffers and where those funds originate from. The latter issue exercised particular controversy prior to *PPERA*, especially with respect to the permissibility of foreign donations and the laissez faire regime governing corporate donations. The phenomenon of donations from abroad was a contentious matter in the 1990s as a string of foreign businessmen of sometimes dubious propriety made significant contributions to Conservative Party funds.[83] The principled objection is however to those who have no vote in the UK having an influence on its politics, albeit through the indirect means of contributing to a political party. A formal residency requirement would obviously be unsatisfactory as it would exclude all those citizens who happen to reside abroad, even if only temporarily. A more functional approach was taken by *PPERA*, focussing on the legitimate interests of potential contributors, as measured by their electoral connection with the UK. Accordingly, section 54 of the Act creates the notion of a 'permissible donor' which for individuals means anyone on the electoral roll whilst section 141 shortens the period that the right to vote may be retained by a non-resident from 20 to 15 years. Although this provision is ostensibly desirable, it has the potential effect of depriving relatively poor national groups of campaign resources from abroad, in particular those groups representing racial and/or ethnic minorities who may rely on foreign resourcing.[84]

For institutional donors, the test of permissibility is not ownership (in the case of businesses) but the place of registration. Thus only companies registered to conduct business in the UK under the *Companies Act 1985* may make political donations and trade unions must be on the list kept under the *Trade Union and Labour Relations (Consolidation) Act 1992*.[85] For institutional donors however, the story does not end there. We have already noted that trade unions have long been subjected to fairly onerous conditions in order to make valid political donations whilst private corporations have been relatively unencumbered. This asymmetry was attacked by the Neill Committee which recommended that corporate donations be subjected to a regime similar to that imposed upon unions.[86] Section 139 of *PPERA* has enacted that recommendation by introducing to the *Companies Act 1985* a new Part XA, as set out in schedule 19 of *PPERA*, which incorporates the principle of shareholder consent, in the form of prohibiting corporate donations or expenditures unless authorised by an approval resolution passed at the company's AGM. These resolutions are valid for four years (unlike those for trade unions which are valid for ten years).[87]

None of this however addresses one of the main concerns of reformers of party funding regulation—the fear that contributions can engender a reliance of political parties on large donors, leading to the preferences of the ordinary electorate

[83] Most famously in relation to the Cypriot fugitive Asil Nadir, the Greek shipper John Latsis and the Hong Kong-Chinese businessman CK Ma. Controversy has also attached to largess of the Belize's Ambassador to the United Nations, Michael (now Lord) Ashcroft.

[84] Although not presently a live issue in the UK, it has been elsewhere, see BE Cain, 'Moralism and Realism in Campaign Finance Reform' (1995) *University of Chicago Legal Forum*, 111 and BD Brown, 'Alien Donors: The Participation of Non-Citizens in the US Campaign Finance System' (1997) *15 Yale Law and Policy Review* 530.

[85] *PPERA*, s 54(2).

[86] Committee on Standards in Public Life, *The Funding of Political Parties in the United Kingdom* (Cm 4057-I, 1998) paras 6.24–6.37.

[87] See J Gray, *Politics and Companies* (1999) 20 *The Company Lawyer* 275–6.

and grassroots members being ignored in favour of quid pro quos. The solution to this problem of corruption, or its appearance, has been dealt with in the USA by the imposition of limits on contributions as low as $1,000 which have been upheld by the Supreme Court on the basis that the limits protected a 'sufficiently important interest [anti-corruption] and employ[ed] means closely drawn to avoid unnecessary abridgment' of associational rights.[88] By contrast, *PPERA* has imposed no limits at all on the quantum of contributions, instead relying on transparency to purge quid pro quos from the system. This reliance is premised on the notion that the public will question what 'millionaire donors' are getting in return for their generosity—that the suspicion will always remain that such large sums are not given out of the goodness of their hearts but in expectation of future reward. However, the argument that transparency and its generation of public distaste for large donations will create a disincentive for political parties to solicit and accept such donations is simply not borne out by experience, viz the flurry of millionaires' donations disclosed in the first few days of January 2001.[89] If transparency continues to fail to limit contributions, and parties continue to rely on large individual donations, it is not unlikely that they will feel beholden to these donors, fearful of offending them, and anxious not to jeopardise repeat donations. Even if not in the mind of party treasurers (unlikely), these considerations will inevitably compromise the party's integrity in the public's perception. The reality or appearance that parties' freedom of action is restricted by large donations can only be undercut by limits on what they can accept. In imposing any such limit, care must be taken to ensure that the political parties are not starved such that they cannot perform those duties we expect of them—will they allow parties and candidates to raise sufficient money for effective advocacy? Even if the limits are set at a relatively high level—say £100,000—that permits large donors to make very substantial donations, these limits create a real problem that impacts disproportionately on the Labour Party, namely, how can contributions from trade unions be accommodated? Imposing a limitation on individual but not institutional donations would be arbitrary from the perspective of corruption avoidance, but we have already noted that *PPERA* purports to meet that challenge by other means. Nonetheless, a principled defence of the continuation of unrestricted institutional donations can be fashioned from the notion that donations ought to represent the desire of individuals to support a political actor of their choice. Trade unions being representative, voluntary, members' organisations, can readily function as the vehicle for transferring the cumulative preferences of their memberships. And under the new regime of shareholder consent, a similar argument can be fashioned for public companies' contributions. This being so, the limits

[88] *Buckley v Valeo* 424 US 1 (1976) at 25. Although limits on contributions were supported by three governmental interests—preventing corruption and its appearance; equalising the ability of citizens to affect elections; and opening the electoral process to more candidates—the court did not need to discuss that latter two, having decided the matter on the basis of the first. More recent cases have been less compliant on this issue, see *Nixon v Shrink Missouri Government PAC* 528 US 337, 926 (2000).

[89] For a different analysis, see Ewing in chp 4 of this volume.

which apply to the contributions of private individuals need not properly apply to institutional donors.

Notwithstanding the anxious scrutiny to which the Neill Committee subjected this issue, the recent Report of the Electoral Commission has looked at the possibility of a donation cap once again. Somewhat in line with the remarks above, the Commission is of the view that transparency has not served to ameliorate all public concerns regarding very large donations. In particular, the suspicion that major donors are able to buy access has been particularly hard to shift. Given then that we are dealing with the *appearance* of corruption, any donations to be introduced would have to lie at a particularly low level. A public mind that is concerned about a £1m donation from Mr Eccleston will not be set at ease by a cap of £500,000, or even £50,000. To the ordinary voter, says the Electoral Commission, that remains a suspicious sum. On that basis, the view taken in the report is that if a cap is to be introduced, and if it is to be effective in assuaging the public's fears of elite quid pro quos, it would have to stand at a level of around £10,000.

Were such a measure to be enacted, a raft of new problems, possibly greater problems than those currently faced, would have to be addressed. Firstly, there would inevitably be constitutional rights challenges to such restrictions on an associational basis. As in *Buckley*, a future court deciding this matter may draw the conclusion that one can effectively exercise one's right of association with a political party or candidate from the moment of contributing one's first pound. In such an event, the limit drawn at the £10,000 would not encounter any difficulties on this basis, but such an outcome is far from certain and in any case not explored in any detail by the Report. Secondly, as discussed above, and in chapter 4 of this volume, any such limit would have a devastating effect on the constitutional structure of the Labour Party. Founded as it is on an intimate relationship with organised labour, and the aggregated subs of members, the Labour Party would be stripped of its most stable and single largest source of income in the event of the imposition of any contribution limit of such a level. Such an outcome would clearly sit ill with the Commission's opening gambit as to the vital role of political parties in our constitutional apparatus. Relatedly, a contribution cap of £10,000 would engender a dramatic shortfall in party incomes. None of the major national parties would be able to withstand such a crippling blow to their finances, and if the much vaunted centrality of the political parties to our system of government is to be taken seriously, then the state would be obliged to step into this financial breach and provide substantial state funding. And here's the rub. While the Commission's research, both qualitative and quantative, has indicated that there is much anxiety surrounding large donations, that same research has revealed even greater hostility to extending public support for politics. Taken together with the delicate situation as regards associational rights and the disproportionate impact a low donation cap would have on the Labour Party, the Commission has found itself in a double bind. This is explored further below, as regards public funding, but the upshot for the purposes of a £10,000 cap is that the Commission has decided that in the absence of satisfactory resolution of the three issues raised, no case can presently be made for recommending any such cap.

Public Funding

The degree of affirmative state action taken to facilitate electoral and party activity in the UK is certainly on the low side when compared with most countries in Europe and North America.[90] Moreover, public funding is, as noted above, organised in a most disorganised fashion. Both of the most common devices of state support—direct subventions to political parties and tax relief on donations—are eschewed in favour of a disparate range of discrete mechanisms including funding the parliamentary work of opposition parties, the provision of free broadcasting airtime, free (though limited) use of the postal system and access to public meeting rooms. *Ad hoccery* in the finest British tradition is clearly at play here, but the relevant issue is not so much the elegance of the architecture but whether it can support the weight it carries. Public funding exists to ensure that parties have the funds they need to operate—to recruit and support candidates; to develop and advance policy; to mobilise voters; and to convey their message to the electorate in a distinctive fashion. If parties are starved of funds and so constrained in their operational capacities (because of restrictive regulations and/or the unwillingness of private donors to finance politics), a presumptive basis for state intervention arises.

The view that such a basis existed was taken by the CSPL, although only in a limited sense. The CSPL rejected suggestions that a 'new system should be introduced whereby the state is obliged for the indefinite future to provide financial support for the political parties',[91] in favour of more directed action against the paucity of resources available to parties for long term policy development. According to the Committee this afflicted both government and oppositional parties, either through the day to day demands of the political melee, or a concentration on campaigning and routine administration. Either way, '[T]he political parties themselves should be one of the major sources of ideas in British politics. They are not always so at present.'[92]

The government's response was the innovation of the 'Policy Development Grant', a global annual fund of £2m to be distributed by the Electoral Commission to political parties for the sole purpose of policy development.[93] Admittedly a modest sum, this ring-fenced sum should provide a significant boost to parties' ability to engage in long term research without fear of diverting scarce resources

[90] Public funding, for example, plays a major role in elections in the USA. Four states—Arizona, Maine, Massachusetts and Vermont—provide for full public financing for those candidates that accept spending limits. Some 22 states (and many more localities) provide public financing for political campaigns and organisations. See MJ Malbin and TL Gais, *The Day After Reform:Sobering Campaign Finance Lessons From the American States* (Albany, NY; Rockefeller Institute Press, 1998). These schemes are separate from the Presidential Election Campaign Fund which, set up in 1976, supports candidates to the presidency who accept certain spending limits.

[91] Committee on Standards of Public Life, *the Funding of Political Parties in the United Kingdom* (Cm 4067, 1998) rec 36. Such a scheme was supported most strongly by the Liberal Democrats, see *Ibid* at appendix V, p 247, para 23.

[92] *Ibid* at para 7.25.

[93] *PPERA*, s 12.

away from quotidian demands.[94] Given that the Electoral Commission has felt unable to recommend donation caps and correlative public funding in its latest report, it is perhaps no surprise that any increases in public funding that it has endorsed are designed to act as incentives to parties to better engage with the electorate. The view has been taken therefore that the Policy Development Grant scheme has been of benefit to the parties and should be extended beyond its present limits of operating only in Westminster to the Holyrood Parliament, the Northern Irish Assembly, the Welsh Assembly and the European Parliament. This seems perfectly sensible but the proposal to increase the current dispensation from £2m per annum to only £3m seems remarkably frugal.

It should also be noted that the CSPL recommended the introduction of a system of tax relief on donations as a means of boosting parties' incomes and civic participation. The government declined to include such a provision on a number of bases, including that it was inappropriate to compel tax payers to contribute to parties they potentially object to; that it would be costly to administer and that it would effectively operate as a subsidy to the Conservative Party alone.[95] Whilst the former two arguments are not strong (tax payers are frequently asked to support causes they disagree with and the administrative costs are surely worth paying if the scheme were meritorious on its own terms),[96] the latter one at least recognises the reality that tax relief on donations will disproportionately benefit those parties whose members are from higher income brackets. Accordingly, the objection is not to public subventions as such but as to the mode of distribution. By comparison, linking state support to a form of electoral success (as recommended by Houghton, see above) or the level of party membership might be seen as less objectionable. The view of the Electoral Commission however has been similar to that taken by the CSPL in 1998. The latter body argued that small donations would be incentivised by granting tax relief on donations up to £500—a sum that was criticised along the lines stated above, and ultimately rejected by the government. The Commission's latest Report is at one with the CSPL insofar as it seeks to create incentives for small donors, but appreciates the class/party bias of a £500 upper limit and so has settled for one of £200.[97] Whether this adequately meets the objection is an open question, but what is certainly welcome is the extension of any tax relief benefits to non-taxpayers—a previously well aired concern.[98]

Conclusion

In comparison with the old regime, *PPERA's* greatest virtue is its comprehensive scope. The Act has ensured that political actors are capable of fulfilling their

[94] For argument that £2m is too small a sum, see HC Deb, col 82, 10 Jan 2000 (MacShane).
[95] For opposition support of tax relief, see Lord Goodhart, HL Deb, vol 624, col 1136-8, 3 April 2000 and Lord Mackay, HL Deb, Vol 619, col 1143, 27 Nov 2000.
[96] HC Deb, vol 342, col 53, 10 Jan 2000 (Young).
[97] Above n 44 at 6.44ff.
[98] See Ewing, ch 4 in this volume.

constitutional functions both within and outside of Parliament, whether in election periods or not. They will continue to be supported almost entirely by private means with only limited support from the state but where once that may have been a cause for concern, with the new provisions regarding the disclosure and reporting of income and expenditure, as well as new constraints on expenditure itself, those fears ought to be assuaged.

It would be somewhat Panglossian to end there, however. As the Electoral Commission's Report has highlighted, there remain serious concerns, emanating substantially from public anxiety, as regards the present expenditure limits and the modes of campaigning that these engender and the absence of donation caps and the occasionally unseemly contributions that are thus sometimes made. Now, the second of these seems the more intractable of the problems since the very same popular hostility to public vice that objects to millionaire donations is the self same attitude that rejects the public purse making an ever greater contribution to the political process. Nor can this be dismissed as an irrational response. Given that public esteem for politicians is not high at present, diverting money away from other spending priorities so that politicians can spend it in contentious ways is likely to be counterproductive—unless controversy is the purpose of the exercise. Estimates indicate that the current system of public funding, in its myriad operations, costs the taxpayer some £100 m in an election year, and £25 m in other years.[99] That is a major expenditure by popular reckoning and more extensive provision would be tendentious in the extreme. The Electoral Commission's background paper (at 4.10) tentatively puts forward the figure of an extra £50m in state funding per annum. Even without index linking, that would amount to over £1/4 bn for the (five year) life of a Parliament. It is inconceivable that that will be received as a 'relatively small addition'. How many schools, hospitals, nurses, teachers . . .

There is certainly virtue in such a parsimonious approach. The tried-and-tested nature of the system—substantially in operation since the War; large parts of it since the Represention of the People Act 1918—has its own attractions. British elections have operated under that regime without either significant scandal or public disaffection at electoral conduct in a manner that is unprecedented in comparable western democracies. More significantly, the current system is consistent with maintaining and strengthening the link between voters and parties, is in accordance with British population's belief that further state funding of politics is not a priority; and a counter to the oft repeated claim that public funding somehow 'cleanses' the politic process. Indeed, the notion that public money somehow cleanses the political processes is one of the great *canards* of party funding. Empirical evidence is wanting. In fact, the evidence suggests that if anything, regimes in which large public funding of the political process features are those very regimes most afflicted by corruption. Germany is one example (and not only in the most recent bout of scandals), Italy another, and the USA a third. The fact

[99] *The Funding of Political Parties—Issues Paper* (London, Electoral Commission, 2003).

is that public funding merely contributes to the quantum of money in a system, creating opportunity structures for malfeasance. The only possibility for state money driving out private contributions (which would include members' dues, small donations, bean feast revenues etc) would be to proscribe completely such donations. Not only would this be contrary to a central pillar of British voluntary politics, it would comprehensively destroy the associational rights that individuals hold in every democratic regime. Compliance with Article 11 of the ECHR and thus the *Human Rights Act* would be a pipedream.

The traditions of politics in Britain have always maintained that political parties are the primary players in democratic politics and that they are voluntary associations, prospering or declining according to those members. More extensive state provision to parties threatens that link as parties move into the care of the state rather than being responsive to members and the membership. It is true that not all mechanisms of state support would entail this outcome but the danger is real (and is one that has afflicted German debates on state support since the 1960s). Any reforms in this area should therefore follow the broad scheme of the Houghton Committee,[100] which was mindful of this risk. It recommended state subventions to political parties on the basis of specified sums per vote gained at the previous election, in three forms: (1) annual grants to political parties nationally which passed a low threshold of electoral support; (2) support to candidates at the constituency level (so as to counterbalance the extra power that (1) may give to the national party) through reimbursement of election expenses and; (3) a scheme similar to (2) but to candidates for local government elections. An alternative system might pay sums on the basis of membership rather than votes gained. Indeed, this system would provide parties with a strong incentive to bolster their ranks with the dual benefits of broadening political participation among the electorate and increasing its own capacity to search out and effectuate the policy wishes of that electorate.

Like the Houghton scheme, any extensions to party funding should be attentive to the reality of voter and/or member support, and the more profound issue of the link between them and the political process. To this end, there may be an argument for extending the current level of support available to parties for essential infrastructural purposes (ie non-campaigning activities). In this way, state money would go towards enabling parties to do their essential tasks, and strengthening the dialogue between grassroots and parties.

[100] Houghton Committee on *Financial Aid to Political Parties* (Cmnd 6601, 1976).

4

The Disclosure of Political Donations in Britain

KD EWING

Introduction

BY 1997 IT was the practice of almost every democratic country in the world that the political parties should be required to reveal the sources of their income. Not in Britain. The parties voluntarily published annual income and expenditure accounts, but they were under no legal obligation to provide even this basic information and there was no one to vouch for the accuracy of the information that was provided. The Labour Party since 1995 published annually the names of those who donated more than £5,000 but did not publish the amount.[1] The Conservative Party refused to publish even the names of donors, with donors' names being said to be 'one of the Party's most closely guarded secrets', locked in the Treasury Department at Conservative Central Office.[2] The information was concealed even from party members who complained about the inadequacy of membership rights, especially in the area of financial accountability.[3] The secrecy was justified—by the then treasurer of the party—on the ground that 'Conservative Central Office is not a charity dedicated to helping the sick and suffering', and that it would be 'the height of folly to expose how such a machine manages its resources or, indeed, how large, or how small these resources are at any one time'.[4]

[1] It was also the case that the information was reported 10 months after the end of the year in which the donation was made. A donation made in January would thus not be disclosed until the October in the following year.

[2] *The Sunday Times*, 27 September 1992.

[3] HC 726 (1992–93), pp 164–5.

[4] L McAlpine, *Once a Jolly Bagman* (London, Weidenfeld and Nicolson, 1997) p 229.

The Road from Secrecy to Transparency

The secrecy of party funding was one of the issues addressed by the House of Commons Home Affairs Committee which conducted an inquiry into *The Funding of Political Parties* in 1993. But in a feeble report, the Conservative dominated Committee concluded that the case had not been made out 'for requiring disclosure of the identity of donors; where donations are made from identifiable and legitimate sources known to the party they should be allowed to remain private'.[5] In so concluding the Committee hid in a fog of arguments based on considerations of principle and overwhelming practical objections. The argument of principle had been provided in oral evidence to the Committee by Sir Norman Fowler, the Chairman of the Conservative Party. Drawing on Sir Norman the Committee was of the view that,

> Privacy in donations was as fundamental a right when giving to political parties as when giving to any other charitable organisation. What individuals did with their own money was entirely a matter for them and was not of legitimate interest to either inquisitive journalists, political opponents, or even the State. To reveal a name would be a breach of a donor's right to privacy, although of course if he wished to disclose his identity, he was at liberty to do so.[6]

So far as the 'particular and substantial difficulties' are concerned,[7] these related to the threshold at which any donation would be subject to disclosure, in view of the widely different proposals made by the range of witnesses to the Committee. There was also concern about the administrative machinery that would be needed to ensure compliance with any such obligation, and reference was made to the experience in Germany where it was said, citing an academic witness to the Committee, that 'the main parties had simply colluded to break the law'.[8]

Unpersuaded and undeterred, the Labour Party included a commitment in its election manifesto of 1997 to require the parties to 'declare the source of all donations above a minimum figure', as well as 'consider how the funding of political parties should be regulated and reformed'.[9] The implementation of that commitment was to become a matter of some urgency when shortly after the election the Labour Party was involved in a sleaze scandal from which it has never really recovered. The story dominated the news in a three week period in November 1997, and started with a disclosure on 5 November that the government was planning to push the European Commission to exempt Formula One from a proposed directive banning tobacco advertising.[10] Accused of 'bowing to intense lobbying from Formula One', and supported by only one other EC Member State, the government 'remained committed to a ban on tobacco advertising but said it should be done in a sensible

[5] Home Affairs Committee, *The Funding of Political Parties* (HC 726 (1992–93) above) para 80.
[6] *Ibid* at para 73.
[7] *Ibid* at para 74.
[8] *Ibid* at para 79, referring to Dr Michael Pinto Duschinsky.
[9] New Labour, *Because Britain Deserves Better* (1997).
[10] *Guardian*, 5 November 1997.

and pragmatic way'.[11] It was subsequently revealed that the Formula One boss—Mr Bernie Ecclestone—had made a substantial donation to the Labour Party before the election, but worse was to follow when it was eventually disclosed that the sum involved was a £1 m and that the Labour Party was negotiating with Mr Ecclestone for another £1 m. A new word entered the vernacular, with a million pounds now being referred to in less reverential circles as a 'Bernie'. But the affair had other consequences, not the least of which was to persuade the Prime Minister of the need to implement with some alacrity his manifesto commitment relating to political parties. The first step in this direction was taken when the matter of public funding was referred to the Committee on Standards in Public Life for examination (in line with the manifesto proposal). After a thorough investigation, the Committee reported in the autumn of 1998, with its 100 recommendations for reform constituting the backbone of the *Political Parties, Elections and Referendums Act 2000*.[12]

Reporting and Disclosure: The New Statutory Regime

The *Political Parties, Elections and Referendums Act 2000* is a wide ranging measure which addresses the problem of party funding in a number of ways.[13] In contrast to the position elsewhere in Europe, it eschews the option of public funding and instead seeks better to regulate what was to remain in essence a system of predominantly private funding. Neither of the two main parties was in favour of public funding, though the Opposition parties were handed a substantial increase in the amount of money provided by the State to assist with their parliamentary activities. This is a scheme—the so called Short Scheme—that had been introduced in 1975 in recognition of the fact that the Opposition parties in Parliament have research and other needs. So far as the new regulatory regime is concerned, the starting point is the introduction of the concept of the permissible donor, defined in such a way as to exclude foreign donations.[14] This is followed by an obligation by the parties to report to the Electoral Commission on a quarterly basis all donations in excess of £5,000.[15] The information is then published on the website of the Commission (itself created by the 2000 Act).[16] Before considering these provisions in detail, it is to be noted that despite the large donation by Ecclestone that precipitated the legislation, there is no limit on the size of a donation from a permissible donor. The Act did, however, introduce a requirement that companies may make

[11] *Guardian*, 6 November 1997.

[12] Fifth Report of the Committee on Standards in Public Life (CSPL), *The Funding of Political Parties in the United Kingdom* (Cm 4057–I, 1998). See L Klein, 'On the Brink of Reform: Political Party Funding in Britain' (1999) 31 *Case Western Reserve Journal of International Law* 1, and N Ghaleigh [1999] *PL* 43.

[13] For a fuller account, see KD Ewing, 'Transparency, Accountability and Equality: The Political Parties, Elections and Referendums Act 2000' [2001] *PL* 542.

[14] *Political Parties, Elections and Referendums Act* 2000, s 54.

[15] *Ibid*, s 62.

[16] *Ibid*, s 1.

donations only if they have shareholder approval, though this is an obligation enforceable under company law rather than electoral law.[17]

The Purpose and Scope of Disclosure

The reporting and disclosure provisions have thus been left to bear a heavy load. The issue of contribution limits was considered only briefly by the Neill Committee, and was not supported by either the Labour or Conservative parties. Arguments from other witnesses that parties receiving large donations allowed wealthy individuals to buy elections were met by the response that 'individuals should have the freedom to contribute to political parties, and the parties should be free to compete for donations'.[18] Arguments that limits should be imposed to prevent the parties being subject to improper pressures were met by the response that disclosure would 'remove illegitimate pressure, whether apparent or real'. In any event, if a party 'becomes over—dependent on a particular source, that is its own affair, provided its dependence is a matter of public knowledge'.[19] And arguments that large corporate donations allowed corporations to exercise influence over public policy were met by the response that the Committee's proposals to reform corporate giving would 'sufficiently address the concerns over such donations'.[20] These were the proposals for shareholder approval, which strictly were about the accountability of a company to its members rather than to the electorate. But the Neill Committee did not place its faith exclusively on the reporting and disclosure regime that it proposed. Also important were the recommendations for electoral spending limits which would 'tend to lessen the need for large donations'.[21]

Following the recommendations of the Neill Committee, the treasurer of a registered party must submit a quarterly donation report to the Electoral Commission, the report to record all donations in excess of £5,000.[22] For this purpose a donation is widely defined to include donations of money as well as donations in kind. It also includes donations from the State in the form of Short money and policy development grants. The latter were introduced by the 2000 Act and are administered by the Electoral Commission which was given an annual budget of £2m for the purpose, to be distributed between eligible parties. Donation reports must be submitted within 30 days of the end of the reporting period to which it relates.[23] Anything of £5,000 or less need not be reported, though if in a subsequent quarter there is another donation of £5,000 or less which together with donations in the previous period exceed £5,000, the combined amount must

[17] *Ibid*, s 139.
[18] Fifth Report of the Committee on Standards in Public Life (CSPL), *The Funding of Political Parties in the United Kingdom* (Cm 4057–I, 1998) at para 6.7.
[19] *Ibid.*
[20] *Ibid.*
[21] *Ibid.* See 2000 Act, note n 14 at ss 72–84.
[22] *Political Parties, Elections and Referendums Act* 2000, s 62.
[23] *Ibid*, s 65.

be disclosed.[24] Once the £5,000 limit has been reached for any one year—whether by way of a single donation or an aggregation of smaller donations—any subsequent donations of more than £1,000 must be recorded and reported. For this purpose there must be a reporting not only of any donation of more than £1,000, but also a reporting of a number of donations which in aggregate exceed £1,000.[25] At the time of a general election, more frequent reports must be made.[26]

The Scope of Disclosure and Party Structure

At first blush, it would appear to be easy enough to evade these obligations, commendable though they are. Just to remind ourselves: all donations over £5,000 (and at £1,000 thresholds thereafter) to the national party—including donations in kind—must be reported and disclosed. Surely it would be easy enough for the donor to give the money to the regional or constituency parties which could spend the money on their own activities or channel it to the national party. This was a loophole in the Canadian system of reporting, so that donations to local organisations might appear somewhere as an internal party transfer without the identity of the donor ever being revealed. The elimination of this risk therefore suggests the need for measures designed to ensure the transparency of donations made to all parts of a party organisation. There is a need not only for transparency to relate party policy nationally to donor activity, but also to relate local party policy and conduct to donor activity. There are a number of ways by which this could be done: each unit of party organisation (constituency party or association) could be required to report donations to the Electoral Commission (as recommended by the Labour Party in its evidence to the Neill Committee); or each national party could be made responsible for reporting all donations to all units of party organisation (as is the case in Germany).

The *Political Parties, Elections and Referendums Act 2000* follows the German example. But it does so in very complex and impenetrable terms. The effect is that the party treasurer is responsible not only for reporting donations to the central organisation of the party, but also to the accounting units of the party (in the case of those parties which have accounting units—which includes all the large parties). There are however modifications, to reflect the fact that a donation in excess of £5,000 annually to a local party would be unusual. So there is an obligation on the part of the Party treasurer to report quarterly any donation of more than £1,000 to any unit of party organisation, or any donations which in aggregate amount to more than £1,000 in any quarter, or which in aggregate amount to more than £1,000 when added to other donations from the same source in previous quarters in the reporting year in question.[27] But what happens if a donation

[24] *Ibid*, s 62(4)(5).
[25] *Ibid*, s 62(6)(7).
[26] *Ibid*, s 63.
[27] *Ibid*, s 62(11).

of £1,000 is made locally and £5,000 nationally? In neither case would the individual donation have to be reported, because in both cases it falls below the reporting obligation. Here the Act provides that any donation to a unit of party organisation which does not have to be reported (because it falls below the more than £1,000 limit) is to be treated as a donation to the central organisation of the party.[28] This means that it would have to be aggregated with donations made to the central party organisation, so that if in aggregate all these donations exceed £5,000, they will have to be reported.[29]

'Sleaze': The Continuing Problem of Political Donations

Although donations are thus widely defined, it is nevertheless quite clear that the *Political Parties, Elections and Referendums Act 2000* has not resolved the problem of political funding. Indeed the ink was barely dry before a series of other scandals erupted in quick succession. Two problems have emerged, as a cloud of sleaze appeared to descend on British politics, providing an opportunity for the media to attack the government and the Labour Party, which was soon to learn about the down-side of disclosure. The first problem is that some extremely large donations were made to the parties just before the Act was introduced on 16 February 2001. These include donations of £2m from each of Christopher Ondaatje (a retired financier), Lord Hamlyn (a publisher) and Lord Sainsbury (a government minister).[30] There was no obligation to disclose these donations which had been raised before the Act was due to come into force, and the reluctance of Labour to identify the donors added to the unease about the donations, which were said to make the party 'unhealthily dependent on a few large gifts from a few rich men'.[31] The Conservative Party also reported a large donation of £5 m from the spread betting tycoon, Stuart Wheeler, making him the biggest one-off donor in British political history.[32]

[28] *Ibid*, s 62(12).

[29] In some countries (such as Australia) reportable donations must be reported by donors as well as political parties. That is not the case in the United Kingdom, with one exception. This arises where a donor makes a large number of small donations to a registered party which in aggregate exceed more than £5000. A small donation for this purpose is a donation of £200 or less. This is another anti-evasion device, designed to deal with the possibility that someone may donate more than £5000 to a party in a series of small parcels of money deposited at different parts of the party organisation. This could arise where an individual makes a small cash donation to a party nationally, and a series of small cash donations to constituency or regional parties. It is perhaps unlikely that anyone would want to go to the trouble of, say, making 25 donations of £200 to 25 local party organisations, as well as a donation of £200 to a party nationally. If they do, none of this would have to be reported by the Party. But it would have to be reported by the donor, by the 31 January after the calendar year in which the donations were made. It is necessary to specify only the aggregate value of the donations, but not to list each of them.

[30] *Guardian*, 5 January 2001. This was said to be a 'troublesome' donation, on the ground that 'it could be read as a form of insurance against dismissal; *Guardian*, 3 January 2001. But the point is unconvincing.

[31] *Guardian*, 3 January 2001.

[32] *The Times*, 18 January 2001.

Although the large donations have dwindled since the Act was brought into force, they have not dried up altogether, as Lord Sainsbury's donation of £2 m to the Labour Party in 2003 made clear. The other problem is a rather different one which erupted in a frenzy of press excitement and indignation in the Spring of 2002, though it has since abated. This relates to allegations that a number of donors to the Labour Party (not those referred to) appeared to benefit from government decisions in their favour, though it should be stressed that there is no evidence to link the decisions with the donations or vice versa. These latter donations were not huge, being in the region of £50,000 to £125,000. Three donations were particularly controversial.

The first was the donation of £100,000 by Richard Desmond at the beginning of 2001, again before the legislation came into force, escaping the new disclosure rules by 'a hair's breadth'.[33] Apart from the timing of this donation, there were two reasons why it was controversial. The first was its source. Mr Desmond was reported in the press as a man who made his money trading in pornography.[34] This was thought by many to make him an improper person from whom the Labour Party should not accept a donation:[35] the *Guardian* was satisfied that 'Labour's latest donor demeans the party'.[36] But that is a matter for the Labour Party, its members and supporters. Following the *Political Parties, Elections and Referendums Act 2000*, electors now have the information to make up their own minds about Labour and the company it keeps. A more serious allegation was that the donation was made around the time when Mr Desmond was seeking to buy the *Daily Express* and its stablemate the *Daily Star*. Added to the government's discomfiture is the fact that Mr Desmond had taken tea with Mr Blair in Downing Street. This meeting had taken place on 26 November 2000, four days after Mr Desmond's Northern and Shell media company had paid £125 m for the Express Newspaper group. On 7 February 2001 the Secretary of State for Trade and Industry announced that he would not refer Mr Desmond's purchase of the *Express* to the Competition Commission, a few days before the Labour Party banked Mr Desmond's £100,000 donation. In deciding not to refer the purchase to the Competition Commission, Mr Byers was acting in accordance with his policy announced on 26 October 2000 to accept the advice of the Office of Fair Trading on takeovers 'save in exceptional circumstances'. In this case the minister followed the advice of the Director-General. Despite the obvious lack of impropriety, unfavourable comparisons were nevertheless made between this case and the case of Mr David Sullivan, also a businessman with adult interests. His attempt to acquire regional newspapers in Bristol in 1990 was blocked on the ground that he was not a fit and proper person to own a national newspaper.[37]

[33] *Evening Standard*, 13 May 2002, accusing Labour of 'losing the moral high ground'.

[34] 'Porn magnate Desmond gives £100,000 to New Labour' (*The Independent*, 12 May 2002); 'Labour defends porn baron's donation' (*Guardian*, 13 May 2002); 'How Blair's tea-time friend ran his porn empire' (*Guardian*, 30 May 2002).

[35] See *The Times*, 13 May 2002; *Guardian*, 13 May 2002.

[36] *Guardian*, 13 May 2002.

[37] *The Times*, 13 May 2002.

The second controversial donation was the donation by Lakshmi Mittal in June 2001. Mr Mittal gave the Labour Party £125,000 in June 2001. Concerns were raised about the fact that on 23 July 2001 the Prime Minister wrote to the Romanian Prime Minister in the following terms:

> I am delighted by the news that you are to sign the contract for the privatisation of your biggest steel plant Sidex, with the LNM Group. This represents an important step forward in the efforts you and your government are making to restructure and modernise your country's economy. I am particularly pleased that it is a British company that is your partner. This should send a very positive signal to investors and businessmen in Britain and more widely. Together with the other measures you are taking, I hope it will stimulate renewed interest by British business in Romania. And it will, I hope, set Romania even more firmly on the road to membership of the European Union, an objective of which the British government remains a staunch supporter.[38]

Not everyone was troubled by this letter, though claims were made that Mr Mittal's name had been deleted as had a reference to him as a friend of the Prime Minister. Hugo Young took the view that 'the alleged service performed, writing a letter after a deal was done, was nugatory',[39] while others claimed that it was the attempt to cover up an embarrassment that caused more difficulty than the Prime Minister's actions themselves.[40] *Guardian* reporters, however, were not so sanguine, pointing out that 'the letter was sent at a crucial moment when the French had intervened, and Mittal had been forced to return to London empty-handed after a postponement of the deal on July 20'.[41] It was also claimed that although Mr Mittal was resident in the United Kingdom, his company was registered in the Netherlands.[42] He had only a small administrative staff based in the United Kingdom, and it was also claimed in the press that the deal would 'bring no jobs and no profits into Britain'.[43] So far as the Romanian plant is concerned, it was said to have been sold to an offshore registered Dutch Antilles firm, LNM Holdings NV, a company said to have been privately owned by Mr Mittal. This called into question claims that Mr Blair was intervening on behalf of British business. A crucial question was whether Mr Blair knew that Mr Mittal was a Labour Party donor. According to *The Independent*, Mr Blair was 'adamant that he did not know', and insisted that it would not have made any difference if he did.[44] On the other hand, it was reported by the *Guardian* that,

> Blair went to a thank-you party for big donors at the house of Lord Levy, his chief fundraiser, in June 2001, the *Guardian* has established. Acquaintances of Mittal say he was one of only three Asians present. The donation was also publicly announced

[38] *Guardian*, 14 February 2002.
[39] *Guardian*, 12 February 2002.
[40] *The Independent*, 14 February 2002.
[41] *Guardian*, 14 February 2002.
[42] *The Independent*, 13 May 2002.
[43] *Guardian*, 14 February 2002.
[44] *The Independent*, 14 February 2002.

> on June 14 in a list compiled by the Electoral Commission. Mittal had also donated a large sum for the 1997 election. Blair no longer repeated the claim of ignorance of Mittal's donor status in Parliament yesterday, conceding instead: 'it was a matter of public record that he was a donor to the Labour Party.[45]

The third donation to give rise to concern was in fact one of a number of donations from Dr (now Lord) Paul Drayson, the owner of a company called Powderject Pharmaceuticals. The reason why these donations (two of £50,000 each) gave rise to concern was that the company was awarded a £32m government contract to supply smallpox vaccine 'to protect Britain against a bioterrorist attack'.[46] The second of these donations was said to have been given 'while the government was deciding who should be awarded the contract'.[47] Concerns were raised when it was suggested that the normal procurement procedures had been waived in the interests of national security. According to press reports, the government claimed that it was not in the public interest to draw attention to the preparations for terrorist attacks by the use of biological weapons. Also according to press reports, the government claimed that Powderject was 'the only company that could quickly produce the millions of doses needed to protect the UK population', though it was also reported that 'other manufacturers say they could have met the requirements if they had been given the details'. For its part, the government claimed that Powderject was the only company that could supply the strain of the vaccine which had been recommended by the security and intelligence services.[48] An investigation by the *Guardian* tends to suggest that there was no impropriety in awarding the contract to Powderject. According to the *Guardian*, John Hutton the health minister 'appears to have been subsequently embarrassed' by the discovery that Drayson 'had been making party donations'.[49] But his request that the matter be reconsidered was overruled at the insistence of the Ministry of Defence which wanted the strain that only Drayson could provide.[50] Any lingering doubts about impropriety were subsequently scotched by a National Audit Office investigation.[50a]

Although these proved to be the most serious cases, allegations and innuendos were made in the press about other donations. Apart from money from Enron, these included claims about donations from individuals and companies linked to the gambling industry who stood to gain from the government's policy of liberalisation.[51]

[45] *Guardian*, 14 February 2002. In the *Guardian* on the following day, Ewan MacAskill and Patrick Wintour reported that 'Mr Blair has admitted that he knew Mr Mittal was a donor, but did not make the connection with his company, LNM, which was bidding for the steelworks.'

[46] *Sunday Times*, 14 April 2002.

[47] *Guardian*, 29 June 2004.

[48] *Guardian*, 13 April 2002.

[49] *Guardian*, 29 June 2004.

[50] Other attempts have been made to link Drayson's donations to government benefits. But they too seem thin and rather spurious; *Observer*, 28 April 2002.

[50a] Comptroller and Auditor General, *Procurement of Vaccines by the Department of Health*, HC 625(2002–2003)(9 April 2003).

[51] *Sunday Times*, 31 March 2002; *The Times*, 8 August 2002.

This was followed by a claim that the Prime Minister used a trip to the Czech Republic 'to promote the sale of jet fighters made by a company [BAE systems] that donated money to Labour', in an affair that was said to have 'uncanny echoes' of Mittal.[52] The currency of claims that donations brought Prime Ministerial influence was, however, beginning to devalue with overuse. Thus,

> Tony Blair used his personal authority to save a £1bn deal to sell Hawk fighter-bombers to the Indian government. The company involved in the deal is British Aerospace Systems which is listed among companies who gave more than £5,000 in sponsorship in both 1998 and 2000.[53]

Nevertheless, other allegations about 'cash for favours' were also made. These included a claim that a law firm that had donated £6,100 was paid more than £8 m by the government to look after miners' compensation claims.[54] But having made the claim under a 'cash for favours' headline, the newspaper also reported that there was 'no suggestion the donation was made in expectation of Government favours'. Several months later a new 'contracts for donors row' erupted following claims by a haulage company that 'it had lost government work during the foot and mouth crisis to a rival that had made a donation to the Labour Party'.[55] Drawing parallels with the Drayson donation, in this case normal public procurement procedures were allegedly not applied, though in this case the £5,000 donation was made after the haulage contract had been awarded. But this was not the end of it. A millionaire Indian food entrepreneur had to insist that there was no connection between his £100,000 donation to Labour and his knighthood in the Golden Jubilee Birthday Honours' List.[56] More recently further concern has been expressed about some of the nominations made by the Conservative Party to the House of Lords: the coincidence between nominations and donations to party funds had not gone unnoticed.[57]

The Labour Party's Response

The introduction of the *Political Parties, Elections and Referendums Act 2000* ought to have been a genuine cause for celebration. Instead the Labour Party was mired in controversy because of donations and the circumstances surrounding these donations. It was thus to discover that transparency comes at a price: it is not enough to report and disclose if what is reported and disclosed causes offence. Reporting and disclosure also require the parties to adapt to the new legal regime

[52] *The Independent*, 15 April 2002.
[53] *The Independent*, 2 June 2002.
[54] *Daily Telegraph*, 25 May 2002.
[55] *Sunday Times*, 4 August 2002.
[56] *Independent on Sunday*, 16 June 2002.
[57] *The Times*, 5 December 2003.

unless they are prepared to be mocked and embarrassed by what is revealed. The Labour Party was particularly stung by the donation from Mr Richard Desmond, the proprietor of a number of 'adult' publications. Apart from the concerns raised about the coincidence between the donation and Mr Desmond's acquisition of the *Daily Express*, concerns were also expressed about the Labour Party's judgment in accepting money from such sources. Those concerned about the latter were hardly impressed by the response of the then Chairman of the Labour Party (Dr John Reid) who is reported as having said that the party would not sit in moral judgment of those who want to make gifts.[58] In this febrile atmosphere Dr Reid was himself to be the target of allegations that he 'had set up a trust fund which concealed the identity of supporters': it was alleged that his election return revealed that 70 per cent of his total election spending (£5,326.07) had been provided by 'John Reid Electoral Expenses Fund, c/o Atkinson Donnelly, Chartered Accountants'.[59] The concerns expressed in the Spring of 2002 led to a number of calls for a fresh round of controls on the funding of the parties, as well as the introduction of State funding. These are matters to which we return. They also induced the Labour Party to take some precautionary measures to deflect further allegations of sleaze by which it was engulfed.

Adapting to the New Regime

The Labour Party was sufficiently chastened by the increasingly adverse publicity surrounding its donations that it moved to introduce a number of safeguards to avoid any repetition of such controversies. Transparency thus does help to alter behaviour, though it is perhaps surprising that the Labour Party should not have been prepared for this. Nevertheless the party in the recent past has a good record on self regulation: before there was any obligation to do so, the party published the names of donors of more than £5,000 and refused foreign donations. That legacy finds more contemporary expression with the announcement in May 2002 of changes in the way that the Labour Party would deal with donations and donors.[60] One of the key features of the new arrangements is the adoption of a Statement for Donors, whereby it is declared that donors to the Labour Party provide support because they are broadly committed to the aims and values of the Labour Party, and accept that they provide this support 'without seeking personal or commercial advancement or advantage for themselves or others'. Quite how this will operate in practice will be revealing, given that the Statement reproduces clause IV of the party constitution which makes clear that the Labour Party 'is a

[58] *Guardian*, 13 May 2002; *Tribune*, 17 May 2002. Fiona McTaggart—described as 'one of Labour's leading feminist MPs' is also reported as rejecting criticism: "If society thinks making money from pornography is legitimate, I think it is legitimate for a political party to take money from pornographers, so long as there is no evidence of influence over policy".'

[59] *Scotland on Sunday*, 10 November 2002. But this did not breach electoral law, though the arrangement was criticised for not complying with the spirit of the law 'to allow transparency and let people see if there were significant donations.'

[60] See C Clarke, 'Committed to a Funding Re-Think', *Tribune*, 31 May 2002.

democratic socialist party'. The Statement also makes clear that 'by supporting the Labour Party with donations, it is understood that this should not of itself disadvantage anyone, whether personally or in terms of business activities'.

In addition to this Statement, another important initiative is the setting up of a new fund-raising committee to 'have oversight in the area of major donors'. This has been referred to in the press as an ethics committee, and is expressly stated by Labour to be designed to build on the legislation. But despite winning plaudits from the right wing press,[61] two problems have been identified with this initiative. One is the composition of the Committee, with difficulty caused in particular by the fact that it includes the Labour Party's chief fund-raiser. Although his influence is likely to be diluted by the presence of five others, it is criticised by some as a text book illustration of conflict of interest: he who raises the money is also judging on whether to receive it. For his part Lord Levy is reported at a press conference announcing these initiatives as being amazed that 'people cannot understand that you can put various areas of your life into different boxes and deal with them accordingly'.[62] The more sceptical, however, saw Lord Levy's presence as raising doubts about whether the Committee will take tough choices.[63] The other problem is the concern that the Committee has no published ethical principles to guide its proceedings and by which it can be held to account. Apart from an alertness to 'potential conflicts of interest', each case it seems is to be judged on its merits, and it remains to be seen whether money would be accepted in the future from people like Mr Desmond.

The Response of Donors

But it is not only the parties which are adapting to the new regime. Donors have gone cold, as the press has become interested in who they are and questions their motives for making donations. The press interest can be sustained and intrusive, and indeed one of the issues raised in the Labour Party's self-regulatory initiative is to condemn much of this coverage and to assert 'the democratic right of individuals and organisations to make political donations', said to be 'vital to the existence and quality of our democracy', while accepting that 'donors should not be treated differently, positively or negatively, because they are donors'. But it may be too late. According to the Labour Party's fund-raiser, 'the big donors are running scared, and it is becoming increasingly difficult to raise money'.[64] Big donors have become quasi-public figures whose conduct is newsworthy on matters quite unrelated to their donation, as in the report that 'Labour donor cuts workers' pensions'. The story was reported in April 2002: the donation referred to in the article was made in 1997.[65] All of which is to suggest that the need for contribution limits may have passed: transparency may be beginning to operate at both the demand and

[61] *Daily Telegraph*, 22 May 2002.
[62] *The Times*, 22 May 2002.
[63] *The Guardian*, 23 May 2002.
[64] *Daily Telegraph*, 25 May 2002.
[65] *The Guardian*, 22 April 2002.

the supply sides to provide an effective form of regulation as the Neill Committee anticipated it would.

But although some may lament the shyness of the donors, it is not necessarily to be deprecated. Indeed it might be argued that there are certain kinds of donor to a governing party who should be actively discouraged, and that the Labour Party procedures do not go far enough in this regard. It is not enough that the donor accepts the aims and values of the party to which he or she is donating, nor is it enough for the Party to be alert to potential conflicts of interest: it ought to be clear beyond argument that donations from certain sources are simply not acceptable by a party of government. In other words, there is a case for developing the idea of the impermissible donor, to complement the existing statutory concept of the permissible donor. This would mean that within the context of the permissible donor, there are some donations which would not be acceptable. It is already the case that donations may not be accepted as an inducement for a political honour, or for a political honour to be given as an inducement for a donation. In the absence of legislation, it ought also to be accepted by the governing party that a donation ought not to be accepted from a government contractor or anyone who may be bidding for a government contract or who is on a list of approved bidders. There are some countries where such donations are unlawful, notably the United States,[66] and there would be a case for similar legislation here. This would eliminate any suspicion—however unfounded—that donations are a prequisite to the granting of a contract and that donations are given as some kind of kickback for favours granted.

Donation Trends: The Labour Party

Some four and half years have passed since the *Political Parties, Elections and Referendums Act 2000* came into force. The donations made before and just after it came into force provided great sport and excited a great media frenzy. But now that the dust has settled, it is timely to reflect on what the information is yielding about the state of political funding in Britain. In the first three years of the new legal regime (February 2001–March 2004) the Electoral Commission reveals that a total of £89 m was donated to political parties. The principal beneficiary was the Labour Party which received more donations and more money, though the average Labour Party donation appears to be smaller than the average donation to either the Conservatives or the Liberal Democrats. Thus we find that 2864 donations to the Labour Party yielded a total of £40,745,680.71; that 1649 donations to the Conservative Party yielded £36,406,491.69; and that 1007 donations to the Liberal Democrats yielded £6,375,993.14. This suggests that the average donation to the Labour Party is £14,226, the Conservatives £22,077, and the Liberal Democrats £6,331.

A striking feature of donations to the Labour Party is the heavy reliance on trade unions. For the moment it is enough to record that of the £40,745,680.71

[66] *Federal Election Campaign Finance Act 1971*, s 441c.

donated to the Labour Party, some £26,455,840.89 was supplied by trade unions. This accounted for 1793 of the Labour Party's 2864 donations. Of these the bulk was provided by the so called 'big four' unions, as follows:

Donor	**Cash**	**Non Cash**
UNISON	4,836,018	13,956
GMB	4,355,359	22,648
TGWU	2,979,635	6,669
AMICUS[67]	5,254,569	506,495
Total	17,425,581	549,768
Total Cash and Non Cash Donations	**17,975,349**	

The total number of donations from each of these unions was 230, 229, 159, and 303 respectively, many of these from union branches to constituency Labour Parties, as well as head office affiliation fees and election donations. Other large union donors included the CWU and USDAW. But between them the four large unions accounted for 44 per cent of the Labour Party's donation income.

The other striking feature of donations to the Labour Party relates to large personal donations. In the period from 2001 to 2004, Labour received six donations in excess of £250,000 from four people:

Donor	**Date**	**Donation**
Lord Sainsbury	25.01.02	2,000,000
Lord Paul Hamlyn	20.12.02	500,000
Lord Sainsbury	01.03.03	2,500,000
William Haughey	05.12.03	330,000
Lord Paul Hamlyn	19.12.03	500,000
Sir Christopher Ondaatje	19.12.03	1,000,000
Total		**6,830,000**

In addition to the above, another five individuals gave six donations of between £100,001 and £250,000 each. These were as follows:

Donor	**Date**	**Donation**
Alan Sugar	09.06.01	200,000
Lakshmi Mittal	28.06.01	125,000
Sir Richard Cohen	14.02.02	200,000
Bill Kenwright	13.06.02	200,000
Sir Richard Cohen	17.02.03	250,000
Sir David Garrard	23.05.03	200,000
Total		**1,175.000**

[67] This includes donations by the two constituent unions (AEEU and MSF) prior to the amalgamation to create AMICUS in 2002.

The combined effect of the foregoing is that the Labour Party relied on only nine people for about a fifth of its donation income. These nine people accounted for more than a half of donation income if trade union donations are removed from the equation. The other issue relating to the funding of the Labour Party is the extent to which it relies on corporate funding. Here the evidence suggests that reports of Labour dependence on corporate money are greatly exaggerated, though many of the individuals who fund the party have made their money in business. But support by businessmen (there are no female 'high value' donors) does not mean support by businesses. According to the Electoral Commission, the Labour Party received 160 donations from companies, these yielding only £948,569.75, which represents c 2.5 per cent of the value of donations to the Labour Party. The average business donation to Labour is in fact under £6,000. All but three donations were £25,000 or less, and the three largest donations were £30,000. Of these one was by the Political Animal Lobby, a company but not a commercial enterprise. The other two were donations of £30,000 from Manchester Airport. These latter had to be returned because the donor had no authority to make them. As we shall see the position relating to the Conservative Party is very different.

Donation Trends: Opposition Parties

Donations to the Opposition parties are unlikely to be as controversial as donations to the governing party, though the questions raised about the Conservative nominated peers in 2004 indicates that the Opposition parties are not immune from scrutiny and criticism. But the current problem with the Opposition parties is the extent to which they have fallen badly behind Labour in fund-raising and badly behind Labour in terms of financial security. The trade union base has been seen to be a remarkably stabilising force for Labour and a remarkable source of financial security. Attempts to erode this in the 1980s have largely failed, and the other parties have no comparable sources of alternative funding. It is a remarkable and paradoxical feature of the financial position of both the main Opposition parties that they are now heavily dependent on the State for their financial security. This is despite the fact that the Conservative Party is opposed to State funding.

The Conservative Party

Between 2001 and 2004 the Conservative Party received 1649 donations, which is significantly less than Labour's 2864, though more than Labour's 1071 donations if trade union donations are deducted from the total. The first striking feature of Conservative funding is the party's heavy reliance on the State. Of the £36 m in donations reported by the Conservative Party, some £11.9 m were in the form of public funds, such as the Short money and policy development grants. That is to say that the party most strongly opposed to State funding depends on public funds for a third of its donation income. A second striking feature of Conservative Party funding is that it is more heavily dependent on large donations than the Labour Party. In the period 2001 to 2004, the Conservatives received four donations in excess of £250,000, as follows:

Donor	Date	Donation
John Wheeler	03.05.01	2,450,000
Sir Paul Getty	11.06.01	5,000,000
John Wheeler	27.11.03	504,000
George Maugham	24.02.04	400,000
Total		**8,354,000**

So although there are fewer very large donations than Labour, their combined value is higher. The Conservatives also received five cash donations of between £100,001 and £250,000, the donors in question being Robert Fleming (£206,000), Roderick Fleming (£200,000), Leonard Steinberg (£110,000), and Sir Stanley Kalms £120,000 and £160,000). These come to a total of £796,500 with two donations in kind (travel) by Corin Graeff (£128,353) and Edward Haughey (£119,816) accounting for another £248,169. Total donations from these six people thus accounted for £1,044,669.

The Conservatives thus relied on just nine people for just under £10,000,000, this representing just under 40 per cent of all donations from private sources. Apart from the heavy reliance of the Conservative Party on the State and the heavy dependence on large personal donations, the Conservative Party also receives more donations from companies than does the Labour Party, and these donations are of a higher average value than the donations to Labour. 456 companies have given £7,052,069, with two of these being over £250,000:

Donor	Date	Donation
Norbrook Laboratories	02.04.01	1,000,000
IIR Ltd	26.03.02	520,000
Total		**1,520,000**

In addition to the foregoing, another 10 companies gave the Conservative Party donations between £100,001 and £250,000, the combined value of which was £1,588,615. High value (in excess of £100,000) company donations thus account for £3,108,615, and the Conservatives rely on companies for just under a third (£7 m) of their private donations (£24 m). If company and personal donations are combined, we find that the Conservatives relied on 23 such donations in excess of £100,000 for more than half (c £13 m) of their donations from private sources. Without public funding and donations in excess of £100,000, the Conservatives would have been required to finance their operations (including a general election and a European election) since 2001 with donations of little more than £12 m, which would be in the region of £4 m annually.

The Liberal Democrats and the Nationalist Parties

The Liberal Democrats received 1007 donations in the period under review, raising £6,375,993.14. Over a third of these took the form of donations from public funds, these donations amounting to £2,421,527.79. A total of £3,468,463.20 was provided by 806 cash donations, with another 131 donations in kind providing £389,625.47. The average cash donation to the Liberal Democrats was thus a relatively modest £4303. The party received no private cash donations in excess of £50,000, and only 11 cash donations in excess of £25,000. These were as follows:

Donor	Date	Donation
Lord Jacobs	31.03.01	31,000
Lord Jacobs	10.05.01	30,000
Lord Jacobs	15.06.01	30,000
P Yeldon	01.12.01	40,000
Liberal Democrat Ball 2001	12.12.01	38,000
D Laxton	16.05.02	40,000
G M Lewis (bequest)	05.09.02	32,730
UNISON	10.04.03	29,000
UNISON	05.08.03	32,730.50
E Lakeman	09.01.04	50,000
Liberal Democrat Ball 2003	18.02.04	45,712.15
Total		**399,172.65**

In terms of company donations, the Electoral Commission records that £1.3 m was provided by companies,[68] though most of these were Liberal Democrat constituency bodies or clubs which are registered as companies. But they do include sponsorship from McDonalds and significant non cash donations from KPMG totalling £108,500.

So far as the SNP is concerned, the Electoral Commission reveals that it received 110 donations in the period under review, these amounting to £1,214,924.45 in total. The bulk of this (£828,916.53) is accounted for as public funds (such as Short money and policy development grants). The SNP received only 32 cash and 13 non cash contributions: the former amounted to £291,714.08, and the latter to £23,806.29. Significant features of SNP fundraising is that it received only 12 cash donations of £5,000 or more, three of which were bequests (£80,234.46; £62,945.16; and £10,000). Apart from bequests, only four donations were for £10,000 or more,

[68] Another £201, 600 was provided by way of donations in kind.

with the highest being £25,000 (A J Tulloch). Otherwise, there was little evidence of corporate funding of the SNP except the 13 non cash contributions of £23,806.29 which were all donated by South of Scotland Power Ltd in the form of staff secondment and accommodation costs. Although modest compared with the other parliamentary parties, the SNP is still more generously funded than Plaid Cymru which has reported 47 donations of £283,045.86. Of these 31 have been provided by public funds (Short money and policy development grants), these accounting for £175,079.05. This means that only £100,000 is provided by private donors, of which £29,450.00 was provided as a non cash donation by a company (Splitside Ltd) in the form of a computer software system. Plaid Cymru received two cash donations of £10,000 and another of £7,000. Otherwise all donations were less than £5,000, with the exception of a bequest of £33,342.47.

Conclusion

The funding of political parties has been transformed by the *Political Parties, Elections and Referendums Act 2000*. Foreign donations are now forbidden, corporate donations are highly regulated and much diminished, and the political parties are subject to tough accountability measures in relation to donations. But the problems of funding have not been fully resolved, as political practice develops some steps ahead of the regulators. There is the question of large donations and the question of allegations (all unsubstantiated) about cash for access, cash for favours, and cash for honours which have not been completely driven from the system. So far as the latter question (access, favours and honours) is concerned, the Labour Party has taken steps to minimise problems by way of self-regulatory internal reforms, but the government may need to do more. The investigation of the Drayson donations by the National Audit Office was a good example of how questions raised by political donations cannot be resolved by legislation or party funding law alone. With this in mind:

- So far as access is concerned, civil service guidance regulates the relationship between civil servants and lobbyists.[69] But there is no corresponding provision of the Ministerial Code dealing with access to ministers by lobbyists, party donors or newspaper proprietors.[70]
- So far as political honours are concerned, this problem will not be resolved while party leaders have a monopoly on who is to be nominated to represent the parties in the House of Lords.[71] This is a problem which is inextricably bound up with another festering sore, namely Lords' reform.

[69] See Cabinet Office, *Guidance for Civil Servants—Contact with Lobbyists*, www.cabinetoffice.gov.uk

[70] For the Ministerial Code, see www.cabinetoffice.gov.uk

[71] This is despite legislation that makes it unlawful to offer money for a peerage or to offer a peerage for money: *Honours (Prevention of Abuses) Act 1925*.

So far as the large donations are concerned, this is a problem which needs to be addressed for a number of reasons. There are two ways by which this might be done. The first is by further regulation which bans such donations. This could be done by introducing a limit on the amount which any donor may give to a political party in any one year.[72] But as we have seen this option was rejected by the Neill Committee as recently as 1998. In addition to the reasons already considered, the Committee cited the problem of compliance, observing that 'the United States of America strikes us as an example of a well-developed system which none the less suffers from frequent incidents of evasion'.[73] The Committee was unwilling 'to propose arrangements which could prove disproportionately cumbersome to enforce'.[74] Contribution caps of this kind nevertheless operate in many countries other than the United States (though by no means all comparable democracies have adopted this form of regulation), and such limits have just been introduced into Canada with personal donors now limited to $5,000 annually. But as we have seen there are problems in terms of enforcing such legislation, and it remains to be seen whether these problems are overcome in Canada. There is also the question of the impact on the parties of banning such donations in the United Kingdom, at a time when they are already stretched as more obligations are piled upon them. It would be difficult for the State to contemplate banning large donations without providing alternative sources of revenue, as in Canada where large scale public funding will replace the private money lost by the contribution cap.

But even if this was model was followed in the United Kingdom, a more difficult question relates to the impact which a limit on donations would have on party structure and autonomy. The problem arises because of the diverse nature of party organisation. It is a particular problem for the Labour Party which is an association of individuals and organisations. The latter include affiliated trade unions and socialist societies (such as the Fabian Society and the Society of Labour Lawyers) which are not only donors to the party but are actually members of the party in their organisational capacity.[75] Indeed the party was founded by trade unions and socialist societies and it was not until 1918 that it became possible to be an individual member of the party. As members of the party, trade unions and socialist societies are integral parts of its constitution—with rights of participation in the election of party leader and rights of representation on the National Executive Committee, at Conference (which meets annually) and on the National Policy Forum. These rights of participation and representation are weighted according to the size of the affiliated organisation, with larger unions enjoying more formal influence than smaller unions.[76] A limit on contributions

[72] For an elegant argument for such an initiative, see J Rowbottom, 'Political Donations and the Democratic Process: Rationales for Reform' [2002] *PL* 758.

[73] Committee on Standards in Public Life, *The Funding of Political Parties in the United Kingdom* (Cm 4057–I, 1998) para 6.9.

[74] *Ibid.*

[75] Membership of the Party is vested in the union not its members, who may also be individual members of the party.

[76] See L Minkin, *The Contentious Alliance* (Edinburgh, Edinburgh University Press, 1992) for a full account.

would undermine this arrangement and would render unlawful the existing constitutional structure of the Labour Party.[77] That would be a step too far: it is not the business of the State to tell political parties how they are to be organised or who their members may be. Ultimately that is a responsibility of the electorate. It would be possible to limit large personal donations while leaving the current arrangements relating to the Labour Party unchanged. But that would create other problems and inequities, and is not a response that it likely to be attractive to the other parties.[78] The structural realities of the British party system suggest that the solution to the donations problem may have to be subtle and indirect: self restraint encouraged by greater State support for core party activities and further reductions of the electoral spending limits, in both cases to reduce the need for the sugar daddies.

[77] For further consideration of this issue, see KD Ewing, *Trade Unions, the Labour Party and Political Funding* (London, Catalyst, 2002).
[78] Contrast G Orr and JC Tham, Submission to the Joint Standing Committee on Electoral Matters, *Inquiry into Electoral Funding and Disclosure* (2004).

5

Access to the Airwaves and Equality: The Case against Political Advertising on the Broadcast Media

JACOB ROWBOTTOM

Introduction

COMMERCIALLY PURCHASED POLITICAL advertisements have never been permitted on the UK broadcast media. While the ban may shock lawyers in other jurisdictions, it is a longstanding feature of UK politics central to limiting the cost of elections and widely accepted by politicians and broadcasters. However, a recent decision by the European Court of Human Rights has suggested the ban may violate Article 10 of the ECHR and called its justifications into question.[1] This chapter will defend the ban on the grounds of political equality, that wealthy groups and individuals should not have disproportionate opportunity to advance their views on the broadcast media. The Strasbourg Court's decision and the justifications for the ban will be examined. While a case can be made for some direct access to television and radio by political groups, commercially purchased advertisements would do little to bring new points of view into the public domain or include new participants in political deliberation. While lifting the ban may seem to permit greater freedom of expression, this chapter will argue that lifting the ban would not provide equal opportunities for expression and could be more harmful to the democratic process.

The ban on advertising does not mean direct unmediated access is prohibited. Political parties are granted direct access through party political and election broadcasts that are distinct from advertisements in length and frequency, are preceded by an announcement and listed like a television programme. The party broadcasts began as part of the BBC's commitment to public service broadcasting, at a time when all advertisements were prohibited on television and radio.[2]

[1] *VgT Verein gegen Tierfabriken v Switzerland* (2002) 34 EHRR 4.

[2] For a more detailed background on political and election broadcasting, see Electoral Commission Discussion Paper, *Party Political Broadcasting Review 2001–2* (2001).

When commercial television was launched in 1956, the distinction was drawn between commercial and political advertisements.[3] Since then, the party political and election broadcasts have been seen to reduce the harsh impact of the ban on political advertising. The broadcasts no longer resemble current affairs programmes running to 20 or 30 minutes as they did in the 1950s and 1960s.[4] While still distinct from advertisements, the two have come closer in format and length with no party broadcast running to more than 5 minutes in the 2001 general election.[5]

The major political parties and broadcasters have largely accepted the ban on advertisements and the provision of time to the parties.[6] On the most recent enactment of the ban, the Secretary of State for Culture, Media and Sport, Tessa Jowell, explained that it aims to protect political equality:

> By denying powerful interests the chance to skew political debate, the current ban safeguards the public and democratic debate, and protects the impartiality of broadcasters.[7]

Broadcasters are under a duty of balance and impartiality in political coverage. While this does not mean all political parties or points of view receive equal time, the lifting of the ban would undermine the balance by tilting political coverage in favour of those able and willing to pay. By outspending the campaigns with a competing point of view, an interest group with a wealthy backer could ensure their message is aired more frequently and to a wider range of people. For example, if an interest group wished to broadcast an advert highlighting the need for stronger regulations against pollution, those industries with a commercial interest against such regulations could simply respond with a flood of advertisements promoting their interest. Those industries would undoubtedly have a greater pool of resources for such advertising. While the interest group may have the opportunity to broadcast its view, it will often be in a weaker position to do so. However, it is not just that political debate would become unbalanced, some groups would remain excluded due to the high cost of television advertising. A single 30-second advert in the middle of Coronation Street costs over £80,000.[8] The opportunities for expression generated by lifting the ban would therefore be limited to those with sufficient resources.

Despite strong support for the ban, its future is uncertain. Following a 2001 decision of the European Court of Human Rights that a similar ban in Switzerland violates Article 10, the Minister introducing the *Communications Act*

[3] *Television Act 1954*, sch 2.

[4] For an account of the techniques of political broadcasting on television and radio, see M Rosenbaum, *From Soapbox to Soundbite* (Basingstoke, Macmillan, 1997) ch 3.

[5] M Harrison, 'Politics on the Air' in D Butler and D Kavanagh (eds), *The British General Election of 2001* (Basingstoke, Palgrave, 2002).

[6] The Fifth Report of the Committee on Standards in Public Life, *The Funding of Political Parties in the United Kingdom* (Cm 4057, 1998) (the Neill Report) para 13.5.

[7] HC Deb, vol 395, col 788 (3 December 2002).

[8] *How to Advertise with ITV*, p20 <http://www.itvsales.com/itv/export/download/pdf/1380v5_ITV_AdvertGuideFINI.pdf>, last accessed 20 April 2005.

2003, which maintains the ban, was unable to make a statement of compatibility with the *Human Rights Act* and made a statement under section 19(1)(b) instead.[9] However, the government does not accept the ban is a violation of Article 10 and promises to make a robust defence of the ban if it is challenged in either the domestic or Strasbourg Court.

Political Advertising and Article 10

Supporting the government's position, earlier Strasbourg decisions on similar issues suggest the ban stands a good chance of surviving an Article 10 challenge.[10] In 1971, an individual challenged the ban after the BBC and independent broadcasters refused to grant an organisation access to television to broadcast its views.[11] The European Commission on Human Rights held that Article 10 does not require every individual or organisation to have access to the television to advance a point of view.[12] The Commission relied on the provision in Article 10(1) that permits the licensing of broadcasting,[13] so long as any interference with expression rights advances a legitimate aim under Article 10(2).[14] In contrast to the US and Australian courts,[15] the Strasbourg Court has held that expression can be restricted for the purpose of furthering political equality and preventing any person or group gaining a political advantage through wealth.[16] So assuming that the ban serves a legitimate aim, the remaining question is whether the ban is proportionate to that aim. The decision in *X and Association of Z* that Article 10 does not require universal access to television does not mean a ban on all political advertisements will necessarily be consistent with Article 10. However, European jurisprudence has previously been tolerant of bans on advertising limited to particular types of media, for example as part of maintaining professional standards.[17] When political expression has been banned in one forum, the presence of alternative forums or media, no matter how qualitatively different, has led to the Strasbourg Court finding the restriction to be proportionate.[18] The ban involves a difficult balance of interests on which different countries in Europe take different approaches, which would also suggest a wide margin of appreciation. For all these reasons, one would expect the Strasbourg Court to find the ban on political adverts to be consistent with Article 10.

[9] HC Deb, vol 395, col 787 (3 December 2002).
[10] For a similar view see Neill Report, above n 6, paras 13.8–13.11.
[11] *X and Association of Z v United Kingdom* (1971) 38 CD 86. See also *Huggett v United Kingdom* (1995) 20 EHRR CD104.
[12] *X and Association of L v United Kingdom* (1971) 38 CD 86 at 88.
[13] *Ibid* at 89.
[14] *Groppera Radio v Switzerland* (1990) 12 EHRR 321.
[15] See *Buckley v Valeo* (1976) 424 US 1 and *Australian Capital Television Pty Co Ltd v Commonwealth* (1992) 177 CLR 106. The distinct approaches are noted in Joint Committee on Human Rights, 19th Report of Session 2001–02, HL Paper 149, HC 1102, para 63.
[16] *Bowman v United Kingdom* (1998) 26 EHRR 1.
[17] *Casado Coca v Spain* (1994) 18 EHRR 1; *Colman v United Kingdom* (1993) 18 EHRR 119.
[18] *Appleby v United Kingdom* (2003) 37 EHRR 38.

With this background, the decision of the Strasbourg Court in *Tierfabriken* is surprising. The court rejected the argument that in refusing the advertisement the broadcaster was merely exercising its contractual freedom, and accepted that positive protection may sometimes be required by the Convention. However, this was not decisive as the statutory ban on political adverts clearly engaged the Convention right. The Court followed the earlier cases in finding the statute pursued a legitimate aim, accepting the danger of wealthy groups gaining control of the media. However, as political speech was at stake, the Court found the margin of appreciation to be reduced.[19] That the ban was applied to broadcasting and not to other types of media was taken to suggest that the goal of the ban is not particularly pressing.[20] The Court also noted that the association wishing to advertise was not a powerful financial group.[21] Although alternative means were available to broadcast the message, national TV was the only way to reach the whole country. Consequently, the ban was found to be a violation of Article 10.

The decision in *Tierfabriken* contrasts with two recent decisions of the Strasbourg Court. In *Murphy v Ireland*, a ban on religious advertising was held not to be in breach of Article 10.[22] On the issue of proportionality, the Court granted a wider margin of appreciation to Member States on personal or moral questions such as religion.[23] Even though the ban was complete, the Court found that the interference was limited as religious groups could advertise in other media and advance their views on ordinary television programmes.[24] While the advert in question was to publicise a meeting and would not cause much offence itself, the Court found it would be impracticable to filter adverts on a case-by-case basis.[25] As Geddis has argued, the reasons given by the Court in *Murphy* can be applied to *Tierfabriken* with equal force.[26] In the political speech case of *Appleby v UK*, the Strasbourg Court found that Article 10 did not require a group of leafleters to be granted access to a private shopping mall. A positive obligation on the state to provide the resources for expression only arises where the opportunities for expression are otherwise destroyed.[27] The impact on the expression right was held to be limited as the applicants could distribute leaflets outside the shopping mall and had access to newspapers and other media.[28] Again, the willingness to rely on alternative means to find the restriction proportionate contrasts with *Tierfabriken*. *Appleby* and *Tierfabriken* are not directly analogous. *Appleby* is closer to a refusal by a privately owned broadcaster or newspaper to carry a political advertisement or point of view. However, both *Tierfabriken* and *Appleby* have the

[19] *VgT Verein gegen Tierfabriken*, above n 1 at para 71.
[20] *Ibid* at para 74.
[21] *Ibid*.
[22] *Murphy v Ireland* (2004) 38 EHRR 13.
[23] *Ibid* at para 67.
[24] *Ibid* at para 74.
[25] *Ibid* at para 77.
[26] A Geddis, 'You Can't Say "God" on the Radio: Freedom of Expression, Religious Advertising and Broadcast Media After Murphy v Ireland' [2004] *European Human Rights Law Review* 181.
[27] *Appleby*, above n 18 at para 47.
[28] *Ibid* at para 48.

effect of restricting the opportunities for political expression to those with sufficient property or wealth. Member States can redress this by providing airtime or access to property for speakers without sufficient resources, but this is not required by the ECHR.

The decision in *Tierfabriken* does not mean the UK ban is automatically a violation of Article 10. The Strasbourg Court noted that a prohibition of political advertising might be compatible with the requirements of Article 10 in other circumstances.[29] This caveat gives some scope for the UK courts and the government to distinguish the UK system from that in Switzerland. Some members of the House of Lords have hinted at a reluctance to follow the approach taken in *Tierfabriken*. In *Prolife Alliance*, Lord Walker stated that the Strasbourg Court's decision 'does not, with respect, give full or clear reasons for what seems to be a far-reaching conclusion', and that the principle of *X and Association of Z*, that no one has an unfettered right of access to broadcasting, still holds.[30] While the UK courts do not recognise any 'right to antenna', where access is granted to one group but denied to others without justification the courts will intervene.[31] That the UK courts have taken an approach that recognises the need to regulate political broadcasting could be an influential factor in any future litigation in Strasbourg. The European Court has in the past been responsive to criticisms of decisions from the UK courts and has modified its approach to accommodate the objections.[32] Such a dialogue between the courts suggests that even if *Tierfabriken* cannot be distinguished from the UK ban, the Strasbourg Court may limit the reach or modify their own jurisprudence in accordance with the UK practice. With this possibility in mind, the remainder of this chapter will examine the justifications for the ban and any alternative measures.

Political Ends and Objects

The ban applies to advertisements 'by or on behalf of a body whose objects are wholly or mainly of a political nature' or 'directed towards a political end'.[33] Consequently, it appears that greater freedom is granted to commercial as opposed to political expression. Given that both the UK and Strasbourg Courts have repeatedly affirmed the importance of political expression, it may seem strange to subject the political to stricter controls. The answer lies in what Lord Walker has described as a 'paradox':

> On the one hand, political discussion or debate is, of all forms of communication protected by Article 10, accorded particular importance . . . But on the other hand,

[29] *VgT Verein Tierfabriken*, above n 1 at para 75.
[30] *Prolife Alliance v BBC* [2003] UKHL 23 at paras 128–9. See also Lord Hoffmann at para 64.
[31] *Ibid*. See also the Privy Council decisions *Benjamin v Minister of Information* [2001] UKPC 8 and *Observer v Matthew* [2001] UKPC 11.
[32] See D Anderson, 'The Law Lords and the European Courts' in A Le Sueur (ed), *Building the UK's New Supreme Court* (Oxford, Oxford University Press, 2004) 208–12.
[33] *Communications Act 2003*, s 321(2).

> there may be good reasons for imposing special restrictions, especially to prevent those with the deepest pockets from exercising too much influence through the most powerful and intrusive means of communication.[34]

However, this is not a paradox at all. The special restrictions imposed on political speech reflect its importance. The regulation of political expression is not so much to reduce political freedom, but to ensure political freedom is secured and shared equally among participants. The importance of political speech means that it should not be treated like a commodity that can be sold to those with sufficient resources. The weight accorded to that form of expression therefore explains the need for restrictions that further other democratic values. The importance of political expression is based on self-government justifications that invoke values that do not apply to commercial expression. In the marketplace for goods and services, economic inequalities are accepted. However, even commercial advertisers are not completely free, as the content and timing of commercial adverts are regulated. With the distinct values underlying the political system, preserving freedom of political expression requires regulation of a different kind.

Political campaigns are already subject to regulations not found in other spheres. The goal of equality in the opportunities for political participation is recognised by the spending limits imposed on political parties, referendum campaigns and third parties. Consequently, even if the ban on political advertising is lifted, political parties cannot spend unlimited amounts of money on advertisements. The ban may therefore look like an unnecessary restriction devised at a time when national political expenditures were unregulated. However, the ban on political advertisements is what makes the system of political funding workable. If political parties were expected to pay for broadcast advertisements, claims would soon arise that the expenditure limits are set too low for an effective campaign. The limits on expenditures could be challenged as a breach of Article 10, where the European Court assesses funding restrictions in its context, including the cost of advertising.[35] Without raising the current expenditure limits, political parties would not be able to purchase much airtime. However, even if the expenditure limits remained in place, lifting the ban would create a demand among the parties to buy the adverts, while restricting the supply of funds. The combination would provide the parties with a strong incentive to find loopholes in the funding laws.

The party funding legislation also limits the potential for third parties to spend money in support of a political party or candidate.[36] While a third party may be able to spend some funds on independent advertising, the expenditure limits would prevent this occurring on a large scale on the broadcast media. However, if the ban on political advertising were lifted, third parties would be able to spend unlimited amounts on political advertisements that do not directly refer to a party or politician. Andrew Scott, however, makes a distinction between advocacy

[34] *Prolife*, above n 30, para 130.

[35] *Bowman*, above n 16.

[36] *Political Parties, Elections and Referendum Act 2000*, s 85.

advertising that is issue centred and electoral advocacy that aims to influence the outcome of an election.[37] According to Scott, the concern of the party funding legislation is limited to the latter, and the breadth of the current ban is not justified by this concern.[38] The ban clearly goes beyond party politics and election issues. The *Communications Act 2003* defines political objects and ends as: influencing the outcome of elections or referendums; bringing about changes in the law; influencing the policies or decisions of local or national governments, or any other body whose public functions are conferred by law or international agreement; influencing public opinion on a matter of public controversy, or promoting the interests of any group or party organised for political ends.[39] Scott proposes a narrower definition that prohibits only party political but not issue advertisements. While the boundary between the two can become blurred, Scott argues that such a line could be drawn, for example prohibiting advertisements only where it aligns with the proposals of a political party.[40] This may still permit some blurring, especially if the issue advertised is associated with a political party. For example, an issue advert on the NHS may not be directly aligned with a specific line in a party's election manifesto, but such advertising on the issue may direct the political agenda onto what is perceived to be a Labour strength. Similarly, the position taken may be associated with a political party even though there is no official party line. For example, a political party may allow a free vote on a moral issue, but it is well known how the two parties are likely to divide. Rather than attempting to draw a line between those types of advert that are permissible and those that are not, it would be easier and clearer to maintain the ban on political advertisements. This at least eliminates the risk of limits on electoral advocacy being evaded through a blurred boundary.

A more important objection to the division between party and issue advocacy, is that the values of political equality are not just present in electoral politics. Debate outside the formal political process should not be influenced by money either. This is not to suggest that political equality requires expenditure limits on the activities of interest groups, but rather that the opportunities to persuade the public on political issues through the broadcast media should not depend on wealth. The problem with lifting the ban on political advertisements would be to allow those groups with the most money to gain greater coverage than their opponents.

The difficulty with this argument is that party politics enjoys a privileged position, compared with political groups operating outside the parliamentary model of politics.[41] Party politics enjoys more coverage in the news and major parties have direct access through political and election broadcasts, all of which mitigate

[37] A Scott, 'A Monstrous and Unjustifiable Infringement?: Political Expression and the Broadcasting Ban on Advocacy Advertising' (2003) 66 *Modern Law Review* 224 at 241.
[38] *Ibid.*
[39] Communications Act 2003 s 321(3).
[40] Scott, above n 37.
[41] A Boyle, 'Political Broadcasting, Fairness and Administrative Law' [1986] *Public Law* 562 at 574 and 581–2.

the harshness of the ban. Critics of the ban have therefore argued that it effectively excludes many interest groups and good causes from advancing their case on the broadcast media at all.[42] When the ban was discussed in Parliament in 1990, two amendments were proposed to allow groups such as Friends of the Earth and Greenpeace to advertise.[43] The issue came before the courts when the Radio Authority refused an advert by Amnesty International on the grounds that its objects were political. While the Court of Appeal upheld the Radio Authority's decision, the formula devised to determine whether an organisation is 'wholly or mainly' political has since been relied on to permit Amnesty advertising after reassessing the objectives of the organisation.[44] While the decision has been criticised for failing to narrowly construe the provision,[45] the broader definition of political has since been confirmed and clarified in the *Communications Act*. However, the objection that this definition still stops some good causes advertising merely isolates one particular consequence of the ban. As Kennedy LJ explained in the Divisional Court in *Bull*:

> Many people, particularly lawyers, admire the work of British Amnesty, and the dedication of those who work for it. But it is worth recognising that something that may appear to be an unnecessary restriction upon a good cause could also usefully restrain something manifestly less worthy.[46]

For example, the broad definition of political stopped Brian Souter, the owner of Stagecoach buses and at that time Scotland's richest man, broadcasting an advert as part of his 'Keep the Clause' campaign in 2000.[47] Without the ban, the campaign would have gained access to the airwaves solely as a result of the estimated £500,000 that Mr Souter was willing to spend. The example of Mr Souter highlights the danger of one extremely wealthy individual being able to pick his or her pet issues and force them onto the political agenda. Even with the ban on broadcast advertising he was able to generate a great deal of publicity. However, the ban at least acted as a restraint on this activity. That the broad reach of the ban applies to well-established groups such as Greenpeace is merely the other side of the ban. If access for such groups is thought to be necessary, then channels other than purchased advertisements should be considered.

Even if political expression in the broad sense requires some regulation for political equality, Professor Barendt argues measures short of an outright ban are

42 Paul Foot, 'Tortuous Drivel from Ministry of Truth', *The Guardian*, 1 August 1994; G Monbiot, *Captive State* (Basingstoke, Macmillan, 2000) 337–42.

43 Robin Corbett MP and Robert Maclennan MP proposed the amendments, The Official Report of Standing Committee F, *The Broadcasting Bill*, 30 January 1990, cols 425–9.

44 *R v Radio Authority, Ex parte Bull* [1998] QB 294 (CA), Brooke LJ at 319–22.

45 D Feldman and J Stevens, 'Broadcasting advertisements by bodies with political objects, judicial review, and the influence of charities law' [1997] *Public Law* 615.

46 *R v Radio Authority, Ex parte Bull* [1996] 1 QB 169 (DC) at 187.

47 'Keep the Clause advert banned by TV watchdog' *The Sunday Times*, 6 February 2000. The campaign sought to persuade the Scottish Assembly to keep Clause 28 that bans the promotion of homosexuality in schools. The campaign continued with adverts on other media and even held its own private referendum on the issue.

sufficient. On the argument that the ban is necessary to stop a wealthy group dominating the airwaves, Barendt responds:

> This is unconvincing. It is perfectly possible to impose limits on the duration and frequency of, and on the charges for, such advertisements, so that some time could be afforded by less well-off groups.[48]

In order to allow access by less well off groups, the charges for broadcast advertising, especially television, would need to be severely limited. If not, minor groups and parties would only be able to purchase advertisements on stations with a smaller audience and not at peak times. In Germany, while political advertisements in the 1998 elections were sold for 45 per cent of the commercial rate, only the major political parties had the resources to take up this offer.[49] If the cost of political advertisements is set considerably lower than commercial advertisements, broadcasters will be less willing to accept such adverts. Broadcasters' would lose revenue from advertising due to the cut price, and consequently would prefer to limit the time allocated to such adverts or receive compensation from the state. If this is the case then it may be just as easy to take wealth out of the equation and require free access time.

If the price of advertisements were to be lowered to make broadcasts accessible to more groups, the demand for time would be far greater than the supply. In order to fulfil the duty of impartiality and balance, Barendt states, advertisements could not be allocated on a first come first served basis. The regulation of this type of advertisement would require broadcasters to decide issues of allocation to preserve balance and impartiality, as they do with party election broadcasts. This could be difficult where one group produces an advert, but those advocating an opposing point of view cannot afford to meet these reduced costs. Even where various points of view are able to advertise, it would still have to be decided whether balance is to be achieved by giving equality to points of view on both sides of an issue or by giving equal time to different organisations. Such questions are not clear cut, especially when most issues do not simply have two sides.

If rates for advertising were cut, effectively to subsidise political speech, and if issues of allocation were to be decided, then it would not be so far from giving free airtime. This could be done by requiring the provision of free access to short broadcasts as a condition of granting broadcasting licences. The administrative difficulties and cost to the broadcaster would not be much greater than with the regulated advertisements Barendt proposes. The difficult issue with free access would be deciding how to allocate the broadcasting time. This could be done if a group presents a sufficient number of signatures, has a large membership, or has a substantial level of expertise. All of these methods are not perfect, but are at least

[48] E Barendt, *Broadcasting Law: A Comparative Study* (Oxford, Oxford University Press, 1993) 169. See also the evidence of Professor Barendt to the Joint Committee on the Draft Communications Bill, HL Paper 169-II HC Paper 876-II, 17 June 2002.

[49] Electoral Commission Discussion Paper, above n 2, paras 6.14–6.16.

preferable to wealth determining access. If the ban on political advertising is thought to be so unjustifiable a restriction on expression, then these questions will need to be addressed. If it is thought to be too great an imposition on broadcasters or raises too many problematic issues, then the ban should remain in place.

Do Political Advertisements Generate an Advantage?

The argument advanced so far has assumed that lifting the ban would give an unfair advantage to wealthy groups and individuals. However, Andrew Scott challenges this assumption and argues that political adverts do not automatically convert people's opinions.[50] The message broadcast has to be persuasive to have any influence. Invoking the marketplace of ideas, Scott argues that the vast range of alternative sources of information will ensure that any misleading or weak arguments will be unmasked.[51] However, while advertising does not guarantee persuasion and some campaigns can backfire, in this marketplace of ideas the different sources of information are hardly on a level playing field. This comes back to the qualitative differences that make the broadcast media so powerful and influential. A newspaper commentary criticising an advertisement is hardly likely to reach the same audience as an advert broadcast on prime time television. In the US, most major newspapers scrutinise the content of political advertisements, but this has not curbed the influence of those advertisements or raised the quality of the content. In so far as the effectiveness of advertising depends on the content and message, this again will give some advantage to the wealthiest groups. Those groups will have the resources not only to employ the most skilled advertisers, but also to employ the pollsters and market research to ensure that the advertisement reaches the target audience. Again, this does not work as a guarantee, but it does give those with greater resources an advantage.

Whether advertisements influence the public is difficult to assess. One obvious point is that if it did not have any effect at all, then no one would bother to invest so much in advertising. The influence is difficult to assess as an advert can have different effects and work in subtle ways. A political advocacy advert would not simply list the facts of an argument and respond to counterarguments. This can be seen with the development of party election broadcasts. Where once a Minister would sit at a desk explaining policies and delivering facts and figures, a political broadcast is now more likely to feature ordinary people (played by actors) indicating their sympathy for a particular policy or party. Similarly, political adverts would rely on anecdotes or imagery, which are harder to test in the marketplace of ideas.

[50] Scott, above n 37 at 237.
[51] Scott, above n 37 at 239.

Empirical studies have suggested that television has at best a limited role in influencing voting behaviour, but that it provides voters with information.[52] However, a study of the 1997 election has suggested that the 'direction' of the television coverage, whether a party is portrayed favourably or unfavourably, has some impact on voter preferences.[53] Such empirical research on the effect of the media will always be problematic, as the media is just one factor that impacts on voting decisions, its influence may develop over a long period of time and will vary according to the audience and type of programme. However, even if the broadcast media has had limited influence so far, this is a product of the regulatory environment that requires balance and impartiality. Lifting the ban on political advertising would alter this environment and potentially alter the influence of the broadcast media. The coverage of politics in the advertisements will not be governed by rules of impartiality and each advertisement would advocate one point of view. Television would therefore play a greater role in the direct persuasion, rather than informing, of voters.[54]

Apart from studies of the impact of overall political coverage on television, several studies have attempted to examine whether party election broadcasts influence voters, which is probably the closest type of broadcast comparable to the political and issue adverts that would be available if the ban were lifted. Some studies have suggested that election broadcasts help smaller parties, such as the Liberal Democrats.[55] This may be as the free airtime helps to overcome the lack of attention in the ordinary media coverage. However, research studying party political broadcasts in the mid-1980s suggests the SDP/Liberal Alliance broadcasts had less impact on voter attitude.[56] This finding is consistent with the argument that with fewer resources, smaller parties will find it harder to resort to the slick advertising that has become the norm for the major political parties.[57] The research seems inconclusive on the effect of these broadcasts. This is partly because at election times voters are provided with information from broadcast and non-broadcast media alike, and the participants are already well known to the electorate with their strengths and weaknesses defined. If the ban on political adverts

[52] See W Miller, *Media and Voters* (Oxford, Clarendon, 1991). For a general discussion of the research see, J Street, *Mass Media, Politics and Democracy* (Basingstoke, Palgrave, 2001) 88–93, and R Negrine, *Politics and the Mass Media in Britain* (London, Routledge, 1994) 156–78.

[53] P Norris, J Curtice, D Sanders, M Scammell and H Semetko, *On Message, Communicating the Campaign* (London, SAGE, 1999).

[54] In his study of the 1987 election, Miller, above n 52, found newspapers to have greater influence on the preferences of the electorate. Political advertisements would be similar to the more partisan coverage currently found in newspapers and potentially influential. See also Norris *et al*, above n 53 on the influence of 'directional' coverage on television.

[55] CJ Pattie and RJ Johnston 'Assessing the Television Campaign: The Impact of Party Election Broadcasting on Voters' Opinions in the 1997 British General Election' (2002) 19 *Political Communications* 333 at 350; JG Blumler and D McQuail, *Television in politics: Its uses and influence* (London, Faber and Faber, 1968).

[56] M Wober, 'Party political and election broadcasts, 1985–87: Their perceived attributes and impact on upon voters' in I Crewe and M Harrop (eds), *Political Communications: The General Election campaign of 1987* (Cambridge, Cambridge University Press, 1989).

[57] Rosenbaum, above n 4 at 68.

was lifted, then such adverts could become more influential for those groups and issues that are less well known, just as political adverts are used in the US to gain name recognition for the challenging candidates. The use of adverts may have a role to play in bringing less well-known groups and issues to the public's attention. However, these smaller groups would be the most likely to be excluded by the cost of advertising.

The research also indicates that advertisements become more influential if not balanced with broadcasts on the opposing point of view. A study based on statistics from the 1997 election showed that party election broadcasts had an impact on the perceptions of which party would be stronger in government. However, when viewers saw an opposing party's broadcast, this influence was cancelled out.[58] Such a finding suggests that the balance in the allocation of party election broadcasts helps to limit the influence of the broadcasts. If political adverts could be purchased, then a danger exists that this balance would be lost, where those groups without sufficient resources could not counteract the advantage gained by their opponents in advertising. As above, a change in the regulatory environment could change the scope for the media to influence voters.

A further way in which political adverts could be used to buy influence is not directly through persuading the public, but by agenda setting. Buying more advertisements for one point of view will create an advantage by bringing a political issue to the public and media attention. Partisan groups would be able to purchase adverts that ensure the issues on the media agenda are associated with a strength or weakness of a particular party. Similarly, an interest group would focus on an aspect of an issue that advances their case best and frames the debate on their own terms. According to this argument, the impact of a political advertisement can go beyond the 30 or 60 seconds of broadcast time. The capacity of political parties to set the media's agenda and the impact of the media's agenda on voter attitudes in the UK has been the subject of empirical research.[59] While the findings of the studies are not conclusive, the lifting of a ban will at least give greater opportunities to set both the media and the public agenda. In the past, attempts have been made by political parties and interest groups to set the political agenda through press conferences or staged events. In election campaigns, the significance of a new billboard poster campaign is not the number of posters that will actually be seen, but the launch of the poster being covered on television news and having the political message repeated into thousands of homes. While the media views such promotions and events sceptically, direct advertising on political issues will be harder to ignore. This can be seen in the US where some controversial broadcasts become a news story and are repeated on current affairs programmes and

[58] Pattie and Johnston, above n 55 at 350.

[59] On the role of parties setting the media agenda, compare H Brandenburg, 'Who Follows Whom? The Impact of Parties on Media Agenda Formation in the 1997 British General Election Campaign' (2002) 7 *Harvard International Journal of Press/Politics* 34, with Norris *et al*, above n 53. On the role of the media setting the agenda of the electorate, see Norris *et al*, above n 53 and Miller, above n 52, ch 7.

discussed at length. Giving more opportunities to set the political agenda to groups other than politicians and the media may have benefits and will be discussed below, but the potential to influence the political agenda should not be based on purchasing power.

Political advertisements may be influential in attempting to persuade elected officials and policy makers. If a policy is likely to trigger a negative response in the form of advertisements, the legislature or executive may be discouraged from pursuing that policy. If the effect of the advert is to bring unpopular policies to the public's attention or require the office holder to justify the existing policy, this is no bad thing. Such an impact reflects a pluralist view in which advertisements made by interest groups represent the views of citizens outside the formal political channels. If a group such as Greenpeace advertises against a policy, it does not just provide information, it shows that interest group's strength of feeling against that particular policy. Such an advertisement would register the unpopularity of that policy with a section of society, and the policy maker targeted would take this into account. The advertisement can therefore serve a broader purpose as part of a lobbying campaign. The difficulty with this arises when the opportunities to engage in such lobbying are dependent on wealth. It is similar to the objection of using cash to get access to ministers, that politicians should not be responsive only to wealthy groups. However, in this case the access is not from a meeting with the policy maker, but through a direct appeal on television.

The value of expression through advertising outlined above is not solely instrumental in informing and shaping the opinions of voters and policy makers. Political expression has an intrinsic value as an act of participation. Giving people the chance to voice their opinions and know that they are being heard enhances the sense of inclusion in the democratic process. Even if this does not lead to a change in public opinion or government policy, it allows people to feel that their side of the argument has been put across. If, however, the avenue of expression is open only to those with sufficient funds, those without the money to buy the advertisements will feel excluded from participating in the political process. If lifting the ban would permit wealthy individuals and businesses to advertise for policy changes that serve their self-interest, only an elite would be able to participate fully in the political process. Looking at the problem from this perspective takes attention away from the question of whether the money buys actual influence, and focuses on the distribution of opportunities for participation. None of this is to say that every individual has a right to access the airwaves, but that the opportunities to put forward the best case for a particular point of view should not be based on the ability to pay.

Why the Broadcast Media?

In *Tierfabriken*, the ECtHR was influenced by the absence of a similar ban on the non-broadcast media in Switzerland. The same is true in the UK. The reasoning of the Strasbourg Court suggests that the ban should be applied across all media or not applied at all. The problem with the Court's reasoning is that if the ban is applied across all media, and therefore consistent in principle, fewer alternative outlets for expression would be available. Such a universal ban would thereby constitute greater interference and potentially violate Article 10. The Neill Committee looked at the historical context to justify the current distinction between broadcast and print media.[60] Billboard advertisements have long been a part of UK elections, whereas political advertisements have never been allowed on the broadcast media. The Committee also found that a ban on newspaper advertisements would force parties to rely on direct mailing or the mediated newspaper coverage. One solution would be to extend the ban to other forms of media, but allow free access to the print media for parties and interest groups. The Committee considered this in relation to billboard advertising and concluded that it would be too costly for a state subsidy to compensate the billboard owners for lost revenue as a result of the free access. The Committee's conclusions reflect a pragmatic compromise. Permitting paid adverts on billboards and in newspapers offsets some of the harsher consequences of the ban on the broadcast media. The possibility of buying advertisements elsewhere provides some alternative means for the expression. The distinction drawn by the Committee may not seem consistent in principle, but preserves the working of the system that avoids an all or nothing approach.

The absence of a ban on newspaper or billboard advertisements may mitigate, but does not balance, the lack of direct access to the broadcast media. The qualitative difference of the broadcast media suggests that the two types of media are not alternatives to one another. This qualitative difference provides one justification for the different regulatory regimes, in particular the intrusive nature of the broadcast media. McCullough J in the Divisional Court in *Ex parte Bull* explained:

> The spoken word is both more compelling and more intrusive than the written. The newspaper reader can immediately turn the page. If the listener switches off he might miss the resumption of his programme, and meanwhile he has to wait.[61]

This argument recognises that messages carried on the broadcast media are much harder to avoid. This is reflected in the current system for political broadcasts that are preceded by an announcement and are listed in the television schedules. A compelling argument against the concern with intrusiveness is that television already allows commercial and other news items to be broadcast into a person's home.[62] As explained above, different considerations may apply to political expression where the need for a level playing field is recognised. Furthermore, commercial advertisements are strictly regulated to ensure the potent media is not abused. The restrictions on commercial advertisements would be hard to apply to

[60] Neill Report, above n 6, paras 13.23–13.33.
[61] *Ex parte Bull*, above n 46 at 192.
[62] Scott, above n 37.

political advertisements.[63] The ban avoids the difficult question of how the content and timing of political advertisements should be regulated to meet the concerns of intrusiveness.

When discussing the intrusiveness of the broadcast media, McCullough J stated that there is no right to subject the listener to opinions they are unwilling to hear. The difficulty with this argument is that a democracy requires that people hear opinions including those they do not agree with. Political debate must go beyond merely preaching to the converted. This does not mean the speakers have free reign to broadcast whatever they like whenever they like. The mediated news coverage may therefore go some way to meeting the need to disseminate diverse viewpoints. However, the stricter regulation of the broadcast media may be due to its broader reach and its capacity to advance a message through sophisticated and subtle techniques. As stated earlier, the effects of the broadcast media on the audience are uncertain, and it is equally unclear if it is more effective than newspapers in persuading people. Lifting the ban may alter the regulatory environment to permit television to play an even more influential role. While paying for advertisements in newspapers and posters may not be ideal for reasons of political equality, it has less potential to distort the democratic process than broadcasts.

A major difference between the types of media is the cost. A 30 second advert on national television is far more expensive than an advert in the national press. Furthermore, broadcast media has much higher production costs than print media. The consequence is that the economic barriers to the broadcast media are far greater. If the ban is lifted the opportunities for expression will be open only to the wealthiest groups. By contrast, in the print media, the lower cost of advertising at least allows more groups to use this channel of expression. This is not to say that unregulated advertising in print is unproblematic, it still means that wealthier individuals and groups can advertise more frequently and more widely, but that the problems of inequality are not as great as broadcast advertising.

Political Advertising as a Check on Inequality

The ban can be criticised from a different perspective, that rather than preserving political equality it merely reinforces the inequalities in the existing system of broadcasting. This section looks at the argument that political advertisements can check the advantages granted to business, the media and government under the current system.

Businesses are allowed to broadcast advertisements encouraging people to buy their products. However, interest groups may be prevented from advertising to

[63] The Electoral Commission recommended that the Code of Practice applied to commercial advertisements should not be applied to newspaper and billboard advertisements, see Electoral Commission, *Political Advertising: Report and Recommendations* (2004).

advise the public not to buy products that, for example, have been manufactured in sweatshops, if such an object comes under the broad definition of political.[64] This highlights that the actions of businesses can have political consequences, blurring the division between the economic and the political. While different values underlie each sphere, it is not clear when the application of those values is appropriate. However, allowing commercially purchased political adverts would not provide a remedy. The business would always be in a better position to ensure their case is broadcast more frequently and to a wider audience. Furthermore, those businesses could be more aggressive in pursuing their political agenda. Going beyond advertisements solely for products, such businesses could begin to use their adverts as part of a strategy in lobbying for changes in government policy. For example, it is easy to imagine an advert for alcoholic drinks that also hints at the potential benefits of liberalising licensing laws. By dismantling the existing framework of regulation, the interest groups that seek to put the case against big business will be forced into a weaker position that will potentially harm their own cause. This is not to say that such interest groups should be denied a place to voice these concerns on the broadcast media, but that permitting commercially purchased political advertisements is not the way.

An even broader argument may be made, that allowing commercial adverts has a political effect in reinforcing people's acceptance of the market economy and the tendency to view the world as consumers. However, for as long as the economy is organised through the market, the institutions of that system will inevitably have such a reinforcing effect. This also has an effect on television programmes. In order to secure the highest ratings, the broadcasters will need to develop programmes that not only get the largest audience, but whose audience consists of the advertisers' target. The broadcaster will have an incentive not to broadcast programmes that lose the target audience nor upset a regular advertiser. However, such criticisms seem targeted at commercial television in general, rather than the ban on political advertising. The tension between commercial television and the public service rationale is not new, and no easy solution exists. Lifting the ban on political advertisements does not provide a solution. While pressure groups would broadcast the occasional advertisement, the airwaves would still be dominated by businesses placing the same pressures on the broadcaster.[65]

A further consequence of the present system of regulation is that the broadcaster's editorial choices determine the political output on television. The ban on political advertising maintains the broadcasters' power by preventing political material outside their editorial control being aired. While this power is held by a small number of broadcasters, the coverage is dominated by a small number of personalities. The opinions of journalists such as Andrew Marr seem to get more airtime than those of politicians or interest group spokesmen.[66] At a time when

[64] Monbiot, above n 42.

[65] In criticising the ban, Andrew Scott notes that political advertising would not give interest groups a structural power over broadcasters, above n 37 at 237.

[66] Harrison, above n 5 at 144.

the influence of journalists is being increasingly questioned, direct and unmediated access to the airwaves by other sections of society may provide a remedy. On this view, the public service broadcasting rationale is served not only through the presentation of issues edited and mediated for impartiality, but also by allowing multiple partisan opinions to be aired. How broadcasting can best provide coverage is still being debated and it is not conclusive that such direct access is the solution. However, even if direct access can offset the slant given by edited coverage by broadcasters, it would be necessary to ensure that diverse views are represented through such access rather than granting access only to those with the money to buy the time.

The ban arguably creates an advantage for the party in government. During election campaigns, broadcasters strain themselves to ensure the fair allocation of time between parties, but even then the party in government will get a fraction more coverage.[67] Outside an election, the party in government inevitably gets more time in current affairs coverage, as its actions are central to the issues and events being reported. In addition to this, the government can use their resources to provide public information about a policy or development. The line between information and persuasion is hard to draw, and both Labour and Conservative governments have been accused of abusing this avenue for partisan advantage. While in Opposition, Tony Blair complained that government advertisements on economic issues and privatisation were being used to promote policies 'in a most partisan and one-sided fashion'.[68] At the same time, the Conservatives made similar allegations about local government and prohibited local authorities from publishing information designed to support a political party.[69] Since gaining power, Labour has been subject to similar allegations by the Conservatives.[70] While this is not the place to consider which party is the worst offender, it seems that information about government policies is required, but can potentially be abused. Such information on new initiatives, even when not partisan, will put the spotlight on the government's latest policies. Furthermore, the capacity of the government to use their central position to influence the media agenda is increasingly sensitive. Much media coverage has focused on the rise of spin in which politicians and their advisors develop close relationships with journalists and offer privileged access in return for favourable coverage. The government is increasingly aggressive in pushing favourable stories and ensuring negative issues receive minimal coverage. The other side to this is that the government tends to complain of media bias against them, with reporters focusing on failures or divisions in the party. These issues may, however, point to the need for some direct access to balance the media coverage, so groups outside of government can influence the media agenda and put across their point of view. This argument suggests

67 Harrison, above n 5 at 133–4.
68 'Publicity or just propaganda?' *The Times*, 25 April 1988.
69 *Local Government Act 1986*, s 2.
70 'Taxpayer "footing Labour propaganda bill"', *The Daily Telegraph*, 26 April 2001; 'Labour is UK's biggest spender on ads', *The Independent*, 13 August 2000.

that if we are to be subjected to political advertisement in the form of government 'infomercials', then at least extend that opportunity to others.

If direct access to the broadcast media can offset the power of business, media and government, it will take more than a simple lifting of the ban on political advertisements. If the direct access has to be purchased, the political adverts may reinforce rather than check the other sources of power. The danger is that if only the wealthy groups can afford the access to the airwaves, the views in those adverts may not conflict with those of the government. This is especially the case where government policy already caters to the interests of the wealthy. Where this is the case, those policies will be supported by a powerful combination of the government's advantage of incumbency, coverage by commercial broadcasters and adverts purchased by wealthy groups. If access to the airwaves is open only to those with sufficient resources, it is unlikely to provide a check.

The experience in Italy highlights such dangers when access to media, ownership and government become aligned. Silvio Berlusconi is Italy's richest man and at the time of writing is Prime Minister. Berlusconi's television company Mediaset has a near monopoly on national commercial television, controlling three channels, Italia 1, Rete 4 and Canale 5. While Berlusconi emphasises that Mediaset channels carry left-wing viewpoints and those critical of his government, the coverage of politics on those channels nevertheless has a pro-Berlusconi slant. It is hard to estimate what impact the use of the media had on the election campaigns, but it has clearly been a major factor facilitating Berlusconi's political successes and political advertisements were central to the launch of his political career in 1994. Just over two months before the elections in March 1994, Berlusconi announced his entry into politics under his new political party Forza Italia. While political advertisements could not be broadcast in the 30 days before the election, before this ban took effect, Berlusconi bombarded viewers of his three commercial channels with short advertisements promoting himself and his party.[71] For the general and European elections in 1994 combined, Forza Italia spent almost 70 per cent of television advertising expenditures by political parties.[72] The use of the media and resources would have been crucial at that early stage in Berlusconi's political career in defining his political identity and message to the electorate. The use of his own media outlets coupled with advertising enabled him to step into the political arena and capitalise on the disillusionment with the established political parties that followed a number of corruption scandals. In the 2001 election, campaign regulations restricted the use of campaign advertisements, forcing greater reliance on mediated coverage and on other types of media.[73] The

[71] G Mazzoleni, 'Patterns and Effects of Recent Changes in Electoral Campaigning in Italy' in D Swanson and Paolo Mancini (eds), *Politics, Media and Modern Democracy* (London, Praeger, 1996) 198–201.

[72] P Statham, 'Berlusconi, the Media and the New Right in Italy' (1996) 1 *Harvard International Journal of Press/Politics* 87 at 94–5.

[73] F Roncarolo, 'Virtual clashes and political games: the campaign in the print and broadcast media' in J Newell (ed), *The Italian General Election of 2001: Berlusconi's Victory* (Manchester, Manchester University Press, 2002) 150.

restriction of political advertising does not create a level playing field, but it at least closes off another opportunity for favourable coverage to be bought. While the extent of this problem is specific to Italy, this example illustrates that far from checking the broadcaster's influence, political advertisements can reinforce that influence where the broadcaster and advertiser share the same interests and view.

Since coming into power, Berlusconi has also gained the advantages of incumbency, extending his control of media to the state owned RAI television channels. In the mid-1970s, the three public television channels were divided between the parties so that one channel each was effectively allocated to the Christian Democrats, the Socialists and the Communists. Under this system, the balance on the public channels meant that whoever could gain the most favourable exposure on the private channels through advertising or general coverage, would have an advantage in the overall television coverage of politics. However, this system of pluralism has since broken down, with the governing party attempting to assert greater control over political coverage on the state owned channels. By appointing allies onto the RAI board of administrators, Berlusconi has exerted indirect control over the presenters and programmes that appear on state television, which has in some instances led to the removal of his major detractors from television.[74] With the ownership of the Mediaset channels and the indirect control of RAI channels, Berlusconi is able to influence the political coverage on channels with a combined 90 per cent share of the audience. This concentration of power raises a number of issues, but it is clear that political advertisements would not offset Berlusconi's advantage. Permitting political advertisements creates the danger of a party backed by wealthy interests gaining power in a system where access to political communications is determined partly by wealth. Once in power, the advantages of incumbency and the advantages of wealth combine to help maintain the grip on office, placing challenging parties in a weaker position. The political advertisements work to reinforce rather than check that power.

The Future of Political Broadcasting

With the proliferation of cable and satellite channels and the advance of other forms of media, some have suggested that the current system of political broadcasting will soon become outdated.[75] So far the approach to these developments has been to extend the ban on political advertisements to new channels. However, due to the fragmentation of audiences fewer people see election broadcasts and viewers can avoid news coverage altogether. That the existing forms of direct access are becoming outdated does not mean the ban on political advertisements

[74] P Ginsborg, *Silvio Berlusconi: Television Power and Patrimony* (London, Verso, 2004) 112–14; MJ Bull, 'Parliamentary Democracy in Italy' (2004) 57 *Parliamentary Affairs* 550 at 562–3.

[75] For a discussion of the ways to develop political broadcasts in the light of these changes, see The Department of Culture, Media and Sport, *Party Political Broadcasting: Public Consultation* (2004).

should be lifted. Other approaches could be taken to adapt the regulation to the changing structure of the media. Extending the free political broadcasts to all channels may help solve this problem, although it would no doubt be unpopular with those broadcasters.[76] Alternatively, shorter but more frequently repeated political broadcasts may help parties reach the voters.[77] However, the difficulty with such a proposal is that the line between political broadcasts and commercial advertisements will be blurred. Shorter broadcasts may also take politics further down the road of the soundbite and promote style over content.[78] Strong arguments exist either way and are beyond the scope of this chapter. It is, however, clear that as the media continues to change, the arrangements for political broadcasting must be continuously reviewed. Any reforms should not be used to provide new opportunities for wealth to disproportionately influence political debate and deliberation.

Conclusion

Following the decision in *Tierfabriken*, it is a matter of time before the ban on political advertisements in the UK is challenged. However, this chapter has attempted to show that the justification for the ban remains as strong as ever. Much of this chapter has acknowledged the importance and power of the broadcast media. Its qualities are distinct from other forms of communication and access can be crucial to a point a view. At the same time, it is a limited resource. It is impossible for every speaker to gain access to this media, especially for times when audience levels are high. Consequently, access to broadcasting can only ever be granted to a limited number of viewpoints on a limited number of issues. The issue is how to determine who will gain access. The argument in this chapter is simply that wealth should not be the determining factor. Attempts to limit the role of wealth by imposing time or expenditure limits are unlikely to be effective. The limits would either still be so high that the least wealthy groups would remain excluded or so low that too many groups could afford access. In the latter case, broadcasting time would have to be allocated on some other basis. If limits are imposed on the cost of advertising and such allocations are to be made, this will be little different to establishing a system of free political access time to parties and interest groups. The problem with this approach is that the basis for allocation will be controversial and if the losses of the broadcaster are to be subsidised, it will be costly. However, if the ban on political advertising really is thought to be an unjustifiable restriction on freedom of expression, this will be the price of a system that opens up the opportunities to broadcast to all sections of society regardless of wealth.

[76] See Electoral Commission, *Party Political Broadcasting: Report and Recommendations* (2003) at 25–7.

[77] *Ibid* at 31–3.

[78] For an argument against such concerns, see M Scammell, 'Political Advertising and the Broadcasting Revolution' [1990] *Political Quarterly* 200. See also, B Franklin, *Packaging Politics* (London, Edward Arnold, 1994) 139–41.

Part III

From State Regulation to State Funding

6

Political Finance Law in Australia

GRAEME ORR

The Spectre of Money Politics

Background

In common with other English-speaking polities, Australia has experienced a long period of political stability. Although disaffection with the major parties has increased over the past two decades, such that 'minor' parties and independents routinely attract 15–20 per cent of the vote, a two-party system of government is entrenched. But a predictable oscillation between the 'major' parties of government—the Australian Labor Party (ALP) and the Liberal-National Coalition—does not guarantee modesty. In common with most western democracies, electoral politics in Australia has become unshackled from ideology and addicted to expensive habits, including heavy reliance on television advertising, direct-mail strategies and market research. In short, the usual features of the 'permanent campaign'.

Major party politics has thus become big business. In the financial year encompassing the 2001 federal election, the conservative Coalition and the ALP reported receipts of A$71.5 m and A$60.9 m respectively.[1] It is in this context that the spectre of money controlling politics excites concern and debate.

The view of Australia as a pioneer in the implementation and development of electoral reforms is now something of an historical conceit.[2] Parties for most of the 20th century hid beneath the radar of the common law. They typically remain unincorporated associations, but in registering to control public funding and secure ballot labels, both common and statutory law now treats them as justiciable

[1] These figures cover monies raised for administration and policy development as well as electoral campaigning; but do not necessarily include monies raised independently by local candidacies.

[2] See A Brooks, 'A Paragon of Democratic Virtues? The Development of the Commonwealth Franchise' (1993) 12 *University of Tasmania Law Review* 208 at 208–9 on the 'myth' of seamless enfranchisement. Compare M Sawer, 'Pacemakers for the World?' in M Sawer (ed), *Elections: Full, Free and Fair* (Annandale, Federation Press, 2001).

and regulable entities.[3] Political finance law in Australia, by international standards, however, is decidedly laissez faire. Post-election there are disclosure obligations covering donations and public funding. But the enforcement mechanisms for disclosure are flaccid and there are no limits on either the amounts or sources of political donations or expenditure.

This chapter focuses on parliamentary politics, especially the national system. Unsurprisingly, in a federation of six states and two internal, self-governing territories, political finance laws are a patchwork of difference and varied development.[4] For ease of reference, the key features of each parliamentary jurisdiction are plotted in the appendicised table. It will be seen that, as well as the federal regime, six of the eight states and territories have donation disclosure regimes, and five have public funding.[5]

Outside the political elites, funding and disclosure laws attracted curiously little scrutiny until recent times. There were occasional voices from the right complaining about public funding,[6] and dissident voices, usually from the left, complaining of loopholes in the disclosure laws.[7] Yet in 1995, a parliamentary library report felt able to conclude 'that the intent of the funding disclosure legislation is being marginally vitiated by current practices but *this is not a matter for serious public concern* (although the situation will have to be continuously monitored)' (emphasis added).[8]

In more recent years, however, even the chief authority, the Australian Electoral Commission (the AEC, an independent and non-partisan agency) has anxiously signalled such concern, even alarm, at the efficacy of the disclosure regime:

> [I]f the disclosure provisions in the *Electoral Act* are to deliver transparency in the financial relationships of political parties, candidates and others associated with them, then a comprehensive review of the legislation and principles underpinning the legislation is required.[9]

Academic researchers, too, are laying the groundwork for informed critique. For some time, published work in the field was left largely to a single political scientist.[10]

[3] S Tully, 'Party Registration and Preselection: A Minefield for Electoral Administrators?' in G Orr *et al* (eds), *Realising Democracy: Electoral Law in Australia* (Annandale, Federation Press, 2003).

[4] Even more so when local government is considered. Referenda finance law is also under-developed: G Orr, 'The Conduct of Referenda and Plebiscites in Australia: A Legal Perspective' (2000) 11 *Public Law Review* 117 at 123–4.

[5] Victoria (2002) and the Northern Territory (2004) are the most recent. Western Australia and the Northern Territory are unusual in imposing the stick of disclosure without the carrot of public funding.

[6] Eg, I Farrow, 'Politicians Inc' (1995) 47(4) *IPA Review* 8.

[7] Eg, D Meadows, 'Open Election Funding or Hide and Seek' (1988) 13 *Legal Services Bulletin* 65.

[8] R Gerritsen, *Election Funding Disclosure and Australian Politics: Debunking Some Myths*, (Parliamentary Research Service Paper No 21, 1995) 1.

[9] AEC, 'Submission to Joint Standing Committee on Electoral Matters Inquiry into Disclosure of Donations to Political Parties and Candidates', 26 April 2004, para 3.0, <http://www.aph.gov.au/house/committee/em/donations/sub11.pdf> URL current as of 14 April 2005, a call it first made in 2001.

[10] E Chaples, 'Public Funding of Elections in Australia' in HA Alexander (ed), *Comparative Political Finance in the 1980s* (Cambridge, Cambridge University Press, 1989) 76.

Since 2000, however, diverse works have appeared tracing the roots of the law,[11] and critiquing the disclosure regime and calling for limitations on political donations.[12] A major research report into corporate donations has also been published.[13]

The field has not, however, been the subject of much litigation,[14] and prosecutions are exceedingly rare, with none on record since the mid 1990s. In part this reflects a cooperative approach to enforcement and reporting by authorities. The AEC, for resource and cultural reasons, considers itself more an administrator of the law than an auditing or policing body: 'The AEC believes that the major responsibility for ensuring the timeliness and accuracy of disclosure returns lies with [whoever completes] the return.'[15] This also reflects difficulties in proving intent in those instances of missing or misleading returns, given that some parties' record keeping is sub-standard.

Nor, with the occasional exception, have trends in donations and expenditure received serious empirical attention,[16] although the media has begun to treat disclosure more seriously. Investigators and researchers alike complain about the presentation and transparency of the data in disclosure reports. For example, annual returns of parties and associated entities only become available on 1 February each year—six months after the reporting year. Further, these returns do not require donations and other receipts to be separately identified, although some parties choose to do so. And despite calls for it, there is still no obligation to give pre-election disclosure, let alone instant disclosure of large donations. The complexity of the law, as evidenced in its bulk, is a further hurdle to interested onlookers. The federal statutory provisions on funding and disclosure alone extend across 60 pages.[17]

Chapter Scope

This chapter outlines the essential federal provisions covering political finance. It also canvasses notable differences in state law. Whilst federal Parliament has limited power over state elections, its influence over political finance is significant, for two reasons. First, whilst the wave of contemporary regulation began at state level—in

[11] D Cass and S Burrows, 'Commonwealth Regulation of Campaign Finance: Public Funding, Disclosure and Expenditure Limits' (2000) 22 *Sydney Law Review* 447.

[12] J Tham, 'Legal Regulation of Political Donations in Australia: Time for Change' in G Patmore (ed), *The Big Makeover: A New Australian Constitution* (Annandale, Pluto Press, 2000) 72; J Tham, 'Campaign Finance Reform in Australia: Some Reasons for Reform' in Orr *et al*, above n 3; G Orr, 'The Currency of Democracy: Campaign Finance Law in Australia' (2003) 26 *University of New South Wales Law Journal* 1. (This chapter is a reworking of the latter piece.)

[13] I Ramsay *et al*, *Political Donations by Australian Companies* (Melbourne, Centre for Corporate Law and Securities Regulation, University of Melbourne, 2001); I Ramsay *et al*, 'Political Donations by Australian Companies' (2001) 29 *Federal Law Review* 177.

[14] An exception is *Hare v Gladwin* (1988) 82 ALR 307, where the AEC successfully asserted the right to demand the production of documents from a trust used by the Country Liberal Party.

[15] AEC, above n 9, para 4.1.

[16] Exceptions are Ramsay *et al*, above n 13 and the NSW Greens Donations Project, <www.democracy4sale.org.au> current at 14 April 2005.

[17] The bulk of this is in the disclosure regime. This figure does not include regulations containing operational detail nor party registration.

New South Wales in 1981[18]—the federal regime has come to provide the regulatory model and setting for normative debates. Second, although federal and state elections are not held at the same time,[19] the federal system of disclosure serves as a backstop. This is because most state and territory branches of parties register federally, to control public funding earned at federal elections, and in accounting terms these branches do not distinguish between their state and federal activities. (State disclosure law remains necessary to cover candidates at state elections.)

The chapter falls into two sections: a description of the legal position, followed by a discussion of areas of concern and potential reform. Tham has argued that the regulation of donations in Australia has been 'ineffectual by design'.[20] Whether by design or neglect, the general consensus is that the entire regime needs significant tightening and constant vigilance. I highlight three areas.

First, the disclosure system is a leaky sieve, and in some respects it is misdirected. Second, the regime has not served its founders' purposes of discouraging reliance on corporate donations. It needs to be strengthened by the (re)introduction of expenditure limits. Despite these arguments, there is unlikely to be meaningful reform for some time: the conservative Coalition won control of both houses of federal Parliament at the 2004 election and, as described below, its reform inclinations are, if anything, to relax political finance regulations rather than to tighten them.

The third issue I highlight is that political finance law ought not obsess over party finances at the expense of tangible incumbency benefits. Both are relevant to the ultimate goals of political equality, fair electoral competition, and limiting the corruption of public power. The vast public resources available to incumbent parliamentarians for self-promotion and to governments for puff advertising threaten to outflank direct regulation of party finances.

In closing, I question the conditions in which a funding and disclosure regime might become so ineffectual as to be worse than none at all. Public choice theorists or post-modernists should not interpret this cautionary note as a call to inaction. Disparities in wealth, and their exploitation to distort democracy, will always be with us; the fluid power of money over politics will always pose sharp regulatory issues. But we are more in danger of underestimating the corrupting influence of the spectre of money politics as we are of becoming paranoid about its apparition.

The Current Legal Regime

The Reform Pendulum: A Brief History of Regulation in Australia

The law's evolution in Australia has been chronicled by Cass and Burrows.[21] Prior to the 1980s, the Australian approach to electoral finance had become dilapidated. Its

18 *Election Funding Act 1981* (NSW).
19 Federal law mandates distinct polling days, *Commonwealth Electoral Act 1918* (Cth) s 394 (CEA).
20 Tham in Patmore (ed), above n 12, 78–80.
21 Above n 11.

schema was inherited from the Victorian English model of deterring 'corrupt and illegal practices', whose genesis lay in the crackdown on corruption in the form of politicians buying votes. The modern concern however is not with politicians buying support (pork-barrelling being another story). On the contrary, the contemporary problem is with businesses and sectional groups buying influence over politicians.

Aside from such direct corruptions, the law has always needed to concern itself with the cost of elections, since political equality is diluted when elections become too costly for all but wealthy interests and the politicians willing to serve them. In that regard little has changed in 150 years. The cost of electoral politics in Australia remains unbounded, by regulation at least. Australian law continues, in effect, to trust, or rather hope, that modesty will prevail.

The contemporary Australian model of public funding, allied to broad disclosure obligations, was first hatched in the 1980s. Whilst it can be understood on its own terms, some history is necessary. This is not mere context, for the history continues to shape assumptions about what is, and is not, possible in the field. It also reveals the resistance of the political caste to regulation.

For most of the 20th century, federal electoral law imposed ostensibly strict limitations on expenses, but they only applied to candidates.[22] The system was fatally flawed for two practical reasons. First, its focus on the promotion of individual candidatures ignored the rise of parties as 'brand labels', the Presidentialisation of politics, and the role of the mass media in a country that despite its geographic size, has little media diversity, regional or otherwise. Following UK case law,[23] these factors outflanked a legal regime focussing on constituency expenditure, which duly fell into disrepair, if not disrepute.

The original expenditure limits of A$500 for Senate candidates (who campaign in multi-member state-wide electorates) and A$200 for House of Representatives candidates (who campaign in single-member constituencies) were revised just once in almost 80 years.[24] This was in 1946, when they were increased to A$1000 and A$500 respectively.[25]

Partly as a result, enforcement was far from stringent.[26] When Tasmania's Supreme Court took more strict state election limits seriously in 1979,[27] apoplexy gripped politicians. Rather than leading to a return to the rule of law, in the form of a crackdown on the cost of electioneering generally, the episode merely led to federal expenditure limits being abandoned altogether. Within a year, a conservative

[22] Cass and Burrows, above n 11, 454–5.

[23] *R v Tronoh Mines Ltd* [1952] 1 All ER 697 (interpreting laws restricting expenditure and 'promoting the election of a candidate' as inapplicable to advertising promoting or denigrating parties generally).

[24] The original limits were set in the inaugural *Commonwealth Electoral Act 1902* (Cth), s 169.

[25] *Commonwealth Electoral Act 1946* (Cth), s 4.

[26] Early on, the Chief Electoral Officer adopted a practice of not prosecuting candidates who made no return, if they happened to be unsuccessful at the polls: P Brazil (ed), *Opinions of the Attorneys-General of the Commonwealth of Australia*: Vol1, 1901–14 (Canberra, Australian Government Publishing Service, 1981) 500–1.

[27] *Re Electoral Act 1907* [1979] Tas R 282 (new elections ordered when several members committed the 'illegal practice' of expenditure in excess of the then constituency limit of A$1500).

federal government had seized the moment to repeal the restrictions on federal candidate expenditures.[28] This ushered in a brief period of total laissez-faire federally. Undaunted, the Tasmanian Supreme Court struck again, strictly interpreting Tasmanian law according to its original intent, so as to outlaw third party expenditure—including any expenditure by parties promoting their 'teams'—unless the expenditure was accommodated within the candidate's limit.[29] But this purgation lasted just one election. The incoming Tasmanian Government watered down that State's expenditure restrictions in 1985.[30]

The period of total federal deregulation also proved short-lived. The ALP won office in 1983 and, central to its overhaul of federal electoral laws,[31] it introduced a public funding and disclosure regime, now found in Part XX of the *Commonwealth Electoral Act 1918* (Cth) ('*CEA*').[32] Most states/territories have followed in whole or part. It is notable that all these regimes have been ushered in by ALP administrations, where necessary with support from other social democratic parties, the Australian Democrats and the Greens.

In 1991, a more radical attempt was made by the federal ALP to introduce a British-style ban on broadcast advertising during elections, in tandem with mandatory free radio and television air-time for party broadcasts.[33] This attempt foundered on an activist, liberalist High Court, which 'discovered' an implied freedom of political communication in the Constitution.[34] Free air-time, limited to the election period, is now only provided by the two public broadcasters.

Current Law: Public Funding and Taxation

In legislating for direct public funding of parties, the ALP relied on three main arguments. One was that elections should be decided on the quality of party policy, not the size of party coffers. A second was that public funding would narrow the difference in financial resources to ensure reasonably fair electoral competition. The third was that it should reduce reliance on private donations, minimising potential corruption.

[28] *Commonwealth Electoral Amendment Act 1980* (Cth).

[29] *Attorney-General v Liberal Party of Australia, Tasmanian Division* [1982] Tas R 60.

[30] Expenditure limits now only apply to the rather 'gentlemanly' Tasmanian upper house, a legislature not dominated by party politics. Exceeding the limit by A$1000 is prima facie grounds for unseating.

[31] *Commonwealth Electoral Legislation Amendment Act 1983* (Cth). The reform was preceded by a wide-ranging inquiry: Joint Select Committee on Electoral Reform, *First Report* (Parliament of Australia, 1983).

[32] For other jurisdictions, see: *Election Funding Act 1981* (NSW); *Electoral Act 1992* (Qld), s 126A, sch; *Electoral Act 2002* (Vic), pt XII; *Electoral Act 1992* (ACT), pt XIV; *Electoral Act 1907* (WA), pt VI; *Electoral Act 2004* (NT), pt X.

[33] *Political Broadcasts and Political Disclosures Act 1991* (Cth). The reasons for the ban are argued in Joint Standing Committee on Electoral Matters ('JSCEM'), *Who Pays the Piper Calls the Tune: Minimising the Risks of Funding Political Campaigns* (Canberra, Parliament of Australia, 1989).

[34] *ACTV v Commonwealth* (1992) 177 CLR 106. Critiquing the case, see KD Ewing, 'The Legal Regulation of Electoral Campaign Financing in Australia: A Preliminary Study' (1992) 22 *University of Western Australia Law Review* 239; E Barendt, 'Importing United States Free Speech Jurisprudence' in T Campbell and W Sadurski (eds), *Freedom of Communication* (Dartmouth, Aldershot, 1994) 57; S Joseph, 'Political Advertising and the Constitution' in Patmore (ed), above n 12, 48.

The federal system provides for post-election payments, according to the number of first preference votes received at both Senate and House of Representatives elections.[35] Registered parties appoint an agent to receive the funding generated by their candidates. Candidates running as independents or endorsed by unregistered parties receive any funding directly.

The amount per vote is indexed and stood at just over A$1.94 for the 2004 election. With well over 12,500,000 enrolments and a compulsory voting system in both Houses, the amount of public funding potentially exceeds A$50 m per triennial federal electoral cycle. The amount, however, is never paid in full since, despite compulsory voting, voter turnout is closer to 95 than 100 per cent. Further, public funding is only earned where candidates poll over four per cent of the formal vote, so that minor parties and independents are under-funded.[36] Federal funding is as of right, however, rather than by way of reimbursement, so that claimants are not required to prove actual campaign expenditure.[37] This has raised fears that a group running under little more than a slogan could profit from an election.

The older New South Wales (NSW) funding model features several notable differences. First, entitlements are capped, so that no one party or candidate can receive more than half of the funding. Secondly, registered parties are entitled to claim partial payments in *advance* of the poll.[38] Thirdly, the threshold of four per cent does not apply to a candidate who is actually elected (which can easily occur at NSW upper house elections, where the quota is low). Fourthly, an extra tier of payments is made via a 'Political Education Fund'.[39] This gives registered parties an annual entitlement equal to the cost of a stamp for every vote received at the last lower house election, for seminars and disseminating information about the party and its policies to members or the public. It cannot be used for electoral campaigning or conventions.[40] Finally, a specialist Election Funding Authority, notionally distinct from the State Electoral Office, administers the law.

The Liberal Party proposed tax deductibility of donations, to encourage private funding of parties, instead of public funding. The ALP insisted tax deductibility be limited, and now opposes it altogether.[41] In 1991, federal tax laws were amended to permit income tax deductions of up to A$100 pa for contributions to or membership of registered parties.[42] The Liberal Party has also recently pushed to substantially increase the deductible amount and extend it to corporate donations. Parties also enjoy tax-free status, and candidates can deduct campaign

[35] *Commonwealth Electoral Act 1918* (Cth), pt XX, div 3.

[36] The actual total paid after the 2001 federal election was A$38.6m.

[37] Compare the states, where expenditure must be receipted. The federal system began on a reimbursement basis, but the AEC and the parties found it administratively burdensome.

[38] *Election Funding Act 1981* (NSW), pt 5, div 5.

[39] *Election Funding Act 1981* (NSW), pt 6A.

[40] Election Funding Authority of NSW, *Political Education Fund Determinations.*

[41] JSCEM, *Who Pays the Piper Calls the Tune*, above n 33, 91. ALP, *National Platform and Constitution* (2004), para 16.37.

[42] *Income Tax Assessment Act 1997* (Cth), s 30–15 (table, item 3). Australian Taxation Office, Determination 92/114.

expenditure privately incurred—the latter is a significant subsidy, claims after the 2001 election averaging A$28,500 per federal MP.[43] However such deductions accord with general taxation principles (being expenses incurred in holding down a job) and for electoral fairness extend to all candidates, regardless of success.

Broadcast Air-Time

A 'blackout' on broadcast (but not press) advertising remains in force for the three days prior to and including polling day at all parliamentary elections.[44] Otherwise, as earlier mentioned, political advertising is open slather. There is no constitutional impediment to requiring broadcasters to provide free air-time,[45] but only the two public broadcasters—the Australian Broadcasting Corporation (ABC) and the multicultural Special Broadcasting Service (SBS)—do so, as an aspect of their public information charters.[46] The impact of these public allocations is limited. The ABC and SBS achieve combined ratings equivalent to around one-sixth of the viewing audience. During federal campaigns, one or two staged debates are televised between the Prime Minister and Opposition Leader. But these are not regulated: their number, nature and very existence are matters of convention and haggling, despite calls for a guaranteed and structured system of debates.[47]

Disclosure of Political Donations and Expenditure

Disclosure laws were a quid pro quo for public funding, designed to achieve transparency and accountability. The reach of these laws has become an ongoing issue and the detail has been amended on various occasions. Here I give a snapshot of the federal position as at the end of 2004.[48] The most important observation is that there are no restrictions on the amount or source of private donations.

The disclosure obligations broadly seek to ensure post-election revelation of certain details of donations and expenditure by candidates and donors. They also require annual disclosure by registered parties and their associated entities, including returns of totals of receipts, expenses and indebtedness.[49] ('Associated entities' are bodies controlled by, or operating substantially for the benefit of, registered parties.[50])

[43] *Income Tax Assessment Act 1997* (Cth), s 25–60 (deductibility of expenditure in excess of public funding); S Maiden, 'MPs Take Double Dip of Poll Cash', *The Australian*, 17 July 2004, 3.

[44] *Broadcasting Services Act 1992* (Cth), sch 2, pt 2, cl3A; *Special Broadcasting Service Act 1991*(Cth), s 70C.

[45] They were only struck down in *ACTV v Commonwealth* (1992) 177 CLR 106 because they were an inseparable part of a particular invalid scheme banning all paid broadcasts.

[46] ABC, *Editorial Policies* (2002) ch 11, <http://abc.net.au/corp/edpol02.pdf>; SBS, *Codes of Practice* (2002) 16, <http://www.sbs.com.au/sbsi/cop.pdf>.

[47] Eg, Editorial, 'Stop the Spin and Start the Great Debates', *The Australian*, 4 October 2001, 10.

[48] A joint parliamentary committee was due to report on the disclosure regime, but that inquiry lapsed with the 2004 election: <http://www.aph.gov.au/house/committee/em/index.htm>.

[49] *Commonwealth Electoral Act 1918* (Cth) (*CEA*), pt XX, div 4 ('Disclosure of donations'), div 5 ('Disclosure of electoral expenditure') and div 6 ('Annual returns by registered parties and associated entities').

[50] *CEA*, s 287 (definition).

Disclosure also extends to third parties who incur expenditure on matter intended or likely to affect voting.[51]

The disclosure scheme is practically reliant on a system of agents. Registered or not, political parties (ie, organisations whose objects include promoting its endorsed candidates for federal election)[52] must appoint party agents. Candidates in turn may appoint agents to handle their personal obligations.[53] Disclosure works on a 'cash accounting basis'. That is, only completed transactions are disclosable. (By delaying banking a cheque, a donation could thus fall outside a reporting period.)

In legal terms, donations are 'gifts', defined to include any disposition of property for inadequate consideration, excluding bequests. In theory, donations include the provision of services other than volunteer labour.[54] Within 15 weeks of polling day, all federal candidates must lodge returns disclosing details of certain gifts received during the 'disclosure period', other than private gifts used for non-electoral purposes. If the candidate stood at the prior election, the period dates back to the previous candidature; for new candidates it only dates back to their announcement of candidature.[55] Disclosure encompasses donor names, addresses and amounts. However, whilst the return must specify the total number of donors and the *sum* of all gifts received, donor details are *not* disclosable if the total of that donor's gifts was under A$200.[56] Donors to candidates have a mirror obligation.[57] Every person or organisation that incurs 'political' expenditure in excess of A$1,000 at an election must also furnish a post-election return of donations received.[58] This applies to lobby groups as well as unregistered parties, and is drafted to attempt to capture conduits of donations, since 'political expenditure' here includes the channelling of gifts as well as the cost of promoting views on any election issue.[59]

Registered political parties must submit returns each financial year. These are to include total receipts, plus names and addresses in relation to amounts (including any gifts, loans or bequests) of over A$1,500 received from any individual source in that financial year.[60] However, as a salve to party administrators of parties—but at the expense of transparency—in calculating the amount received from a single source, individual receipts of less than A$1,500 from that source need not be counted or disclosed by the party.[61] Similar annual returns must be made by entities 'associated' with registered parties.

[51] *CEA*, s 4 (definition). This applies to definitions of both 'political expenditure' (s 305(3)—attracting an obligation for 'third party' donation disclosure) and 'electoral expenditure' (s 308—attracting an obligation of post-election expenditure return).

[52] *CEA*, s 4 (definition).

[53] *CEA*, pt XX, div 2 ('Agents').

[54] *CEA*, s 287 (definition).

[55] *CEA*, s 287 (definition).

[56] See *CEA*, s 304 generally for candidate returns.

[57] *CEA*, s 305A.

[58] *CEA*, s 305.

[59] *CEA*, s 305(3).

[60] *CEA*, ss 314AB(2)(a), 314AC.

[61] *CEA*, s 314AC(2).

Annual reporting requirements also apply to donors who make annual gifts totalling A$1,500 or more to any registered party or branch, whether the total was achieved through several small donations, or a single large donation. Gifts via an intermediary are also meant to be disclosed; similarly, an organisation that channels contributions must disclose details of any individual gifts over A$1,000 that helped form a gift of A$1,500 or more to a party.[62] The obligation on donors to make annual disclosure, although not always widely understood, is meant as an auditing 'check' on the accuracy of party returns. A proposal to increase the minimum disclosable amount to A$3,000 pa may soon be enacted.[63]

It is unlawful to receive anonymous donations in circumstances that might undermine disclosure obligations. Thus, parties are not to receive gifts of A$1,000 or more, nor candidates gifts of A$200 or more, unless the true details of the donor are known at the time.[64] Reflecting a similar tenderness over non-commercial loans, the law now also renders it unlawful for parties or candidates to receive loans of A$1,500 or more unless they keep a record of the loan's terms and conditions, and the lender's name and address. Yet there are no restrictions on foreign donations.

Expenditure disclosure is also governed by a two-phase system: partly post-election, partly annual. As with donations, there are no limits to the amount that can be spent. Candidates must make post-election returns of electoral expenditure incurred with their authority, not including expenditure made or authorised by a registered party or branch. 'Third parties' that incur total electoral expenditure in excess of A$200 are also required to detail that expenditure after polling day.[65] In this context, 'electoral expenditure' means the cost of disseminating matter intended or likely to influence voting, including opinion polling.[66]

Annual expenditure returns are required of registered parties and their associated entities. However, to ease the accounting burden, these returns only require total expenditure and not its detail.[67] Total indebtedness must also be declared, including the source and amount of outstanding debts of A$1,500 or more from particular sources.[68]

Media outlets are also required to make post-election returns of electoral advertising carried by them during the campaign.[69] The Coalition government is seeking their abolition.[70] Such returns should be retained: in disclosing the charges for advertising, they may act as a check on media profiteering, a distinct possibility since parties are captive consumers of advertising space during campaigns.

[62] *CEA*, s 305B.
[63] *Electoral and Referendum Amendment (Enrolment Integrity and Other Measures) Bill* 2004 (Cth). An A$3,000 threshold was the majority recommendation of JSCEM, *The 1998 Federal Election*, (Parliament of Australia, 2000) 128. The ALP minority report opposed it at 158–9.
[64] *Commonwealth Electoral Act 1918* (Cth) (*CEA*), s 306.
[65] *CEA*, s 309.
[66] *CEA*, s 308(1), incorporating reference to 'electoral matter', defined in *CEA* s 4.
[67] *CEA*, ss 314AB(2)(b), 314AEA(I)(b).
[68] *CEA*, ss 314AB(2)(c), 314AEA(I)(c), 314AE.
[69] *CEA*, ss 310–11.
[70] *Electoral and Referendum Amendment (Enrolment Integrity and Other Measures), Bill* 2004 (Cth).

Some of the loopholes in this labyrinthine disclosure regime are discussed below. At this point, it suffices to note that whilst the AEC is given potentially broad investigatory powers,[71] the consequences of breaching the disclosure laws are far from draconian. Indeed maximum fines are risibly low:[72]

(1) for failure to make timely returns, A$5,000 for party agents, A$1,000 for others;
(2) for incomplete returns or record-keeping, A$1,000;
(3) for knowingly misleading returns, A$10,000 for party agents A$5,000 for others.

Similarly, politico-legal consequences of disclosure breaches are virtually non-existent. Breaches of disclosure obligations do not taint an offender's political rights, and non-compliance is not grounds for invalidating an election.[73]

Reform Debates

Disclosure Law Under Challenge—Some Illustrations

Before detailing reform proposals, it is worth crystallising the issues by outlining several recent examples of activities that have revealed flaws in the disclosure regime.

One concerns the Liberal Party and its Greenfields Foundation Trust. The Party's treasurer discharged a multi-million dollar bank loan to the Liberal Party, in his personal capacity as a wealthy businessman. The debt was then assigned to the Foundation, with the Party repaying it on an interest-free basis. Disclosure of these arrangements only occurred (and then by the Party, not the businessman) after an AEC investigation.[74] Since then, provisions relating to associated entities, and in particular to the disclosure of indebtedness and the recording of loans from non-financial institutions have been enacted. But broader questions were raised about why guarantees were not treated as 'gifts', and how to identify and enforce the law against associated entities, in particular trusts.

The problem of identifying associated entities surfaced again when it was revealed a Liberal Party Minister had organised a trust fund to help fund legal action against a rival, nationalist party, whose registration was in doubt. The fund had trustees of different political backgrounds. The AEC initially took the Minister's assertion that the fund was not an associated entity at face value,

[71] See especially *Commonwealth Electoral Act 1918* (Cth) (*CEA*), s 316.
[72] See *CEA*, s 315 for offences.
[73] *CEA*, s 319.
[74] AEC, *Funding and Disclosure Report Following the Federal Election Held on 3 October 1998* (AEC, 2000) pt 5.

without seeking its own legal advice or even sighting the trust deed. Five years later, its status has still not been resolved. The fund, ironically, was called 'Australians for Honest Politics'.[75] Aside from being an example of unrigorous policing of disclosure law, the case also highlights conceptual problems in a regime hatched to cover 'campaign' finance rather than 'political' finance.[76]

Both major parties have attracted criticism over general fundraising techniques that muddy disclosure. The ALP's use of a professional fundraising firm called Markson Sparks is a case in point.[77] The firm organises events including auctions of memorabilia associated with Party icons, which can raise hundreds of thousands of dollars. Generally the fundraiser only need disclose the total amount, and the donors and purchasers of items neglect to make disclosure. If a party—or even an associated entity—ran such auctions, donations of auctionable items worth A$1,500 or more would be disclosable, as would have the winning bids (allowing for difficulties in determining the fair market price, and hence the 'gifted' consideration).

Revenue through the sale of memorabilia, however, pales by comparison with the sums that firms will pay for tables at fundraising dinners and privileged status at party conventions and so-called policy 'round-tables' and 'forums'. Disclosure of such payments is lax, with parties sometimes treating payments as ordinary receipts, and the payers often treating them as business expenses rather than donations.[78]

There is real danger in swallowing the corporate view that such payments are valuable consideration, shelled out as part of doing business. Indeed one AEC handbook states that 'value [ie, consideration] includes gaining access to lobby government ministers'.[79] On that reasoning, even large-scale donations ought to be tax deductible as a kind of sponsorship to gain attention! (As of 2004, the AEC now advocates that all payments at fundraisers be deemed to be donations.) No matter how perfect the disclosure law, if the sale of political favours is accepted as part of the 'commerce' of politics, then politics collapses into a business, not a public endeavour. That is, accountability concerns aside, the prostitution of political access is a corruption of political equality. This issue comes on top of the perception of the sale of governmental favours, raised

[75] For a detailed account, see M Kingston, 'Not Happy, John! Defending Our Democracy' (Camberwell, Penguin, 2004) ch 15.

[76] Similarly, the law's application to party pre-selections is unclear. Historically these have been low-key, branch affairs, but high profile, even millionaire candidacies have recently occurred. Also, at least one party, the Australian Democrats, runs leadership ballots of its entire membership, and questions were raised about why a consultant donating his time to one of its leadership contenders generated no disclosure obligation: AEC, 'Submission to the Joint Standing Committee on Electoral Matters Inquiry into Electoral Funding and Disclosure', Submission No 15, 3 August 2001, para 2.1.5 <http://www.aph.gov.au/house/committee/em/f_d/subfifteen.pdf> URL current as of 14 April 2005.

[77] L Oakes, 'Labor's Soft Money Loophole', *The Bulletin*, 5 September 2000, 24. The ALP now accepts that all fundraising bodies should make full disclosure.

[78] For examples, see Tham in Patmore (ed), above n 12, 74–5, and Orr, above n 12, 18–19.

[79] AEC, *Funding and Disclosure Handbook for Third Parties* (2000) pt 2, 1.

recently over the exercise of discretion by an Immigration Minister in relation to Liberal Party donors.[80]

Specific Reform Proposals—the Official View

Institutional scrutiny of federal finance law is guaranteed, each electoral cycle, through two mechanisms. The AEC is required to produce a *Funding and Disclosure Report* after each election.[81] Then, the federal Parliament's Joint Standing Committee on Electoral Matters ('JSCEM') investigates and reports on the overall conduct of the election.

A host of AEC recommendations about funding and disclosure remain on the table, some dating back over seven years. In 2000, the JSCEM was specifically briefed to conduct a 'Funding and Disclosure Inquiry'. But that inquiry has twice been left to lapse by the conservative Coalition.[82] The AEC made several detailed submissions to those inquiries, calling for urgent amendments to redress a host of 'the most pressing problems' in disclosure law, its second submission written in a mixture of frustration and resolve.

Some of these recommendations would represent a considerable tightening of the disclosure regime. They include nullifying any arrangements entered into to obviate disclosure obligations, with significant penalties for such contrivances. Undisclosed donations would be subject to forfeiture; anonymous donations to double forfeiture. Overseas donations would also be liable to forfeiture, at least where the donor failed to declare them. Party returns would be clarified so that donations were clearly distinct from other receipts, and accompanied by an independent audit report. Continued failure to lodge proper returns would be grounds for party deregistration. And the definition of associated entities would be clarified and broadened so, eg, that a right to appoint a majority of directors/trustees would explicitly amount to party control of the entity, and a significant link in membership would be an alternative test for 'associatedness'.

Specific Reform Proposals—Parties and Observers

The parties, of course, have their own agendas for reform, some resembling ambit claims. The organisational wing of the Liberal Party, whose approach to campaign finance has always been libertarian, wanted disclosure thresholds raised to A$10,000 pa. Recalling that parties register their state/territory as well as national branches, if such a large threshold applied one could donate at just below the

[80] L Tingle and T O'Loughlin, 'Ruddock is a Man of Discretion', *The Weekend Australian Financial Review*, 14–15 June 2003, 22–3; Senate Select Committee on Ministerial Discretion in Migration Matters, *Report* (Parliament of Australia, 2004). This echoes a similar recent controversy involving the British Labour government.

[81] *Commonwealth Electoral Act 1918* (Cth) *(CEA)*, s 17(2).

[82] <http://www.aph.gov.au/house/committee/em/f_d/index.htm> (original inquiry), <http://www.aph.gov.au/house/committee/em/donations/index.htm> (reconvened inquiry).

threshold to each branch, and contribute nearly A$90,000 pa to a party without proper disclosure. The parliamentary Liberal Party removed some of the ambit from that claim, when it sought, unsuccessfully, to legislate an A$5,000 threshold.[83] It is likely now to pass that increased threshold.

It is hard to see why the disclosure threshold needs to be significantly raised. Currently, a donor can donate up to nine lots of A$1,499 pa to each registered element of a federally-organised party, and no specific disclosure by either party or donor is required. Indeed it is lawful to make standing donations of, say, A$1,499 per month to the same party branch and the party as recipient is not required to disclose the details: only the donor must disclose. Given that donors are much less likely to know the law, and are harder to police than parties, this inverts the natural order. Parties *solicit* donations. They are in the best position to know and enforce the law (thus, in the ACT for example, it is an offence for parties and MPs to fail to advise donors of their reporting obligations). The status quo is defended as administratively easier, but in a computerised age why should parties not disclose *all* donations with a low cap, set to say average weekly earnings?

Relatedly, it is unclear why the disclosure provisions in this regard are tighter for candidates than parties. This is unfair to independents. Further, the federal disclosure laws should require national party secretariats to amalgamate donation disclosures to include totals received from the same source, regardless of which branch received the donation (just as branches currently must report on all receipts of their sub-branches and campaign committees.)

A second *cause célèbre* for the Liberal Party is increased tax deductibility. It unsuccessfully promoted a Bill to extend deductibility to corporations. Its organisational wing called for a hundred-fold increase in deductibility of donations,[84] though its parliamentary wing proposed a more modest figure, mirroring the disclosure threshold.[85] In the standoff over these issues, the most pressing tax reform, for political equality, fell by the wayside: there is no deductibility for supporters of independent candidates or unregistered parties.

In contrast to the Liberal Party, others have sought a considerable tightening of disclosure and donation law. The Australian Democrats want *instant* publicisation of donations exceeding A$10,000, and a ceiling on donations from any single corporation or organisation.[86] The Democrats, supported by the ALP, succeeded in gaining mandator AEC auditing of donations over A$25,000.

A leading author in the field, Tham, joins the Democrats in advocating caps on donations, if not outright bans.[87] He argues, quite persuasively, that sizeable corporate donations, at least from certain industries, have become 'normalised' (banking and finance federally, and the pub/club industries at state level are

[83] *Electoral and Referendum Amendment Bill (No 2)* 1998 (Cth).
[84] To A$10,000 pa. JSCEM, Parliament of Australia, *The 1996 Federal Election* (Canberra, Parliament of Australia, 1997) paras 8.28–8.30.
[85] *Taxation Laws (Political Donations) Bill* 1999 (Cth).
[86] JSCEM, *The 1998 Federal Election*, above n 63, 174, 176. See also A Murray and M Rock, 'The Dangerous Art of Giving' (2000) 72(3) *Australian Quarterly* 29.
[87] Tham in Patmore (ed), above n 12, 81–6 and Tham in Orr (ed), above n 12, 128.

noteworthy). That is, far from encouraging a general modesty in donations across the board, the 'sunshine' of disclosure has perversely created an atmosphere where significant donations are par for the course—perhaps unsurprisingly in an age where corporations rival governments in terms of power.[88] Disclosure may have exacerbated the tendency of corporations to donate roughly equal sums to both major parties. This may create a more level playing field between those parties, but it only reinforces concerns about selling access to power and the creation of 'cartel' parties to the exclusion of other electoral competitors.

The AEC, however, recommends against donation limits, citing problems of definition and enforcement.[89] The definitional questions raise issues of equal treatment. For instance, since the ALP receives significant 'affiliation' fees from unions, caps on donations would have to include all 'contributions'. Further, to rework an argument of one conservative US scholar, should caps not also apply to the time individual activists commit to, or the number of words polemicists write in support of, political causes?[90] The answer to this objection is not to descend into arid debates about what is 'speech', but to accept that there is a legitimate aesthetic aversion to an excess of money in politics that does not apply to self-expression. Being active and generating ideas about public affairs, after all, is the core currency of politics, not geld.[91]

The larger concern with caps on donations, however, is their workability. It is generally assumed that ruses would be adopted to avoid caps. Given the Australian experience with the use of associated entities and fundraising agencies to place donations at a formal remove from the parties,[92] this seems a real possibility. Nonetheless, albeit partly at a symbolic level, limits on donations are being mooted. The ALP legislated in Victoria to cap donations from casinos,[93] and has renounced contributions from the tobacco industry. The NSW Greens promoted a Bill to forbid donations by major developers.[94]

The Democrats have also led calls for shareholder control and accountability over corporate donations. Their policy includes requiring shareholder approval of 'donation policies' of public companies, and full donation disclosure in company annual reports. Ramsay *et al*, in their study on corporate donating, support this proposal.[95] Such a reform would be commendable, but may prove a leaden

[88] Tham in Patmore (ed), above n 12. See also J Tham and D Grove, 'Public Funding and Expenditure Regulation of Australian Political Parties: Some Reflections' (2004) 32 *Federal Law Review* forthcoming, table 2 and discussion.

[89] AEC, 'Submission to the Joint Standing Committee on Electoral Matters Inquiry into Funding and Disclosure', Submission No 7, 17 October 2000, paras 8.8–8.13 <http://www.aph.gov.au/house/committee/em/f_d/subseven.pdf>, URL current as of 14 April 2005.

[90] JO McGinnis, 'Against the Scribes: Campaign Finance Reform Revisited' (2000) 24 *Harvard Journal of Law and Public Policy* 25.

[91] I develop this in 'The Ritual and Aesthetic in Electoral Law' (2004) 32 *Federal Law Review* forthcoming.

[92] Eg, L McIlveen and S Morris, 'Fronts Obscure Political Handouts', *The Australian*, 4 February 2003, 3.

[93] *Electoral Act 2002* (Vic), pt 12, div 3.

[94] *Developer Donations (Anti-Corruption) Bill 2003* (NSW).

[95] Above n 13.

political football. The ALP might not oppose reforming corporate donating per se, but this would implicate ALP sensitivities about the freedom of unions to contribute affiliation fees and donations—although unions, unlike companies, are democratically organised, and lack the 'corporate veil' that renders the true source of many donations impervious to onlookers.[96]

Expenditure Limits Reprised?

The model I advocate involves retaining public funding but with campaign expenditure limits and expenditure accountability.[97]

Critics of public funding allege that it accelerates the atrophying of 'grassroots' political activity. It is far from clear that this is a product of public funding. Public funding defrays campaign debts after an election, but it hardly covers all the expenses of a party's administration or policy generation. The financial, as well as intellectual and moral health of parties will always require an engaged membership.

The real problem is that, in the absence of expenditure limits, parties have every reason to rely as much as possible on large private donations. Naturally, the affection and attention of party apparatchiks turns away from party membership, when grassroots fundraising inevitably pales in comparison to corporate donations. If donation caps were feasible, this would be a strong argument in their favour.

In any event, public funding is a significant boost to electoral competition. It forms a much more significant share of the revenue of popular minor parties, who do not attract corporate or union largesse: on Tham's figures, the parties of government receive between two and four times the amount of private funding per vote than the minor parties.[98]

Admittedly, the original conception of public funding as a means of weaning parties off private donations proved overly ambitious. Who can be surprised? The Achilles' heel of the project was the failure to link public funding to expenditure limits. Strongly audited expenditure limits, now a feature of comparable democracies such as the UK and Canada, are essential to sustaining a modest campaign culture. Otherwise, like sporting clubs competing without a salary cap, the parties are locked into an escalating war. And as Cass and Burrows argue, there is no reason why well-tailored expenditure limits, including limits on non-party campaigning, should fall foul of constitutional liberalism.[99] After all, candidate limits existed for almost 80 years federally and remain in place in the Tasmanian Upper House.

It will be objected that, like pressing down on the proverbial waterbed, expenditure limits may only cause a flow of money away from parties and candidates to

[96] For examples, see M Bachelard, 'Loopholes that Keep Donors in the Shadows', *The Australian*, 7 February 2004, 1.

[97] Compare D Tucker and S Young, who, whilst arguing that funding levels are not ungenerous, suggest restricting private fundraising as a prerequisite for public funding, 'Public Financing of Election Campaigns in Australia—a Solution or a Problem?' in Patmore (ed), above n 12.

[98] Tham, above n 12, tables 1–3 and discussion.

[99] Cass and Burrows, above n 11, 457–60.

third parties. Or that political elites will simply invent ways of circumventing expenditure limits, such as creating 'front' groups to engage in electoral advertising? In Issacharoff and Karlan's famous metaphor, regulation confronts the 'hydraulics' of campaign finance: money is fluid and seeks its own level.[100]

But to assume that money is an uncontainable acid is to take an odd view of electoral culture in Australia. Australia is not the US. It lacks a deeply-rooted history of expression through civic associations, behind which a proliferation of electoral speech, sham or otherwise, can manifest. In Australia, a more statist culture has prevailed, creating a preference for a more ordered approach to electoral lobbying, generally limited to a few well-known and peak union, environmental, professional and business groups. In short, there is no cacophony of political speech into which mouthpieces for party interests, active only around election time, could easily blend. Culture, though, is admittedly mutable—recently an apparently professional website appeared, conducting anonymous negative campaigning.[101]

Unlike donations, which occur in private, electoral expenditure—particularly advertising and general canvassing—is inherently public. Controls on expenditure are thus more susceptible to enforcement, not least since rival parties are in a position to monitor one another.

Abuses of Incumbency

Incumbents, for better or worse, attract the lion share of public attention. But this is not a 'benefit' of concern to political finance law. Rather, it is the differential access to—and misuse of—public resources that threatens fair electoral competition and political equality.

Parliamentarians and governments alike, of course, need to communicate their work and public service information. Without that, including access to modern methods of grabbing attention, public affairs will be relegated to secondary status, subordinate to consumerist capitalism's saturation of the media, indeed the physical landscape.

But as Young has argued, executive governments and parliamentarians have indulgently overseen a blowout in expenditure and blurring of the line between information and self-promotion for electoral gain.[102] Federal parliamentarians, for instance, enjoy an A$125,000 annual printing allowance, much of which is devoted to puffery such as electorate 'newspapers' adorned with flattering images of the member and promotion of her party's policies, and mail-outs luring electors to give information about issues of concern to them—information then fed into databases for personalised targeting of direct mail around election time. None of this amounts to real communication between governor and governed.

[100] S Issacharoff and PS Karlan, 'The Hydraulics of Campaign Finance Reform' (1999) 77 *Texas Law Review* 1705. No less pithy is DH Lowenstein, 'On Campaign Finance Reform: The Root of All Evil is Deeply Rooted' (1989) 18 *Hofstra Law Review* 301.

[101] Eg, <www.johnhowardlies.com>.

[102] S Young, 'Killing Competition: Restricting Access to Political Communication Channels in Australia' (2003) *AQ* (May–June) 9.

Even more insidious is the misuse of tens of millions of dollars of unrestrained government advertising, which floods the airwaves prior to elections. The cost of advertising promoting federal government policies or positions alone, in the run-up to the 2004 election is estimated to exceed A$150 m.[103] The federal government has failed to enact Auditor-General guidelines aimed at separating 'political' from unexceptional government advertising, even though a parliamentary committee on which government members formed a majority endorsed those guidelines, and even though they are far from onerous.[104] Admittedly, it is not easy to determine if a single advertisement, on its face, is 'political', although governments admit as much by nugatorily 'tagging' all issue advertising, eg, 'Authorised by the Commonwealth Government, Canberra'. But taken as a whole, the size and tenor of most of these campaigns are clearly disproportional to their effectiveness or stated aims. Many contain almost no information but plenty of debatable spin about contentious policies and programmes. That these campaigns are co-ordinated to boost governmental stocks is revealed by the fact that spending on them spikes dramatically in election years.[105] The ALP, risking charges of hypocrisy since the trend began in its previous administration, has pledged to establish an independent body to review government advertising campaigns, to claw-back, from party entitlements to public funding, the cost of any found to be political. A bright-line solution would be to cap the cost of government advertising and permit no more in election years than other times.

The federal government is easily the biggest spender on advertising in Australia: A$665 m alone in the first eight years of the present Coalition administration. A secondary concern with abuse of government advertising is that it creates a dependency in the private media on government largesse. Normally such media is loud in its opposition to public sector waste.

Abuse of incumbency benefits wreaks a hierarchical distortion of electoral equality. Governing parties benefit more than the Opposition, who benefit more than minor parties. And all inside the tent benefit over challengers.

Conclusion—The Limits of Regulation

It is almost universally accepted that elections require some level of disclosure law. It is also understood that the fierce competition for power militates against political culture spontaneously developing a self-enforcing ethic about its own financing. The sub-text of the specialist literature on political finance is that the law is enmeshed in a continuing 'cat and mouse' game. But we commit to the game because of an implicit belief that despite—or perhaps through—this struggle,

[103] M Schubert, 'Howard's $151 m Ad Blitz', *The Age*, 22 June 2004, 4.
[104] Joint Committee of Public Accounts and Audit, *Report 377: Guidelines for Government Advertising* (Canberra, Parliament of Australia, 2000).
[105] Australian National Audit Office, *Taxation Reform: Community Education and Information Programme* (Auditor-General, Audit Report No 12, 1998) 28–30.

incremental progress is achieved, given vigilance and regulatory courage in the face of vested interests and creative lawyering. At the root of this rationalist faith is an unstated assumption that *some* regulation is better than none, and that, other things being equal, *more* regulation, rather than less, is necessary.

It may, however, be possible to reach a point in a funding or disclosure system where the imperfections are such that some law becomes worse than none. At first this might seem paradoxical. General regulatory theory also deals with systems of benefits and penalties, and 'need' and 'wrongdoing'. Yet no one argues that, simply because the law cannot be perfectly policed, or an equal distribution of benefits achieved, the law must give up the regulatory game. It is better to catch a few wrongdoers than none; it is better to pay some welfare even if other deserving cases miss out.

But this theory is based on a simple, linear idea. If we remove dirt then hygiene is advanced; if we give welfare then poverty is mitigated. But administering and policing electoral politics is more complex. If some types of political actors are more likely to get caught in the disclosure net, or to have their fundraising or campaign finance position affected than others, then the law may distort more than it equalises. Such distortion may affect core values like fair electoral competition and improving the diversity and strength of political culture.

This may happen when certain restrictions and benefits apply differentially. A classic illustration is the threshold to 'earn' public funding, which affects the ability of small parties to establish themselves. For example, a party that achieves exactly four per cent of the Senate vote evenly across Australia will receive close to A$1 m. Such a sum would maintain a national office and fund a modest campaign at the next election. A party receiving three per cent of the vote can expect nothing. This situation historically advantaged the Democrats who, to take the 1998 Senate election as an example, received more than 11 times the funding of the Greens, its rival for the progressive vote and the balance of Senate power, although it polled only three times their vote.

Of course any cut-off will have arbitrary effects. Some may even see the funding threshold as desirable, to encourage minor parties of a similar hue to amalgamate.[106] So consider a more subtle distortion. A minor party that can launch with a 'bang' and garner over four per cent will secure the funding it needs to perpetuate and grow. The eruption of the nationalist and racialist One Nation Party ('ONP') is salutary. It benefited from its own controversy and its charismatic leader. The resultant splash earned it very substantial sums of public funding at elections in its first years. This is not to say that the ONP did not 'deserve' the funding: populism is rewarded because the system ties funding to individual voter choices. Rather, the lesson is that minor parties with less attention-grabbing positions but more comprehensive policies, face two obstacles: media occlusion, since

[106] A Democrat-Greens alliance was once suggested given their policy sympathies. The financial argument must have been enticing. Even if it did not increase their combined vote, it would have been worth approximately A$380,000 in public funding for Senate votes alone (1998 figures).

what is less scandalous is less newsworthy and a discriminatory funding apparatus that is not truly pro-rated.

One could multiply similar examples. They are just instances of a well-recognised general phenomenon. The differential receipt of public subsidies can distort a competitive environment. What is perhaps less well considered is whether *disclosure* laws might operate in a similar way.

This might seem paradoxical. Disclosure is knowledge. Science tells us that any knowledge is a good thing, assuming its veracity. From this point of view, partial disclosure is better than none, since it at least sheds some light. But since electoral politics is competitive by nature, the disclosure process itself is inherently political in the sense that media attention to disclosure can have political ramifications. This insight is not new at the margins: radical political groups have long feared that disclosure may deter their supporters, who may risk retribution or social sanctions.

The imperfect policing of complex disclosure may create two problems. Parties or candidates who are less well organised or advised are more likely to fall foul of the law through ignorance, or slavishly follow official guidelines. Conversely, parties and donors who are well resourced are better placed, as the 'Australians for Honest Politics Trust' proved, to obtain professional advice in designing their structures and negotiating with the authorities, to avoid disclosure.

Second, the electorate may receive a distorted picture. Donors who are open about their activities may receive attention more fairly directed at secretive donors. Similarly, scrupulous parties open themselves to greater public scrutiny than others. Such openness may be used to advantage (eg through the virtuous refrain, 'We are open; are our opponents?'). But there is also a danger that public impressions will be tilted against those who are most open. If that is the case, imperfect disclosure laws may be less valuable than other kinds of informational regimes, such as an anonymous survey of business donations, or 'clean politics' systems, such as channelling donations through an official 'clearing house'.

There is also a danger that unintentionally selective enforcement, or selective promotion, will create false impressions of the nature of the overall problem. The issue of political finance reform receives secondary attention in both parliament and the media, compared to crude electoral offences such as personation and multiple-voting, which occur on quite limited scales. Crude electoral fraud is to money politics as blue-collar crime is to white-collar crime.

In the end, the question for the Australian funding and disclosure regime is whether its manifold imperfections are fatally flawed or remediable. The range and tone of recommendations for reform raise the question of whether disclosure is more a labour of Sisyphus than a 'cat and mouse' game, and whether the equivocal benefits of disclosure justify the effort. There is probably the institutional energy in Australia for one more round of disclosure law reform. But as I have argued here, 'comprehensive review' must embrace not just root and branch tightening of disclosure, but both expenditure limits and a crackdown on the milking of incumbency benefits.

Appendix: Australian Political Finance Laws—Key Features

Jurisdiction (by size)	Public Funding	Party Registration	Donation Disclosure	Expenditure Returns	Expenditure Limits	Tax Relief
Federal	Post-election, as of right. Four per cent vote threshold.	500 members or federal Member of Parliament required.[107]	Post-election by candidates, donors and political expenders. Annual returns by parties, associated entities and party donors.	Post-election by candidates and media (advertising). Annual returns by parties and associated entities (summaries only).	None	Deductibility of donations up to A$100pa (corporations excluded). Candidate expenditure deductible.
New South Wales	Post-election, capped by actual expenditure.[108] Four per cent vote threshold. General and constituency funds: no-one entitled to more than half of fund.	Register of parties and candidates. 750 members required.	Post-election by registered parties, candidates and other political expenders.	Post-election by registered parties, candidates and other political expenders.	None	As above

continued over

[107] The federal registration requirements survived constitutional challenge in *Mulholland v AEC* [2004] HCA 41; (2004) 209 ALR 582.

[108] NSW alone also allows for a limited advance (ie pre-election) payment of anticipated public funding. It also provides a 'political education' fund to assist internal party communication.

Victoria	Post-election, capped by actual expenditure. Four per cent vote threshold	500 members.	Registered parties merely to file copy of annual federal return with State Commission.	Post-election, audited statement of total expenditure only (to claim public funding)	None	As above
Queensland	Post-election, capped by actual expenditure. Four per cent vote threshold	500 members or Queensland Member of Parliament required.	Post-election by candidates, donors and political expenders. Annual returns by parties and associated entities.	Post-election by candidates and other political expenders. Annual returns by parties or associated entities (summaries only)	None	As above
Western Australia	None	500 members.	Post-election by candidates, non-party groups and political expenders. Annual returns by parties and associated entities.	Post-election by parties, candidates, non-party groups and other political expenders.	None	As above

continued over

South Australia	None	150 members or any Australian Member of Parliament.	None	None	None	As above
Tasmania	None	100 members.	None	Post-election returns by Legislative Council candidates (including receipts for expenses over A$20).	Legislative Council (Upper House) only: candidate expenses limited to A$ 10,000.[109] Expenditure by others prohibited.	As above
Australian Capital Territory	Post election as of right. Four per cent threshold.	100 members.	Post-election by candidates, non-party groups, donors and political expenders. Annual returns by parties, associated entities, MPs and donors to parties/ MPs.	Post-election by candidates, parties, non-party groups, political expenders and media (advertising). Annual returns by parties, associated entities and MPs.	None	As above

continued over

[109] 2005 figure. The amount increases by increments of A$500 annually.

Northern Territory	None	200 members or federal registration.	Post-election by candidates, donors and political expenders. Annual returns by registered parties and associated entities.	Post-election by candidates and media (advertising). Annual returns by registered parties and associated entities.	None	As above

Postscript: In mid-2005 the Australian government announced plans to significantly liberalise the law. It is anticipated that the disclosure threshold will rise to A$5,000 and individuals will be able to claim tax deductibility of party donations at a similar level.

7

Revisiting Transparency and Disclosure in Japanese Political Reform[1]

AKIKO EJIMA

Introduction

IN JULY 2004 the Japanese press reported that, three years prior in July 2001, Japan's Prime Minister at the time, Ryutaro Hashimoto, had received a ¥100 million cheque (approximately $1 million) from a former chairman of the Japan Dental Association (JDA)—the lobbying arm of the Japan Dentists Federation—at a *ryotei*—a very expensive and private type of Japanese restaurant often used by politicians to have confidential conversations and negotiations among themselves and/or business leaders—in the presence of two other Liberal Democratic Party (LDP) heavyweights. Even though Japan's Political Fund Control Law (PFCL) requires political organisations to disclose all income in an annual balance report, the LDP made no record of this contribution. Prime Minister Hashimoto, who until recently headed the LDP's largest faction, the *Heisei Kenkyukai*, told reporters that he did not remember receiving the cheque and denied his involvement in the affair, although subsequently the *Heisei Kenkyukai* itself acknowledged the donation and re-filed its 2001 political funds report. On 29 August 2004, prosecutors indicted Toshiyuki Takigawa, former LDP treasurer, on suspicion of violating the PFCL with the omission, and subsequently indicted Kanezo Muraoka, former Chief Cabinet Secretary, on whose advice Takigawa stated he had been acting. However, it is very unlikely that prosecutors will charge Mr Hashimoto himself, even though the donor stated that he had handed the cheque directly to the former Prime Minister.

This scandal revealed the existence of a common practice at the LDP: the party receives donations from other political organisations—donations which

[1] The initial draft of this chapter appeared in the Bulletin of the Institute of Social Sciences, Meiji University, vol 26, no 24 (March 2004). The author has updated her facts and analysis to incorporate recent events, particularly the 2004 scandal involving the former Prime Minister and a new proposal for amendment to the Political Fund Control Law.

individual politicians could never take due to legal regulations in the PFCL—and issues receipts to the donors, after which the LDP distributes the money to its politicians. This practice obviously functions as a loophole in the PFCL, and raises the question of whether the PFCL effectively keeps political funding clean enough for the public to continue trusting political parties and politicians. To deal with the problem, the Japanese government is currently proposing a Bill which would set a ¥50 million ceiling on donations among political groups, but while this is a very typical reaction by the LDP to political scandal, as is explained in the next section, the author does not think that it is an effective solution. The explanation of this opinion requires an analysis of the history and present situation of political funding in Japan.

Japanese politics are notorious for the huge cost of electoral and political activities and for incessant political corruption.[2] But this does not mean that the government has never done anything to cope with problems. On the contrary, the cyclical exposure of major political scandals, accompanied by strong anger and distrust on the part of the public, has been a powerful stimulus toward amending regulations of party funding and election finance. However, all attempts to curb political and electoral expenditures and thereby to prevent political corruption have failed so far. It is time to examine not only solutions but also the process through which these solutions are chosen and implemented. Structural factors may prevent the taking of more appropriate and effective measures.

The latest example of this cycle of scandal and attempt at a solution is the Political Reform of 1994. This reform was triggered by the Recruit Scandal in 1988, after which the degree of disgust with existing politics and the desire for change were so overwhelming among the public—and even among politicians themselves—that the LDP lost power for the first time in four decades. In 1993 a coalition government of opposition parties was established, and to it fell the task of political reform. This complete reform not only adopted severer regulations (tightening upper limits on donations, prohibiting certain types of donations and requiring more transparency and disclosure), but also introduced direct public funding to political parties for the first time in Japanese political history. Moreover, the reform succeeded in including changes in the electoral system, on the premise that such change may contribute to the transformation of politician-centred politics into party-centred politics. However, it is doubtful that the reform was successful in curbing the expenditures of politicians and political parties—and thereby lessening the possibility of political corruption—since new problems are now emerging. It is still too early to say that Japanese politics is party-and policy-centred.

The main purpose of this article is to analyse and evaluate the Political Reform of 1994 in order to shed light on what advantages and limitations legal regulations and structural reforms have in the control of political funding. Moreover, the effect of public money is examined by looking at the effects of newly introduced direct public funding regulations on Japan's political parties. In this article the author utilises a classification of three different reform models: the regulation

[2] J Bouissou, 'Gifts, Networks and Clienteles: Corruption in Japan as a Redistributive System' in D Della Porta and Y Meny (eds), *Democracy and Corruption in Europe* (London, Pinter, 1997).

model, the self-regulation model and the structural reform model.[3] The first section of this article explains the history of legal control of political funding in Japan. Specifically, the major political corruption scandals which triggered the legislation in question are examined in order to evaluate how effective the particular regulation model is. The second section examines the present system (after the 1994 Political Reform) in order to clarify the fundamental problem of the Japanese system. For five decades Japan has incorporated various measures that together constitute every factor of the above three models. Therefore, it is useful to classify all the measures that the Japanese government has taken according to the said three models. Thereby, each characteristic of these measures will be analysed and clearly understood. The third section proposes a possible alternative that would be helpful in improving the present situation, taking into account current problems, amendments and nascent awareness among the public.

The History of Legal Control of Political Funding and Election Finance in Japan

Overview: Various Solutions

Presently legal control of Japanese political funding and election finance comprises three major pieces of legislation. First is the PFCL,[4] which regulates the income and expenditures of political activities of politicians, political parties and political organisations. Secondly, the Public Offices Election Law (POEL)[5] regulates income and expenditures during elections. Lastly, the Political Party Subsidies Law (PPSL)[6] introduces state funding and requires political parties to submit a report on how the subsidies are used. These laws were not instituted at once. They have been amended and augmented over five decades, mostly in response to political scandals. They can be classified according to three models.[7]

The first is the 'legal regulation' model, by which laws aim to curb the income and expenditures of politicians and political parties directly by limiting donations and electoral expenditures, by restricting some political activities that are likely to entail bribery and by setting penalties for violations. While this is the most direct approach in terms of restraining political finance, there is also the danger of restricting political freedom more than is necessary. Furthermore, an effective and efficient mechanism of enforcing the law is necessary for this model to function properly. The experiences of various countries[8] have proven that it is difficult to

[3] A Ejima, 'Three Models for Tackling Political Corruption: An Appraisal of the Japanese Political Reform of 1994' (2001) 69 *The Women's College Journal, Meiji University* 1.

[4] *Seiji Shikin Kisei Ho* (in Japanese).

[5] *Koshoku Senkyo Ho* (in Japanese).

[6] *Seito Josei Ho* (in Japanese).

[7] The following derives from A Ejima, above n 3.

[8] Japan is certainly one of the appropriate examples as explained later.

implement such a model and that, even if it is possible to implement it, there are often loopholes which allow politicians to get around regulations when they feel they really must raise money. Under stricter regulations, financial activities to gather political funds tend to take place behind the scenes where corruption is likely to occur and where it is more difficult to discover. In order to cope with these more secretive activities, still stricter laws and more resources for administration are required. Compounding this problem, these severer regulations make the general public feel that political activities are more dubious and immoral than they actually are. Moreover, there is a danger that the law itself, useless and ineffective, becomes a mockery. Loopholes in, and violations of, regulations encourage politicians to feel that avoidance is not a serious crime and that everybody does it if there is a chance.

The second model is the 'self-regulation' model, which requires transparency and disclosure of political finance. The PFCL, POEL and PPSL require political parties, political organisations and politicians to submit reports to the government. Theoretically under the supervision and criticism of the public who are well-informed by the reports, the parties and politicians have to self-regulate in order to gain public trust and support. This model's merit is that it can avoid direct interference into politics by the state so that fundamental freedoms, such as the freedom of expression, are maintained. Moreover if politicians can regulate themselves, their regulations should reflect reality and administrative costs might thus be saved. However, in reality, most people in Japan are not interested in such reports, neither is it easy to become interested in them.

The third and last model is the 'structural reform' model. It focuses on the structural element of the problem of political finance and political corruption. Under this model, changing the electoral system itself and introducing a public funding system are hoped to be helpful in establishing a more frugal and corruption-free political system. Japan, following this model, adopted both measures in 1994 for the first time.

It is noteworthy that in Japan the original legal controls followed the second model, and then included the first one, ie more direct regulations. Only when this did not work was the third one introduced, in the 1990s. It can be argued that because the original reform was triggered by political corruption scandals, the solutions tended to focus on harsher regulation, which was backed by public opinion until the 1990s. Only when, at the end of 1980s, the ineffectiveness of this approach was proven did the argument for structural reform become more persuasive and plausible. However, now it is necessary to examine whether structural reform is effective in controlling political finance. Therefore, it is time to examine the present system, namely the amalgam of regulations, from the viewpoint of controlling political finance.[9]

[9] Y Yoshida, 'Seiji Shikin no Kisei to sono Rekisiteki Igi' in Seiji Shikin Kenkyukai (ed), *Seiji Shikin to Hoseido* (*Political Finance and Legal System*) (Tokyo, Nihon Hyouronsha, 1998).

Origin: Enactment of the Political Fund Control Law 1948

It should be noted that the original Japanese system had its origins in the United States Federal Corrupt Practices Act of 1925, as it was the outcome of cooperation between the US occupation authorities (GHQ) and the Japanese government during the occupation period after World War II. Because of this, the primary focus of the system was on transparency and disclosure in the first place, rather than on direct restrictions of the income and expenses. The basic principle was that politicians and political parties should regulate themselves under public supervision that is equipped with the necessary information (the self-regulation model). However, incessant emergence of political corruption proved that self-regulation is not enough, nor is it effective in coping with the reality of political finance, as will be explained later.

After World War II, Japan returned to parliamentary democracy under the supervision and with the support of GHQ, for whom the democratisation and liberalisation of Japan had priority over everything else. GHQ's General MacArthur demanded women's suffrage, promotion of the establishment of unions, liberalisation of school education, democratisation of the economic system by banning monopolies, and the protection of the freedom of the individual by abolishing the abusive and arbitrary police system. With GHQ's support in promoting liberalisation and democratisation, numerous political parties were established. However, as many of them were simply groups of several individuals or operated only locally, they often could hardly be described as political parties in the modern sense.

The great confusion of party politics in the post-war situation of social and political upheaval brought about an outstanding result in the first post-war election for the House of Representatives (hereinafter HR)[10] in April 1946. The voting age limit was lowered to 20 and women's suffrage was allowed for the first time. Moreover a multi-seat large-sized constituency system for the HR (*Daisenkyokiu Seigen Renkisei*)[11] was introduced which facilitated the participation of small parties in the election. There were 1364 candidates for 466 seats and 267 parties joined in the election. Three hundred and seventy seven new MPs (81% of total seats) occupied these seats since the GHQ had purged many of the MPs from the pre-war parties.[12] Seventy-nine female candidates ran in the election and 39 (8.4%) won.[13] None of the parties could form a majority: There were 140 seats for

[10] *Shugiin* (the Lower House of the Diet).

[11] Each *Todohuken* (Tokyo, Hokkaido, Kyoto, Osaka and other prefectures) forms a constituency and each voter has two votes. This system was used only once and was replaced by the medium-sized constituency system in 1947. The conservative parties had initially supported the single-seat constituency system. Therefore, the adoption of the medium-sized constituency system is the product of compromise between the conservative parties such as the Liberal Party and GHQ.

[12] R Hrebenar, 'The Changing Postwar Party System' in R Hrebenar (ed), *Japan's New Party System* (Boulder, Westview Press, 2000). Of the incumbent Diet members of the Progressive Party, 260 out of 274 were purged; in addition, 30 of the 43 Liberal Party Diet members, 21 of 23 Cooperative Diet members, and even 10 of the 17 Socialist Diet members were prevented from running for public office.

[13] It was the highest record up to now. Presently there are 36 female MPs (7.5%) in the HR (February 2002). There are 18 female MPs (15%) in the House of Councilors (February 2002).

the Liberal Party (*Jiyu-to*), 94 for the Progressive Party (*Shinpo-to*), 97 for the Japan Socialist Party (JSP, *Shakai-to*), 14 for the Cooperative Party (*Kyodo-to*), 5 for the Japanese Communist Party (JCP, *Kyosan-to*), 38 for other parties and 81 for Independents. Consequently, the mergers and regrouping of political parties were repeated and there was a suspicion that money had been used in order to form a majority in the Diet by unifying several political parties artificially. Therefore, the control of political parties and the prevention of corrupt practices rose to the top of the political agenda. The Home Ministry (*Naimu-sho*) undertook this task with the help of GHQ. In October 1946, GHQ and the Home Ministry held a preparatory meeting to discuss the drafting of legislation for political parties in order to cope with the rapid increase in fringe political parties and to prevent political corruption.

After some futile attempts to draft a Political Party Bill, GHQ suggested that it would be better to concentrate on the issue of preventing political corruption first. In 1948 the PFCL passed through the Diet. Because of the significant role of GHQ in this reform, the Federal Corrupt Practices Act of 1925 was used as a model. Thus, the concept of transparency and disclosure played a vital role in the PFCL. The law itself did not ban particular donations but the public could know who received how much money from whom and thereby judge whether such receipts were appropriate. Political parties and political organisations were required to submit income and expenditures reports. However, these ideas did not work well in practice. Japanese politics remained tainted by corruption, without any serious effort to cope with it,[14] until one of the biggest scandals blew up in 1966. Incessant political corruption and many violations of electoral law persuaded the government to establish the First Electoral System Council (*Dai 1-ji Senkyo Seido Shingikai*). The Council's report suggested that corporate donations should be banned. However, it also suggested that an immediate ban was not appropriate and the timing for the ban had to be considered carefully.

Simultaneously, the courts considered the illegality and constitutionality of corporate donations. In the *Yahata Seitetsu* case, the Tokyo District Court held that donations made by its Director violated corporate law.[15] In the court's view a corporation is an organisation whose purpose is to generate profits, and its non-profit activities—other than social philanthropy—are violations of its bylaws. Moreover donations to political parties and religious organisations could not be considered philanthropic activities. This decision was criticised by those who claimed broader rights for companies[16] but was supported by those who argued for the cleanup of politics.[17] The Third Electoral System Council (*Dai 3-ji Senkyo Seido Shingikai*) also discussed the prohibition of corporate donations, and one of

[14] A few minor efforts, such as the 1950 Amendment and the 1962 Amendment, were made.
[15] The judgment of 5 April 1963, 14–4 *Kaminshu* 657.
[16] See T Omori, *Shinpan Kaishaho Kogi* (Tokyo, Yushindo, 1971) 18 and T Suzuki, *Shoho Kenkyu III* (Toyo, Yuhikaku, 1971) 292. In general, see K Saegusa, '*Seiji Shikin no Shihouteki* Approach', in NZ Gakkai (ed), *Seiji Shikin* (Tokyo, Gakuyo Shobo, 1991).
[17] N Kobayashi, *Nihon niokeru Kenpou no Doutai Bunseki* (Tokyo, Iwanami, 1963) 174.

the Council members even proposed such a ban, to take effect within five years. However, the Japanese Supreme Court, upholding a decision of the Tokyo High Court, overruled the judgement of the Tokyo District Court. The Supreme Court held that political parties were indispensable elements of parliamentary democracy and that therefore it was acceptable for companies to make political donations in their socially-acceptable role of supporting the healthy development of government. It should be pointed out that the Court interestingly included corporate donations as one of the political freedoms protected by the Constitution of Japan.[18] This had the effect of reinforcing the argument that companies have the freedom to carry out political activities, including political donations.

The 1975 Amendment of the Political Fund Control Law: Restriction on Donations

The Black Fog (*Kuroi-kiri*) Scandal in 1966, accompanied by the dissolution of the HR, necessitated a complete reform of the PFCL. The Fifth Electoral System Council (*Dai 5-ji Senkyo Seido Shingikai*) urgently set up a special committee in order to discuss the problem of political finance. In 1967 it submitted a report proposing restraints on donations and a further increase of transparency and disclosure accompanied by severer penalties. Thus, at this stage, the necessity for more direct regulations was clearly recognised because of the realities of money politics. Interestingly, the report indicated that the sources of political funding should be limited to individual donations and party membership fees. However, it also argued that it was not realistic to ban corporate donations as most political parties depended heavily on them and if they were banned, the parties' financial difficulties would lead to political disorder. The report added that corporate donations could be banned after the modernisation and restructuring of political parties. After this, political parties would be able to survive on individual donations and membership fees alone.

The Sato government immediately undertook to draft an amendment based on the report. It was submitted, in vain, to the 55th Diet in June 1967. Several similar attempts by the government failed in 1968, 1969 and 1972.[19] These, however, were followed by the 10th election of the House of Councilors (hereinafter HC).[20] This election reflected the reality of contemporary political finance: its electoral expenses were so high that it was called the Money-Tainted Election (*Kinken Senkyo*). The Miki government was formed in December 1974, after the Tanaka government resigned in the wake of criticism of the election and Tanaka's own money scandals. Prime Minister Miki himself argued for the prohibition of corporate donations but the LDP, then the ruling party, was strongly opposed to it. Finally the government submitted the amended PFCL in 1975, made possible by postponing a review of corporate donations to some future date. After passing the

[18] The view of the Supreme Court has been heavily criticised by constitutional law experts.
[19] Opposition parties also submitted their own Bills to the Diet.
[20] *Sangiin* (the Upper House of the Diet).

HR, the Bill passed the HC with 117 votes for and 117 against, and the supporting vote of the Speaker of the HC.

The principles of self-regulation—of the control through transparency and disclosure—had had to be critically reconsidered, and more direct regulations were introduced. The primary amendment was the introduction of a limit on donations. However, it must be noted that the limit was on the total amount only. Specifically, the total amount of donations that any one company can give annually depends on its capital, which means that the biggest companies in Japan can donate a maximum of ¥100 million (approximately $900,000) to parties and political organisations (fundraising organisations for politicians).[21] In addition to this cap, there were improvements in disclosure and tax deductions for individual donations, and the definitions of political parties and political organisations as recipients of donations were clarified in the PFCL for the first time.

The 1980 Amendment of the Political Fund Control Law

The exposure of the Lockheed Scandal in 1976 instigated further political finance reform. This scandal greatly shocked and angered the public; there were aggressive debates in the Diet and former Prime Minister Tanaka and the former Minister of Transport were both arrested. Tanaka had received bribes from Lockheed for his influence in establishing a contract between Lockheed and Japanese airline companies. Therefore, this reform focused on transparency and disclosure of each individual politician's finances. However, neither the Miki government nor the Hukuda government could enact specific measures for the prevention of political corruption.[22] Then the US Securities and Exchange Commission disclosed another suspicious payment by McDonnell Douglass and Grumman concerning the purchase of airplanes. This convinced the public that factors of corruption were structural and inherent in Japanese politics,[23] and that it was necessary to implement more fundamental measures to improve the situation and to prevent corruption. Succeeding Hukuda, the Ohira government felt that the establishment of political ethics was one of the most important items on the political agenda. Ohira set up a private consultative body for this purpose. It submitted a proposal emphasising that the cleanup of politics had to be achieved by the efforts of politicians themselves. Particularly it put emphasis on the following four points. First, it is necessary to shift from politician-centred politics to party-centred politics that will lead to less expensive elections. Secondly, a distinction had to be made between the income and expenditures of the political activities of politicians and the income and expenditures of politicians as private individuals, and for this purpose more transparency and a reporting system are

[21] US $1 is approximately equal to ¥133 on 1 March 2002.

[22] Only the amendment of penalty for the crime of bribery was submitted to the Diet in 1977 and passed in 1980 after carrying over for several sessions of the Diet.

[23] Those corruptions were described as a structural corruption (*kozo-oshoku*). The thorough research on Tanaka done by journalist Takashi Tachibana had a strong impact. See T Tachibana, *Tanaka Kakuei Kenkyu* (Tokyo, Koudansha, 1976).

necessary. Thirdly, an ethics committee in the Diet and an ethical code of conduct should be established. Fourthly and finally, in order to promote better political ethics, public awareness should be heightened. On receiving the proposal, government and the LDP discussed specific measures and an amendment Bill was submitted to the Diet in April 1980, although it did not succeed. The Suzuki government also made efforts to establish ethical politics and submitted a similar Bill in the same year which finally passed the Diet. The main point of the amendment was that it required an individual politician to submit a report of income and expenditure. For this purpose individual politicians have to specify one of their supporting organisations (*koenkai*) as a specified organisation that can receive political donations on behalf of the politician and submit a report on income and expenditure. Further, the Diet Act was amended in order to add a new chapter on political ethics. Each House set up principles of political ethics and a code of practice according to this chapter and established a review committee for political ethics. However, these amendments proved to be useless in curbing political expenses[24] and in preventing political corruption. There continued to be incessant political corruption scandals, including the Recruit Scandal in 1988.

The Political Reform of 1994 and Beyond

The Recruit Scandal in 1988 and other successive political corruption scandals[25] shocked and enraged the public. These scandals had modern and unique features compared with older scandals, which could be described as individual crimes. Contrastingly, the Recruit company distributed bribes not only to influential and senior LDP members of both Houses, ministers and high public officials related to Recruit's business (traditional recipients of bribes), but also to less influential or much younger LDP members and opposition members, the journalists and even to some academics.[26] The bribe itself was symbolic of the period of the 'Bubble' boom economy. Recruit offered recipients an opportunity to purchase new shares in Recruit that were not yet being sold on the stock market but which were strongly expected to sell at a premium in the economic boom of that period. The fact that many recipients actually gained a huge profit from selling them after purchase without feeling any shame or the slightest hesitation disgusted the public, whose trust in politics and politicians again plummeted. The approval rate of the LDP Takeshita government was only 15 per cent (March 1989)—having fallen from 41 per cent (October 1988)—and the disapproval rating was 68 per cent, increasing from 31 per cent. In 1989 the LDP lost its majority in the HC, after which the Takeshita government resigned. The recovery of public trust was a high priority. It was thought that the previous method, ie adding or reinforcing regulations concerning political finance, couldn't solve the problem fundamentally.

[24] See Figure 6 below.
[25] The most important are the Kyowa Scandal (1991), the Tokyo Sagawa Scandal (1991), the Kanamaru Scandal (1993) and the Construction Firm (*Zenekon*) Scandal (1993).
[26] About 70 people in total allegedly received bribes.

The emphasis was put on the structural aspect of politics. Therefore, not only more restrictions on donations and more transparency, but also electoral reform and public funding were proposed.

Succeeding Takeshita, the Uno government established the Eighth Electoral System Council (*Dai 8-ji Senkyo Seido Shingikai*). The Council pointed out fundamental principles of the reform in its reports; in order to achieve party and policy-centred politics, it suggested not only additional political finance regulations, but also structural reform of the electoral system and the introduction of public funding. After Uno's resignation, triggered by a scandal of his own making, the Kaifu government submitted Political Reform Bills in vain. The Miyazawa government, succeeding Kaifu, only succeeded in adding minor amendments to the PFCL (Emergency Political Reform) in 1992. After the LDP government's successive failure to carry out political reforms, a coalition government of opposition parties was established following the 1993 general election. The LDP lost its majority in the HR for the first time in almost four decades.

This Hosokawa coalition government gave priority to political reform and submitted its own political reform Bills. These Bills—the 1994 Amendment of the PFCL, the 1994 Amendment of the POEL, The Political Parties Subsides Law of 1994 and the Constituency Boundary Council Law of 1994—passed the Diet in 1994 after many twists and turns. The previous PFCL had been heavily criticised as ineffective because of its many loopholes (it was described as a 'strainer' law because it could not stop illegal money from going in and out of politicians' pockets). Therefore, the 1994 Reform had to be capable of effectively dealing with loopholes. The 1994 Amendment increased transparency of income and expenditures and reinforced penalties (tightening the guilt-by-association system); it forbade companies and other bodies (such as trade unions) from making donations directly to members of either House and also to politicians. Donations could not be made other than to political parties, political fund organisations (PFOs)[27] and fundraising organisations (FROs).[28] In both cases the party or the politician must file a report concerning their political organisation to the Home Affairs Minister[29] or the relevant Election Administration Committee. Although total prohibition of corporate donations was strongly advocated during the legislative debate, it did not happen. Rather, it was agreed that donations by companies and trade unions to fundraising organisations would be banned five years after the date when the reform went into force and that donations by companies and trade unions to political fund organisations would be reconsidered at the same time. This agreement was incorporated in the 1994 Amendment (sections 9 and 10 of the Appendix).

[27] A political party can specify only one political organisation as its political fund organisation (*seiji shikin dantai*) whose purpose is to offer financial support to the political party and receive donations for the party from individuals, corporations and other political organisations.

[28] A politician can specify only one political organisation as his or her fundraising organisation (*shikin kanri dantai*) whose purpose is to receive political funding for the politician.

[29] The General Affairs Minister replaced the Home Affairs Minister in 2001. The Ministry of Public Management, Home Affairs, Posts and Telecommunications replaced the Ministry of Home Affairs when the governmental system was overhauled and restructured in 2001.

Just a few months before January 2000—the deadline for this reconsideration—the Prime Minister announced a ban on donations by companies and trade unions to FROs. However, a clause stipulating a future reconsideration of donations by companies and trade unions to PFOs was eliminated without serious reconsideration. This means that the total ban on corporate donations that had been initially aimed at was not accomplished. This is in contrast with the views of many companies, which had hoped that political finance would be provided by public funding and individual donations.[30]

As far as structural reform is concerned, the 1994 Reform took steps to incorporate two epoch-making measures to encourage the transition from politician-centred politics to party and policy-centred politics. First, the previous multi-seat medium-sized constituency system of the HR, which had lasted for almost four decades, was replaced by combination of the single-seat constituency system (first-past-the-post system) and the proportional representative system (1994 Amendment of POEL). Secondly, the PPSL of 1994 adopted a comprehensive public funding system for the first time.

It is important to keep in mind that successive governments appeared to be eager for reform but in reality hesitated to introduce effective measures to prevent political corruption because money is a matter of life and death for political parties and politicians. This has always resulted in a compromise among influential political parties and politicians. Therefore, the real aim of reform was always perverted by the real politics of power. Many similar examples have appeared since then, and the 1994 Reform was no exception.

The Current Regulatory System of Political Finance: An Evaluation of the Political Reform of 1994

Legal Status of Political Parties

Before explaining the current regulatory system, it is helpful to describe the post-war development of political parties in Japan. The Japanese Constitution does not stipulate that political parties should exist. However, it is understood that the Constitution admits their existence as the most powerful medium for stimulating political awareness among the people and for allowing the smooth development of parliamentary democracy.[31] There is no particular independent statute dedicated to political parties in Japan, although there was an attempt to establish one just after the war as has already been explained. However, several laws exist to regulate political parties, such as the PFCL and the PPSL, and the PPSL was accompanied by the Political Party's Legal Person Status Law of 1994 (PPLPSL, *Seitou Houjinkaku Huyo Ho*), which granted legal entity status to political parties so that

[30] *Asahi Shimbun*, 17 November 1999.

[31] Judgment of the Supreme Court, 24 June 1970, 24–6 *Minshu* 625.

they could receive public subsidies. It follows that when political parties wish to accept a subsidy, they have to apply for legal entity status. A Japanese political party, as defined by the PFCL, is a political organisation which (a) has more than five members in the HR or the HC, or (b) has obtained more than two per cent of the total votes of the previous election for the HR or the HC. The PPSL and LPSP-PL adopt the same definition of a political party.

In 1955 the LDP was established, integrating a group of conservative parties after intense power struggles. It became the most powerful political party in Japan, and this one-party-predominant system lasted from then until 1993. This fact should be borne in mind when the reasons for the failure of Japanese political reform are examined. The LDP has received more corporate contributions than any other Japanese political party while at the same time, as the ruling party, it has been under pressure to prohibit such donations. It is too optimistic to believe that the LDP would take effective action against corporate contributions when so doing would cut away its own sources of money. Therefore outside pressure was necessary. However, none of the major post-war opposition parties—the Japan Socialist Party (JSP, *Shakai-to*), the Democratic Socialist Party (DSP, *Minsha-to*), the Komei Party (KP, *Komei-to*) or the Japanese Communist Party (JCP, *Nihon Kyosan-to*)—nor any opposition coalition had succeeded in displacing the LDP.

The LDP's power was broken in the great political upheaval of the early 1990s, triggered by successive political scandals and public distrust and anger. During the ensuing process of political reforms, power struggles within the LDP fractured the party, leading to the birth of several new ones, and the LDP lost its majority in the 1993 general election. A coalition government consisting of the JSP, the KP, the DSP, the United Social Democratic Party (*Shaminren*), the Shinsei Party (*Shinsei-to*), the Japan New Party (*Nihon Shinto*), and the New Party Sakigake (NPS, *Shinto Sakigake*) took power. The LDP's fall into the role of opposition party was recognised as a landmark in the history of Japanese politics, described as the end of the 1955 system.[32] However, the LDP's fall was not permanent, and it returned as the ruling party by forming a coalition government of its own with the JSP and NPS.[33] This movement brought about the further creation, division and integration of political parties, and the Japanese political scene changed completely.

Presently (February 2002), the LDP, New Komei Party (NKP, *Koumei-to*)[34] and the New Conservative Party (NCP, *Hoshu-to*) form a coalition government that has ruled since October 1999. The current opposition parties are the Democratic Party of Japan (DPJ, *Minshu-to*),[35] The Liberal Party (LP, *Jiyu-to*), the Social

[32] 1955 was the year when the LDP was established and since then it had occupied the status of the ruling party.

[33] The JSP had to make many compromises to remain in the coalition government, including recognition of the constitutionality of the Self-Defense Force. The JSP had previously argued for the abolition of the SDF by claiming that it was against Article 9 of the Japanese Constitution. These compromises lessened the JSP's identity and hence its support.

[34] The majority of the KP was incorporated into the New Frontier Party (NFP, *Shinshin-to*) in December 1994. However, in November 1998 the NKP was established after the dissolution of the NFP.

[35] The DPJ became the biggest opposition party by absorbing several newly created parties, which appeared after the dissolution of the NFP.

Democratic Party (SDP, *Shakai Minshu-to*),[36] the JCP and the Association of Independents (AI, *Mushozokunokai*).[37] The fact that none of the opposition parties other than the JCP existed before 1993 eloquently demonstrates how dramatically the political scene has changed since that year.

Present Legal Control of Political Funding and Election Finance and Attendant Problems

The current regulatory system is mostly based on the system established by the 1994 Political Reform, which targets political organisations—including political parties, political fundraising organisations and other political organisations[38]—and politicians. Through an evaluation of the 1994 Reform, this section tries to describe how well the present system is working, what kinds of problems still remain and what kinds of new problems are emerging.

Transparency and Disclosure

The present system requires three kinds of reports, which can provide information to help understand the finances of political parties. First, the PFCL requires all political organisations, including political parties, to submit a report disclosing all income and expenditures to the General Affairs Minister[39] or to the relevant Election Administration Committee.[40] Secondly, the POEL requires an electoral candidate to keep an account book and submit a report of all income, including donations[41] and expenditures, on electoral campaign activities to the relevant Election Administration Committee. Thirdly, the PPSL requires a political party to submit a report detailing how public subsidies are used to the General Affairs Minister.[42]

[36] The JSP numbers dwindled as some members seceded from it in order to join other new parties. It finally changed its name to the SDP.

[37] The allocation of seats in the HR (7 February 2002) were: 242 (10) seats for the LDP, 31 (3) for the NKP, 13 (1) for the NCP, 125 (6) for the DPS, 22 (1) for the LP, 20 (4) for the JCP, 19 (10) for the SDP and 13 (1) for the AI. The allocation of the seats in the HC (22 February 2002) were: 116 (11) for the LDP, 24 (4) for the NKP, 60 (8) for the DPS, 20 (9) for the JCP, 15 (2) for the LP, 7 (4) for the SDP and 4 Independents. The number in the parentheses shows the number of female MPs.

[38] See Figure 1 below.

[39] The General Affairs Minister took over the work of the Home Affairs Minister after the reform of the governmental system in 2001. See n 29, above.

[40] There are various Election Administration Committees according to the type of election: the Central Election Administration Committees for the general election of the HR based on the proportional representative system and the election of the HC based on the proportional representative system; the Election Administration Committees of Prefectures for the election of the HR based on the single-seat constituency system (first-past-the-post system), the election of the HC based on the multi-seat prefectural constituency, the election of the prefectural and metropolitan (Tokyo) assemblies and the election of the head of the local government; the Election Administration Committee of Municipalities for the election of the municipal assemblies and the election of the head of municipalities.

[41] The name, address and employment description of the donor, and the amount and the date of the donation should be reported.

[42] Particularly, when a certain expense from the subsidy exceeds more than ¥50,000 ($455), the name of the recipient, the amount, the date and the purpose of this expense shall be detailed in the report.

The General Affairs Minister or the relevant Election Administration Committee must make a public summary of all the reports in the official daily gazette or the public bulletin. The original report is available for public inspection at the Ministry of Public Management, Home Affairs, Posts and Telecommunications or the relevant Election Administration Committee for three years after its submission. As far as the report required by the PFCL is concerned, 82.8 per cent of Japanese political organisations (4325 of 5221 organisations) submitted annual reports to the relevant authorities in the year 2000. All the major political organisations have submitted reports regularly.

The 1994 Amendment of the PFCL promoted transparency of political finances by requiring recipients of donations to disclose the names of donors and the amount of the donation whenever a donation exceeded ¥50,000 ($454) or a particular donor had contributed more than ¥200,000 ($1818) on fundraising party tickets. This tightened the previous standard, which was ¥1 million ($9091) in the case of donations to political organisations other than political parties and political fundraising organisations and ¥1 million in the case of party tickets, but ¥10,000 ($91) in the case of the donations to political parties and political fund organisations.[43] This made reports more transparent. In the 1995 report, which was the first report after the amendments, each donor's name and the amount donated can be traced for 82.2 per cent of all donations.[44] In the previous year only 3.8 per cent donor's names and contribution amounts were identifiable.[45] Moreover, it can be argued that disclosure of the names discouraged many companies from making donations: In 1995 corporate donations were ¥16.5 billion ($15 million), an immense drop of 39 per cent from the previous year. However, it is too early to judge whether the heightened disclosure requirements truly contributed to the curbing of corporate donations. There are two reasons for caution.

First, it is true that companies hesitated to make political donations immediately after notorious political scandals such as those of the early 1990s, but that effect may not be permanent. For a while companies even stopped gathering donations through the Federation of Economic Organisations (*Keidanren*), where donations were collected by a quota system according to the size of the capital of each company, but now they have resumed. Corporate donations increased again to ¥17.8 billion ($162 million) in 1996.[46] After that they declined slightly (¥16.1 billion in 1997, ¥15.3 billion in 1998, ¥14.6 billion in 1999) until 2000, when corporate donations to political organisations other than political parties and their political fund organisations was finally prohibited by the amendment.[47]

[43] On this point the PFCL was eased to encourage donations to political parties by the 1994 Reform.

[44] This increase of transparency made it possible to obtain meaningful data for the first time, and thus enabled research concerning members of the Lower House by a group of researchers and journalists funded by the Ministry of Education (*Monbusho*). See T Sasaki *et al*, *Daigishi to Kane* (MPs and Money: The Report of National Survey of Political Finance) (Tokyo, Asahi Shimbun-sha, 1999).

[45] *Asahi Shimbun*, 13 September 1996.

[46] The 1996 general election also helped to push up corporate donations.

[47] During January, February and March 2000 companies were still allowed to make donations to fundraising organisations and corporate donations amounted to ¥5.4 billion. It was reported that some MPs urged companies to give larger donations during this period to cover yearly donations.

Secondly, it is possible for companies to make donations through different channels, such as fundraising party tickets and making donations to local branches of political parties (many of which are in reality the offices of politicians). The income from fundraising party tickets was ¥9.1 billion ($83 million) in 1995, an increase of nearly 50 per cent over the year before. Moreover, this income continued to increase year by year thereafter: ¥10.1 billion in 1996, ¥12.2 billion in 1997, ¥12 billion in 1998, ¥13.4 billion in 1999 and ¥13.1 billion in 2000.[48] This occurred because of the differences in disclosure limits between donations (¥50,000) and fundraising party ticket fees (¥200,000). This is a good example of how politicians can effectively find a loophole in the system.

Although disclosure is supposed to be a key factor in regulating political finance and it is described in the regulatory system as such, there are difficult problems concerning the disclosure of party finances from the viewpoint of effective self-regulation. Firstly, to what extent do the reports reflect reality? Who can check the reports effectively and efficiently? In the Japanese system there is no inspection body[49] with the authority to check whether the figures in the reports show the truth or not. Instead, false reports are sometimes discovered by accident. One such case was the Kanemaru Scandal, in which a donation by the Sagawa Company of ¥500 million to Shin Kanemaru, the then Deputy Prime Minister of the LDP, was disclosed through the investigation of another political scandal, the Sagawa Scandal. Under the PFCL, it is illegal for politicians to receive donations of more than ¥1.5 million ($13,636) from the same organisation in any one year, so Kanemaru received a summary penalty of ¥200,000 ($1818). This showed not only that politicians but also the regulatory body of the government did not take the accuracy of the report seriously. It can be argued that there must be many reports which are false but are unknown. Furthermore, the penalty for violation of the PFCL is so trivial that politicians do not mind violating it. Hence, it is very doubtful that all income and expenditures are properly and fully reported.[50] Several prosecutions of MPs for false reporting, just after the Reform, revealed how problematic the real situation was.[51]

Restrictions on Donations

The PFCL comprises various kinds of restrictions on donations (see Figure 1). First, the PFCL prohibits political parties from receiving donations from certain persons or organisations: any company subsidised by or invested in by the government or local government, any company who has had an operating deficit for

[48] The Reports of the Political Fund 1996, 1997, 1998, 1999 and 2000. *Asahi Shimbun*, 8 September 2000.

[49] In the case of reports of electoral income and expenditure, the Election Administration Committee can require the candidate to report or submit related materials to investigate the report.

[50] It is argued that the income and expenditure disclosed by reports (particularly the LDP) are just the tip of the iceberg. It is a well-known saying among LDP candidates that the winner of the general election spent ¥500 million, while the loser spent ¥400 million (*gotou shiraku*).

[51] The most resent case was the indictment of Yamamoto, a former Democratic Party MP. *Asahi Shimbun*, 23 September 2000.

three years, any foreigner or foreign corporation, and any corporation whose major members are foreigners. Moreover, political parties must not accept a pseudonymous or anonymous donation. Secondly, the PFCL caps the total amount of donations both of the donor and of the recipient. Thirdly, the PFCL prohibits companies and other bodies such as trade unions from making donations to MPs and politicians (since 1995) and to fundraising organisations (since 2000).

The PFCL adopts two kinds of upper limits on donations: a total limit and an individual limit (again, see Figure 1). An individual cannot donate annually more than ¥20 m ($181,818) total to political parties and political fund organisations, or more than ¥10 m total to other bodies (fundraising organisations and other political organisations). Moreover, an individual contributor cannot donate more than ¥1.5 m ($13,636) annually to the same

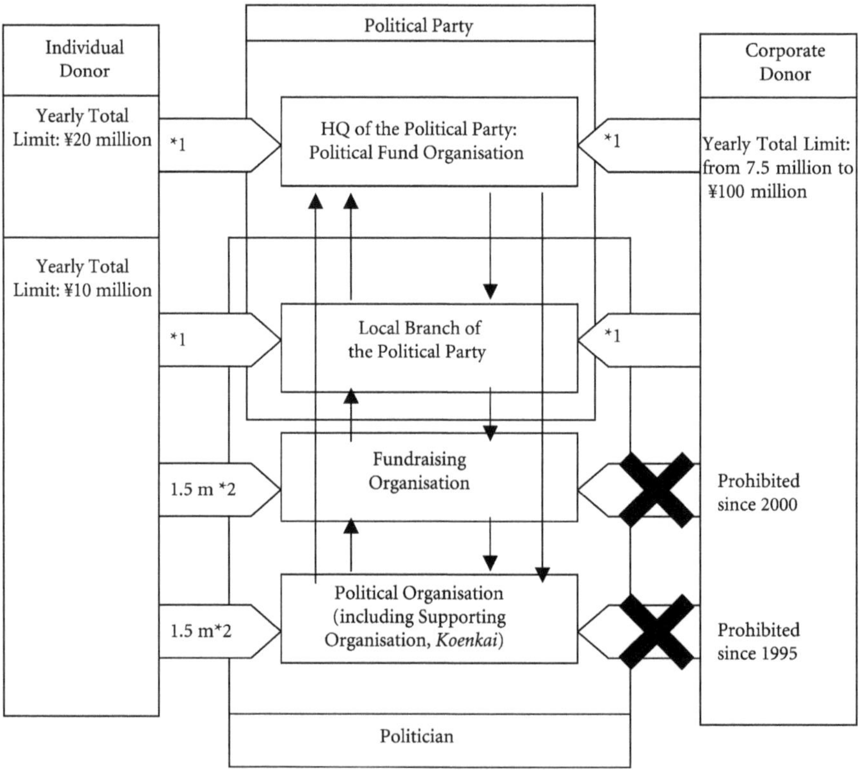

*[1] There is no upper limit of donations to political parties or its local branches unless this exceeds the upper limit for the total donations from the same donor.
*[2] The upper limit of donations to the same organisation is ¥1.5 million ($13,636).

↑: The arrows show the flow of political funds. There are no limits on circulation of money among political parties, political fund organisations and political organisations

FIGURE 1: The Flow of Political Funds under the Political Fund Control Law.

fundraising organisation or political organisation. In the case of donations by a company or trade union, the upper limit depends respectively on the capital of the company or the number of members of the trade union. The upper limits of the total donations to political parties and political fund organisations vary from ¥7.5 million ($68,181) to ¥100 million ($909,909), which is the maximum. The upper limits of total donations to fundraising organisations also vary from ¥3.75 million ($34,091) to ¥50 million ($454,455), which is the maximum. A company or a trade union used to be able to donate less than ¥500,000 a year to the same fundraising organisation, but this was banned by the 2000 Amendment to the PFCL. Furthermore, an organiser of a political fundraising party cannot receive more than ¥1.5 million in ticket fees for fundraising parties from the same person or organisation.

The 1994 Amendment's prohibition of donations from corporations and other bodies such as trade unions to members of both Houses and also to politicians directly, and the 2000 Amendment's prohibition of the same parties from making donations to fundraising organisations should not be underestimated. Because of these, companies can donate only to political parties (headquarters and local branches) through the political fund organisations. The problem of the 1994 system, however, is that it cannot avoid loopholes, such as the abuse of the local branches as receivers of corporate donations and the purchase of fundraising party tickets, which makes the other regulations meaningless.[52] One of the serious loopholes of this reform is that local branches of political parties have been used as another way of funding candidates. It is often the case that a local branch of a political party is in fact a particular MP's office. A politician's fundraising organisation cannot receive more than ¥500,000 from the same company whereas there is no such limit on the donations to a political party. There is significant evidence that political funding of local branches of political parties tripled in 1995 and doubled in 1996.[53] Moreover it was reported that politicians would ask companies which donated more than ¥500,000 to donate this amount to a local branch of the political party rather than to a politician's FRO, after which the local branch would transfer the funds to the FRO instead.[54] In 2000, 122 MP's fundraising organisations received donations from the local branches of their parties. This amounted to about ¥1.8 billion ($16 million) in total. In the previous year only 53 fundraising organisations received ¥630 million ($5.7 million). Therefore, it is obvious that this loophole is becoming ever more utilised.[55] Figure 2 shows that presently companies donate to the local branches of the political party. The average income of these MPs is made up of the income from the local branch of the political party and the income from the FRO of the MP. From Figure 2, LDP MPs are clearly much better off than MPs from other parties because companies mainly donate money to the LDP.

[52] This will be discussed later.
[53] *Asahi Shimbun*, 28 November 1997.
[54] *Asahi Shimbun*, 11 September 1998. This kind of donation is banned under the 2000 Amendment.
[55] *Asahi Shimbun*, 21 December 2001.

Average Income of MPs from Party Local Branches and from FROs in 2000

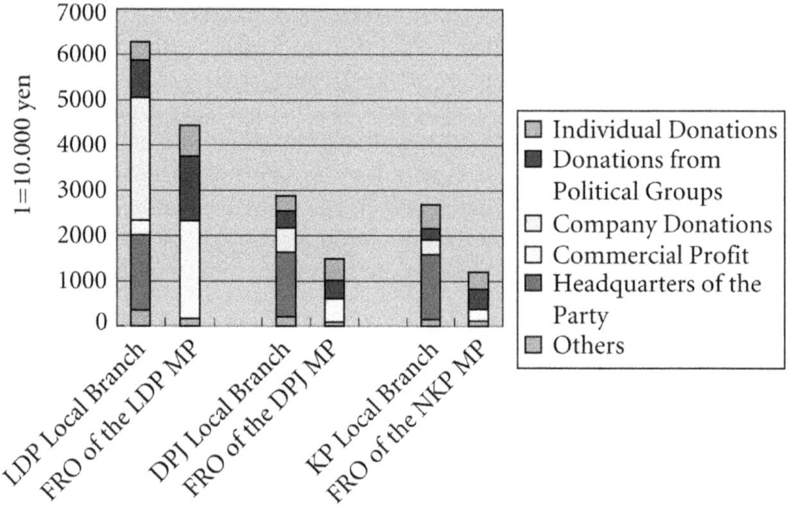

Source: *Asahi Shimbun*, 21 December 2001

FIGURE 2

Apart from the above direct restrictions on donations by the PFCL, the POEL provides several indirect regulations, such as an upper limit on electoral expenditure for each candidate. This limit depends on the numbers of the electorate in the relevant constituency. For example, in the case of a single-seat constituency of the House of Representatives, the upper limit is obtained by multiplying the numbers of the electorate by ¥15 ($0.14) and adding a fixed amount (¥19,010,000 = $172,818). This comes to between ¥23 million ($209,091) and ¥28 million ($254,545). Moreover, the law imposes very severe restrictions on electoral campaigns: a total ban on canvassing, a restriction on the number and size of posters and leaflets, a total ban on electoral campaign broadcasts except free public electoral campaign broadcasts, a restriction on the period of the campaign and a total ban on campaign activities by public officials.[56] On the whole, the regulation of electoral finance in Japan is quite strict. However, politicians often get round the upper limit of electoral expenditure by counting electoral expenses as part of political activity expenses. Moreover, many candidates begin their campaigns before the start of the legal period for the electoral campaign.[57] It is illegal to campaign before this period but it is very difficult to distinguish in practice between electoral campaign activity and political activity.

[56] *Sarufutsu* case, judgement of the Supreme Court, 6 November 1974, *Keishu* 28–9–393. It was held that the prohibition of allocating and advertising of the posters of a candidate of the HR by a lower-level post office official does not violate of Article 21 of the Constitution (freedom of expression).

[57] Eg, 12 days for the election of the House of Representatives.

Public Funding

Although 1994 was the first time that comprehensive direct public funding had been adopted in the political history of Japan, it should be recalled that before the introduction of political party subsidies, other various forms of state aid to political parties (through candidates) had already existed under the guise of 'official elections' (*kouei senkyo*). Many measures relating to electoral campaigns are provided for by the government: free electoral campaign broadcasts on behalf of political parties,[58] free mailing, free posters, free poster advertising, free press advertising, free meeting rooms for campaign speeches, official bulletins concerning campaign pledges, free public transportation, free use of campaign cars etc. These subsidies were based on the idea that severe restrictions on electoral activities and highly government-subsidised elections could diminish the possibilities of political corruption. However, considering the incessant political scandals, most of the above measures do not seem to have curbed political corruption or prevented electoral offences. Therefore, it is doubtful that more general public funding like that adopted in the 1994 Reform can curb political and electoral expenses or prevent political corruption. Therefore re-examination of the existing quasi-state subsidy must occur before adopting more general state subsidy.

The total amount of political party subsidies is about ¥30 billion ($272 million), which is the population of Japan (125 million) multiplied by ¥250 ($2.27). This figure is based on the argument that state subsidy must cover one third of the total expenses of political activities by political parties. From the past political expenses, total expenses have been estimated as ¥90 billion ($818 million). But there are questions about the appropriateness of the amount of the present state subsidy. First, the past political expenses had been reproached as too high and the curtailment of the political expenses was the priority of the reform. Therefore, it is not appropriate to decide the necessary amount of state subsidy by using the past figure. Secondly, why state subsidy has to cover one third of the total political expenses is not clear.[59]

Political parties eligible to receive subsidy are defined as follows: (i) a political party which has more than five members of the HR or the HC, or (ii) a political party which has more than one member in the HR or the HC and has obtained more than two per cent of the valid votes in the election for the HR or the HC.[60] State subsidy is allocated according to numbers of the members of each House (50%) and the number of the votes cast in elections (50%). There is no upper limit, although originally a cap at two thirds of total income had been discussed. While it was assumed that an upper limit might encourage political parties to raise more donations in order to receive more subsidies, this regulation was abolished before being enforced because of strong opposition by all parties.

[58] Broadcasts by individual candidates of HR elections for single-seat constituencies were prohibited by the 1994 Amendment.

[59] During the deliberation in the Diet it was suggested that the price of a cup of coffee would be acceptable for the public.

[60] It has been argued that it is inappropriate to qualify political parties according to past results of elections and that the above qualifications are too severe for minor parties and new parties.

Nevertheless, considering the present situation, it can be argued that by abolishing the upper limit, parties' dependency on subsidy has increased (see Figures 9 and 10). Political parties or their regional branches are obliged to keep accounts, have them audited and submit an annual report with an audit report to the Home Affairs Minister or the relevant Election Administration Committee. The summary of the report is published in the official daily gazette. If a political party does not submit a report, the subsidy grant will be suspended.

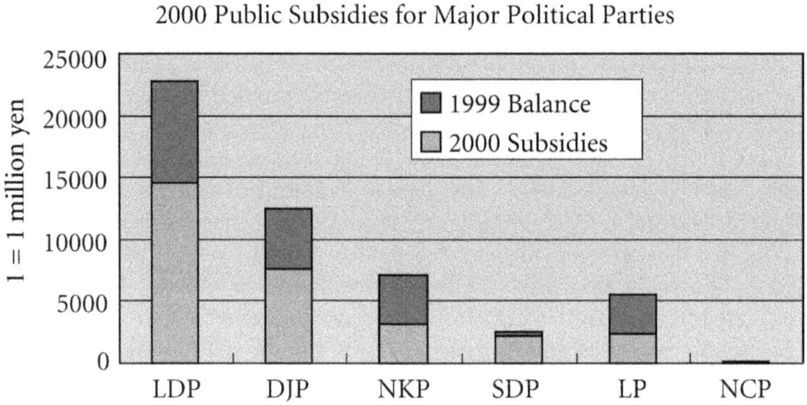

Source: The 2000 Report of Public Subsidies

FIGURE 3

In 2000 the LDP received 46 per cent (¥14.5 billion, or $132 million) of total public subsidies. When the balance carried forward from the year 1999 is added to the 2000 subsidy, the LDP's financial predominance is strikingly clear (see Figure 3). It is not surprising if one takes into account that the present electoral system selects 300 MPs (out of a total of 480 MPs for the HR) by the first-past-the-post system, which is advantageous to a bigger, nationwide party like the LDP. Moreover, Figures 4 and 5 show that many parties retained public subsidies without using them.

The present law does not regulate the usage of public subsidies; how the subsidies are used is totally up to the political parties. The only requirement is that when a particular expenditure of subsidy money exceeds ¥50,000, the name of the recipient, the amount, the date and the purpose of this expense shall be particularised in the report. In practice major items are running costs, political activity costs (mainly printing costs) and the reserve fund for elections (see Figure 4). In 1995 the LDP formed an internal code of practice for subsidies and specified inadmissible items (eg, a ban on food expenses). This is a good example of self-regulation. By contrast other parties did not set up any policy and therefore various items, such as donations to candidates and *koenkai,* food, hairdressing costs, alumni association fees and the purchase of a building for the headquarters of the party, can be allowed. Moreover, it is noteworthy that many parties reserve a certain amount of the subsidy for their electoral fund. For example, the New Frontier Party (NFP, *Shinshin-to*)[61] reserved half of the subsidy for its electoral fund in 1995. Several cases of misuse of subsidies were reported. One of the most striking cases was that of Yojiro Nakajima, a former MP. He misused public subsidy for his private expenses and submitted false reports to disguise his misconduct. He was sentenced to two years and nine months in prison (without a suspended sentence) for this act and other criminal acts including bribery.

Despite the fact that it does not seem appropriate to pay some expenses with public money, legal regulation of such usage could be considered a state infringement on political freedom. It is more desirable to leave the parties to make their own rules under public supervision. Thus disclosure and accessibility of the necessary financial information are crucial. Additionally if the subsidy is paid with

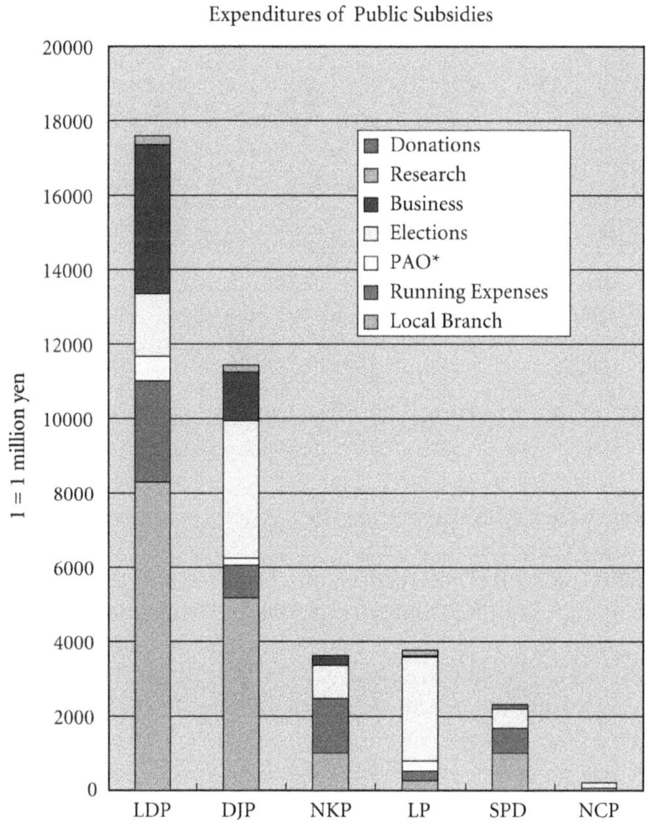

Source: The 2000 Report of Public Subsidies

*PAO: Organisational Political Activities

FIGURE 4

[61] The NFP came out of the integration of the Shinsei Party, the KP, the Japan New Party and the DSP. It was dissolved in December 1997 and split into seven new parties.

public taxes it is proposed that the party should spend more money on making policy, for research activities and for better communication between the party and the electors. Figure 5 shows that few parties spent subsidies on research activities. On the contrary, some opposition parties, such as the DJP and LP used the subsidies for electoral expenses. It should be remembered that this political reform of 1994 was replaced by electoral reform. Public funding to political parties and politicians was the bait for those who had hesitated to accept severer regulations for their financial problems.

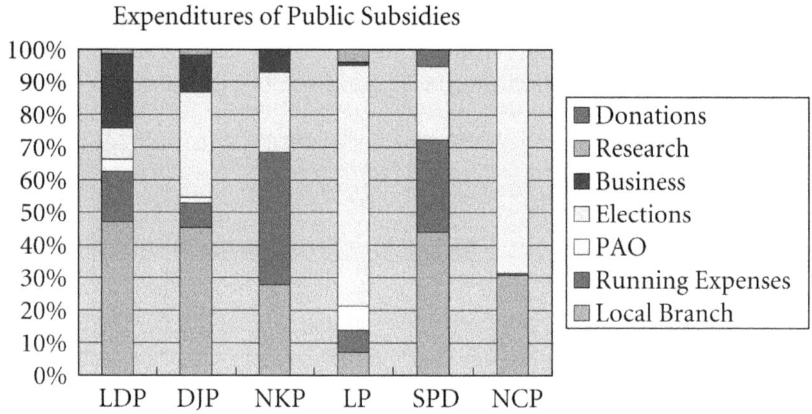

Source: The 2000 Report of Public Subsidies

FIGURE 5

Evaluation of the 1994 System: Present Situation of Political Funding

Now it is time to question whether the 1994 system succeeded in curbing political income and expenditures. According to the 2000 Report of the Political Fund, political parties, political fund organisations, fundraising organisations and other political groups raised ¥156.9 billion ($1.43 billion) in political funds in 2000, an increase of 3.4 per cent from the previous year. Although this number plummeted to ¥148.5 billion (the lowest since 1978) in 1994, it has fluctuated since then. Nineteen ninety–eight marked the highest level of political funding (¥186.5 billion) because of the 1998 general election for the HR. Therefore, it is difficult to say that the 1994 Amendment contributed to the restraint of political funding (see Figure 6).

In 2000 political parties and political fund organisations (including local branches of the political parties) raised ¥110.4 billion ($909 million), an increase of 12.4 per cent from the previous year and making up 70.4 per cent of all political funds. On the other hand, other political organisations raised ¥46.5 billion (29.6%), a decrease of 14.2 per cent from the previous year. The major sources of income were commercial income, public subsidies and donations. The details of

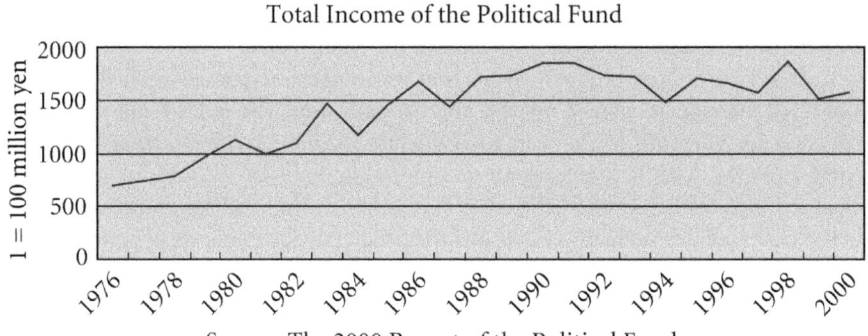

Source: The 2000 Report of the Political Fund

FIGURE 6

income are as follows: commercial income ¥55.3 billion (35%, mainly for issues of the political bulletin), others include ¥37.4 billion (24%, mostly public subsidies), donations ¥35.5 billion (23%), membership fees ¥14.3 billion (9%), loans ¥9.7 billion (6%) and internal grants ¥4.6 billion (3%).

Donations are obviously declining (see Figure 7). The 2000 Amendment prohibited corporate donations to FROs, which caused overall corporate donations to decline. On the other hand individual donations have been slightly increasing. However, the final effect of the 2000 Amendment remains to be seen since organisational donations are increasing and the function of local branches as loopholes is revealed. Therefore, it is difficult to say that the 1994 system is encouraging individuals to take part in politics. Furthermore, the increase of individual donations cannot cover the decrease of corporate donations. It is still too early to say that party-centred politics is achieved.

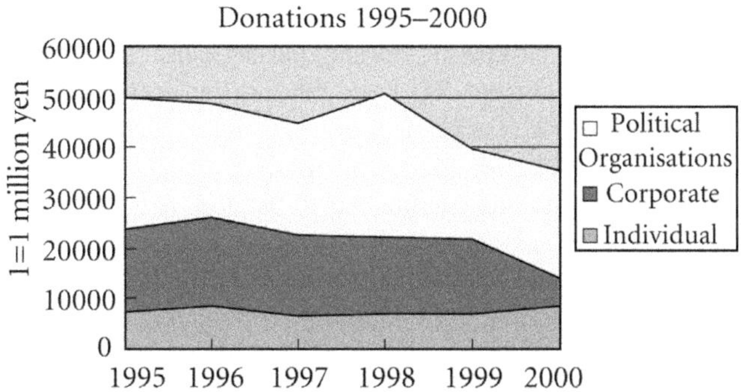

Source: The 1995–2000 Report of the Political Fund

FIGURE 7

Total political party income reported in 2000 is as follows: the JCP ¥32.8 billion ($298 million), the LDP ¥27.1 billion, the NKP ¥15.9 billion, the DPJ ¥11 billion, the SDP ¥4.4 billion, the LP ¥3.8 billion, the Liberal Association ¥2.8 billion, NCP ¥0.7 billion, the Independents ¥0.3 billion, the Sakigake ¥0.3 billion and the Dai-niin Club ¥0.1 billion. Figure 8 shows that well-organised parties such as the JCP and NKP manage to balance income and expenditures. The JCP's main income is the commercial profit (86% of its total income in 2000) made by the issue of the party bulletin. The JCP refuses to accept public subsidy by arguing that it is against the Constitution. On the other hand the income and expenditures of the LDP fluctuated dramatically because of the financial requirements of general elections which make it difficult to keep a balanced budget.

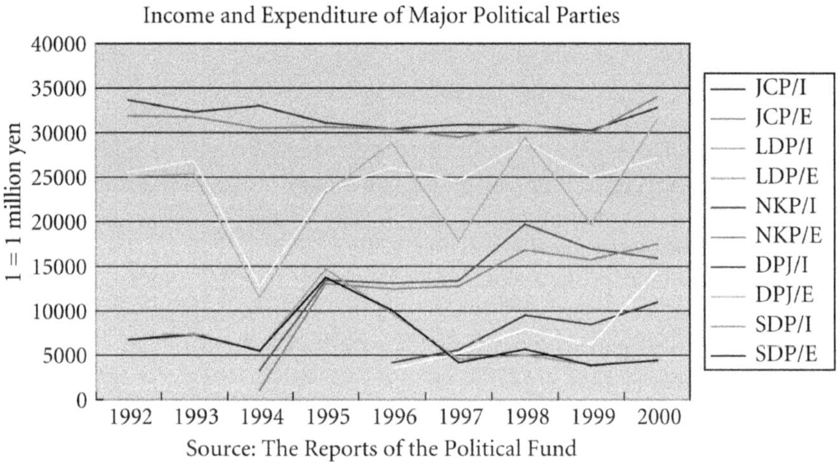

FIGURE 8

It is clear that political parties are now hugely dependent on public subsidies. Figure 10 shows that more than half of the income of the major parties, including the LDP (53%), DPJ (70%) and LP (65%), comes from public subsidy. Furthermore most of the income of the small parties is in the form of public subsidies: Dai-niin (99%), Sakigake (76%) and the Independents (75%). The significance of membership or affiliation fees among major parties is low: JCP ¥1.3 billion (4.5% of its total income), LDP ¥1.8 billion (6.8%), NKP ¥1.1 billion (7%), LP ¥3 million (0.1%), SDP ¥0.4 billion (8.6%). Smaller new parties did not gain membership fee income.

The 2000 Report declared that the expenditures of the parties and other political groups during 2000 totalled ¥174.5 billion, an increase of 24 per cent from the previous year. The political parties spent ¥112.2 billion in total. The itemised expenses of the party are as follows: ¥16 billion (14% of the total expense) for the operating expenses, ¥12.6 billion (11%) for political activity expenses, ¥12 billion (10%) for electoral expenses, ¥36 billion (32%) for publishing (business), ¥27 billion (24%) for donations and ¥6.9 billion (6%) for others. The average expenditures of LDP members is ¥72 million while the DPJ's ¥43 million.[62] It is

[62] *Asahi Shimbun*, 21 December 2001.

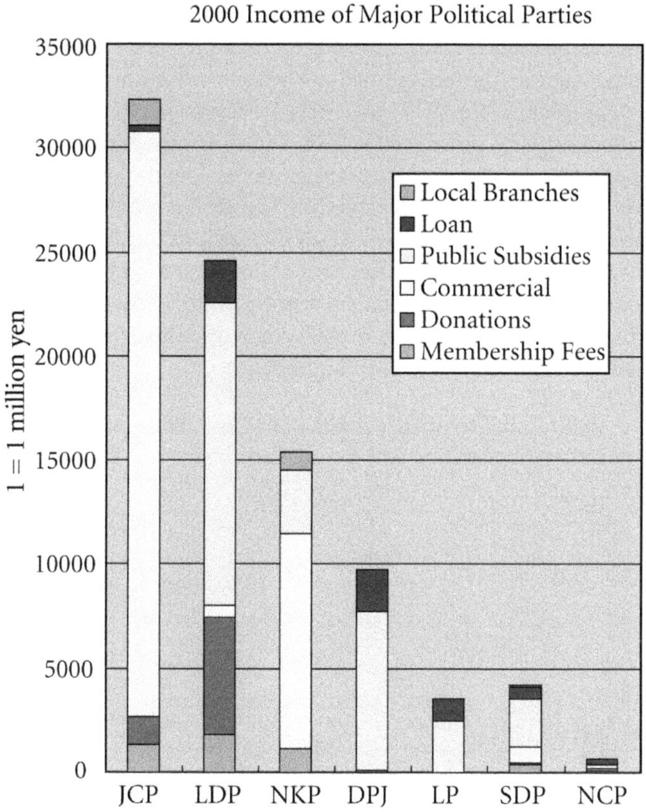

Source: The 2000 Report of the Political Fund

FIGURE 9

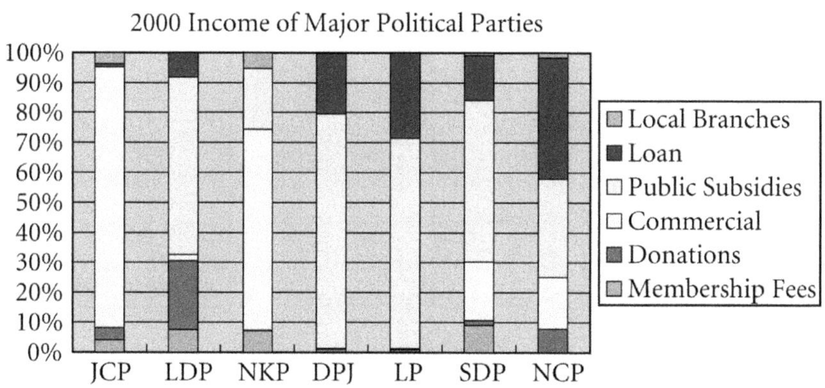

Source: The 2000 Report of the Political Fund

FIGURE 10

interesting that many parties not only receive donation but also give donations (see Figure 11). It can be argued that parties began to play a role to receive donations for politicians and afterwards redistribute to them because corporate donations to politicians was prohibited in 1995 and corporate donations to politician's fundraising organisations also was prohibited in 2000. More organised parties such as the CJP and NKP spent their funds on business expenses (mainly the issue of the party bulletin). On the other hand the newly established parties such as the DPJ, LP, SDP and NCP spent quite a proportion of their funds on elections (see Figure 12).

These results lead to the conclusion that the 1994 system has not succeeded in curbing income and expenditures or preventing political corruption. Conversely, several problems, such as loopholes in the system and the dependency of political parties on public subsidies, have been highlighted.

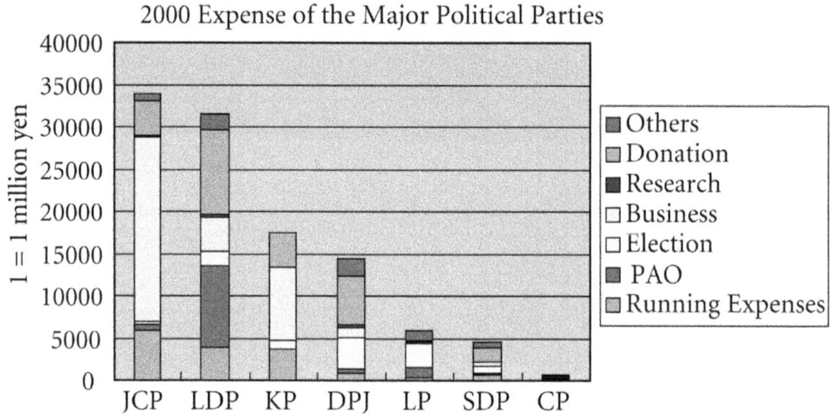

Source: The 2000 Report of the Political Fund

FIGURE 11

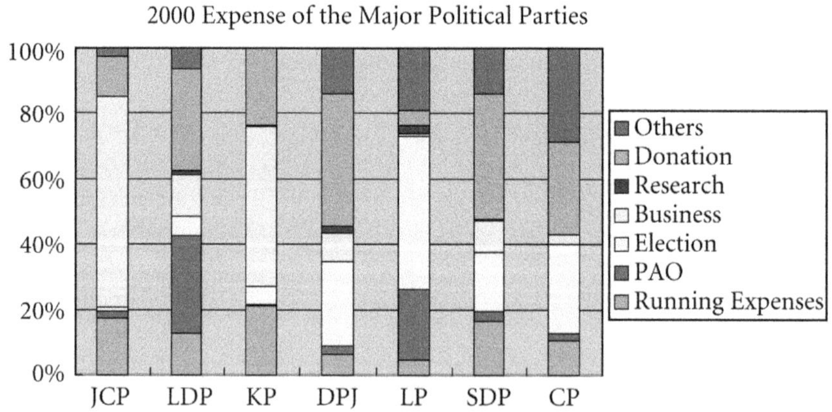

Source: The 2000 Report of the Political Fund

FIGURE 12

Conclusions: Revisiting Transparency and Disclosure

So far as one aspect of the regulation model in the 1994 Reform is concerned, it is difficult to say that the 1994 Reform played a fundamental role in changing the structure of political funding: The current scandal of former Prime Minister Hashimoto clearly revealed that the mindset of LDP politicians has not changed, and that they continue to try to find loopholes in the law instead of reforming the funding system. The acceptance of such a huge amount of money as ¥100 million without declaring it can be interpreted by the general public as an indication that the LDP and/or politicians are working only for organisations with money. It should be noted that the revelation was accidental and that the PFCL system itself does not have any authority to check whether funding reports submitted by political parties are accurate or not.

More clear evidence of this lack of change is the current abuse of the local branches of the political parties. Although corporate donations to FROs were prohibited in 2000, it has been revealed that this prohibition is ineffective because politicians can receive the same donations through the local branch of their political party. In 2000 local branches of the LDP received corporate donations six times as large as the previous year's.[63] It can also be argued that the exchange of political funding among FROs and their supporting organisations can bypass the donations limits. This circulation of money among the three types of organisations is tantamount to money laundering.[64] Politicians skilfully juggle these three purses according to the nature and amount of the donations. To cope with this loophole, a restriction on the number of local branches would be effective. The DPJ limits the number of its local branches voluntarily, currently to about 480. On the other hand, the LDP has established 6931 branches up to now. It is said that the LDP accepted the prohibition on corporate donations to FROs only because it understood that local branches could be used to raise the same money.[65]

Even though closing loopholes by tightening regulations and introducing new regulations is effective, it should be noted that there are already an enormous number of regulations in the Japanese electoral and political systems. Depending on the nature of the violations, the law imposes fines, imprisonment, suspension of the right to vote and stand for election, and the invalidation of a politician's election. It is true also that the 1994 Reform reduced electoral violations by tightening up the guilt-by-association system, increasing fines and adopting the suspension of civil rights in cases of bribery. Nevertheless, several political scandals were reported even after the 1994 Reform.[66] Current suspicions concerning the

[63] *Asahi Shimbun*, 21 December 2001.

[64] Sasaki, n 44 above at 45.

[65] *Asahi Shimbun*, 21 December 2001.

[66] The KSD Scandal (2001) involving leading LDP MPs Koyama and Murakami. Currently LDP MP Suzuki is alleged to have been involved in rigging bids for government-funded projects, including the construction of a 'House of Friendship' on Kunashiri Island, off the northeastern coast of Hokkaido, which is part of Suzuki's constituency.

mediation of MP's private secretaries for example led to a suggestion to amend the Law for Punishment of Public Officials' Mediation,[67] which would prohibit the mediation by the people in public office and MP's public secretaries, so as to include private secretaries. The history of Japanese politics teaches us that stricter regulations either do not work or work only for a limited period. Severer regulations cannot change the mindset and customs of politicians and companies. On the contrary, if politicians need money, they will always find loopholes. Therefore, tightening regulations for political finance and adding restrictions on electoral campaign activities in Japan can only do so much to curb expenditures and thereby prevent political corruption. Moreover, it has a negative effect on the public because stricter regulations lead to more loopholes, and this makes the public feel that political activities are more dubious and disgusting, leading in turn to political apathy.

So far as structural reform is concerned, there is no evidence that electoral and public funding reform have realised the goal of party and policy-centred politics, the fundamental aim of the 1994 Reform. Contrastingly, some minor reforms that seemed to be inconsistent with the above aim of the 1994 Reform were added afterward. First, the reduction of seats for the HR was proposed and seats for the HR selected from the proportional representative system were curtailed from 200 to 180 but the seats selected from the single-seat constituency system (first-past-the-post system) were intact. Taking into account that the proportional representative system is supposed to encourage party-centred politics, this curtailment cannot be considered as favourable to the aim of the 1994 Reform. Secondly, the reform of proportional representative system in the election for the HC enables the electorate to write the name of a candidate in a ballot instead of the name of a political party to which the candidate belongs. This brought about an unusual electoral offence perpetuated by high-ranking public officials in the postal service.[68] They asked the post office heads in official meetings to campaign for Koso, an LDP candidate who used to be a high official in the Ministry of Posts and Telecommunications. Koso was elected by a huge majority but resigned afterward because this offence was disclosed. This incident tells us that the reform encouraged a move toward politician-centred rather than party and policy-centred politics. Furthermore, negotiations have taken place among the ruling parties to return to the previous multi-seat medium-sized constituency election system because the present system is not advantageous to the NKP whose cooperation the LDP wishes to retain. It is doubtful that the ruling parties support the aims of the reform. They utilise it when it is useful (for example, the introduction of political funding) and ignore it when it is not advantageous to them. In fact, newly introduced public funding is not effective in curbing expenses but merely makes political parties dependent on it and they tend to take it for granted and make fewer efforts to appeal to the general public.

[67] It was established in 2000.

[68] Judgment of Osaka District Court, reported in *Asahi Shimbun*, 17 January 2002.

Thus, it is worthwhile to return to the initial principle of the system of control of political finance: transparency and disclosure. These are the keys to encouraging political parties and politicians to self-regulate under public scrutiny. The 1994 Political Reform should not be dismissed from the perspective of transparency and disclosure although these aims have not been fully realised yet. The legacy of the 1994 Reform is the promotion of transparency. Recipients are required to disclose the name of the donor and the amount of donations when these are more than ¥50,000 (the previous threshold was ¥1 million).[69] Thereby a more accurate and detailed statement of political finance has been revealed to the public for the first time. It means that the public can now evaluate the political activities of political parties and politicians more precisely and appropriately through the presentation of concrete figures,[70] not by anecdotal or superficial evidence.

Yet, the more fundamental problem concerning transparency and disclosure is the gap between principle and practice. The present system of disclosure premises that the influence of donations and the propriety of the use of public subsidy are assessed by the electorate who are provided with the appropriate information from the annual reports through the official daily gazette or the press. In reality very few people read and understand the official gazette, which enumerates only names and amounts of donations and expenditures but does not show important details or information helpful for a full understanding. Most people do not know which political fund organisation is related to which political party and which fundraising organisation is related to which politician (the name of the organisation does not often suggest their relation). The press usually reports on the results of the annual report of political funding only when the report is published (ie once a year). People are surprised at the huge amount of money reported and deplore it. Yet it seems to be difficult to maintain their feelings until the next general election. Moreover, very few journalists or experts go to view the original reports at public offices. Furthermore, copying original reports is prohibited, one can only read them and take notes.[71] The website of the General Affairs Ministry now shows the outline of the PFCL report and PPSL report (since 1998) and its more detailed summery (since 2000).[72] It is a significant step, compared with previous practice. However, it is urgently proposed that the content of the reports must be sorted, analysed and published so as to enable ordinary people to easily understand them. The introduction of data processing and online searching is

[69] The current argument for relaxation of this threshold from the LDP shows their reluctance to transparency and disclosure.

[70] Sasaki, n 44 above. This is the first overall survey of political finance in Japan as a result of cooperation between academics and journalists. The improvement of transparency through the 1994 Reform enabled it to take place.

[71] The Osaka Election Administration Committee has just started to allow the copying of reports in August 2000.

[72] <http://www.soumu.go.jp/senkyo/2001/010914.html>, <http://www.soumu.go.jp/senkyo/kanpo/shikin.html, http://www.soumu.go.jp/senkyo/2001/0912.html>, and <http://www.soumu.go.jp/senkyo/kanpo/kohukin.html>.

desirable to attain this end.[73] On this point, the US disclosure system of the Federal Election Commission is extremely suggestive. It provides not only the electronically filed reports but also the actual financial reports scanned on its website, and the public can search the data by words.[74] Moreover, voluntary efforts on the side of the political parties to disclose at least the detailed use of the subsidy should be encouraged since the subsidy is paid through public taxes.[75] It is time to establish an accessible and easy system to analyse a huge bulk of financial information. Otherwise, this information is just numbers on paper. Also, there is a new aggressive tendency on the part of the public. For example, recently 72 policyholders sued the presidents of insurance companies to claim for the return of political donations of ¥170 million which were paid to the LDP by companies.[76] The 1994 Reform is a starting point towards more meaningful and lasting reform.

[73] Therefore, the current decision of the Ministry of Public Management, Home Affairs, Posts and Telecommunications not to upload the details of the reports on its website is retrogressive.

[74] <http://www.fec.gov/disclosure.shtml>.

[75] The New Party Sakigake started to disclose its income and expenditures on its internet homepage five years ago. Now Niin Club has followed this example. See *Asahi Shimbun*, 8 September 2000.

[76] The Osaka District Court (18 July 2001 1120 Hanrei-times 115) and the Osaka High Court (11 April 2002 1120 Hanrei-Times 119) dismissed their claim. They appealed to the Supreme Court which dismissed their claim, saying that there was no constitutional issue, on 27 February 2003 (*Asahi Shimbun* 28 February 2003).

8

Financing Parties at the Grass-Roots Level: The Québec Experience

LOUIS MASSICOTTE

FEDERATIONS HAVE OFTEN been described as political laboratories, because the multiplication of sub-national units and the autonomy they enjoy increase the likelihood that new policies be tested and later be emulated on a wider scale if they prove successful. This is true not only for substantive policies, but also for institutional arrangements. Though in mature federations the basic design of regional governments and parliaments tends to be patterned on the national one, there is plenty of room for experiment.

The regulation of political finance in the Province of Québec, Canada, tends to support that view. Prior to the so called Quiet Revolution of the 1960s, Québec was far less prone to institutional and electoral innovation than, say, the Western provinces of Canada. Indeed, the distinctiveness of Québec in these days found its expression in a tendency to lag behind the rest of the country: Québec was the last province to abolish its unelected upper house and to enfranchise women, while even in the late 1960s its electoral boundary delimitation was one of the most unfair of the whole continent.

Yet, in the field of political finance, Québec's existing arrangements are original, they have inspired other jurisdictions, and they have been claimed to be a model for emerging as well as mature democracies. These are good reasons for providing a critical overview of this topic.

Origins and Contents of the Québec System for Regulating Party Funding and Election Finance

It is not unfair to say that prior to the Quiet Revolution in the 1960s, political finance was unregulated, and the way electoral campaigns were conducted in the Province was a cause of shame for many. Two attempts at cleaning up electoral corruption were made in the 19th century. Both followed scandals that had led to the downfall of a Premier. In 1875, in the wake of the *Scandale des Tanneries*, provision was made for candidates to appoint election agents, and for detailed returns of election expenses to be made and published in the Official Gazette.[1] The latter requirement was abolished in 1892 but re-established in 1895, following the *Railway Scandal*. At the same time, the legislature went further by imposing a ceiling on candidates' election expenses.[2] This was repealed in 1903, while the publication of returns of election expenses was abolished in 1926 and official agents were dispensed with from 1932. From then on, and until 1963, election expenses were entirely unregulated.[3] There was never any legislative attempt to control the way political parties operated and raised funds: Québec's legislation followed the (then) common practice in Commonwealth countries to regulate political activity as if political parties did not exist.

Electoral politics in Québec have been traditionally considered quite corrupt, though anyone familiar with the way political machines operated in American cities prior to the New Deal can hardly be impressed by the extent of the corruption that prevailed in Québec at the same time. However, such practices survived well into the 1950s, under Premier Duplessis, giving the Province an embarrassing reputation. Francophones were then much poorer than the Canadian average and many were inclined to see the electoral process as an opportunity for improving their lot rather than to express their will. Following the 1956 election, the extent of corruption was documented in detail and widely condemned.[4] The defeat of Duplessis' party, the *Union Nationale*, in 1960 opened the way for reform.

The existing political finance regime in Québec is composed of two layers. The election spending side is still regulated by provisions first enacted in 1963 at the initiative of the Liberal Party. The second layer, fundraising (ie political contributions) is covered by provisions adopted in 1977 at the initiative of the other major provincial party, the *Parti Québécois* (PQ). Several amendments, mostly technical in scope, have been brought to these legislations thereafter, the latest in 2001.

Election Expenses

When they reached office in 1960 after 16 years on opposition benches, Québec Liberals were highly motivated to reform electoral legislation and practices. Throughout its long tenure in office, the *Union Nationale* had gathered a huge warchest, and was able to outspend opponents at the 1956 election by as much as eight to one, according to one source.[5] Further, provincial Liberals were

[1] Statutes of Québec (hereafter cited as SQ) 1875, ss 278–88.

[2] SQ 1895, c 9, ss 289–309.

[3] On Québec's earlier legislation, see A Bernard and D Laforte, *La législation électorale au Québec 1792–1967* (Montréal, Cahiers Sainte-Marie, 1969) 166–8.

[4] Standard sources are Pierre Laporte's series of articles, 'Les élections ne se font pas avec des prières' in *Le Devoir*, 1956, and L O'Neill, *Le Chrétien et les élections*, (Montréal, Éditions de l'Homme, 1960).

[5] HM Angell, 'The Evolution and Application of Québec Election Expense Legislation', Committee on Election Expenses Report (Ottawa, Queen's Printer, 1966) 284.

handicapped by the tendency of some of their more wealthy federal cousins to reach local deals of non-aggression with sitting *Union Nationale* Members or Deputies, and badly needed sources of money of their own. As they were committed to the eradication of patronage, they had every interest in creating a level playing field when it came to election spending.

In 1963, the Liberal government headed by Jean Lesage introduced a sweeping reform package dealing with election expenses.[6] From the British *Corrupt Practices Prevention Act* of 1883, they borrowed three basic principles: (1) election expenses would be made through agents only; (2) election expenses would be disclosed; and (3) their amount in constituencies would be limited. No comparable scheme then existed elsewhere in Canada.

However, the 1963 election expenses legislation went beyond the original British model in three ways.

First, while it did not provide for the recognition of political parties as public bodies that could be sued in the courts, the legislation at least acknowledged their existence, provided they fielded at least 10 candidates (there were then 95 electoral districts), and requested the leaders thereof to appoint also an election agent, who would fulfil on behalf of the party the role performed for candidates by their agents. Likewise, party spending had to be reported and was to be limited. The electorate was thus provided, if *post facto*, with a full picture of political spending during election campaigns. This was a marked improvement over the British model, which at that time dealt with candidate expenses, but did overlook party spending.

Second, provision was made for the reimbursement by the government of a portion of the election expenses of the most preferred candidates, though party expenses were initially not eligible for reimbursement. This was the first step towards public funding of parties.

Third, the 1963 law established that *only* agents could spend money for the purpose of supporting or opposing, directly or indirectly, a candidate. The law also provided, if implicitly, that those who did not stand as candidates, be they corporations, labour unions or other interest groups, may not incur election expenses. In other words, the law prohibited US style independent campaign spending.

Following the most recent amendments,[7] election expenses in Québec are defined as the cost of any goods or services used during an election period to promote or oppose, directly or indirectly, the election of a candidate or the candidates of a party; to propagate or oppose the program or policies of a candidate or party; to approve or disapprove courses of action advocated or opposed by a candidate or party; or to approve or disapprove any act done or proposed by a party, a candidate or their supporters. Fourteen items are specifically excluded from the ambit of that definition. They include articles and editorials in the media, public affairs broadcasts, the costs of nomination meetings (not to exceed $4,000), personal

[6] For a detailed description, *Ibid* at 279–320.
[7] *Election Act*, Revised Statutes of Québec (hereafter cited as RSQ), c E-3.3, ss 401 to 457.210.

expenses of candidates, and advertising expenses of private intervenors (not exceeding $300).[8]

Election expenses can be made only by agents appointed by parties and candidates. There is a distinction between party expenses and candidate expenses. Province-wide, parties may spend up to 60 cents per registered elector in those electoral districts where they field candidates. In addition, in the 125 electoral districts, candidates, whether sponsored by a party or not, may spend up to one dollar per registered elector.[9] Since 2001, these amounts have been readjusted for inflation on a yearly basis. At the 2003 general election, with an electorate of 5,490,551, a party with a full slate of candidates could spend a maximum of $3,404,025, while its candidates could spend in the aggregate $5,754,188, which adds up to a total of $9,158,213. At by-elections, parties may not incur expenses, but the ceiling on candidates' expenses is increased by 60 cents per elector. No advertising relating to the election may be made in electronic and printed media on the first seven days of the campaign and on polling day. Both parties and candidates must file with the Chief Electoral Officer a return of all their election expenses.

Candidates are reimbursed 50 per cent of the election expenses they incurred. Not all candidates though, as this advantage is granted only to the winning candidate and to candidates who obtained at least 15 per cent of the vote in their riding. An advance of 35 per cent of the maximum election expenses is to be paid by the Chief Electoral Officer to eligible candidates upon receipt of the election results, with a final adjustment to be made upon receipt of the election expenses return some three months later.

Initially, unlike candidates' expenses, party expenses were not eligible for reimbursement. Since 1992, parties are reimbursed 50 per cent of their election expenses. No threshold was provided then, but since 1998, only parties that obtained one per cent of the vote province-wide are reimbursed.

The threshold for reimbursing candidates became an issue for litigation in recent years. Under the 1963 law, reimbursement was provided to candidates elected or having polled 20 per cent of the vote. However, reimbursement was also guaranteed, well before the result of the election was known, to the winner of the *previous* election (either a general or a subsequent by-election), and to candidates sponsored by parties whose candidates ranked first or second in the riding at the *previous* general election. The inner logic of that provision was followed to its conclusion in 1984, when such candidates were granted in addition, at the beginning of the election campaign, an amount equal to 35 per cent of the spending ceiling, as an advance on the reimbursement of their election expenses.

This was a unique privilege, not found in any other comparable legislation in Canada and indeed, to this author's knowledge, in the world.[10] It meant that while

[8] All dollar figures quoted in this chapter are, of course, in Canadian dollars.

[9] Provision has been made for higher spending in five remote ridings. In four huge ridings in Western and Northern Québec, the amount is $1.25 per elector, and reaches $1.70 in the small district of Iles de la Madeleine, a group of islands on the Eastern Atlantic coast.

[10] This provision was called 'most inequitable' by an authority on the subject: see KZ Paltiel, *Political Party Financing in Canada* (Toronto, McGraw-Hill, 1970) 128.

other candidates had to poll 20 per cent of the vote in order to qualify, incumbent Members and their challengers from the other main party in the district were guaranteed the reimbursement of their expenses right from the start of the campaign, and whether or not they later reached the 20 per cent threshold.[11] Further, the privileged candidates received a substantial cash payment at the beginning of their campaigns, while other candidates, if eligible for reimbursement, had to wait more than three months after polling day.

The scheme was a self-serving provision, obviously designed to provide a safety net for established parties. It did not prevent one of them, the *Union Nationale*, from disappearing within the next 15 years, or the *Parti Québécois*, starting from scratch, from becoming one of the main parties. Nevertheless, this clause was one of the few oligopolistic provisions of the legislation and arguably infringed on the principle of equal opportunity. As such, it was bound to be challenged one day or another. The *Action Démocratique du Québec* (ADQ), a breakaway party created in 1994, came to appreciate how inconvenient the scheme was for an emerging party, and how vulnerable it might be to a court challenge. In *Hébert v Procureur général du Québec* (1998), against the wishes of both main parties, the Superior Court of Québec ruled the provision to be an infringement on both the Canadian and Québec Charters, and invalidated it.[12] In 2001, the provision attacked was formally struck out from the legislation, and at the same time the threshold was lowered from 20 per cent to 15 per cent.[13]

Until 1998, independent spending was prohibited, and election expenses could be made only by parties and candidates. The same rule had been extended to referendums, except that individuals and organisations not affiliated to one of the referendum committees were allowed to spend a maximum of $600. In 1997, the Supreme Court of Canada struck down the latter provision as too restrictive and as an infringement on freedom of expression, and it was assumed that this necessitated greater flexibility in the *Election Act* as well. In response, the legislature provided for an elector or an unincorporated group of individuals to be authorised in each riding as a 'particular intervenor' (*intervenant particulier*). Individuals or groups seeking authorisation must state that they do not intend to favour or disfavour, directly or indirectly, a candidate or a party; that they are not members of any party; and that they are not acting directly or indirectly for a party or candidate. They are prohibited from becoming members of a party during the campaign, and may not incur an expense in agreement, collusion or association with another person. Expenses made by particular intervenors must be made out of

[11] For example, in 1966, one major party candidate polled less than 6 per cent of the vote and was nevertheless reimbursed, because his party had come second at the previous general election, while no less than 54 third-party or independent candidates at the same election were not, though they had obtained a higher proportion of the vote.

[12] *Hébert v Procureur général du Québec*, Cour Supérieure du Québec, 11 December 1998, reported in [1999] RJQ 267.

[13] *Loi modifiant la Loi électorale et d'autres dispositions législatives*, SQ 2001, c 2.

their own funds. They are not deemed to be election expenses except for some purposes, must be disclosed in a post-election report and must not exceed $300.[14]

Political Contributions

The 1963 legislation was acclaimed as a milestone and some of its authors were shortly thereafter invited to Ottawa to recommend the adoption of a similar system for federal elections.[15] But at the same time, contributions to parties and candidates remained undisclosed and unlimited. Despite the veil of secrecy which covered the private funding of parties, it was well known that corporations were contributing princely sums to the warchest of both the Liberal Party and the *Union Nationale.*[16] For that reason, more radical reformers such as René Lévesque (one of the main architects of Québec's so called Quiet Revolution), could still claim that secrecy surrounding the source and amount of political contributions allowed powerful and wealthy interests to influence in a decisive way the decisions made by governments of whatever party. There is every reason to believe that they at least guaranteed access to decision-makers.[17] The victory of Lévesque's *Parti Québécois* in 1976 paved the way for a full-scale reform of political party financing which, despite numerous readjustments, has remained in force ever since.

In a nutshell, the 1977 legislation, rushed into the legislature after the PQ victory, obliged all parties to raise money more or less the same way the PQ had been doing since its creation in 1968. Notably, contributions from 'legal persons' (ie corporations, labour unions and other associations or interest groups) were banned and the right to contribute to parties was reserved to electors qualified under provincial legislation.

Following the most recent amendments to the provincial *Election Act*, political contributions are now subject to the following rules. Sections 87 and 90 enshrine the cornerstone of the 1977 legislation, that contributions may be made only by qualified electors, and must be made by electors themselves out of their own property.

Contributions may be made only to entities registered with ('authorised' in Québec parlance) the Chief Electoral Officer. Four kind of entities may be authorised: political parties, 'party authorities' (ie constituency and regional associations), independent Members of the National Assembly, and independent

[14] *Election Act*, ss 457.2 to 457.22, as enacted by SQ 1998, c 52, s 77.

[15] The Federal Committee on Election Expenses was chaired by Alphonse Barbeau, one of the chief architects of the Québec law. The report of this committee, known as the Barbeau Report (1966) led ultimately to the passage of the *Election Expenses Act* of 1974 (SC 1973–74, c 51).

[16] Secret contributions allow for any kind of unwarranted speculation, but it has been firmly established by the Malouf Royal Commission of Inquiry that two large engineering companies, Régis Trudeau & Associés and Desjardins Sauriol, had contributed no less than $748,000 to the Québec Liberal Party between 1970 and 1976. The two companies received a substantial share of contracts concluded in relation to the building of the Montréal Olympic Stadium in the 1970s. See *Rapport de la Commission d'enquête sur le coût de la 21e Olympiade*, Vol 4, 1980, p 88–109, and Pierre O'Neill, 'Des "rapports étroits" avec la caisse du PLQ' *Le Devoir*, 6 June 1980, 5.

[17] P Fournier, *Le Patronat québécois au pouvoir: 1970–1976* (Montréal, Hurtubise HMH, 1979) 114–17.

candidates. In order to be authorised, a political party must undertake to present official candidates in at least 20 electoral districts at any general election, and its application must be supported by the names, addresses and signatures of at least 25 electors per electoral district in 20 electoral districts, declaring they are members or supporters of the party. If a party later proves unable to field 20 candidates as promised, its authorisation is withdrawn. Party authorities are authorised upon application by the party leader. Would-be independent candidates must wait three years after a general election in order to apply for authorisation in anticipation of the next general election. Their request must be supported by 100 electors. No restrictions apply to independent Members of the National Assembly, except they must request authorisation within 30 days of acquiring that status.

Contributions are defined as sums of money donated to a party, services rendered and goods furnished to it free of charge for political purposes. The maximum amount an individual may contribute to each political party (including its constituency organisations) within a year is $3,000.[18] Volunteer work, anonymous donations, loans, membership dues (up to $50), entrance fees to political activities (up to $60), free time or space in the media, transfers of funds within a party, as well as State funding of any kind, are not considered as contributions, though they must be disclosed.

Donations from civil society were intended to remain the chief source of revenue for parties. However, they are supplemented by State subsidies to political parties. Starting in 1975, a sum of $400,000 was appropriated to be shared yearly among political parties according to the percentage of the popular vote each got at the previous election.[19] Two years later, possibly in order to compensate for the loss of corporate revenue anticipated under the new legislation, the subsidy was increased to 25 cents per registered elector (then about $1 million a year).[20] In 1992, it was further increased to 50 cents per elector (now about $2.7 million a year), not an unreasonable move in view of the cumulative effects of inflation meanwhile. This adds to the reimbursements provided to candidates since 1963, and to parties since 1992.

For each calendar year (every six months until 1981), chief financial officers of authorised entities must file with the Chief Electoral Officer an audited and detailed report including, inter alia, a general statement of revenues and total expenditures, the number and amount of contributions received, together with the name and address of each donor of more than $200. Failure to do so exposes the party leader to legislative disqualification.

Finally, there is a tax incentive for political contributions, that has become more generous over the years. Upon its introduction in 1977, the tax credit was 50

[18] Before 1989, the ceiling was $3,000 for contributions to *all* authorised entities.

[19] The eligible parties were those that had 12 Members in the Assembly (there were then 110 seats) or had secured 20 per cent of the vote at the most recent general election, or had fulfilled either criterion at the general election held prior to the most recent one.

[20] At the same time, every party represented in the Assembly (there were five in 1977, two from 1981) was made eligible to public funding. From 1989, every authorised party, whether represented or not in the Assembly, has received some public funding.

per cent of the first $100 contributed, plus 25 per cent of the next $100, for a maximum of $75. In 1983, this was increased to 50 per cent of the first $280 contributed, up to a maximum of $140. A further increase in 1995 brought the credit to 75 per cent of the first $200, plus 50 per cent of the next $200, up to a maximum of $250.

Like the 1963 legislation on election expenses, the 1977 law on political donations blended original features with provisions derived from other jurisdictions. Registration procedures, reporting of donations, a ceiling on contributions and a tax credit for political donations were inspired by corresponding legislations in the neighbouring Province of Ontario or at the federal level. However, the prohibition of corporate and labour union contributions was rather alien to the Canadian mainstream.[21]

Which raises the question: why did Québec go that way? After all, few societies have gone that far, and the conventional wisdom at that time was that no party could rely solely on individual contributions.[22] Though the US federal legislation also bans corporate donations, contributions by political action committees (PACs) are tolerated, which re-introduces some element of collective action in a system otherwise premised on the supremacy of the individual. How can we explain that Québec opted for that solution?

In my view, the roots of the Québec approach to political finance lie in two sets of interrelated factors. The first one is the very nature of the political party which enacted it. The *Parti Québécois* in its early formative years was quite unique in North America insofar as it blended hard-line nationalism with strong social-democratic inclinations. Both beliefs were anathema to big business, whose contributions were consequently channelled to rival parties, namely the Liberal Party and the *Union Nationale*.

The PQ might have tried to find alternative funding from the powerful and increasingly nationalistic labour unions operating in the province. They did not, for a variety of reasons. Chief among those was the will of its leader not to become the political instrument of trade unions. The fact that some trade union practices, especially long lasting strikes in the public health system, were widely unpopular with many electors, may also have been a contributing factor. Certainly, there was no evidence that formal trade union support could be a vital asset anyway on the electoral scene. The lack of success of the Québec wing of the New Democratic Party in federal elections, despite support from the Québec Federation of Labour, was not very auspicious. Further, within trade unions, some activists considered the PQ too 'bourgeois' to be worthy of support. Being snubbed by big business without enjoying or accepting full support from big labour, the PQ could not do

[21] A Canadian federal statute formally banned corporate contributions in 1908 (SC 1908, c 26). It was never really effective, except to hinder trade union contributions to Labour parties. For that reason, this law was repealed in the 1930s at the initiative of a Labour Member of Parliament.

[22] KZ Paltiel, 'Campaign Finance: Contrasting Practices and Reforms' in D Butler, HR Penniman and A Ranney (eds), *Democracy at the Polls. A Comparative Study of Competitive National Elections* (Washington and London, American Enterprise Institute, 1981) 142–3.

otherwise than relying on contributions from its members and sympathisers, essentially middle-class individuals working mostly in the public sector.

Another option might have been to accept foreign funding. For decades, rumours circulated that a huge amount ($300,000) had been received from the French government by the *Parti Québécois*, and were denied as a flat lie.[23] It is now established that after the 1970 election, a senior official in the Quai d'Orsay who had a strong sympathy for Québec nationalists, had indeed offered the treasurer of the PQ a contribution of $350,000, but that René Lévesque refused the proposal outright when he heard of it, because he foresaw the dangers that foreign funding would create for his party, should it be disclosed later. The offer was deemed to be serious enough to warrant sending a party envoy to Paris in 1971, who transmitted directly to the French official a confidential letter outlining the party's refusal.[24]

The emphasis put by the PQ on individual contributions was thus far from disingenuous. In following that principle, they largely made virtue of a necessity. When they imposed it on other political parties, some of which had hitherto depended on corporate contributions, they were certainly not hampering their own cause.

Another line of explanation lies in the rather unique relationship of Francophone Québeckers in general with economic power. Perhaps one should say: the lack of such relationship, for it is well known that up to the 1980s, Francophones were glaringly absent from economic decision-making centres in a province where they account for about 80 per cent of the population. Countless studies have documented the dominance of the Province's economy by English and American interests, the concentration of Francophones in low-paid jobs and traditional sectors and the predominance of the English language in corporate decision-making centres. In a province where big business spoke English, corporate contributions were perceived as English money, an important channel for ensuring that the privileged position of Québec Anglophones would be protected.[25]

[23] A disgruntled PQ member, Dr Marc Lavallée, claimed, in a book published in 1982, *Adieu la France, Salut l'Amérique* (Montréal, Stanké, 1982) 105–24, that in his capacity as a member of the party's Executive Committee, he had been asked by René Lévesque to explore in Paris with French bureaucrats and politicians the possibility of contributions to the party, that he asked in February 1970 a senior official of the Quai d'Orsay, Jean-Daniel Jurgensen, for a contribution of $300,000, and that no immediate answer was provided. Lavallée never claimed, however, that the money had actually been given, but claimed that Jacques Parizeau had taken charge of that file and had gone to Paris in the midst of the 1970 campaign. Lévesque denied that Lavallée had been asked to do so, and Parizeau denied having travelled to France at that time. Both claimed they had refused any money that 'might' come from France, but made no mention that a firm offer had been made. That rumour, that had surfaced in Ottawa in the early 1970s, was used as a justification by the Royal Canadian Mounted Police to raid secretly the headquarters of the *Parti Québécois* in 1973 in order to find evidence of that contribution. None was found.

[24] P Duchesne, *Jacques Parizeau: Vol 1, Le Croisé* (Montréal, Québec/Amérique, 2001) 596–609. See also N Lester, *Enquêtes sur les services secrets* (Montréal, Éditions de l'Homme, 1998) 326–7, and C Roldan, 'Le Québec et les visées secrètes de De Gaulle', 1998 26(2) *Cité Libre* 36–44.

[25] See the speech by René Lévesque (then an Opposition MLA) in *Débats de l'Assemblée Nationale*, 15 October 1969 (p 3099): '*Dans une collectivité qui est petite et fragile comme le Québec, où tant de leviers nous échappent, en particulier dans le domaine économique, et où les partis qui alternent au gouvernement sont sans doute les principaux centres de décision que nous ayons en main, comme population, c'est encore plus vrai que partout ailleurs*'.

That situation infuriated supporters of independence, but was also resented by a large number of non-separatist Francophones as well.[26]

Such specifics help us to understand why the individuals-only political funding system not only originated in Québec, but remained for long an example of Québec exceptionalism rather than an exportable commodity. They were apparently overlooked by those Progressive Conservative Members of the House of Commons from Québec who, from the mid 1980s, advocated the adoption of the Québec model as a response to the numerous scandals which were then undermining public support for their party. The idea was rejected largely because all three main federal political parties depend heavily either on corporate (Liberal, Progressive Conservative) or labour union (New Democratic Party) contributions and had no interest in cutting such sources. Further, English Canadians never felt historically alienated from the business community to the same degree as Francophone Québeckers did.

Yet, there are indications that the Québec approach may not remain that exceptional after all, as it has been emulated in recent years by a few jurisdictions where public trust for politicians had been previously shattered by scandals: this occurred in France (1995),[27] Belgium (1994)[28] and Manitoba (2000).[29] In 2003, the Parliament of Canada adopted the same kind of approach, though parties will depend much more on government subsidies than on individual contributions.[30]

How Well the Current Regulatory System is Working

Election and Referendum Expenses

Election expenses have been controlled at the provincial level for over 40 years now, while comparable rules have been extended in 1978, *mutatis mutandis*, both to referendums[31] and to municipal elections.[32]

There are indications that the implementation of the spending provisions of the legislation was not very tight before 1977. First, some candidates did not submit a return of their election expenses, and their proportion tended to increase

[26] Premier René Lévesque had only disdain for businesspeople, be they Francophone or Anglophone. See P Godin, *René Lévesque, Vol 2* (Montréal, Québec/Amérique, 1997) 159–68; *Vol 3* (Montréal, Québec/Amérique, 2001) 10, 107, 150, 189, 196, 204–5, 289, 311. A typical quote (*Vol 3*, p 83) runs as follows: 'René Lévesque believes bankers (*les financiers*) are sly enemies. He knows that no small country can rely on them in order to exist. These people worship a single god: money' [my translation].

[27] France, *Loi no 95–65 du 19 janvier 1995 relative au financement de la vie politique* (JO, 21 January 1995 p 1105), Art 4 (now Art L.52–8 of the *Code électoral*).

[28] Belgium, *Loi du 4 juillet 1989 relative à la limitation et au contrôle des dépenses électorales engagées pour les élections des Chambres fédérales ainsi qu'au financement et à la comptabilisation ouverte des partis politiques*, Art 16*bis*, as enacted by Law of 19 May 1994.

[29] *The Election Finances Act*, CCSM 2000, c E–32, sub-s 41 (1).

[30] An Act to amend the Canada Elections Act and the Income Tax Act (political financing) LC 2003, c 19.

[31] *Referendum Act* (*Loi sur la consultation populaire*), RSQ, c C–64.1.

[32] *Loi sur les élections et les référendums dans les municipalités*, RSQ, c E–2.2.

with years, reaching 14 per cent in 1976. Second, no less than 21 candidates (five of whom were elected) filed returns indicating they had spent more than the limit (one by as much as 37.6 per cent) though there is no record that they were sued for that. Third, while returns indicate that all parties and the vast majority of candidates complied with the spending ceilings, research by political scientists cited candid admissions by some election organisers that in practice candidates had spent much more than they were allowed to, a finding that threw doubts on the accuracy of reports.[33] Since then, there have been no allegations of that nature.

Government advertising proved to be the first major hurdle for the spending legislation, and the law failed that test utterly. The problem has remained minor at general elections, though governments have been accused of broadcasting messages with political overtones. However, the stringent limits imposed on the two referendum committees at the 1980 referendum on sovereignty-association were a total failure. Formally, each committee complied with the $2 million ceiling, but the federal government launched a major advertising blitz in the midst of the referendum campaign. This looked like a major breach of the law, as any spending made outside referendum committees was conspicuously banned. The official then in charge of the implementation of the spending provisions of the Act, Québec's Director General of Political Party Financing, thereupon went to the Superior Court of Québec in order to secure a court order prohibiting Ottawa's advertising campaign. The Court answered that the Director General, though a lawyer by training, had addressed the wrong court, as the law explicitly granted to a three member special court known as the Referendum Council the power to rule over referendum law disputes. A few days later, when the request was at last directed to the proper forum, the Council ruled that the Government of Canada (or, for that matter, the Government of Québec) was not bound by the provisions of the Act, due to a section of the *Interpretation Act* providing that no law affected the rights and privileges of the Crown unless the Crown had specifically assented to it.[34]

This ruling left the door of the barn wide open: federal advertising expenses during the 1980 referendum have been variously estimated at $2 million, $5 million, or even $17 million. As each referendum committee could not spend more than $2 million, even the lowest of these figures is equal to the whole spending of the 'No' Committee. There is no evidence that this carried the day, but it remained a standing grievance for 'Yes' supporters.

There was no blitz of the same magnitude at the 1992 referendum on the Charlottetown Accord. However, at the 1995 referendum, another major breach occurred during the last week of the campaign. When opinion polls suggested that

[33] D Latouche *et al* (ed), *Le processus électoral au Québec* (Montréal, Hurtubise HMH, 1975) 47–52; A Bernard, *Québec: Élections 1976* (Montréal, Hurtubise HMH, 1977), 87.

[34] *Directeur général du financement des partis politiques v Médiacom*, Cour Supérieure du Québec, 13 May 1980; *Directeur général du financement des partis politiques v Médiacom*, Conseil du référendum, 16 May 1980; L Massicotte, 'Une réforme inachevée: les règles du jeu électoral' (1984) 25 *Recherches sociographiques* 43; P Patenaude, 'La publicité propagande électorale et référendaire' (1981) 41 *Revue du Barreau* 1045.

the supporters of secession might win, a major demonstration, known as the 'March for Unity', was organised in Montréal a few days before the vote. Demonstrators were bused or flown from other provinces.[35] In a typical case, the Algonquin College Student Association was sued in court by Québec's Chief Electoral Officer. In 1997, the Superior Court of Québec ruled that Québec courts had no jurisdiction to rule over the alleged breach, as it had been committed outside the limits of the province.[36]

A more serious blow came later the same year when the Supreme Court of Canada invalidated key provisions of the *Referendum Act* banning independent spending. The decision originated from a challenge launched in 1992 by Robert Libman, leader of the Equality Party (a party defending the interests of the English-speaking minority in Québec), who alleged that the law infringed on the freedoms of association and expression by forcing all political forces to join one of the two umbrella committees in order to participate in the referendum campaign.

Such a challenge could be anticipated since the enactment in 1982 of the *Canadian Charter of Human Rights and Freedoms*. The US Supreme Court had decided that spending limits were unconstitutional in the *Buckley v Valeo* decision (1976). In 1984, an Alberta lower court had similarly taken the view that the prohibition by the *Canada Elections Act* of independent expenditures (known here as 'third-party spending') was an infringement on freedom of expression that could not be reasonably justified in a free and democratic society.[37] There was every reason for the Québec government to be nervous when the Libman challenge was launched.

The law survived a first test in July 1992. In a substantial decision, the Québec Superior Court agreed that the provisions of the referendum legislation infringed on such freedoms, but concluded that they could nevertheless be allowed to stand as a reasonable limit that could be justified in a free and democratic society. The judge noted that the objective of the legislation was to create conditions for a fair campaign, that such an objective was important and legitimate, that the spending limits were an appropriate means to reach it, and that they were proportionate to that goal insofar as they allowed groups outside umbrella committees to spend up to a maximum of $600. The judge even quoted with approval a statement that Canadian elections were more free than American elections because they were more fair.[38] This ruling was upheld in 1995 by the Québec Court of Appeal, with one of the three judges dissenting.[39]

While refraining from endorsing the rationale behind the *Valeo* decision, the Supreme Court of Canada overruled the two Québec courts.[40] In a unanimous

[35] Chief Electoral Officer, *Référendum du 30 octobre 1995. Bulletins rejetés – Marche pour l'unité. Rapport du Directeur général des élections* (Québec, 1996) 47–60.

[36] *Algonquin College Student Association v Directeur général des élections du Québec*, Cour Supérieure du Québec, 2 April 1997.

[37] *National Citizens' Coalition v Attorney General for Canada*, Alberta Court of Queen's Bench, [1985] 11 DLR (4th) 480.

[38] *Libman v Procureur général du Québec* [1992] RJQ 2141.

[39] *Libman v Procureur général du Québec* [1995] RJQ 2015.

[40] *Libman v Procureur général du Québec* [1997] SCR 569.

decision issued in October 1997, the Court, while lauding the objectives of Québec's *Referendum Act*, invalidated some of its key provisions. The $600 ceiling on independent expenditures was deemed to be unnecessarily restrictive and not proportional to the goal pursued. This had the side effect of jeopardising the actions launched in court against the organisers of the March for Unity by the Chief Electoral Officer, which had to be dropped shortly thereafter. The Québec legislature might have used the so-called 'notwithstanding clause' of the Canadian Constitution in order to protect the law from the Court's decision.[41] However, after careful consideration of the issue, Premier Bouchard decided to comply with the decision and to amend the Act accordingly. 'Private intervenors' were allowed at a referendum to incur advertising expenses not exceeding $1,000. Had he done otherwise, any referendum on secession held in the future would have been governed by a legislation ending with a statement that it applied notwithstanding both the Canadian and Québec Charters of Rights, a feature that international observers and foreign governments might have held against Québec's secessionist government.

Contributions

The most original and creative part of the Québec system is the contribution side. How has this system worked in practice? Since 1978, parties have reported on each year details on contributions and other revenue as well as spending. These reports have been reproduced in a document made public in April of each year by the Chief Electoral Officer. I have reviewed in earlier works the financial life of Québec political parties since 1978, as reflected in these audited reports.[42] For the purposes of this chapter, I will assume that these reports reflect the financial reality of the parties though, as we shall see, there are increasing doubts over that.

On the surface, as Table 1 suggests, Québec's provincial political scene is quite multi-party, as there have been never been less than six, and as many as 21, authorised parties each year since 1978. Yet, these numbers are quite misleading. Taken together, the two larger parties, the secessionist *Parti Québécois* and the federalist Liberal Party, got 95 per cent of the vote in both 1981 and 1985, 90 per cent in 1989, 89 per cent in 1994 and 86 per cent in 1998. In 2003, the rise of the ADQ reduced that figure to 79 per cent. Apart from the ADQ, most other authorised

[41] Under s 33 of the *Constitution Act 1982*, Parliament or a provincial legislature may provide for a law to apply notwithstanding a court ruling declaring that it was unconstitutional. This derogatory clause has been used very sparingly since then.

[42] L Massicotte, 'Party Financing in Québec. An Analysis of the Financial Reports of Parties, 1977–1989', in FL Seidle (ed), *Provincial Party and Election Finance in Canada*, Vol 3 of Research Studies of the Royal Commission on Electoral Reform, (Ottawa, Department of Supply and Services, 1991) 3–38; L Massicotte, 'Popular Financing of Parties in Québec 1978–1989' in AG Gagnon and AB Tanguay (eds), *Democracy with Justice. Essays in Honour of Khayyam Zev Paltiel* (Ottawa, Carleton University Press, 1992); and L Massicotte, 'Political Finance in Québec: Potential Lessons for Emerging Democracies', paper presented at the joint conference ITAM-Université de Montréal, Mexico, April 1993, 28 pages, published as 'Financiamento de partidos politicos en Québec: Lecciones potentiales para democracias emergentes' in BJ Stevenson, P Martin and A Noël (eds), *Interpretaciones de la Québec contemporanea* (Mexico, Porrua, 1996).

TABLE 1: *Number of Authorised Entities on March 31 of Each Year*

Year	Parties	Party organizations		
		Electoral districts	Regions	Province-wide
1978	6	0	0	0
1979	7	255	36	0
1980	9	257	36	0
1981	12	292	13	0
1982	12	291	13	0
1983	15	294	14	1
1984	17	298	14	1
1985	17	309	14	1
1986	12	376	14	2
1987	14	392	14	1
1988	17	394	14	1
1989	17	395	14	1
1990	16	339	13	0
1991	14	313	15	0
1992	12	275	16	0
1993	14	255	16	0
1994	21	260	16	0
1995	16	296	18	0
1996	16	295	18	0
1997	17	301	18	0
1998	18	376	19	0
1999	10	376	19	0
2000	10	376	19	0
2001	11	376	22	0
2002	14	375	24	0
2003	a	n/a	n/a	n/a
2004	a	n/a	n/a	n/a

Source: Annual Reports of the Chief Electoral Officer. Information office of the Chief Electoral Officer.

parties were little more than empty shells that secured few votes, if indeed they fielded any candidates. In recent years, the criteria for a party being authorised have been made more stringent, possibly in order to deter freak parties.[43]

[43] Under s 39 of the 1977 law (SQ 1977, c 11), the following could be authorised: the party of the provincial Premier; the party of the Leader of the Official Opposition; any party which at the previous general election had 10 official candidates; and any party whose leader was elected at a convention, which had constituency associations in at least 10 electoral districts, and undertook to present candidates in at least 10 electoral districts at the next general election. In 1984, the new *Election Act* (SQ 1984, c 51, s 325) dispensed new parties from having a leader elected at a convention and deleted the requirement for 10 constituency associations, but required instead the signatures of 60 electors in each of 10 electoral districts in support of the request for authorisation. Five years later, another brand new *Election Act* (SQ 1989, c 1, s 47) required that a new party undertake to present candidates in at least 10 electoral districts, and required in addition that the application for authorisation be supported by the names, addresses and signatures of 1000 electors declaring that they were members or supporters of the party, while any reference to the residence of these supporters was struck out. Under this liberal requirement, the number of authorised parties peaked at 21 in 1994, including a *Parti Citron* (Lemon Party) and a *Parti Chevreuil du Québec* (Deer Party). A 1998 amendment (SQ 1998, c 52, s 8) raised the number of required candidates to 20, and demanded in addition the name, address and signature of 25 electors in each of 20 electoral districts. The number of authorised parties dropped afterwards to 11. There is no obvious indication that the democratic process in the Province has been much impoverished.

Five parties were represented in the National Assembly when the 1977 legislation was adopted. In addition to the larger two, they were the old *Union Nationale*, and the younger *Ralliement Créditiste* and *Parti National Populaire* (PNP). All three had vanished by 1981. Apart from the short-lived Equality Party in 1989, the most serious challenge to the two-party system emerged in 1993 with the *Action Démocratique du Québec* (ADQ), a group of breakaway French-speaking Liberals disgusted with the party's return to the federalist fold in 1992. The ADQ obtained six per cent of the vote in 1994, 12 per cent in 1998, and 18 per cent in 2003. During the last six months of 2002, the party even led in the opinion polls.

Table 2 provides the revenue and spending of all authorised entities and of the two larger parties since the new fundraising rules came into force. The first thing that strikes an observer after a casual review of figures is the dominance of the two larger parties. From 1978 to 1989, they accounted for about 96–7 per cent of all

TABLE 2: *Revenue and Spending of Authorised Entities*

Year	Liberals		Parti Québécois		All entities	
	Revenue	Spending	Revenue	Spending	Revenue	Spending
1978	$2 195 078	$1 465 370	**$2 266 418**	**$3 728 049**	$4 663 368	$5 565 308
1979	**3 150 692**	2 811 013	2 918 001	**5 550 033**	6 246 201	8 809 645
1980	3 105 955	5 172 982	**4 295 935**	**7 802 151**	7 533 874	13 417 645
1981	1 076 871	6 143 899	**4 927 671**	**10 134 543**	6 372 288	17 024 500
1982	2 631 877	2 919 475	**3 536 731**	**3 171 996**	6 319 840	6 361 837
1983	**3 746 839**	**3 763 625**	2 910 274	2 916 652	6 800 185	6 894 704
1984	**5 863 762**	**4 602 996**	2 902 318	3 003 741	8 857 120	7 765 206
1985	**10 130 019**	**7 197 380**	6 906 030	4 249 929	17 549 608	11 869 439
1986	**8 801 947**	**4 199 635**	2 010 347	1 602 528	10 995 918	6 002 635
1987	**8 364 091**	**5 079 554**	1 805 436	1 995 240	10 414 003	7 321 085
1988	**9 773 675**	**6 989 152**	2 240 690	1 891 009	12 200 239	9 098 030
1989	**6 716 743**	**12 202 222**	5 803 344	6 091 621	13 009 184	18 789 033
1990	**7 238 583**	**6 060 099**	3 620 500	2 435 220	11 111 572	8 712 595
1991	**7 225 506**	**6 775 822**	3 783 462	2 718 918	11 281 876	9 730 579
1992	**6 417 020**	**7 811 913**	6 356 029	5 669 081	13 068 329	13 743 687
1993	**8 033 163**	**5 567 436**	4 878 613	4 353 227	13 226 424	10 213 928
1994	10 352 770	**13 974 481**	**10 718 839**	11 884 508	22 481 432	27 425 842
1995	7 371 082	6 924 286	**9 572 868**	**8 404 941**	17 420 748	15 701 814
1996	3 989 000	3 574 312	**5 655 040**	**5 339 278**	10 076 780	9 333 680
1997	4 394 199	3 843 355	**5 740 611**	**4 798 774**	11 000 587	9 474 297
1998	11 306 168	**14 161 998**	**11 656 088**	12 588 610	24 564 197	28 364 775
1999	5 638 803	4 575 787	**6 069 766**	**5 397 249**	12 293 702	10 543 714
2000	**5 865 015**	4 976 677	5 629 769	**5 352 245**	12 049 053	10 823 922
2001	**7 475 381**	**5 430 248**	5 876 285	5 240 754	14 101 588	11 330 854
2002	**8 462 344**	**7 646 946**	5 797 436	5 481 756	16 793 353	14 802 540
2003	**14 560 624**	**14 696 016**	11 477 646	13 655 801	33 062 990	38 135 091

Bold type figures indicate that a party raised more or spent more than the other main party.

funds raised and spending made by all registered bodies. Their share of cash contributions, of party membership dues and of donors were in the same range. This pattern survived throughout the 1990s, with the two larger parties together accounting for 95.5 per cent of all revenues raised and for 96 per cent of spending made. Donors to both parties were 97.6 per cent of the total. In 2002 and 2003, however, the share of the two larger parties fell to 85 per cent and 79 per cent of all revenues, and to 89 per cent and 74 per cent of all spending.

The reason is, of course, the rise of the ADQ. Until 2001, the respectable showing of the ADQ in the polls had never been matched financially. Its portion of all parties revenues ranged from 1.6 per cent to 5.4 per cent. The party was then heavily dependent on State funding (reimbursement of election expenses and State subsidy), which accounted for fully 60 per cent of all its revenue for the period. However, the ADQ's revenues were 14 per cent of the total in 2002, and 20 per cent in 2003, while its share of spending reached 10.5 per cent and afterwards 24 per cent.

Party revenues have been anything but stable over time, and indeed have varied quite dramatically from year to year. For example, total revenue went from \$8.9 million in 1984 to \$17.5 million in 1985, crashed to \$10.9 million the next year, rebounded to \$13 million in 1989, and to \$22.5 million in 1994, going down to \$10 million in 1996, and rising to \$33 million in 2003. Much of this roller-coaster pattern is due to the occurrence of elections and referendums. The average revenue for all parties was \$19.5 million for election years, \$12.7 million for referendum years, and \$10.9 million for other years. Another factor is the strength of party, as reflected by opinion polls. In particular, the PQ had serious financial difficulties in 1986–88, a period when its electoral prospects were at their lowest.

Table 3 shows the sources of revenue for all authorised entities since 1978. Contributions have remained the chief source for political parties, but their relative share has tended to decline over the years: from 64 per cent in the 1980s, to 60 per cent in the 1990s. Membership dues, admission fees and anonymous donations have remained comparatively marginal. This is in keeping with the spirit of the law. The other main sources have come from the State: the reimbursement of election expenses, and the State subsidy (which accounts for most of the 'other' sources).

However, the number of donors (Table 4) and the average contribution size (Table 5) have varied dramatically since the law came into force. Contributions have remained the main source of party funds, but they have become larger on average and tend to come from a much smaller number of donors than before.

Financial reports of authorised entities do not indicate explicitly the number of donors. Rather, they reveal the number of receipts issued by the entity. Prior to 1989, there was no obligation for parties to consolidate figures, so that a single receipt would be issued by the entity to each single donor. Assuming the number of donors is roughly equivalent to the number of receipts issued, the contrast is striking between the first five (1978–82) and the most recent five (1999–2003) years: the average number of receipts issued for contributions

TABLE 3: *Sources of Revenue, all Authorised Entities*

Year	Contributions	Membership dues	Admission fees	Anonymous donations	Reimburs. electoral expenses	Other	Total
1978	$3 760 957	$557 007	$276 666	$68 738	*	*	$4 663 368
1979	5 070 458	848 958	251 780	75 005	*	*	6 246 201
1980	6 085 200	1 186 350	186 365	75 959	*	*	7 533 874
1981	4 402 038	1 705 864	205 258	59 128	*	*	6 372 288
1982	3 052 390	1 112 174	384 002	20 655	*	$1 750 619	6 319 840
1983	3 529 929	1 054 784	543 349	18 248	*	1 653 875	6 800 185
1984	5 216 555	1 270 306	628 110	19 417	*	1 722 732	8 857 120
1985	10 703 941	1 894 233	553 565	39 958	$2 669 338	1 688 573	17 549 608
1986	7 521 116	896 274	323 234	13 791	773 451	1 468 052	10 995 918
1987	7 522 201	881 084	324 774	5 713	79 870	1 609 361	10 414 003
1988	8 568 505	1 018 697	739 879	7 363	51 808	1 813 987	12 200 239
1989	6 568 782	1 339 130	276 856	23 993	2 631 301	2 169 122	13 009 184
1990	7 000 851	936 860	437 203	10 737	931 501	1 794 420	11 111 572
1991	7 784 398	998 130	791 589	10 505	68 111	1 629 143	11 281 876
1992	9 122 476	1 051 912	412 874	13 109	12 512	2 455 446	13 068 329
1993	8 213 973	1 139 033	113 962	4 070	71 332	3 684 054	13 226 424
1994	11 153 584	1 339 055	172 311	18 888	5 995 545	3 802 049	22 481 432
1995	11 718 723	1 050 328	184 842	8 317	1 207 403	3 251 135	17 420 748
1996	5 962 511	795 305	244 650	2 943	228 951	2 842 420	10 076 780
1997	6 466 640	757 353	412 874	4 858	194 033	3 164 829	11 000 587
1998	13 367 378	1 338 721	175 519	12 512	6 776 188	2 893 879	24 564 197
1999	7 260 828	705 055	168 645	13 102	943 880	3 202 192	12 293 702
2000	7 774 842	710 493	603 447	7 917	99 318	2 853 036	12 049 053
2001	9 923 241	840 844	224 944	18 557	197 408	2 896 594	14 101 588
2002	12 220 540	1 016 334	277 149	10 005	340 380	2 928 945	14 802 540
2003	17 543 427	916 644	257 588	37 052	10 446 257	3 862 022	38 135 091

* Were not included in financial reports in these years.

TABLE 4: *Number of Donors*
(Number of Receipts Issued for Contributions)

Year	Liberals	Parti Québécois	All authorised entities
1978	64 535	**93 941**	163 910
1979	**124 439**	107 569	235 139
1980	103 337	**154 170**	259 072
1981	11 049	**168 910**	185 803
1982	29 815	**77 748**	111 235
1983	**50 009**	49 143	100 181
1984	54 120	44 963	99 680
1985	61 791	**61 895**	128 391
1986	**45 286**	23 620	71 354
1987	**66 524**	22 118	96 864
1988	**53 349**	34 355	89 339
1989	11 821	**66 582**	82 027
1990	31 783	**50 483**	84 751
1991	25 637	**49 348**	77 156
1992	23 016	**91 020**	115 719
1993	28 442	**47 840**	77 373
1994	22 451	**82 739**	108 901
1995	27 057	**86 741**	114 544
1996	20 219	**42 941**	64 513
1997	16 925	**38 337**	56 700
1998	25 133	**62 133**	90 337
1999	19 195	**30 989**	51 909
2000	18 774	**33 289**	54 346
2001	23 644	**31 821**	58 082
2002	26 212	**31 318**	63 786
2003	26 276	**39 685**	75 982

Bold type figures indicate that the number of donors for a party was higher that year than for the other main party.

dwindled from 191,000 to 60,800. Figures for 1996, 1997, 1999, 2000, 2001 and 2002 (non-election years) were the lowest since the came into existence. Figures for 1992, 1994, 1995, 1998 and 2003 (election or referendum years) were also lower than at any election year except 1989. The pattern of fluctuations has been much the same as for revenue: 163,112 on an average referendum year, 112,933 on an average election year, and 91,014 on other years. This trend is worrying, since the tax credit for contributions has been increased twice meanwhile.

Comparing the average size of contributions for the same years, we find that the average contribution size went from \$23–\$27 (1978–82) to \$140–\$231 (1999–2003). When adjusted for inflation, the data indicate a substantial,

TABLE 5: *Average Contribution Size*

Year	Liberals	Parti Québécois	All authorised entities	
			In dollars	In 2001 $
1978	**$27**	$20	$23	61
1979	21	**22**	22	54
1980	**23**	23	23	51
1981	**65**	20	24	47
1982	**33**	25	27	48
1983	**36**	33	35	59
1984	**64**	38	52	84
1985	**104**	64	83	129
1986	**145**	35	105	157
1987	**98**	38	78	111
1988	**136**	36	96	132
1989	**254**	49	80	104
1990	**157**	37	83	104
1991	**207**	48	101	119
1992	**198**	49	79	92
1993	**196**	54	106	122
1994	**216**	67	102	117
1995	**181**	77	102	114
1996	**110**	83	92	102
1997	**146**	100	114	124
1998	**246**	107	148	159
1999	**165**	126	140	148
2000	**198**	117	143	148
2001	**234**	129	171	171
2002	**242**	128	192	190
2003	**319**	148	231	222

Bold type figures indicate that the average contribution for a party was higher that year than for the other main party.

though less dramatic, increase: from an average $52 (1978–82) to an average $176 (1999–2003).[44] Even taking inflation into account, the average donation has substantially increased. The tendency of the Liberal Party to raise larger contributions than the PQ, already obvious in the 1980s, has continued unabated into the 1990s. Average donations to the ADQ have been $330 in 2002 and $376 in 2003, the highest among the three parties.

[44] Dollar figures from the parties' financial reports were converted in 2001 dollars using the inflation calculator found on the website of the Bank of Canada (<*http://www.bankofcanada.ca/en/inflation_calc.htm*>).

There is further evidence that contributing to a political party in Québec still remains a rather elitist activity. Financial reports do not provide any data on donors other than the name and address of those who gave contributions exceeding $200 ($100 until 1992). However, provincial taxation statistics provide interesting data on donors, provided they claimed the tax credit they were entitled to. These figures are to be taken with some caution, as many donors did not claim their tax credit (see Table 6). Nevertheless, a sample of more than three-fifths is normally instructive.

Table 7 reveals that donors tend to come from upper revenue brackets. The proportion of donors and the average size of their contributions both increase substantially as one moves to upper revenue brackets. In 1997, taxpayers with a revenue of $50,000 or more accounted for 10 per cent of all taxpayers, 43 per cent of donors, while 63 per cent of contributions came from that source. The inclination to contribute, as well as the amounts contributed, both increased markedly

TABLE 6: *Basic Data on the Tax Credit for Political Contributions*

Year	Number of tax credit claimants	Number of donors	% donors claiming tax credit	Tax credits
1978	50 401	163 910	31	$1 125 000
1979	77 631	235 139	33	1 508 000
1980	90 358	259 072	35	1 727 000
1981	69 034	185 803	37	1 267 000
1982	50 708	111 235	46	926 000
1983	32 671	100 181	33	1 045 000
1984	43 103	99 680	43	1 454 000
1985	54 449	128 391	42	2 237 000
1986	37 023	71 354	52	1 749 000
1987	29 813	96 864	31	1 525 000
1988	44 543	89 339	50	1 936 000
1989	41 028	82 027	50	1 546 000
1990	47 676	84 751	56	1 807 000
1991	47 378	77 156	61	1 956 000
1992	53 851	115 719	46	2 404 000
1993	38 170	77 373	49	1 893 000
1994	54 457	108 901	50	2 525 000
1995	56 014	114 544	49	4 330 000
1996	36 685	64 513	57	2 506 000
1997	34 541	56 700	61	2 652 000
1998	63 346	90 337	70	5 897 304
1999	22 467	51 909	43	1 826 914
2000	40 136	54 346	74	3 468 000
2001	49 455	58 082	85	5 178 000

SOURCE: Figures provided by Gouvernement du Québec, Ministère du Revenu, Direction générale de la planification, des programmes et du budget, Direction des études statistiques. Ministère du revenu du Québec, *Statistiques fiscales des particuliers.*

TABLE 7: *Contributions to Authorised Entities for Which Tax Credit was Claimed by Revenue Bracket, 1997*

Total revenue of taxpayer	% of all taxpayers	No of taxpayers who made contributions	%	Total amount contributed by those taxpayers	%	Average donation
$0–$20 000	54	5 812	15	$455 898	8	$78
$20–$30 000	16	5 451	14	$533 550	9	$98
$30–$40 000	12	5 625	15	$618 284	11	$110
$40–$50 000	7	4 735	13	$576 438	10	$122
$50–$100 000	9	11 756	30	$1 963 904	34	$167
$100 000 +	1	4 849	13	$1 700 464	29	$351
TOTAL	99	37 728	100	$5 848 538	101	$155

SOURCE: Figures provided by Gouvernement du Québec, Ministère du Revenu, Direction générale de la planification, des programmes et du budget, Direction des études statistiques; Ministère du revenu du Québec, *Statistiques fiscales des particuliers 1997.*

as one moved upwards in the revenue ladder. The group of taxpayers earning $100,000 or more (one per cent of the total), included 13 per cent of donors and was the source of 29 per cent of all contributions in 1997. The pattern has been the same for earlier and following years. These data suggest that while there are many positive sides in the Québec system, calling it 'financement populaire' borders on overselling the commodity.

Taxation statistics for more recent years no longer include the amount contributed by each taxpayers bracket, but still indicate the number of donors in each. They suggest that elitism remains. Table 8 shows that in 2001 as in earlier years, donors were disproportionately found among males, professionals and people in their 40s and 50s. This is hardly surprising: men are more prosperous than women, and they tend to be wealthier in middle age. On the whole, revenue appears to be by far the most significant independent variable. Taxpayers earning $50,000 and more (14 per cent of all taxpayers) included 46 per cent of all donors in 2001.

Increasing Dependence on Public Funding

When the law was passed, political scientist Vincent Lemieux predicted that relying on individuals to finance parties would work in a period of creative politics like the late 1970s, but that in calmer times that source would prove unable to satisfy party needs, and that parties would then increasingly become dependent on public funding.[45] The first decade did not appear to confirm that prediction. In the long run, however, Lemieux appears to have been right.

[45] V Lemieux, 'Réforme à l'image du Parti québécois' *Le Soleil*, 16 July 1977, B2.

TABLE 8: *Profile of donors who claimed a tax credit for a political contribution, 2001 (85 per cent of all donors for that year)*

Variable	Percentage among:	
	All taxpayers	Donors
AGE:		
Less than 35	29	8
35 to 49	32	29
50 to 64	22	37
65 and over	17	26
SEX:		
Male	50	68
Female	50	32
TOTAL REVENUE:		
Less than $25,000	58	21
$25,000–$49,999	28	33
$50,000–$99,999	12	30
$100,000 and more	2	16
MAIN SOURCE OF REVENUE:		
Wage-earners	57	50
Pensioners	18	27
Unemployed	2	0.5
Investors	3	5
House renting	1	4
Capital Gains	0.2	0.5
Business	4	4
Professionals	1	6
Other	14	4

Source: Gouvernement du Québec, Ministère du Revenu, *Statistiques fiscales des particuliers. Année d'imposition 2001*, Québec, Novembre 2003.

The strongest case in favour of the view that parties are in danger of becoming wards of the government is a table prepared in May 2000 by the office of the Chief Electoral Officer. Public funding accounted for 69.7 per cent of all party revenues in 1996, 49.7 per cent in 1997, 43.3 per cent in 1998 and an astounding 77.5 per cent in 1999. However, these figures need qualification. First, they did not square either with those found in the parties financial reports for the same years, as edited by the office of the Chief Electoral Officer, or with those of Québec's Department of Revenue for tax credits. Second, these percentages were arrived at by assuming that tax credits for political contributions should be considered as public funding, but also that *tax credits should therefore be deducted from the contributions given by electors*, which is a more debatable accounting convention. Tax credits are monies designed to encourage electors to contribute, and in my view, it is a questionable operation to equate them with a straight subsidy. If tax credits are not deducted from contributions, public funding accounts for 26.8 per cent in 1996, 24.8 per cent in 1997, 31 per cent in 1998 and 41.7 per cent in 1999. The higher figures for the latter two years, it must be pointed out, are due to the fact that the election held in late 1998 brought substantial reimbursement of election spending to parties and candidates, thus increasing temporarily the relative weight of public subsidies.

Yet, even so adjusted, public funding accounts for a higher proportion of party revenue than it did a few years ago. In 1985, another election year, reimbursements of election expenses and the public subsidy accounted for 19 per cent of the revenues of the Liberal Party, and 27 per cent of the revenues of the PQ. The turning point appears to be 1992, when party election spending was made eligible to a 50 per cent reimbursement, and when the amount of the public subsidy was doubled. Both measures suggest that parties had some trouble attracting individual contributions, and found it necessary to open further the faucet of public funding.

A Potemkin Village?

Much more disturbing is the charge that individuals may contribute to a party with the understanding that they will be reimbursed by the corporation they own or manage, either through extra bonuses or faked expense accounts. As a consequence, what formally looks like an individual donation amounts in reality to a camouflaged corporate donation. Partners in engineering firms or legal studies, or members of the same family, may agree together to contribute up to $3,000 each to a party, thus magnifying the impact of their individual support.

To the extent that such practices become commonplace, the paradoxical result of the legislation is to camouflage group contributions rather than eliminate them. Indeed, in order to find out how much money a company which got a government contract gave to the ruling party, one has to track down the names of all its owners or senior managers in the list of donors and to sum up their individual donations, while under federal legislation, one has simply to look for the name of the company to get the equivalent figure.

Some investigative journalists have tried to do just this. For example, in the middle of the controversy generated by the insistence of the provincial government to relocate a downtown hospital in the outskirts of Montréal in 1992, opponents of the move were able to point out that all contracts relevant to the move had gone to some 30 architect and engineering firms whose partners had together contributed some $178,000 (over a period of three years) to the Liberal Party. The Minister responsible for the move replied that this was simply coincidental, that these firms had been selected on the basis of professional criteria, and that *all* engineers in Québec had contributed to the Liberal Party anyway as, he claimed, they had donated money to the PQ during its years in office. No legal proceedings have followed.[46]

[46] See P O'Neill, 'Le dossier, 'rouge' de l'Hôtel-Dieu', *Le Devoir*, 12 February 1993 A1 and A8; L Lévesque, 'Tous les ingénieurs contribuent à la caisse du Parti libéral' *La Presse*, 13 February 1993, B1.

So far, the most damning piece of evidence is a study conducted by the 1000 member *Association professionnelle des ingénieurs du Gouvernement du Québec* (APIGQ) on the basis of the financial reports of parties for 1998 and 1999. In a letter to the Minister of Electoral Reform in November 2000, the President of the Association outlined some of its findings. There were many instances (400 in 1998, 170 in 1999) of individuals who gave *to both parties*, a common practice for corporations who view political contributions as a business investment.[47] Contributions from these 'bicephalic donors' totalled about $300,000 to each party. There were indications that many of them had tried to hide their 'ambivalent' feelings by modifying the spelling of their name or of their address. The letter pointed out that donors of $3,000 (the maximum allowed) included government contractors in the building industry. There were instances of individuals breaking the law by contributing more than $3,000. The letter noted that 'social activities' were no longer confined to the Liberal Party, and that the PQ relied increasingly on the same technique. Large ($1,000) and very large ($3,000) donations to the PQ had increased substantially (by 92 per cent and 181 per cent respectively) after the party came to office.

In a series of articles, journalist Kathleen Lévesque disclosed the main findings of that study. Further, she interviewed some businesspeople who confirmed that the law was circumvented on a large scale. Former PQ Cabinet Minister Yves Duhaime, now recycled in the private sector, was quite blunt:

> When a senior company executive is donating $3,000, do you believe that money comes from his own salary? He is granted by his boss a $6,000 bonus. Assuming a taxation rate of 50 per cent, this includes $1,500 for federal income tax, $1,500 for provincial income tax and $3,000 for the party. This is what happens. It always worked. Professionals working for companies do the same.[48]

In the same article, other businessmen revealed they were solicited by ministers' assistants and that not contributing meant they would be blacklisted: 'If you are in business and you are not seen at [then Premier] Landry's cocktail, notice thereof will be taken. So, in order to be in the game, I buy tickets'.[49]

Possible Solutions

Up until recently, Québec's fundraising system had been hailed locally as a tremendous achievement and proposed to the whole world both as evidence that

[47] During the Spring of 2002, it was revealed that the Liberal candidates at by-elections had contributed to the *Parti Québécois*. One of them was heading a company working on public roads. See A Duchesne, 'Le candidat libéral Pierre Delangis a donné plus au PQ qu'au PLQ' *La Presse*, 10 June 2002, A5; S Paradis, 'Une candidate libérale qui a déjà contribué à la caisse du PQ' *La Presse*, 22 March 2002.

[48] K Lévesque, 'Financement des partis politiques. Comment contourner la loi' *Le Devoir*, 22 February 2001, A1 and A8. My translation.

[49] *Ibid*. My translation.

Québec was a most democratic society and as a model to follow. In a political context of intergovernmental rivalry, one of the objectives of the legislation was to restore public trust in the Québec government, both within and outside Québec. The excellence of the law was quoted as an argument reinforcing the credibility of referendums on sovereignty: whatever international and Canadian constitutional law might dictate, surely the outcome of a referendum organised under such exemplary rules had to be obeyed.[50] Its originality was interpreted not as an indication that Québec was way out, but as additional evidence that 'Québec's democracy' was different—and better—than Canadian democracy. The legislation was supported even by parties that had been initially lukewarm. Québeckers were proud to point out that compared with neighbouring jurisdictions, their own provincial politics had been scandal-free since 1978.

Whether this enthusiasm was warranted is increasingly questioned. Routine praise for the system in Québec among election officials and media elites has not been matched by systematic and critical study of how the law actually worked. One of the conclusions of this chapter is that even when judged on its own terms, the actual working of the Québec system is far from perfect: the number of individual donors has decreased sharply, the average contribution size has increased, and parties are becoming increasingly dependent on the State, as the various sources of government funding and the tax credit had to be made more generous, especially in the 1990s. Most of the money given to parties comes from the upper-middle class.

For years, scepticism has been mounting as to whether the law was actually complied with, and whether the parties' financial reports reflected reality. Prominent businessmen hinted privately, and sometimes uttered publicly, that the law was routinely evaded and that in practice the system had degenerated into a sham: interested corporate contributions were still channelled to parties, but were so efficiently camouflaged that the net impact of the law was to deceive the public by projecting a reassuring picture. Rather than being a pious religious image, Québec's fundraising laws were likened to a triptych: the outside panels featured the Lady surrounded by angels, but opening the panels revealed a much darker picture of little devils perpetrating their usual business.

The latter view is in the process of becoming prevalent. Québec's former Chief Electoral Officer, Pierre-F Côté, who had been for years a staunch defender of 'René Lévesque's legacy', astounded his audience—and many others—in late 1999 by calling the system a failure and by suggesting that corporations be allowed to contribute to parties.[51] Coming from a former official who had previously

[50] See for example the presentation of former Liberal leader Claude Ryan to the Legislative Committee of the Canadian House of Commons on Bill C–20, *An Act to give effect to the requirement for clarity as set out in the opinion of the Supreme Court of Canada in the Québec Secession Reference*, 21 February 2000, <http://www.parl.gc.ca/InfoComDoc/36/2/CLAR/Meetings/Evidence/clarev05e.htm#1645>.

[51] PF Côté, 'Financement des partis politiques: adapter les règles pour améliorer l'éthique' in AG Bernier and F Pouliot (eds), *Éthique et conflits d'intérêts* (Montréal, Liber, 2000) 59–63; D Lessard, 'Pierre-F Côté propose de permettre aux compagnies de financer les partis politiques' *La Presse*, 27 November 1999, B11.

brushed aside criticisms of the law as if they amounted to an attack on Québec's identity, this turnaround spoke volumes. At the same time, the federal wing of the PQ, the Bloc Québécois, faced with a sharp drop both in the number of donors and of the amounts contributed, abandoned its previous policy of refusing corporate contributions though the latter were allowed under federal legislation.[52] Both mainstream parties hesitate to launch a debate on the issue, as each is likely to see its own public image, not to speak of Québec's reputation in Canada and abroad, being shattered. Yet, as the APIGC study suggests, what was hitherto dismissed as cynical attacks coming from opponents of popular financing might later be confirmed.

The first six months of 2002 were marred by serious allegations of corruption at all three levels of government. The director general of the *Parti Québécois* had to resign his position after revelations that he had received princely sums to act as a lobbyist. Too cosy relations with another lobbyist led to the resignation of Minister Gilles Baril. A tough bill regulating lobbying was passed by the Assembly shortly after. Opinion polls published at that time cast doubt on the assumption that Québec provincial politics is cleaner, or at least is perceived to be so.[53]

What can we do? One option is to stick to the existing legislation, but to enforce it in a much more stringent way. After all, lawbreaking in itself is no convincing argument for making legal what the law prohibits. Instances of drunken driving, tax evasion, plagiarising, are regrettable indeed, but few would conclude that they warrant the repeal of the *Criminal Code*, of the *Income Tax Act* or of copyright legislation. A more appropriate conclusion in each case may be that the law should be more strictly enforced.[54] This would require both the powers of inquiry and the legal staff of the Chief Electoral Officer to be increased. Tracking hidden corporate contributions would be made easier by obliging major donors to disclose the name of the company they work for. Yet, this begs the question: what will be left if camouflaged corporate contributions are taken out of the picture? Will parties find enough money to carry out their activities?

Another option is lifting the ban on contributions from legal persons, while disclosing them, as advocated by Yves Duhaime.[55] This would align Québec legislation on those in force in Ottawa until 2003 and in most other provinces. Contributions could be limited in size, though it would be easy to circumvent such ceilings by creating dummy companies. The rights of individual shareholders and trade union members might be protected by demanding, as Britain does,

[52] L Plamondon, MP, 'Financement des partis politiques: le Bloc québécois tente de s'adapter à la réalité fédérale' *Le Devoir*, 18 January 2000, A6; JD Bellavance and A McIntosh, 'Bloc diverted money to pollster' *The National Post*, 21 January 2001, A1 and A10. For a criticism of the Bloc's decision, see D Monière, 'Le Bloc ne doit pas ressembler aux vieux partis pour son financement' *Le Devoir*, 18 January 2000, B3.

[53] Léger Marketing, 'Les Canadiens et la corruption des gouvernements. Rapport', a poll conducted in early April 2002; JD Bellavance, 'Le favoritisme à Ottawa et à Québec: c'est du pareil au même, selon CROP' *La Presse*, 12 April 2002, A1–4.

[54] At present, offenders are liable to fines ranging from $100 to $10,000.

[55] K Lévesque, 'Le soutien financier aux personnes morales devrait être permis' *Le Devoir*, 25 February 2001, A2.

that political contributions be approved by majority vote instead of being decided privately by the leadership. The Liberals might welcome that solution, as they have every reason to expect generous funding from the business community, but nothing excludes that the PQ, by now an established party with some record of business friendly moves, would not receive its share (as does Blair's New Labour Party), in addition to labour union funding. How would public opinion react? One should not assume too quickly that the public at large would be outraged: the unanimous praise in Québec media for the banning of corporate contributions conceals the fact that a substantial proportion of Québeckers, according to a poll conducted in 1990 for the Royal Commission on Electoral Reform, supported such contributions.

There is a third option, put forward by a former Chief Electoral Officer, whereby corporations would be allowed to contribute, subject to disclosure of large donations and to a ceiling, but contributions would be transferred to a trust account maintained by the Chief Electoral Officer and distributed among parties on the basis of the popular vote for each.[56] This implies that corporations could not direct money to a specific party, and would have no control over which party would get the money. This suggestion seems exceedingly naive, insofar as there is doubt that corporations would be interested in contributing under such terms.

Another option is that contributions from civil society, be they coming from corporations, labour unions or even individuals, be banned altogether, and that parties rely henceforth exclusively on public funding. One could imagine then the State subsidy to be increased markedly and to be apportioned among parties according to their electoral performance. There are obvious drawbacks: parties would be exposed to degenerating into empty shells relying on government funding rather than on militant activity; they would become wed to an interventionist government and might be perceived by the general public as being in a standing conflict of interests, as it is the prerogative of the legislature to determine the total amount to be apportioned; they would be protected, at least until the next general election, against the reaction of angry militants dissatisfied with the policies of their own government; the emergence of new political forces would be made more difficult because public funding is mostly based on past electoral performance.

As of the Summer 2004, party finance had disappeared from the public agenda in Québec, not the least because the adoption by the federal Parliament in 2003 of a new legislation largely inspired by the Québec approach, led many to conclude that the latter was after all the best possible system, or the least of all evils. The record suggests, however, that new loopholes might be eventually exposed publicly in the future, leading to some hard questions being asked.

[56] Côté, above n 51 at 62.

Part IV
Regulation and Judicial Review

9

Throwing in the Towel: The Constitutional Morass of Campaign Finance

SAMUEL ISSACHAROFF

'MONEY, LIKE WATER, will always find an outlet.'[1] So informs the lead opinion of Justices Stevens and O'Connor in the Supreme Court's latest pronouncement on campaign finance regulation. And so it undoubtedly will. In light of the developments of the twenty-five years following *Buckley v Valeo*,[2] described by Professors Briffault and Persily in the chapters that follow, the Court's confidence that it can predict how the latest regulatory endeavor will play out is dramatically shaken. The 1974 rendition of the *Federal Election Campaign Act*, truncated by the *Buckley* divide between contributions and expenditure regulation, yielded an innovative array of 'outlets,' first in the form of the trickles of PACs and finally in the torrents of soft money.

But the distinctive feature of American campaign finance over the past 20 years has been that the organising regulatory force has come from an increasingly complicated if not contradictory set of opinions from the Supreme Court. The flow of campaign funds, particularly through innovative channels of evasion of regulatory limits, has been shaped by the odd juxtaposition of limited private funding at the contribution level and unbounded largesse at the expenditure level. In light of the most recent combination of the *Bipartisan Campaign Reform Act* and a surprisingly pliant Supreme Court, the regulatory environment has shifted again, this time to some remove from the overarching strictures of the Constitution.

The early evidence is that Bipartisan Campaign Reform Act (BCRA) will follow its regulatory predecessors in prompting new forms by which money seeks to influence, cajole, inform, capture, and even corrupt—*Buckley's* enduring if ill-defined contribution to the constitutional arsenal of regulation. Only those weak in history and firm in self-assured prognostication would venture how the new regulatory environment will direct the flow of campaign funds. Perhaps money will move to the newest entrants, the so called '527 organisations' who walk a

[1] *McConnell v FEC* 124 S Ct 619, 706 (2003).
[2] 424 US 1 (1976).

finely drawn line between seeking to influence elections and express advocacy.[3] Perhaps the most significant feature will prove to be the relatively unreviewed expansion of hard money which, combined with innovative fundraising techniques, has already propelled the main presidential contenders to opt out of the federal financing system altogether. Perhaps as well, the bundlers of hard money will emerge as the first new institutional force, akin to PACs after *Buckley*.

Or perhaps, this is much ado over nothing. A regime that liberalises the flow of hard money directly to candidates and parties may remove some of the politics of circumvention. The limitation on expression during critical periods of the campaign cycle—the times when public discourse turns to the issues of the day—has troubling political and constitutional overtones, but is restricted to the pariahs of political expression: corporations and labor unions.[4] There is an odd quality to the gingerly protection of expressive activity for the myriad interest groups of the American political spectrum, but for the exclusion from the public arena of labor and capital. How far we have come from the 19th and 20th century political theories that were the contending forces that drove the engine of history.

It is possible to engage the Court's latest handiwork on many different levels. For example, there is the curious clustering of unions and corporations as nothing more than compelled accumulations of wealth whose hapless constituents, absent campaign finance regulation, are forced to endure whatever political endorsements their organisations fancy. Unmentioned is the vast regulation of union internal life under the *Beck/Abood* line of cases that require segregation of all political funds and allow for objecting union members to demand the rebate of any union dues spent on political activity.[5] Or perhaps it is the malleability of the concept of the 'appearance of corruption,' a concern that threatened to swallow the First Amendment in *Austin*[6] and now returns with a vengeance in *McConnell.*[7] Or perhaps it is the Court's disturbing and sudden humility in allowing congressional expertise to reign supreme in the matter of—what else—how best to elect a Congress. Given my prior writings on the need to be vigilant when incumbent power threatens to undermine the competitive accountability of politics, there is more than a touch of recognition when Justice Scalia warns of the risks of incumbent self-protection in closing off potential sources of electoral criticism.[8] But for now I wish to leave all of these important issues to the side. I have always been more taken by the issue of the paradoxical effects of campaign finance regulation[9] and for such an assessment, as Chou en Lai is once reported to have quipped about the French Revolution, 'it is too early to tell.'[10]

[3] *Ibid* at 678, n 67.

[4] *Ibid* at 687.

[5] See *Communications Workers of America v Beck* 487 US 735 (1988); *Abood v Detroit Beard of Education* 431 US 209, 236 (1977).

[6] *Austin v Michigan Chamber of Commerce*, 494 US 652 (1990).

[7] *McConnell v FEC* 124 S Ct 619, 661 (2003).

[8] *Ibid* at 721 (Scalia, J, concurring in part and dissenting in part).

[9] See S Issacharoff and P Karlan, 'The Hydraulics of Campaign Finance Reform' (1999) 77 *Texas Law Review* 1705.

[10] Quoted in G Roeder, Jr, 'People's Century: History Made Visible' (1997), available at <http://businessweek.com/bwdaily/dnflash/apr2004/nf2004045_3567_db056.htm>, last accessed 12 May 2005.

Despite my discomfort with incipient restrictions on speech during the critical facets of the election cycle, and despite my sympathy for Justice Scalia's worries over self-serving regulation over the powers that be, I find much to commend the Court's basic holding. I say this with substantial hesitation because I agree with Justice Kennedy that a constitutional foundation based on vague notions of appearance of corruption is 'unbounded and susceptible to no limiting principle,'[11] and may easily threaten bedrock conceptions of political competition that ensure that '[d]emocracy is premised on responsiveness.'[12] But, nonetheless, I share the sense that the Court has proven not particularly successful at managing its increasingly regulatory role in campaign finance law. So it is difficult not to welcome the Court's humbling acknowledgment that, '[w]e are under no illusion that BCRA will be the last word on the matter. Money, like water, will always find an outlet. What problems will arise, and how Congress will respond, are concerns for another day.'[13] Not only are congressional findings entitled to deference, announces the Court, but so are its 'predictive judgments.'[14]

While the new regulatory regime unfolds in practice, it is possible to examine *McConnell v FEC* not so much for how it will play out in the cold-blooded world of political influence but for how the Court came to its conclusion. Put another way, what is the Court's view of the relation between constitutional law and the political process that explains how it handled the challenge to BCRA? After all, it was the Constitution itself that the Court used as the template for fashioning much of the campaign finance regulatory regime of the past several decades. When taken as a lens through which to gauge the Court's jurisprudence of the political process, *McConnell* unfortunately yields at least three competing, somewhat coherent, yet largely incompatible approaches to the constitutional law of politics, thereby carrying forward the central and unreconciled tensions in this entire area of law. The remainder of this introductory chapter on American law will be directed to the principles underlying the Court's response to the world of politics.

Rights, Deference and Process

The Rights Domain in Politics

From the most basic right-to-vote cases, through the minority vote dilution cases, through *Baker v Carr* and the reapportionment revolution,[15] the Court's political process jurisprudence has always had a strong element of enforcement of individual rights. There have been debates on and off the Court about the role that rights

[11] *McConnell v FEC* 124 S Ct 619, 747 (2003).
[12] *Ibid* at 748.
[13] *Ibid* at 706.
[14] *Ibid* at 673.
[15] See S Levinson, 'One Person One Vote: A Mantra in Need of Meaning' (2002) 80 *North Carolina Law Review* 1269, 1296.

discourse could or should legitimately play in claims defined by aggregation. But whatever the limitations, the Court has returned time and again to the language of first-order constitutional rights when intervening in the political sphere. Sometimes the rights component is rather self-evident, as with challenges to limitations on the ability to register to vote on account of a poll tax or a residency durational requirement.[16] Other times, the rights component is more of a reach, as when the Court in *California Democratic Party v Jones* crafted a strong right of associational autonomy to prevent the imposition of a blanket primary requirement in California.[17]

Rights claims necessarily put courts in conflict with the democratic processes. When properly functioning, democracies respond ultimately, if imperfectly, to majoritarian commands. A rights claim may properly challenge a majoritarian determination that an out-group be prohibited from participating, as historically has been done for reasons of sex or race or wealth or duration of residency. A rights claim may similarly assert that majoritarian processes render minorities incapable of participating effectively, as with minority vote dilution suits. Insofar as campaign finance regulation inescapably burdens expressive activity, First Amendment arguments are invariably a part of the litigation landscape.

Without entering into the merits of the First Amendment claims in BCRA, there can be little doubt, after *Buckley,* that there must be a significant rights overlay to the expressive dimension of campaign finance regulation. The First Amendment approach would require some elevated showing of both need for the regulation and tightness of fit between state objectives and means taken. A striking feature of *McConnell* is the almost complete absence of such conventional First Amendment concerns. The opinion is replete with references to the congressional interest in forestalling the poorly defined 'appearance of corruption.'[18] Not only does the Court repeatedly announce its intent to defer to congressional judgments, but extends this to what Congress 'may' have concluded or what may be 'reasonable'[19] or, in one passage, to the value of 'common sense' in determining the ambit of congressional regulatory authority.[20]

What is most striking, however, is the sudden and inexplicable resurgence of First Amendment formalism with regard to—of all people—minors. Stunningly, in light of the radically diminished First Amendment protections minors receive in general, Chief Justice Rehnquist announces that the restrictions on contributions by minors 'may . . . impinge on the protected freedoms of expression and association' and that, accordingly, the burdens of BCRA must be subject to heightened scrutiny.[21] The rejoinder that contributions through children appear to be an invitation to evasion, an argument that carries the day with regard to

16 See *Guinn v United States* 238 US 347, 363 (1915).
17 530 US 567, 581–2 (2000).
18 *McConnell v FEC*, 124 S Ct 619, 661 (2003).
19 *Ibid* at 672–3.
20 *Ibid* at 661.
21 *Ibid* at 711.

contributions to parties, all of a sudden fails because, 'the Government offers scant evidence for this form of evasion.'[22]

The sudden emergence of conventional First Amendment scrutiny cannot be attributed to the different authorship of separate parts of the opinions of the Court; both Rehnquist and Stevens/O'Connor write the holdings of the Court. What emerges instead is a perfectly viable First Amendment lever with real clout as to restrictions on burdening expressive activity—but with no predictable mechanism for determining when it will be pulled.

Deference to Political Judgments

As opposed to the invitation to judicial scrutiny of the rights domain, a distinct jurisprudential tradition would leave the political process largely to political determinations. Whether dressed up formally as the political question doctrine, or more typically, as the regulatory domain for managing elections, the Court has reserved for the political process a significant area relatively immune from constitutional scrutiny. Hence the repeated invocations throughout the opinion of the importance of deferring to congressional judgments, even beyond the boundaries of actual fact finding.[23]

The difficulty comes with drawing the line between the inherently expressive quality of participation in the political process and the need to permit coherent regulation of the political process. A critical example comes with the act of getting on the ballot. Because the state must print a ballot with a presumably finite number of candidates, all rules requiring preconditions for appearing on the ballot impose a direct burden on political participation. The Court's response has been to treat most ballot access matters (eg, signature requirements to get on the ballot) as regulatory affairs guaranteeing the orderly administration of elections, while reserving more exacting constitutional scrutiny for specific access restrictions that attempt more directly to regulate speech.[24] Unfortunately, it is not easy to tell ex ante which side of the regulatory/expressive divide any particular form of regulation will fall on. Once categorised as a matter of regulation of the electoral arena, the Court's decision to defer to the political and administrative judgments of state electoral authorities appears unassailable. The trick, however, lies in the categorisation.

Consider, for example, the disclosure requirements that form the core of the regulations upheld in Title II of BCRA. Among the provisions upheld were those requiring disclosure of the sponsors of anything falling within the sweeping category of 'electioneering communication.'[25] Relying on *Buckley*, the Court

[22] *Ibid.*

[23] See, eg, *McConnell v FEC* 124 S Ct 619, 661 (2003). For examples of the Court's prior strictness in requiring congressional fact finding, see *United States v Morrison* 529 US 598, 614 (2000); *City of Boerne v Flores* 521 US 507, 536 (1997); *United States v Lopez* 514 US 549, 564 (1995).

[24] See, eg, *Cook v Gralike* 531 US 510 (2001); *McIntyre v Ohio Elections Commission*, 514 US 334 (1994).

[25] 2 USCS section 441(d) (2003).

eliminated any possible claim of First Amendment privilege by invoking the state's regulatory interest in,

> providing the electorate with relevant information about the candidates and their supporters; deterring actual corruption and discouraging the use of money for improper purposes; and facilitating enforcement of the prohibitions of the Act.[26]

Viewed in its regulatory light, there is no question but that the Court should defer to the congressional determination that disclosure measures preserve the integrity of the electoral process. But should disclosure be seen as a mere regulatory device or as a form of compelled speech that threatens to disrupt the free flow of information in the political marketplace of ideas?

For the Court in *McConnell*, the answer appeared so obvious that the issue was never meaningfully engaged. But compare for a moment how the Court, in another opinion by Justice Stevens, condemned an Ohio law prohibiting the publication of anonymous leaflets on electoral matters because 'the category of speech regulated by the Ohio statute occupies the core of the protection afforded by the First Amendment.'[27] In *McIntyre v Ohio Elections Commission*, the Court invoked the Federalist Papers for the historical pedigree of anonymous speech in the political domain and even speculated that anonymity may enhance the expressive quality of speech: 'Anonymity thereby provides a way for a writer who may be personally unpopular to ensure that readers will not prejudge her message simply because they do not like its proponent.'[28] As if in rapture, the Court goes on to extol the centrality of anonymous (and presumably critical) speech in the constellation of constitutional values:

> The decision in favor of anonymity may be motivated by fear of economic or official retaliation, by concern about social ostracism, or merely by a desire to preserve as much of one's privacy as possible. Whatever the motivation may be, at least in the field of literary endeavor, the interest in having anonymous works enter the marketplace of ideas unquestionably outweighs any public interest in requiring disclosure as a condition of entry. Accordingly, an author's decision to remain anonymous, like other decisions concerning omissions or additions to the content of a publication, is an aspect of the freedom of speech protected by the First Amendment.[29]

I do not intend this discussion as a condemnation of disclosure. Indeed, I rather favour disclosure as a limited, information-enhancing mechanism to identify the role of money in politics. Instead, the focus is on the absence of doctrinal mooring for the Court's willingness to cede to political judgments in the freighted arena of politics. The Court could have moved in the direction of process, and directed

[26] *McConnell*, 124 S Ct 619, 647–8 (2003).

[27] *McIntyre v Ohio Elections Comm'n* 514 US 334, 346 (1995).

[28] *Ibid* at 342. For an extended discussion of the privacy concerns in anonymity, see W McGeveran, 'Mrs McIntyre's Checkbook: Privacy Costs of Political Contribution Disclosure' (2003) 6 *Pennsylvania Journal of Constitutional Law* 1.

[29] *McIntyre*, above n 26 at 341–2.

its attention to the public outcry over moneyed influences in politics, or it could have looked to the ubiquity of campaign finance restrictions in jurisdictions that allow for referendum mechanisms that bypass legislative self-interest, or it could even have looked to congressional reluctance to regulate this arena as evidence of lack of anticompetitive motivation. But instead, the Court purports to defer to legislative fact findings on the ephemeral claim of appearance of corruption. As *McIntyre* shows, however, such appearances are as readily trumped by the virtue of political speech as they are predictable grounds for electoral regulation.

Integrity of the Political Process

The rights approach assumes an active judiciary critically engaging the outputs of the majoritarian process, while the deference regime requires courts to cede to the institutional expertise of the very same majoritarian legislative processes. A third alternative, grounded conceptually in the *Carolene Products* [30] and the tradition of John Ely's *Democracy and Distrust*,[31] would have the judiciary selectively intervene to protect the process integrity of politics. As I have addressed on many previous occasions,[32] the core idea here is that the legitimacy of democratic processes turns on the processes that protect the competitive accountability to the electorate, and further that courts perform an invaluable service in securing the integrity of the process.

Process integrity has been a critical, if often not fully explicated, factor in many of the most inflammatory interventions of the Court into the political process in recent years. For example, and most controversially, there is Justice Scalia's defence of the Court's injunction against further recounts in Florida in the 2000 election on the grounds that the Court needed to ensure 'election results that have the public acceptance democratic stability requires.'[33] A similar, if less controversial, concern for process regularity is found in the Court's first opinion on Florida 2000 requiring reassessment of Florida law to assure compliance with 'a principle of federal law that would assure finality of a State's determination [of election results] if made pursuant to a state law in effect before the election . . .'[34] It is also possible to read the Court's *Shaw v Reno* line of cases[35] as expressing a concern that the extravagance of district-line manipulations in a way that conveyed a political process distorted by racial concerns. While each of these examples will no doubt provoke bitter rejoinders, the point is that the Court has within its arsenal analytic approaches to process distortions that have commanded decisive majorities in historic cases.

[30] *United States v Carolene Prods Co* 304 US 144, 152 n 4 (1938).

[31] John Hart Ely, *Democracy and Distrust: A Theory of Judicial Review* (Cambridge, Harvard University Press, 1980).

[32] See, eg, S Issacharoff, 'Gerrymanders and Political Cartels' (2003) 116 *Harvard L Rev* 593; S Issacharoff & R Pildes, 'Politics as Markets: Partisan Lockups of the Democratic Process' (1998) 50 *Stanford LJ* 643.

[33] *Bush v Gore* 531 US 1046, 1046 (2000).

[34] *Bush v Palm Beach County Canvassing Board* 530 US 70, 78 (2000).

[35] Eg, *Miller v Johnson* 515 US 900 (1995); *Shaw v Reno* 509 US 630 (1993).

In *McConnell,* it was Justice Scalia who forcefully took up the argument for process integrity:

> [BCRA] forbids pre-election criticism of incumbents by corporations, even not-for-profit corporations, by use of their general funds; and forbids national-party use of "soft" money to fund "issue ads" that incumbents find so offensive . . .
>
> If *all* electioneering were evenhandedly prohibited, incumbents would have an enormous advantage . . .
>
> Is it accidental, do you think, that incumbents raise about three times as much "hard money"—the sort of funding generally *not* restricted by this legislation—as do their challengers?[36]

This argument goes essentially unanswered in *McConnell.* It may be that the Scalia's assessment of BCRA as nothing more than an incumbent-protection scheme rings hollow in light of the clear reformist history of the Act—although the Act's provenance does not necessarily explain its final form. Or it may be that Scalia's process integrity rhetoric is simply a rhetorical parry—it was Scalia who authored the lead opinion in a case the same Term that was most hostile to any judicial role in thwarting the most egregious of incumbency preservation mechanisms: the sweetheart gerrymandering of non-competitive districts.[37] My aim, once again, is not to claim that incumbent featherbedding is the salient feature of BCRA. Rather, it is that, as with the rights claims and the invocation of deference of legislative judgments, intervention for reasons of process integrity is a cognisable and coherent approach to judicial superintendence of the political process. Unfortunately, like the witches in MacBeth, there is a fleeting and unpredictable quality to the apparitions of such doctrines.

Conclusion

There is no escaping that, as well captured by my colleague Richard Briffault, *McConnell* is 'a stunning triumph for campaign finance reform.' The Court has given broader latitude to regulations encroaching on expression than even the most intrepid advocates of reform could reasonably have hoped for. But for an opinion in such a volatile and visible area of law, there is a marked absence of structured argument, let alone inspired language. Rather, the opinion reads of resignation, of a Court confronted with the intractable conflict of limiting the role of private money in an increasingly expensive system funded by that same private money. Whether BCRA is the latest manifestation of the law of unintended consequences in the domain of campaign finance remains to be seen. How sophisticated actors will seek to game the system, and whether they succeed also remains to be seen. For now, the Court has thrown in the towel. Perhaps just as well.

[36] *McConnell v FEC* 124 S Ct 619, 720–1 (2003).

[37] *Vieth v Jubelirer* 541 US 267(2004).

10

Soft Money, Congress and the Supreme Court

RICHARD BRIFFAULT

Introduction

ON 27 MARCH 2002, President George W Bush signed the *Bipartisan Campaign Reform Act* of 2002 ('BCRA' or 'the Act') into law. The culmination of a six-year legislative and political struggle, BCRA is the most significant change in federal campaign finance law in nearly thirty years. The Act addresses a broad range of campaign finance issues, including fundraising on federal property, contributions by foreign nationals, modification of the contribution limits for congressional candidates facing high-spending self-funded opponents, donations to the presidential inauguration committee, electronic filing and internet access to campaign disclosure reports, and penalties for the violation of campaign finance laws. But the heart of the Act is the regulation of political party soft money. The Act sharply curbs the ability of state parties to use soft money in federal elections and completely bars the national parties from using soft money.

The soft money restrictions were immediately challenged on the grounds that they violate the First Amendment rights of political parties and party adherents. In December 2003, the Supreme Court, in *McConnell v FEC*,[1] upheld all of BCRA's major provisions, including the restrictions on political party soft money. *McConnell* is the single greatest legal victory for campaign finance regulation since the modern era of campaign finance law was ushered in three decades ago by the enactment of the *Federal Election Campaign Act* (FECA) of 1971, the FECA Amendments of 1974, and the decision in *Buckley v Valeo*.[2]

This chapter will trace the development of soft money, examine BCRA's soft money provisions, and analyse *McConnell*'s treatment of constitutional questions posed by soft money restrictions. It will conclude by briefly considering the impact of BCRA on campaign finances and the implications of *McConnell* for the future of campaign finance law.

[1] 540 US 93 (2003).
[2] 424 US 1 (1976).

The Rise of Soft Money

Soft money emerged out of the political complications of federalism. Federal campaign finance law regulates only federal elections, but federal and state elections often occur concurrently, with candidates for federal and state offices appearing on one ballot. Party committees undertake campaign efforts that simultaneously assist both their federal and state candidates. Spending on federal candidates must satisfy FECA's dollar limitations and source prohibitions—such as the bans on contributions by business corporations, unions, and government contractors—but spending in state elections is beyond FECA's scope and subject only to state law. Many state campaign finance laws are far less restrictive than FECA. Some permit corporations or unions to support candidates; some do not limit individual or political action committee ('PAC') donations.

In the late 1970s, party committees pressed the Federal Election Commission ('FEC') to let them use funds that do not comply with FECA to finance campaign efforts that would help the party ticket as a whole, including both federal and state candidates. In 1978 the FEC determined that a state party could use funds impermissible under FECA to defray a portion of administrative overhead, voter registration, and voter mobilisation activities that benefit both federal and state candidates. In 1979, the FEC went further and decided that national party committees could also accept contributions otherwise barred by FECA to finance expenditures in support of a portion of its expenditures on behalf of a combined federal-state ticket. As a result, a party committee could receive and spend contributions from corporations and unions—otherwise barred by FECA—and donations from individuals and PACs in excess of FECA's dollars ceilings on (i) nonfederal election activities, and (ii) the nonfederal portion of activities in support of combined federal-nonfederal election efforts. Soft money—that is, money that has an effect on federal elections but is not subject to federal contribution, expenditure or disclosure rules but is technically aimed at nonfederal election activities—was born.

Soft money donations to the national parties rose from an initial $19 million in 1980 to $45 million in 1988.[3] Soft funds were used to build up the infrastructure of the national parties—to hire staff, acquire office space, develop direct mail, polling and issues research operations, acquire data processing equipment, and create and improve facilities for mass media communications—on the theory that since some portion of these activities is aimed at state and local elections, a portion of the cost could be defrayed by money not subject to FECA's restrictions. The national parties also transferred millions of dollars in soft money to state parties to build their infrastructures and to fund shared voter mobilisation programs. In 1990, the FEC, in response to years of prodding by campaign finance

[3] Prior to 1990, the FEC did not require the parties to report on their soft money accounts, so the numbers in text are only estimates. See H Alexander & M Bauer, *Financing the 1988 Election* (Boulder, Westview Press, 1991) 37.

reformers and the courts, issued rules requiring party committees to report their soft money funds and regulate the allocation of expenses for shared activities between federal and nonfederal accounts. The rules limited the ability of party committees to shelter some funds for shared expenses in nonfederal accounts, but,

> [t]he general effect of the guidelines was . . . to give party organisations a clearer sense of how to spend soft money legally, and, at least in some instances, to permit them . . . to pay a greater share of their costs with soft money than they had been before.[4]

Soft money exploded in the 1990s. In 1991–92, the two national parties raised $86 million in soft money, or double the amount for 1987–88. Soft money accounted for 17 per cent of total national party receipts in the 1992 election cycle. By 1995–96, national party soft money receipts trebled to $263.5 million and accounted for 30 per cent of total national party income. In 1999–2000, soft money receipts for the two major parties nearly doubled again to $495.1 million, and soft money accounted for 40 per cent of the party fundraising—and nearly 50 per cent of the funds received by the Democratic Party.[5]

The growth in soft money reflected two developments. First, a substantial number of donors were willing to make very large soft money contributions. According to the Center for Responsive Politics, in the 1995–96 cycle, 150 individuals or entities donated $250,000 or more in soft money—including five corporations and two unions that made contributions in excess of $1 million.[6] An additional 25 entities made contributions of between $600,000 and $975,000 each. In 1999–2000, approximately $300 million in soft money (or 60 per cent of the total) came from just 800 donors.[7] The average donation in this group of top donors was, thus, approximately $375,000. The rise of soft money, thus, mocked the campaign finance laws, providing large contributors with a major opportunity to circumvent FECA's contribution restrictions.

Second, the parties discovered a major new use for soft money—issue advocacy advertising. In *Buckley*, the Supreme Court, driven by First Amendment concerns, read FECA's disclosure requirements narrowly to apply only to advertising that 'expressly advocates' the election or defeat of clearly identified federal candidates. All other advertising, even ads that were plainly election-related, were deemed to be 'issue' advocacy if they lacked the 'magic words' of express advocacy. Such issue ads were outside the scope of federal campaign finance regulation.

[4] A Corrado, 'Party Soft Money' *in* A Corrado, *et al* (eds), *Campaign Finance Reform: A Sourcebook* (Washington, DC, Brookings Institute, 1997) at 175.

[5] FEC, 'FEC Reports Increase in Party Fundraising for 2000,' <http://www.fec.gov/press2001/051501partyfund/051501partyfund.html> (24 April 2005) (in 1999–2000 soft money accounted for $495 million out of total national party receipts of $1.236 billion, and for $245 million out of total national Democratic party receipts of $520 million).

[6] Center for Responsive Politics, 'Top Overall Contributors,' <http://www.opensecrets.org/pubs/btl/topover.html> (24 April 2005).

[7] See C Holman & L McLoughlin, *Buying Time 2000: Television Advertising in the 2000 Federal Election* (New York, Brennan Center for Justice at New York University School of Law, 2001) at ch 8 p 12.

Issue ads were initially the province of independent committees, but in 1995–96 the parties began to air issue ads that criticise or promote a candidate and use soft money to pay for them. In the 1996 election, the parties spent an estimated $68 million on issue ads.[8] In the 2000 election, the parties spent $162 million on electioneering issue ads,[9] and issue ads accounted for 37.8 per cent of party soft money spending during the 1999–2000 election cycle.[10] This ability to deploy soft money for the direct support of federal candidates both dramatically expanded the role of soft money in financing federal election campaigns and provided a powerful impetus for the solicitation of further soft money donations.

BCRA's Restrictions on Political Party Soft Money

BCRA restricts soft money by adding new section 323 to FECA. The first subsection, section 323(a), prohibits national political party committees from soliciting, receiving, or transferring or directing to another person or committee any funds that do not comply with FECA's dollar limitations, source prohibitions and disclosure requirements. As Justices Stevens and O'Connor put it in their co-authored opinion[11] for the *McConnell* Court, section 323(a) 'takes national parties out of the soft-money business.'[12]

The other principal soft money provisions address the activities of state and local political parties. This is critical to any effective control over soft money since a ban limited to the national parties would most likely lead donors and party leaders to redirect their efforts to the state and local parties.[13] However, since a portion of state and local party spending is undoubtedly aimed at nonfederal elections, a complete ban on state and local party soft money comparable to the restriction on national parties would effectively federalise state and local election campaign finances.

[8] D Beck, *et al*, *Issue Advocacy Advertising During the 1996 Campaign: A Catalog* (Philadelphia, Annenberg Public Policy Center at the University of Pennsylvania, 1997) 3, 34, 55.

[9] See *Buying Time*, above n 7 at Figure 4–5.

[10] See *Buying Time* above n 7 at Figure 8–5.

[11] The opinion for the Court in *McConnell* actually consists of three separate opinions with four authors. In an unusual arrangement, Justices Stevens and O'Connor co-authored the opinion dealing with BCRA's Titles I and II, including soft money and issue advocacy. This opinion was joined by Justices Souter, Ginsburg, and Breyer. Other opinions dealing with other parts of the Act were authored by Chief Justice Rehnquist, and by Justice Breyer.

[12] 540 US at 133.

[13] Even before BCRA's enactment, when national party committees were free to accept and spend soft money, state and local committees played a pivotal role in the soft money system. Under the FEC's rules for combining hard and soft money in the financing of mixed federal/nonfederal activities, the state parties could generally pay for a significantly greater portion of their activities from soft money than their national counterparts. Consequently, in recent elections the national parties directed or transferred millions of dollars of soft money to the state parties. In 1999–2000, the national party committees reported transferring $265 million in soft money (or more than half of their total soft money receipts) to state and local party committees. See J Dunbar, M Sylvester and R Moore, 'State parties collected nearly $570 million in contributions, soft money transfers in 2000: States used as a $263 million back door for soft money' <http://www.statesecrets.org> (26 June 2002).

Avoiding the difficult federalism question that comprehensive federal regulation of state and local parties would pose, BCRA adheres to FECA's focus on federal elections, but widens the definition of state and local party federal election activity to include expenditures that benefit federal candidates even though they are not aimed at federal candidates explicitly or exclusively. Thus, section 323(b) prohibits state and local parties from using soft money to finance 'Federal election activit[ies],' which are defined to consist of:

(i) voter registration activities within 120 days before a regularly scheduled election for federal office;
(ii) voter identification, get-out-the-vote activity or generic campaign activity conducted in connection with an election in which a candidate for federal office appears on the ballot[14];
(iii) public communications that refer to a clearly identified candidate for federal office and promote or oppose that candidate; and
(iv) services provided by party staffers who spend more than 25 per cent of their time working in connection with a federal election.

Three additional provisions further extend the soft money ban. Section 323(d) prohibits political parties from soliciting funds for or donating funds to tax-exempt organisations which participate financially in federal elections. Section 323(e) prohibits federal candidates and office holders from soliciting, receiving, spending, transferring, or directing soft money in connection with any election for federal, state, or local office.[15] Section 323(f) prohibits state and local candidates and officeholders from spending soft money on public communications that support or oppose federal candidates.

McConnell and Soft Money

McConnell upheld all the soft money restrictions. Four of the five subsections were upheld by 5–4 votes; the fifth, section 323(e), was validated by a vote of 7 to 2.

The National Party Soft Money Ban

The national party soft money ban required the Court to address and resolve four questions: First, should the ban be subject to the lower standard of review which the Court has applied to restrictions on contributions even though the ban

[14] There is one significant exception to these restrictions on soft money. Individuals may donate up to $10,000 per calendar year to state and local political parties for use on voter registration and mobilisation and generic party activity, provided the activities do not refer to a clearly identified candidate for federal office.

[15] Federal officeholders running for state office may solicit, accept and spend soft money for their state campaigns provided they comply with applicable state laws.

applies not just to donations to the parties but to party solicitations, expenditures, and the donation and direction of funds to others? Second, even if the soft money ban is treated as a contribution restriction, can it be justified by the governmental interest in preventing the corruption and the appearance of the corruption of public officials—which are the only constitutional bases for limiting donations—given that soft money is, by definition, contributed not to candidates and officeholders but to political parties? Third, even if some donations to political parties present dangers of corruption and the appearance of corruption because of the use of the donated funds to benefit particular candidates, does that justify a sweeping, blanket ban on all national party uses of soft money? Finally, does the ban unconstitutionally burden the ability of the national political party committees to work with their state and local counterparts? The majority answered the first three questions 'yes,' and the last one 'no.'

The majority, in the opinion co-authored by Justices Stevens and O'Connor, easily concluded that the less rigorous contribution limit standard of review should apply. Although the soft money ban nominally limits the spending as well as the receipt of soft funds, the spending limit focuses only on soft money contributions; it does not cap total party spending or spending on particular activities. '[F]or purposes of determining the level of scrutiny, it is irrelevant that Congress chose in section 323 to regulate contributions on the demand rather than the supply side.'[16] Similarly, the solicitation limit is aimed at the solicitation of soft money; it does not limit the number of potential donors who can be solicited for funds, or the ability of the party to combine its request for funds with political messages. So, too, the limit on party donation and direction of funds to others applies only to party support that involves soft money, not a cap on party support of other committees generally. Thus, despite the references to activities other than contributions, the soft money ban is really aimed solely at limiting the size and source of donations to the parties by forcing all money handled by the national parties to comply with the hard money limits.

Second, the Court found the limits on donations to parties were justified by the need to prevent the corruption and the appearance of corruption of federal candidates and officeholders. Although soft money is contributed to the parties, the record demonstrated that federal officeholders and candidates play a major role in soliciting soft money; that the parties offer soft money donors special opportunities to meet with high-level federal officials as an incentive to donations; and that soft money is frequently used to fund activities that benefit particular candidates so that 'candidates would feel grateful for such donations and that donors would seek to exploit that gratitude.'[17] Soft money had emerged to enable campaign participants to evade FECA's restrictions on contributions to candidates. The Court found,

> evidence in the record shows that candidates and donors alike have in fact exploited the soft-money loophole, the former to increase their prospects of election and the

[16] 540 US at 138.
[17] *Ibid* at 145.

> latter to create debt on the part of officeholders, with the national parties serving as willing intermediaries.[18]

'Both common sense and the ample record'[19] confirmed that soft money contributions to the parties enable donors and candidates to evade the statutory limits on donations to candidates and are the basis for corrupting relationships between donors and officeholders, and of the appearance of donor-candidate corruption.

Third, perhaps the most difficult issue for the national party soft money ban was its comprehensive scope. In 2001, in *Federal Election Commission v Colorado Republican Campaign Committee ('Colorado Republican II')*[20] the Court had upheld FECA's limits on party spending coordinated with the party's candidates, finding that parties could serve as conduits for donations from contributors to candidates, so that limits on party spending limited the ability of donors to get money to candidates. *Colorado Republican II* involved party expenditures coordinated with particular federal candidates. But section 323(a) applies to *all* national party expenditures including those spent in off-year state and local elections, such as the October 2003 California gubernatorial recall, when no federal candidates are even on the ballot.

Relying on a floor statement by one of BCRA's House sponsors and the expert reports of several political scientists, the Court determined that the close institutional relationship of the national parties and national elected officials justified the regulation of *all* donations to the national party committees. As the Court noted,

> the national committees of the two major parties are both run by, and largely composed of, federal officeholders and candidates. Indeed, of the six national committees of the two major parties, four are composed entirely of federal officeholders.[21]

The Court concluded that,

> [g]iven this close connection and alignment of interests, large soft-money contributions to national parties are likely to create actual or apparent indebtedness on the part of federal officeholders, regardless of how those funds are ultimately used.[22]

As a result, the interests in preventing corruption and the appearance of corruption were found 'sufficient to justify subjecting all donations to national parties to the source, amount, and disclosure limitations of FECA.'[23]

Finally, the Court dismissed the argument that section 323(a) would impermissibly interfere with national party cooperation with state and local party committees, including the planning of campaign finance strategies. The Court found that

[18] *Ibid* at 146.
[19] *Ibid* at 145.
[20] 533 US 431 (2001).
[21] 540 US 155.
[22] *Ibid.*
[23] *Ibid* at 156.

BCRA continues to permit 'a wide range of joint planning and electioneering activities,' including the soliciting and expenditure of hard money, and national party officer participation in discussions concerning state party uses of soft money.[24]

The State and Local Party Soft Money Restrictions

Much as national party soft money developed as a device for circumventing FECA's limits on hard money contributions to candidates and parties, both Congress and the Court recognised that limits on national party committees would simply stimulate new efforts at evasion. As Justices Stevens and O'Connor put it:

> Congress recognised that, given the close ties between federal candidates and state party committees, BCRA's restrictions on national committee activity would rapidly become ineffective if state and local committees remained available as a conduit for soft-money donations.[25]

Indeed, even prior to BCRA's enactment, the national parties had actively solicited soft money for and funneled soft money to the state parties to take advantage of FEC rules that permitted state parties to use soft money to fund a far greater fraction of so-called 'mixed activities' that national parties were allowed to do. Noting this practice, the Court found Congress' determination that restrictions on state and local party committees were necessary to prevent the circumvention of FECA's limits to be 'firmly rooted in relevant history and common sense.'[26] The only question was whether the state and local party restrictions were sufficiently narrowly tailored to federal election activities to avoid unnecessarily burdening state and local party freedom to participate in state and local elections.

Relying on expert testimony and other evidence in the record, the Court agreed that the first two categories of BCRA-defined 'federal election activities'—voter registration and mobilisation activities within 120 days of a regularly scheduled election and generic party activities in connection with an election—'confer substantial benefits on federal candidates,' who are appropriately grateful for the contributions that fund those efforts. The 120-day rule focuses the federal restriction 'on the subset of voter registration activity that is most likely to affect the election prospects of federal candidates.' The generic election activity restriction applies only to elections when federal offices are at stake. As a result of these 'temporal and substantive limitations' these provisions were a 'reasonable response' to the corruption danger created by contributions to state and local parties to fund these election activities.[27]

The Court gave even shorter shrift to the challenge to the prohibition on the use of soft money for state and local party 'public communications' that promote or attack a candidate for federal office. The 'public communications' restriction

[24] *Ibid* at 160.
[25] *Ibid* at 161.
[26] *Ibid* at 165.
[27] *Ibid* at 167–8.

arises at the intersection of soft money with BCRA's other central concern—issue advocacy. The Supreme Court in *Buckley*, in order to avoid unconstitutionally vague and overbroad restrictions, had limited FECA's regulation of independent expenditures to express advocacy. If *McConnell* had followed *Buckley* on this point, BCRA's 'public communications' restrictions might have been held unconstitutional. Instead, the Court summarily noted the 'abundant' evidence in the record that public communications that support or oppose a federal candidate 'directly affect[]' federal elections and 'benefit directly federal candidates.' Restrictions on the use of soft money to pay for such public communications could be justified by anti-corruption concerns. The Court tersely rejected the argument that the definition of 'public communication' was too broad, finding instead that by focusing on advertising that promotes or opposes federal candidates the provision is 'closely drawn to the anticorruption interest it is intended to address.' The claim of unconstitutional vagueness drew even less concern. In a footnote, the Court concluded that the statutory terms 'clearly set forth the confines within which potential party speakers must act in order to avoid triggering the provisions.' These terms were sufficiently explicit to regulate the activities of party committees 'since actions by political parties are presumed to be in connection with election campaigns.'[28]

The Court easily concluded that preventing the circumvention of the soft money restriction also justified the requirement that state and local parties spend federal funds to pay the salary of any employee spending more than 25 per cent of his or her compensated time on federal election activities.

The Court also summarily dismissed the argument that BCRA's extensive regulation of state and local parties, and its inevitable impact on state and local party participation in state and local elections held at the same time as federal elections, violates principles of federalism.

Other Soft Money Restrictions

Tax-Exempt Organisations

The Court concluded it was 'entirely reasonable'[29] for Congress to act prophylactically to prevent the parties from soliciting soft funds for, or making or directing soft money contributions to, politically active tax-exempt organisations which could use those funds to participate in federal election campaigns. Evidence in the record demonstrated that the parties had engaged in this practice even prior to BCRA's enactment. The only real issue was whether section 323(d) was narrowly tailored since the provision does not simply restrict political parties from donating or soliciting soft money for tax-exempt organisations but flatly bans all party aid to such organisations, including hard money. A complete ban on hard money donations would prevent parties from giving any support to these organisations

[28] *Ibid* at 169–70 and n 64.
[29] *Ibid* at 174.

but do 'little to further Congress' goal of preventing corruption or the appearance of corruption of federal candidates and officeholders.' The Court solved the constitutional problem by looking to BCRA's legislative history, and its particular concern with soft money, to limit section 323(d) to the solicitation and donation of soft funds only, and then upheld the subsection.

Federal Candidates and Officeholders

Seven members of the Court approved section 323(e)'s restrictions on the raising and soliciting of soft money by federal candidates and officeholders. The majority found the ban 'closely drawn' to prevent corruption or the appearance of corruption.[30] Justice Kennedy, joined by Chief Justice Rehnquist, concurred, finding that the provision—which contains exceptions permitting candidates to speak at fundraising events, to solicit or direct unlimited funds to organisations not involved in federal election activity, and to solicit or direct donations of up to $20,000 per year from individuals to organisations involved in federal election activity—is sufficiently 'narrowly tailored to satisfy First Amendment requirements.'[31] This was the only soft money restriction that garnered the support of any of the Justices outside the Stevens-O'Connor group.

Public Communications by State and Local Candidates and Officeholders

The Stevens-O'Connor majority upheld section 323(f)'s prohibition on state and local candidates and officeholders spending soft funds to pay for 'public communications' that promote or support, or attack or oppose, a clearly identified candidate for federal office. This measure, like the other restrictions on soft money, was justified by the anticircumvention concern. Given the prior history of successful efforts to evade campaign finance limitations, Congress was 'eminently reasonable' in predicting that state candidates and officeholders would 'become the next conduits' for the use of soft money in federal campaigns.[32]

McConnell and the Expansion of the Idea of 'Corruption'

Since *Buckley v Valeo* the prevention of corruption and the appearance of corruption have been 'the only legitimate and compelling government interests thus far identified for restricting campaign finances.'[33] Contributions may be limited because, according to the Court, they present the danger of corruption and the appearance of corruption. By contrast, candidate expenditures and independent expenditures by parties, individuals and interest groups on efforts to communicate

[30] *Ibid* at 182.
[31] *Ibid* at 314.
[32] *Ibid* at 185.
[33] *Federal Election Commission v National Conservative PAC* 470 US 480, 496–7 (1984).

with and persuade voters may not be limited because they do not present the danger of corruption. The Court, however, has been maddeningly imprecise in its definition of corruption. *Buckley* focused on the concept of the quid pro quo, finding that '[t]o the extent that large contributions are given to secure a political quid pro quo from current and potential office holders, the integrity of our system of representative democracy is undermined.'[34] *Buckley*, however, declined to define what it meant by quid pro quo, indicating only that the term was more inclusive than outright bribery. '[T]he giving and taking of bribes' are 'only the most blatant and specific attempts of those with money to influence governmental action.'[35] Subsequently, in *FEC v National Conservative Political Action Committee* ('*NCPAC*'), the Court treated corruption as a form of financial exchange: 'The hallmark of corruption is the financial quid pro quo: dollars for political favors.'[36] More recently, *Nixon v Shrink Missouri Government PAC*[37] defined corruption to include the 'broader threat from politicians too compliant with the wishes of large contributors.'[38] Citing *Buckley*, *Shrink Missouri* asserted '[t]hese were the obvious points behind our recognition that the Congress could constitutionally address the power of money to "influence governmental action" in ways less "blatant and specific" than bribery.'[39] However, in our political system individual and interest group efforts to influence governmental action are not only normal and expected, but also normatively desirable and constitutionally protected. *Shrink Missouri*, like *Buckley* before it, gave little guidance as to what efforts to influence government are permissible—indeed, constitutionally protected—and what efforts count as corrupt.

McConnell addressed three aspects of the corruption problem. First, as in earlier cases, the Court considered what candidate or officeholder response to a campaign contribution would be considered a *corrupt result*. Second, the Court examined what constitutes an *exchange*. Implicit in *Buckley*'s focus on the quid pro quo is the idea of an exchange between donor and donee, but BCRA's soft money regulations do not address contributions by individuals to candidates, or even by individuals to parties for ultimate contribution to candidates. Rather, BCRA regulates gifts to parties—and the parties' use of such gifts—not expressly tied to specific candidates. Does this present the danger of corruption or the appearance of corruption? Finally, what evidence would Congress have to produce to justify a restriction as necessary to prevent corruption or the appearance of corruption?

On the first question, the Court expanded the concept of corrupt result to include the 'special access'[40] to officeholders that donors obtain from their contributions. The Court repeatedly focused on the use of donations to 'buy preferential access to federal officeholders'[41] and thereby 'open the doors of the offices of

[34] *Buckley v Valeo* 424 US 1 at 26–7 (1976).
[35] *Ibid* at 28.
[36] 470 US at 497.
[37] 528 US 377 (2000).
[38] *Ibid* at 389.
[39] *Ibid*.
[40] 540 US 150.
[41] *Ibid* at 156.

individual and important Members of Congress and the Administration.'[42] So, too, the Court emphasised the corruption inherent in the 'peddling'[43] and 'sale'[44] of access to donors and potential donors in order to obtain contributions. Although the Court had previously made clear that corruption was not limited to outright vote-buying, the Court's language of undue influence had nonetheless focused on the effects of large contributions on government decision-making. By focusing on special access, *McConnell* reframed the corruption analysis from the consideration of the impact of contributions on formal decisions to their effect on the *opportunity to influence* government actions. While surely the ultimate concern with special opportunities for influence is the effect of such influence on government, the Court treated preferential access as a problem in itself, and found that Congress could take steps to eliminate a campaign finance device that creates incentives to officeholders to give special access to donors.

Justice Kennedy's dissent blasted the Court, finding that,

> '[a]ccess in itself . . . shows only that in a general sense an officeholder favors someone or that someone has an influence on the officeholder. There is no basis, in law or in fact, to say favoritism or influence in general is the same as corrupt favoritism or influence in particular.[45]

In his view, the Court 'adopts a definition of corruption that . . . is at odds with standard First Amendment analysis because it is unbounded and susceptible to no limiting principle.'[46]

Justice Kennedy's dissent is to some extent unfair. The Court did not state that all unequal access or unequal influence was corrupt. Indeed, it specifically held that 'mere political favoritism or opportunity for influence alone is insufficient to justify regulation.'[47] The Court emphasised that only access *sold* in exchange for campaign contributions, not other forms of influence, could be regulated as presenting the danger of corruption or the appearance of corruption. Nor was Justice Kennedy more successful at coming up with a limiting principle that would provide a clear distinction between corruption and the appropriate interaction between interest groups and officeholders. At one point Justice Kennedy implied that only 'actual corrupt, vote-buying exchanges' could be regulated, but he, too, agreed that *Buckley* permitted the regulation of 'undue influence' broader than vote-buying.[48]

Certainly Justice Kennedy was correct in stating that private access to and influence with government decision-makers—and government responsiveness to such access and influence—are not harmful per se, but rather are inherent in the

[42] *Ibid* at 148, n 46 (quoting Judge Kollar-Kotelly, quoting the declaration of a donor). See also *ibid* at 165, n 61.
[43] *Ibid* at 150.
[44] *Ibid* at 155.
[45] *Ibid* at 296.
[46] *Ibid.*
[47] *Ibid* at 153.
[48] *Ibid* at 293.

nature of representative government. 'Democracy,' as he noted, 'is premised on responsiveness.'[49] And he was certainly right in suggesting that in order to protect the constitutional right to seek to influence government while also recognising government's efforts to preclude corrupting influence, the Court needs a standard that can 'distinguish good political responsiveness from bad.'[50] But Justice Kennedy presented no such theory. Instead, as discussed more fully below, he focused not on the officeholder's response to the campaign contribution but on the closeness of the relationship between a donor and a candidate.

As for the access theory of corruption itself, it has the benefit of focusing the corruption inquiry less on the ultimate actions of public officials and more on the processes of decision-making. Special access is likely to be easier to prove than 'undue influence.' It is often difficult to know whether a particular individual or interest group had any influence over a government actor or whether that influence was either dispositive or 'undue.' Access is more measurable and it is easier to determine whether access is related to the solicitation and receipt of contributions. We can tell if a large donor was invited to a White House breakfast or a policy retreat with Congressional leaders, much as we can tell whether special meetings or briefings are offered as a reward for large donations. Moreover, special access is certainly closely connected to the idea of appearance of corruption. Indeed, special access is typically the channel through which undue influence flows. Special access provides the large donor with an extra opportunity to make her case, to be heard during negotiations while a bill is in committee, to be briefed on what is happening while a bill is being marked up, or to speak to a member of Congress concerning which bills should be treated as priorities. If special access to officeholders provides the opportunity for the exercise of special influence, then '[t]he best means of prevention is to identify and remove the temptation.'[51]

To be sure, the Court merely asserts, without really defending, its fundamental premise that special access procured by money—as opposed to friendship, family ties, ideological affinity, or prior support—is uniquely corrupt.[52] However, the idea that the influence of money contributions to elected officials raises the danger of corruption has been at the heart of campaign finance law since *Buckley*. Even the dissenting justices assumed that the use of money to influence governmental action is corrupt; they just would have limited the category of corrupt officeholder response to a contribution to a formal vote or something close to it.[53] But it is not clear why the concept of corrupt response should be so limited. If it is 'troubling to a functioning democracy' that 'officeholders will decide issues not on the merits or the desires of their constituencies, but according to the wishes of those who have made large financial contributions valued by the officeholder,'[54]

[49] *Ibid* at 297.
[50] *Ibid.*
[51] *Ibid* at 153.
[52] *Ibid* at 355 (benefits to federal candidates and officeholders from newspaper endorsements) (Rehnquist, CJ)
[53] *Ibid* at 259 (Scalia, J); *Ibid* at 269 (Thomas, J); *Ibid* at 291–8 (Kennedy, J).
[54] *Ibid* at 153.

then Congress should be able to respond to the campaign finance practices that create the unequal access that make it more likely that decision-makers will act 'according to the wishes' of large donors.

The second way *McConnell* expands the concept of corruption involves the notion of corrupt *exchange*. In *Buckley*, the danger of corruption arose from contributions to candidates and political committees. This squarely raised the issue of a quid pro quo between donor and candidate. *Buckley* and later cases also applied the concept of the corrupt exchange to include contributions by individuals to intermediary organisations, or by intermediary organisations to candidates, where there was evidence that the intermediary would function as a conduit linking the original donor to the candidate.[55] In *Colorado Republican II*, the Court specifically found that party expenditures coordinated with candidates function as conduits for the transmission of funds from donors to candidates. BCRA's national and state political party soft money restrictions involve a more attenuated relationship between donors and candidates than in previous cases. Soft money donations pass from the original individual or interest group donors to party committees which use the funds not to make a contribution to or a coordinated expenditure with a particular candidate, but to undertake an expenditure—on voter registration, voter mobilisation, generic party speech or public communications—that benefits that candidate, along with, possibly, other candidates supported by the party committees. In the case of the national party committee, the expenditure might help state rather than federal candidates. Soft money funds do not move from donors to parties to candidates, but rather remain with the parties where they are used in many ways, not all of which benefit party federal candidates.

McConnell expanded the concept of corrupt exchange to include such soft money donations. The Court found federal officeholders enjoy a 'special relationship and unity of interest'[56] with their political parties, particularly the national

[55] See, eg, *Buckley*, 424 US 1, 38 (1976) (upholding FECA's limitation on an individual's total contributions in any calendar year—in addition to limitations on donations to candidates, political committees, and parties—on theory that aggregate limit 'serves to prevent evasion' of limits on donations to candidates 'by a person who might otherwise contribute massive amounts of money to a particular candidate through the use of unearmarked contributions to the candidate's political party'); *California Medical Association v Federal Election Commission* ('*CalMed*') 453 US 182, 197–8 (1981) (upholding limit on amount organisation can give its own PAC; although there was no danger that the organisation could corrupt its own PAC, the provision would 'prevent circumvention of the very limitations on contributions that this Court upheld in *Buckley*') (plurality opinion); see *Ibid* at 203 (concurring opinion of Blackmun, J) ('contributions to multicandidate political committees may be limited to $5,000 per year as a means of preventing evasion of the limitations on contributions to a candidate or his authorised campaign committee'); *Colorado Republican II,* above 20, 533 US at 456–7 (limits on party expenditures coordinated with candidates justified by need to prevent donors from using parties as conduits); *FEC v Beaumont,* 539 US 146 (2003) at 155 (limits on corporate contributions justified in part to prevent corporate officers and directors from using corporations as conduits for contributions to candidates).

[56] 540 US at 145. See also *Ibid* at 152 ('the close ties that candidates and officeholders have with their parties'); *Ibid* at 154 ('the close relationship between federal officeholders and the national parties'); *Ibid* at 156, n 51 ('the record demonstrates close ties between federal officeholders and the state and local committees of their parties').

committees. Given the unique role parties play in placing their candidates on the ballot, mobilising voters, and organising Congress, the Court found that parties have structural ties to candidates unmatched by any other interest groups.[57] This creates at least the theoretical possibility that donations to party committees raise the same corruption dangers as donations to the candidates. Moreover, the Court—noting the many ways in which candidates do in fact benefit from soft-money-funded activities; the candidates' awareness of the identities of soft money donors and of the use of the soft funds and of the candidates' consequent gratitude for the soft money donations; the role of federal candidates and officeholders in running party campaign committees and soliciting soft funds; and the parties' use of access to federal officeholders as an incentive to and a reward for soft money donations—found the danger of corrupt exchanges through the parties was reflected and reinforced by campaign finance practices.

McConnell, thus, makes an important new statement about the nature of political parties. In recent cases, the Supreme Court has seen the parties as organisations vital to citizen participation in the political process and has emphasised the First Amendment rights of the parties.[58] *McConnell*, however, emphasises a different aspect of the parties, at least of the two major parties that have long dominated the American political scene: Parties play a central role in organising the executive branch and Congress, linking elected officials together, and shaping government decision-making. The parties are a part of both our campaign finance system and our governance structure, much as government officials play an important role in directing the parties. As the raison d'etre of campaign finance law is controlling the influence of campaign money on government actions, the Court found that it made sense to apply the same laws to the party committees that interconnect election campaigns with the elected officials.

Justice Kennedy sharply dissented. He stressed the need for a 'limiting principle' that would prevent concerns about corruption and the appearance of corruption from resulting in undue regulation of contributions. The limiting principle for him was the need for a direct link between the donor and the candidate.[59] Contributions to the parties not earmarked for specific candidates and not involving solicitation by candidates or officeholders could not be corrupt because they do not involve such a direct connection

Justice Kennedy's position on this point is completely unpersuasive. If, as seems possible, (i) spending by a party—on issue research, voter registration, voter mobilisation, or public communications—can help its candidates even though the spending does not involve a contribution to the candidate or an expenditure coordinated with a candidate; (ii) candidates know this and are therefore grateful to the donors who fund these activities; and (iii) donors know this and make contributions to a candidate with the expectation of candidate gratitude, then why

[57] *Ibid* at 188.

[58] See, eg, *California Democratic Party v Jones* 530 US 567 (2000); *Eu v San Francisco Co Dem Central Comm* 489 US 214 (1989); *Tashjian v Republican Party of Connecticut* 479 US 208 (1986).

[59] 540 US 296–8.

cannot soft money donations to the parties raise at least the possibility of corruption?[60] And does not the role of federal officeholders in soliciting soft funds—including funds that will benefit party candidates other than themselves—and in making access to themselves available as an incentive to and reward for soft money donations provide evidence that soft money functions this way at least some of the time? To be sure, this does not prove that all donations to the parties raise the danger of corruption. The targeted restrictions on state and local party soft money may correlate more closely with the dangers of corruption than the absolute ban on national party soft money. But surely, there is a sufficiently strong theoretical and empirical basis for rejecting Justice Kennedy's categorical assertion that soft money contributions do not raise any danger of corruption that Congress may regulate.

With respect to the third question—the evidence needed to sustain the party restrictions—the Court built on its prior *Shrink Missouri* decision, which had held that the amount of evidence needed to sustain a contribution limit is not great and which had upheld a state contribution limit on a fairly slim evidentiary showing.[61] Indeed, the record in *McConnell* concerning soft money fundraising practices, the uses of soft money in federal elections, and the impact of soft money on Congress was enormous.[62] To be sure, although *Shrink Missouri* relied on relatively little evidence, all of it involved claims of government actions that were linked to campaign contributions,[63] whereas the evidence cited by *McConnell* involved either the exchange of contributions for preferential access or broad assertions by donors, present and past officeholders, consultants and political scientists about the pervasive effects of contributions on the political process. The Court cited relatively little evidence of the impact of particular donations on specific government decisions.[64] This, however, is entirely consistent with the Court's redefinition of corruption in terms of special access.

The Court cited relatively little evidence to justify the restriction of *all* donations to the national political parties, rather than just those donations solicited by candidates or officeholders or used to pay for activities that benefit federal candidates. Again, however, this is consistent with the Court's expansion of the concept of corrupt exchange and its finding of a close structural relationship between national party committees and federal officeholders and candidates affiliated with the parties. Relying on the statements of three political science experts and one of

[60] Justice Kennedy himself acknowledged that '[a]s a conceptual matter, generic party contributions may engender good will from a candidate or officeholder.' *Ibid* at 301.

[61] 528 US at 393–4 (citing the affidavit of the co-chair of the state legislature's Interim Joint Committee on Campaign Finance Reform; a handful of newspaper accounts; and the referendum vote for contribution limits).

[62] The findings of fact relating to BCRA's soft money provisions compiled by the *McConnell* three-judge district court came to approximately 270 pages in Federal Supplement 2d. See 251 F Supp 2d at 331–56 (Henderson, J), 439–525 (Kollar-Kotelly, J), and 815–74 (Leon, J).

[63] Above n 37 at 393–4.

[64] The statement that '[t]he evidence connects soft money to manipulations of the legislative calendar, leading to Congress' failure to enact, among other things, generic drug legislation, tort reform, and tobacco legislation' *McConnell* 540 US at 150 (citing two of the district court opinions and the declarations of Senator McCain and former Senators Simpson and Simon) is the only specific linkage of soft money to congressional action.

BCRA's sponsors, the Court concluded that the national parties and federal officeholders are so 'inextricably intertwined'[65] that 'large soft-money donations to national party committees are likely to buy donors preferential access to federal officeholders no matter the ends to which their contributions are eventually put.'[66] Due to the deep and ongoing ties between officeholders and their national parties, the Court found that donations to the national parties are likely to earn the gratitude of officeholders and provide large donors with special access to government decision-makers.

This seems a reasonable assumption. As the Court notes, 'the national committees of the two major parties are both run by, and largely composed of, federal officeholders. Indeed, of the six national committees of the major parties, four are composed entirely of federal officeholders.'[67] Although some money donated to the national parties may not be used in federal campaigns, national party leaders—who are often federal officeholders—take a leading role in dealing with big donors, soliciting funds, arranging opportunities for special meetings with Congressional leaders and executive branch officials, and deciding how those funds will be used. They are likely to be aware of who the donors are and to be grateful in their capacities as party leaders and federal officeholders—even if they are not directly benefited by the donations as candidates. As a result the structure of the national party-officeholder relationship itself is sufficient to meet the evidentiary burden of justifying a complete ban on national party soft money.

Conclusion

Campaign Finance Under BCRA

Prior to BCRA's enactment some critics were concerned that soft money reform would devastate the parties. As of this writing, the United States is only part-way through its first federal election cycle under BCRA, but it is clear the parties are flourishing financially. Aided by BCRA's significant increase in FECA's hard money limits on individual donations to the parties,[68] the parties are raising more in hard money than they had previously done in hard and soft money combined. As of 30 June 2004, the political parties had raised $762.4 million in hard money alone, as compared with $657.3 million in combined hard and soft money at the same point in the election cycle in 2000.[69] In other words, the parties have fully

[65] *Ibid* at 155 (quoting statement of Rep. Shays).

[66] *Ibid.*

[67] *Ibid.*

[68] BCRA raised the maximum individual hard money contribution to the party national committees from $20,000 to $25,000 per year. BCRA also significantly raised the aggregate cap on total contributions an individual can make.

[69] See FEC, 'Party Fundraising Continues to Grow,' <http://www.fec.gov/press/press2004> (6 August 2004).

replaced the $268 million in soft money they had obtained by this point in 2000. In short, BCRA does not appear to have hurt the parties financially.[70]

On the other hand, as some sceptics predicted, with contributions to the parties more tightly restricted, hundreds of millions of dollars have begun to flow to independent organisations. The principal beneficiaries are the entities known colloquially—after the section of Internal Revenue Code under which they are organised—as Section 527 committees. These committees can raise and spend money in connection with federal elections but, if they do not have a 'major purpose' of funding express advocacy in support of or in opposition to a federal candidate, they are not subject to FECA. Although the Court in *McConnell* upheld the various provisions in BCRA that went beyond *Buckley*'s 'express advocacy' test, BCRA did not address the 527s.[71] The FEC spent much of 2004 grappling with whether and how to apply *McConnell*'s new approach to the definition of election-related expenditures to the activities of 527 committees before concluding, on August 19, to table the matter until after the election.

527s are not entirely beyond regulation. They are subject to Internal Revenue Code disclosure requirements, although these rules are less extensive than FECA's. A 527 committee can neither contribute to nor coordinate its activities with a candidate. Like other entities, a 527 committee may not spent corporate or union treasury fund contributions on electioneering broadcast ads within 60 days of the general election. But, more importantly, under current law 527 committees can accept unlimited individual donations and contributions from corporate and union treasury funds. They are, thus, well-positioned to re-introduce soft money into national politics.

It appears they are doing just that. Based on its examination of IRS findings, the Center for Public Integrity reports that as of 20 August 2004, the 527 committees had spent $248 million in 2003–04, although roughly $45 million of that was spent by committees involved primarily in state elections.[72] Not all of this is new money diverted by BCRA. The Center for Public Integrity found that 527

[70] BCRA has not hurt candidates either. As of 30 June 2004, congressional candidates had raised $798.7 million or an increase of 32% over the comparable period in 2001–02. See FEC, 'Congressional Fundraising Continues to Grow,' <http://www.fec.gov/press/press2004> (18 August 2004). As of 31 July 2004, presidential candidates had raised $650 million, or 88% more than the $345 million raised by candidates by the same date in 2000. See Campaign Finance Institute, 'Candidates' Receipts Up 88% from 2000; Small Contributions Quadrupled; Large Contributions More Than Doubled,' <http://www.cfinst.org> (25 August 2004).

[71] Although *McConnell* did not directly address the 527 committees, the Court referred to its past approval of FECA's $5000 limit on contributions to multicandidate political committees as a means of precluding candidates and donors from using these committees to avoid the limits on donations to candidates—even though the limits on donations to these committees may also affect their ability to engage in constitutionally protected independent spending 540 US at 152 n 619. This suggests the anti-circumvention concern so central to *McConnell* could support regulation of the 527 committees. On the other hand, the Court's validation of BCRA's soft money restrictions indicated that political parties are 'entities uniquely positioned to serve as conduits for corruption.' *Ibid* at 156 n 51. This may make it more difficult to impose similar restrictions on 527 committees not controlled or formally affiliated with parties, candidates or officeholders.

[72] See Center for Public Integrity, 'Silent Partners: How political non-profits work the system,' <http://www.publicintegrity.org/527> (25 April 2005), 2003–04 Running Total as of 20 August 2004.

committees spent $149.7 million in the 2000 election cycle and $192.3 million in the 2002 cycle.[73] Nevertheless, some wealthy donors, who formerly gave to candidates or parties, are now giving to 527 committees instead.[74]

Plainly the rise of the 527s threatens to outflank BCRA. Because 527s are, by definition, supposed to be acting independently of candidates and parties their activities may pose less of a 'corruption' danger than political party soft money. Yet, the ability of such transparently election-related quasi-partisan organisations as the Media Fund, a pro-Democratic group led by long-time Democratic operative Harold Ickes, the George Soros-backed America Coming Together, or the now-notorious Swift Boat Veterans for Truth to evade FECA's restrictions and requirements is plainly as important a challenge to campaign finance law as political party soft money was in the 1990s and the 2000 election.

The Future of Campaign Finance Doctrine

McConnell is the rare Supreme Court decision that answers more questions than it opens. *McConnell* completely resolves the debates over the constitutionality of soft money restriction and issue advocacy regulation that marked the last decade. Moreover, the case settles, rather than unsettles, major points of campaign finance doctrine, including, inter alia, the use of a less rigorous standard of review for contribution limitations.

One fundamental question was not raised in *McConnell*: *Buckley*'s determination that expenditure restrictions are subject to strict judicial scrutiny and that the interests in equalising either political influence generally or the financial resources available to competing candidates cannot justify limits on independent spending or candidate spending, including a candidate's spending of his personal wealth. Although Congress is unlikely to adopt spending limits any time soon, more activist states and localities, particularly those that permit voter-initiated legislation, may be tempted to do so. What, if anything, are the implications of *McConnell* for future efforts to limit campaign spending by candidates or independent groups?

There are three possible answers to this question.

First, *McConnell* in no way challenges *Buckley*'s determination that such spending limits are unconstitutional. Indeed, in applying the contribution standard to soft money, the Court emphasised the differences in constitutional burdens posed by contribution, as opposed to expenditure, limitations, as well as the special dangers large contributions may pose for the integrity of the political process.[75]

The second answer, however, is that although *McConnell* carefully limited itself to contribution restrictions, the tenor of the decision may have opened the door to reconsideration of the Court's position on expenditure limitations. The central

[73] See Center for Public Integrity, 'Overall Expenditures Made by 527 Committees,' <http://www.publicintegrity.org/527/> (25 April 2005).

[74] See Center for Public Integrity, A Knott and A Armendariz, '527s Attract New Donors as Others Abandon System in Wake of BCRA,' <http://www.publicintegrity.org/527> (29 August 2004).

[75] 540 US at 134–8.

themes of *McConnell*—that campaign finance restrictions promote democratic values; that election law involves a balancing of competing constitutional concerns; and that a significant measure of deference is due to the political actors who have a greater understanding of the implications of campaign finance practices for the realities of political life—have direct implications for the question of the constitutionality of spending limitations.

The communication of political ideas that results from unlimited campaign spending is surely a crucial democratic concern. Spending allows candidates to make their case, enables challengers to contest incumbents, and provides vital electoral information to voters. But unlimited campaign spending also implicates, and potentially compromises, other vital democratic concerns, including voter equality and competitive elections. Voter equality is a central premise of our democratic system, yet surely it is undermined when some voters and groups of voters, due to their enormous wealth, are able to spend far more campaign money, and potentially have far greater influence on campaign outcomes than most Americans. Electoral competitiveness is also threatened when, as is typically the case in our system, one candidate, usually the incumbent, is able to raise and spend far more money than his opponent. Certainly unlimited expenditures, by enabling incumbents and personally wealthy candidates to spend all the money they can raise, may burden competitiveness by driving up the spending level and thus increasing the amount of money necessary to fund a competitive race. The ability of an incumbent or wealthy candidate to drastically outspend competitors may discourage these competitors from entering the fray at all.

A Court following *McConnell* 's concern with the 'integrity of the [electoral] process' and its recognition that limits on money can actually 'benefit public participation in political debate'[76] might be willing to reopen the question of the constitutionality of spending limits, particularly in situations, like the spending of a candidate's personal wealth, that seem to most directly challenge equality norms while discouraging participation by other candidates.[77] This is not to say that the Court should treat spending limits as deferentially as it now treats contribution limits. Spending limits present constitutional dangers as well as potential benefits. If set too low, they could favor incumbents, and throttle debate. But, following *McConnell*, the Court could take into account the potential for appropriate spending limits to promote public participation and advance democratic values and move away from *Buckley*'s absolute opposition to such limits and their use to promote voter equality and financially fairer contests between candidates. *McConnell* could lead to more of a pragmatic, balancing approach, in which the values to be advanced by a spending limit, and the level of the limit in light of recent spending practices in the relevant jurisdiction, would be taken into account and weighed against the potential harm to robust debate and the opportunity for challengers and interest groups to make their views known. Certainly, following

[76] *Ibid* at 136–7.

[77] Compare *Shrink Missouri*, above n 37, 528 US at 405 (Breyer, J, concurring) (suggesting that *Buckley* might be reconsidered to make 'less absolute the contribution/expenditure line particularly in respect to independently wealthy candidates').

McConnell, the Court should be willing to take seriously evidence presented by Congress or a state or local legislature that a reasonable spending limit can promote fairer contests, encourage participation, and increase voter confidence in the integrity of elections, without abdicating its responsibility to assure that limits do not unduly curtail the opportunity for vigorous debate.

A change in the Court's position on spending limits would also alleviate the dissonance between the Court's general position that only corruption and the appearance of corruption can justify restrictions on the use of campaign money—with corruption defined as a transaction, direct or indirect, between a donor and a candidate or officeholder—and its validation of the limits on the independent expenditure of corporate and union treasury funds.[78]

There is, however, a third possibility—that *McConnell* may hang by a thread. The critical portions of the case were decided by 5–4 votes. Moreover, several justices are plainly sceptical of *Buckley*'s deferential standard of review for contribution restrictions.[79] Justices Scalia and Thomas are ready to overturn *Buckley* on this key point. The other two—Justice Kennedy and Chief Justice Rehnquist—purported to apply *Buckley*, but Justice Kennedy's opinion, which Chief Justice Rehnquist joined—was highly critical of *Buckley*'s deferential standard of review of contribution restrictions.[80] They would require far more evidence of the corrupting effects of a campaign finance practice—and would use a far more constrained definition of corruption—than the majority. These justices are not reconciled to a deferential approach to contribution limits—let alone willing to consider expenditure limits.

The long-term significance of *McConnell* is, thus, both uncertain and hostage to future changes in the composition of the Court. The case could exemplify a pro-reform shift that might culminate in a reconsideration of *Buckley*'s approach to expenditure restrictions. Alternatively, it could be the high-water mark of reform, to be followed, upon a change in the membership of the Court, by a reopening of *Buckley*'s deferential approach to contribution restriction. Or, if the current division on the Court is maintained, it could demonstrate the persistence of *Buckley*'s contribution/expenditure distinction, despite critical academic commentary and the criticism of many members of the Court. That would not be a surprising outcome.

[78] See 540 US at 203. *Austin v Michigan Chamber of Commerce* 494 US 652 (1990).

[79] Four members of the Court—Chief Justice Rehnquist and Justices Kennedy, Scalia and Thomas were also ready to reverse *Austin v Michigan Chamber of Commerce* and invalidate the longstanding federal bans on the use of corporate and union treasury funds in federal elections.

[80] 540 US at 308–12. In his separate dissent, Chief Justice Rehnquist did not criticise *Buckley*, but only *Buckley*'s application to the soft money limits. However, he also joined Justice Kennedy's opinion 'in full.' *Ibid* at 350.

11

The Law of American Party Finance

NATHANIEL PERSILY

FOR THOSE LOOKING into the American system of political party financing from the outside, the combination of labyrinthine rules and amorphous constitutional constructs appears unique and bewildering. The complexity of the rules and impenetrability of the guiding concepts, however, grow from the peculiar place of political parties and political money in the American constitutional design. Indeed, the 'problem' of party financing can serve as a lens through which to view the distinctness of America's regime of political regulation. This chapter attempts to analyse this problem in a way that highlights the unique features both of the constitutional law of American party finance and of the relevant parts of the political system that produce it.

Beginning with an explanation of the constitutional law of American party financing, this chapter describes a continuing clash between grand American values of free speech and clean government. Parties, on the one hand, occupy a constitutional space of sacred First Amendment activity (that is, speech and association), and on the other, they have historically served as repositories for anti-democratic tendencies of corruption, oligarchy, disfranchisement and patronage. Regulations of party financing and the related constitutional jurisprudence have attempted to control the excessive tendencies of parties while, at the same time, they try not to undermine parties' core functions. Second, this chapter explains the difficulty of fitting party financing into the dominant mode of constitutional argument over campaign finance which limits the discussion to a state interest in combating actual or apparent corruption and creates a bright line between contributions and expenditures. It then moves to a description of the structural features of the American party system that present unique difficulties when it comes to regulating party financing. Parties exist vertically at every level of American federalism, horisontally in the executive branch and two houses of the legislature, and functionally in the formal party apparatuses and the less formal groupings of party adherents. Because the American party system is porous and decentralised, regulating party financing poses both insurmountable burdens and unique constitutional risks. The chapter closes with a discussion of whether recent reforms of American party financing have weakened political parties, as many had warned.

Measuring party 'strength'—let alone the effect of reforms on that strength—turns out to be a difficult task. Recent reforms may have weakened parties according to some measures while strengthening them according to others and, perhaps more accurately, have shifted power in the party system away from some incarnations of the party and toward others.

Where We are and How We Got Here: The Law of American Party Finance

To understand the current regime of regulation of party financing one needs to understand the constitutional limits the courts have placed on laws that seek to regulate money flowing into and out of political parties. Although the next section will challenge the reasoning of the relevant caselaw, a few fundamentals are useful to understanding why the current legal regime looks the way it does. The relevant constitutional constraints include the bright line distinction between campaign expenditures and contributions, the treatment of parties as similar to other interest groups, and the overarching importance of preventing actual or apparent corruption as the only court-sanctioned state interests for regulation of campaign finance.

The Expenditure-Contribution Distinction

Since the landmark decision in *Buckley v Valeo*,[1] the courts have drawn a bright line between expenditures, which implicate core political speech and receive the strictest constitutional scrutiny, and contributions, which do not. Constraining an individual's expenditure of money restricts the actual amount of speech uttered, the argument goes, and independent expenditures do not pose the same threat of corruption as do financial transactions between a contributor and a candidate. In contrast, the Court has considered contribution restrictions as primarily implicating the freedom of association between the contributor and candidate and implicating speech by proxy. In other words, contributions enable the candidate's speech, but by themselves contributions only express a generalised message of support ('I support X candidate'). That message remains intact so long as one retains the ability to contribute something to the candidate, and the Court has not viewed such a message as amplified by the amount an individual could contribute. Finally, contribution restrictions target the interaction between a contributor and a candidate and are therefore better tailored toward preventing corruption or its appearance than are expenditure restrictions. Contribution limits prevent large amounts of money from changing hands and reduce the possibility that campaign contributions will buy political favours (that is, quid pro quos).

[1] 424 US 1 (1976) Much of the foregoing discussion is drawn from N Persily, 'Contested Concepts in Campaign Finance', (2003) 6 *University of Pennsylvania Journal of Constitutional Law* 607.

Political parties can serve as contributors, recipients of contributions or as organisations that make expenditures. Consistent with the general constitutional distinction, the courts have upheld regulations of both contributions to the political party or contributions from a political party to a candidate, while striking down regulations of party expenditures.[2] However, because some party expenditures are not truly independent—that is, some kind of joint agreement or concerted action often exists between the party and a candidate—the courts treat those 'coordinated expenditures' as if they were contributions, which can therefore be regulated. As will be discussed in the next section, political parties pose unique conceptual difficulties for the anticorruption rationale that undergirds American campaign finance jurisprudence. Suffice it to say for the moment, however, that the Court has viewed parties as potentially corrupting of candidates, as possibly corrupted by contributions, but as non-corrupting when they spend money independently.

A special corporate and union exception exists to the general rule dividing unprotected contributions from protected expenditures. Because of judicial recognition of their potential to corrupt the democratic process, corporate and union treasury money can be banned outright—that is, the Constitution does not prevent the state from banning contributions or even expenditures of corporate or union treasury funds.[3] Therefore, the Court has upheld laws that ban corporations from using their treasury money to make contributions to candidates or parties and upheld laws that ban corporations from making expenditures on candidate-specific advertising close to an election.

The Primacy of the State Interest in Combating Corruption or its Appearance

Within these constitutional guidelines, the state can limit contributions to candidates and parties as well as limit independent expenditures by corporations and unions for two reasons only: to combat corruption or the appearance of corruption. From *Buckley v Valeo* to *McConnell v FEC*, the Supreme Court has never sanctioned alternative interests—beyond the actual or apparent corruption rationales—as constitutional justifications for regulating campaign finance. What the Court has meant by 'corruption,' however, has vacillated somewhat over time and between contexts. *Buckley* clarified that this notion of corruption included political quid pro quos but extended beyond simple bribery by way of campaign contributions. It extends to 'undue influence on an officeholder's judgment'[4] as manifested in 'the broader threat from politicians too compliant with the wishes of large contributors.'[5]

[2] See *Colorado Republican Federal Campaign Committee v FEC* 533 US 431 (2001) (*Colorado Republican II*); *Colorado Republican Federal Campaign Committee v FEC* 518 US 604 (1996) (*Colorado Republican I*).

[3] See *Austin v Mich Chamber of Commerce* 494 US 652, 660 (1990); *FEC v Beaumont* 123 SCt 2200 (2003); *McConnell v FEC* 124 SCt 619, 677 (2003). But see *First National Bank of Boston v Bellotti* 435 US 765 (1978) (striking down limits on corporate expenditures in a campaign to defeat a popular initiative).

[4] *Colorado Republican II*, 533 US at 441.

[5] *Nixon v Shrink Mo Gov't PAC* 528 US 377, 388–9 (2000) (quoting *Buckley v Valeo* 424 US at 28).

'Corruption is a subversion of the political process. Elected officials are influenced to act contrary to their obligations of office by the prospect of financial gain to themselves or infusions of money into their campaigns.'[6] 'Just as troubling to a functioning democracy as classic quid pro quo corruption is the danger that officeholders will decide issues not on the merits or the desires of their constituencies, but according to the wishes of those who have made large financial contributions valued by the officeholder.'[7] In the special case of corporate expenditures, corruption has expanded to include, 'the corrosive and distorting effects of immense aggregations of wealth that are accumulated with the help of the corporate form and that have little or no correlation to the public's support for the corporation's political ideas.'[8]

The anticorruption interest is not limited to actual evidence of these modes of political distortion or undue influence; it extends to the appearance of corruption as well. In the *Buckley* Court's words,

> of almost equal concern as the danger of actual quid pro quo arrangements is the impact of the appearance of corruption stemming from public awareness of the opportunities for abuse inherent in a regime of large individual financial contributions.'[9]

For example, the sale of access for campaign cash, regardless of the effect on actual policy or votes, creates an appearance that 'money buys influence'[10] even if the dots between a campaign contribution and a representative's vote cannot be connected. The state has an interest in avoiding these ugly appearances because 'public awareness' of the mere opportunity for influence could erode public trust in representatives and representative institutions:

> Congress could legitimately conclude that the avoidance of the appearance of improper influence "is also critical . . . if confidence in the system of representative [g]overnment is not to be eroded to a disastrous extent."[11]

In furtherance of these interests in combating actual or apparent corruption, Congress enacted and later amended the *Federal Election Campaign Act* (FECA) and then two years ago enacted the *Bipartisan Campaign Reform Act* of 2002 (BCRA) to close loopholes that were discovered or carved into the earlier law. The history of American campaign finance law can be seen as a series of stages of legislative innovation, followed by judicial and sometimes administrative modification, accompanied or succeeded by exploration on the part of entrepreneurs seeking to get around these new legal constraints, followed by another round of

[6] *Federal Election Comm'n v National Conservative Political Action Comm* 470 US 480, 497 (1985).
[7] *McConnell*, 124 SCt at 666.
[8] *Austin v Michigan Chamber of Commerce* 494 US 652, 660 (1990).
[9] *Buckley*, 424 US at 27.
[10] *McConnell*, 124 SCt at 666.
[11] *Buckley*, 424 US at 26–7 (quoting *Civil Service Comm'n v Letter Carriers*, 413 US 548, 565 (1973)). See also *McConnell*, 124 SCt at 660–2.

legislation to plug up loopholes discovered or created in the extant regulatory regime. The most recent round of reforms focused on political parties, which had become the avenue of choice for otherwise prohibited contributions to candidates, particularly from corporations, unions and wealthy individuals.

The Bipartisan Campaign Reform Act (BCRA)

Acting within the constitutional constraints described above, Congress passed and the President signed the *Bipartisan Campaign Reform Act* of 2002. The limits entailed in the new law are depicted in Table I. One of the law's primary targets was so called 'soft money,' which refers principally to corporate and union treasury money, as well as large contributions from wealthy individuals, that influenced federal elections through contributions to political parties. Political parties spent soft money on party-building activities, which often included candidate-specific television advertisements that promoted favoured candidates or attacked their opponents. BCRA attempted to choke off corporate and union treasury money from the national parties, limiting both the parties' acceptance and spending of such funds, while also ensuring that all contributions by individuals and interest groups (known as 'hard money') would be made within strict limits.

As it banned soft money, BCRA raised the hard money limits. An individual can now contribute $2000 per election (that is, for both primary and general election) to a candidate; $25,000 per calendar year to a national party committee, and $10,000 per year to a state party committee's federal account (that is, the state party's trough of money used for federal election purposes). However, an individual can only give $95,000 in the aggregate over two years to federal candidates and parties combined. Political Action Committees (PACs), which are interest groups that ordinarily organise to support multiple candidates in an election year, can give $5000 per election to a Senate, House, or Presidential candidate, $15,000 per calendar year to a national party committee, and $5000 per calendar year to a state party committee's federal account.

In addition to these restrictions on the sources and amount of money that can flow into the party, the law places limits on how much money can flow out of the party to the candidate. National party committees can give $35,000 per year (adjusted for inflation) to a Senate candidate, and $5000 per election to each House candidate and Presidential candidate. State parties can contribute $5000 per election to House, Senate, and Presidential candidates. However, these contribution limits are largely meaningless, since most party activity in a candidate's campaign is done through coordinated expenditures, which are limited through complex inflation adjusted formulas pegged to 1974 dollar limits, or independent expenditures which are unlimited. For a given Senate race, for example, both the national party committee and the state party committees can make coordinated expenditures in an amount totaling two cents (adjusted for inflation) times the voting age population of the state. The limits range from $74,620 (for the 10 least populated states) to $1,944,896 for California. Such expenditures are effectively

Regulated Activity	**National Party Committees**	**State Party Committee (federal accounts)**
Personal Contribution Limit to Party Organisation	$25,000/year for each national committee[a]	$10,000/year to each state or local party committee[a]
Aggregate Personal Contribution Limits	$57,500 every two years, less the amount donated to PACs[a]	$37,500 every two years[a]
Political Action Committee (PAC) Contribution Limit to Party Organisation	$15,000/year	$5000/year
Source Restrictions	corporations and unions: from segregated funds (PACs) only	corporations and unions: from segregated funds (PACs) only
Contribution Limit: Party Organisation to Senate Candidate	$35,000/election[a] from national party committee and Senate campaign committee combined; additional $5,000/election from Congressional campaign committee	$5000/election[a]
Contribution Limit: Organisation to House Candidate	$5,000/election[a] by each national party organisation (national party committee, Senate campaign committee and Congressional campaign committee)	$5000/election[a]
Independent Expenditure Limit	Unlimited	Unlimited
Coordinated Expenditure Limit: Organisation to Presidential Candidate in General Election	approximately $16 million for the 2004 election	(state coordinated expenditures are deducted from national party coordinated expenditure limit and must occur with national party committee permission)
Coordinated Expenditure Limit: Organisation to Senate Candidate	two cents[a] times the voting population of the state (range from $74,620 to $2,000,000, for the 2004 election)	two cents[a] times the voting population of the state (range from $74,620 to $2,000,000, for the 2000 election)
Coordinated Expenditure Limit: Organisation to House Candidate	$37,310[a] for 2004 election ($74,620 for states with only one representative)	$37,310[a] for 2004 election ($74,620 for states with only one representative)

[a] Contribution limits for individuals and parties are adjusted annually for inflation.

TABLE I. *Contribution and Expenditure Limits for Federal Races*

contributions since the party and the candidate agree on how the money should be spent. Furthermore, even once the coordinated spending limit is reached, both state and national parties can still make unlimited independent expenditures for the benefit of their candidates, owing to the Supreme Court's decision referenced above that held such expenditures as protected by the First Amendment.

Doctrinal Difficulties

This set of somewhat bizarre and incongruous regulations flows from the constitutional doctrine described above. On the one hand, parties are like candidates, such that contributions to them can be regulated in order to prevent corruption. On the other hand, parties are like outside groups in that their contributions may corrupt candidates, but their independent expenditures are uncorrupting, unregulable, and constitutionally protected. But what does it mean for a party to corrupt a candidate? And how might a contributor corrupt a party? These are difficult, but central, questions that the courts have only begun to answer. Three different notions tying corruption to political parties have emerged in the caselaw—corruption of the party, corruption by the party, and corruption through the party. Figure A depicts these concepts graphically. The solid arrows represent contributions or coordinate expenditures, the dotted arrows represent independent expenditures.

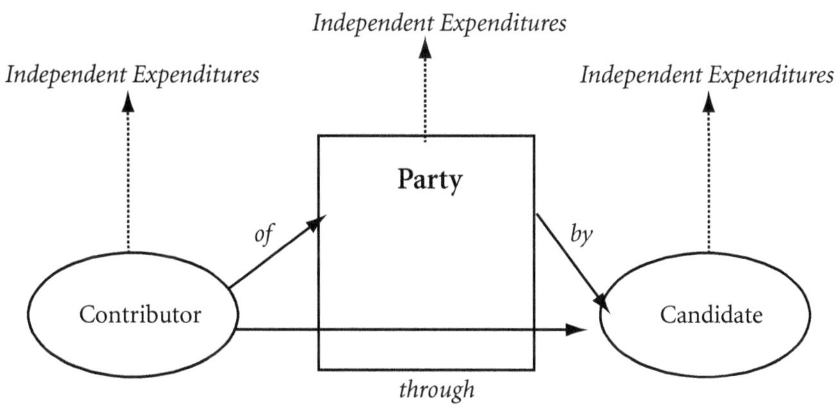

FIGURE A: Corruption of, by, and through the Party

Corruption of the Party

Corruption of the party occurs when contributors gain influence over a party due to their campaign contribution or expenditure. If the state has an anticorruption interest in regulating contributions to a political party for the party's own benefit, it must be because the party, like a candidate or officeholder, controls some measure of state power that can be used for the contributor's benefit. Just as an officeholder can help pass a bill, get someone a patronage appointment or contract, or otherwise dole out official favours, so too a party and its leaders, the argument goes, can use their formal and informal powers to pay back contributors for their generosity. It is essential to understand that this type of corruption does not depend on how the political party spends the money it receives. The assumption here is that the mere donation of funds to the party will make the party beholden to the contributor and likely to use its influence to pay the contributor back.

Assuming for the moment that 'the party' is a definable and identifiable entity, what does it mean for a contributor to have 'undue influence' over the party? Of course, the notion of undue influence is a problem, in general, for campaign finance law, because it assumes that a baseline amount of 'due' influence exists.[12] Undue influence does not mean merely unequal influence: candidates' family, friends, and constituents, let alone the leaders of industry and interest groups, will have greater influence than the average voter. Rather, in the rhetoric of campaign finance, influence becomes 'undue' when the recipient feels beholden to the contributor *because of* the money the contributor donates to the campaign.

In the case of corruption of a political party, though, the concept of undue influence becomes even more problematic. How much influence should an average voter or party member have over a party? How do we know when a contribution has purchased excessive influence? And most important, how do we know when and how the party has paid back the contributor? The paradigmatic case of undue influence over a candidate comes in the form of money for votes on bills. When it comes to undue influence over a party, the forms of possible 'payback' depend on the dimension of the party to which one pays attention. In theory, the party organisation could pay the contributor back by giving the contributor access and influence over party operations, by allowing the contributor to place a thumb on the scales when it comes to nominating decisions, or by changing a platform plank according to the contributor's wishes—eg, dropping handgun reform from the platform once the National Rifle Association (NRA) ponies up.

When reformers concentrate on corruption of a political party though, they usually focus on the party-in-government. Under this view, the party pays the contributor back by using its governmental arm to push through or obstruct legislation, redirect patronage, or otherwise make use of the formal machinery of government to satisfy contributor demands. A contributor gives money to the chairman of the Democratic National Committee (DNC), for example, and in return, he urges Democratic members of Congress to vote in certain ways, telling them it would be good for the financial health of the party. There might be several variants of this type of party corruption, but the formula is simple: contributor gives to party leader, party leader coerces/urges representatives in government to cater to contributor's wishes.

Sometimes the representative from the party organisation might be an unelected official, such as the leader of the DNC, but the leader could also be an elected official, such as the President or the members of Congress that lead their parties' respective congressional campaign committees. In return for the contribution to the party organisation, not only might the elected officials, who lead the party, pay the contributor back with their own votes etc, but they might be able to use the

[12] See S Issacharoff and P Karlan, 'The Hydraulics of Campaign Finance Reform' (1999) 77 *Texas Law Review* 1705.

carrots and sticks that come with their leadership position to coerce their colleagues to satisfy the contributor's demands. Indeed, contributors might find that contributions to party leaders are the most efficient way to gain influence over legislation. If a contributor is concerned about obstructing certain pieces of legislation, why should she waste time giving small contributions to many candidates when she could place a large cheque in the hands of someone who controls committee assignments for half the House? Such contributions have presumably become more effective in recent years as party leadership in the Congress has became more hierarchical and power more concentrated among a few members.

Corruption by the Party

Corruption by the party occurs when a party uses its financial clout so as to gain undue influence over its candidates or officeholders. Corruption by the political party entails a wholly different dynamic and set of concerns than corruption of the political party. In this context, the constitutional debate revolves around undue influence of party leaders over members of the party-in-government due to party leaders' control of party contributions to candidates. In other words, the leaders' control of party pursestrings allows them to extort votes out of incumbent officials who depend on party money to run an effective campaign. Reformers point to this type of corruption to justify limits on party contributions to the candidate or expenditures on behalf of the candidate.

As the focus shifts from the contributor's corruption of the party to the party's corruption of its candidates, parties assume the qualities of interest groups, corporations, or other outsiders with the potential to corrupt the candidates beholden to them. The idea of party corruption of candidates may seem a bit bizarre at first, but the view has gained several adherents at the Federal Election Commission (FEC), in the judiciary, and among good government groups. As Justice Stevens explained in his dissent in *Colorado Republican I*, the 'interdependency [between a party and a candidate] creates a special danger that the party—or the persons who control the party—will abuse the influence it has over the candidate by virtue of its power to spend.'[13] In describing and agreeing with the FEC's position in *Colorado Republican II*, the dissenting judge in the Tenth Circuit panel explained, 'limits on party contributions are necessary to prevent unscrupulous party officials from furthering their pet interests, thereby corrupting or appearing to corrupt the legislative process.'[14] And as one Supreme Court amicus brief put it in *Colorado Republican II*:

> When individual members of Congress become increasingly powerful within the institution, not by virtue of their legislative abilities and achievements, but instead because of their control of the campaign spending decisions of the political parties, there is a potential for a corruption of the democratic processes. Individual members of Congress may become afraid to buck the pet interests of individual party leaders, even when the party itself lacks a firm position on the issue.[15]

[13] *Colorado Republican I*, 518 US at 648 (Stevens, J dissenting).
[14] *FEC v Colorado Republican Federal Campaign Committee* 213 F3d 1221, 1244 (10th Cir 2000).
[15] Amicus Brief of Brennan Center for Justice at NYU School of Law, *Colorado Republican II* at 27.

Under this view, the state's interest in preventing party corruption of candidates justifies setting limits that force candidates to fund their campaigns from individuals and organisations. Just as one corporation, interest group, or contributor should not have undue influence over a candidate, the argument goes, so too the financial voice of the party should not be the loudest one the candidate hears.

This view of parties as just another type of organisation with excessive influence due to campaign contributions has some obvious problems. Unlike other interest groups, parties *exist* to have influence over their candidates. Campaign finance issues aside, political parties remain the principal organising entity both for elections and for legislatures. Candidates usually must be nominated by the party members or the party organisation, they run under the party label in the general election, and once elected, they become part of the party's caucus in the legislature, which itself organises leadership positions, committees etc along party lines. If parties' undue influence over their candidates is a problem, then parties, not money, is the problem.

To understand the deficiencies of the corruption-by-parties argument, one must first realise that the argument does not depend at all on the source of the party's funds. In other words, a party can corrupt a candidate under this theory even if its funds are 'clean'—part of a state funding scheme, a bake sale or whatever. All that matters is that the party has 'too much influence' because of the money it might contribute to a candidate's campaign. Undue influence manifests itself when representatives vote with the party, subordinating their conscience or constituents to the campaign cash value of a party vote. Defection from the party line, under this view, entails more than the cost of losing favour in the party's eyes; it comes with the risk that the party might withhold funds from a reelection campaign or even worse, throw its financial weight behind an opponent in the primary.

Corruption through the Party

Most reformers would argue the real problem with parties and money is not corruption of or by the party, but corruption through the party: that is, the use of parties as mere conduits for the transfer of cash from contributor to candidate. By treating the parties as mere bank accounts into which contributors deposit and candidates withdraw, contributors use parties to get around the restrictions on individual contributions to candidates. In both *Colorado Republican II*[16] and most recently in *McConnell v FEC* the Court found the conduit corruption argument to be the most persuasive justification for regulating party participation in the funding of campaigns.

The concept of conduit corruption is not uniquely applicable to political parties. In theory, any individual or organisation could serve as a transit point for contributions en route from contributor to candidate. The Court in *Colorado Republican II* said as much:

[16] See *Colorado Republican II* 533 US at 452–4.

> [W]hether they like it or not, [parties] act as agents for spending on behalf of those who seek to produce obligated officeholders . . . [T]his party role, which functionally unites parties with other self-interested political actors . . . accordingly, provides good reason to view limits on coordinated spending by parties through the same lens applied to such spending by donors, like PACs, that can use parties as conduits for contributions meant to place candidates under obligation.[17]

In fact, because of their uniquely close relationship to candidates, parties are in the best position to serve as conduits for contributions. They have developed elaborate tallying systems and various other legal equivalents to winks and nods to keep track of which party funds were raised by and are therefore deserved by which candidates.[18] It would be difficult to disagree with the proposition that insofar as direct contributions corrupt a candidate, indirect contributions going through a party conduit can do so almost as well.

The basic problem with the conduit corruption argument is conceptual, not empirical, however. It runs into difficulties when it is used to justify restrictions on the flow of money both into and out of the party conduit. Once the flow of money is restricted at one end of the party conduit, the state's interest in combating corruption at the other end vanishes. A simple example might help prove the point. Suppose a campaign finance law limits individuals to contributing $2000 to candidates and $8000 to a party and limits parties to contributing $40,000 to candidates. The total amount of potential corruption of a candidate per donor would be $10,000 ($2000 + $8000). However, because the party is limited in how much money it can reroute, only five donors could achieve that level of corruption (5 × $8000 = $40,000). After the fifth donor gives as much as he can, the sixth donor (and every donor thereafter) can only give $2000; any money given to a party that has maxed out its contribution to the candidate is wasted as far as the contributor is concerned and free of corrupting potential as far as the candidate is concerned. The cap on party contributions, therefore, forces donors to compete against each other to squeeze through the party conduit to get to the candidate. This competition would occur even if the $8000 limit on contributions to political parties were to disappear.[19]

Where the Justices Stand

Three basic schools of thought have emerged on the Court when it comes to fitting parties into the corruption-preoccupied framework of the constitutional law of party finance. The prevailing view of Justices David Souter, Sandra Day O'Connor, and Stephen Breyer treats political parties as just another species of interest groups, deserving no special constitutional protections nor subject to special burdens. Thus, the decisive plurality on the Court has interpreted the First Amendment as guaranteeing a party's right to make unlimited independent

[17] *Colorado Republican II* 533 US at 452.

[18] *Colorado Republican II* 533 US at 453, 457–60.

[19] Although, then one individual could potentially give a $40,000 contribution to the party that would then be forwarded on to the candidate.

expenditures in support of a candidate[20] while allowing restrictions on contributions from the party to the candidate that serve to combat real or apparent corruption.[21] For these three, the danger of corruption lies principally in the use of parties as passthroughs for otherwise prohibited contributions to candidates—'conduit corruption' or 'corruption through the party.' Under this view, parties exist as bank accounts or, less affectionately, money launderers: contributors deposit and candidates withdraw.

The two other camps on the Court treat political parties as having a special role in campaigns and a unique relationship to candidates that earns them different treatment than that for other groups. For Chief Justice William Rehnquist and Justices Anthony Kennedy, Clarence Thomas and Anthony Scalia, parties' special relationship or the 'practical identity of interests'[22] between parties and candidates argues for greater First Amendment protection of political parties, since their speech is constitutionally indistinguishable from that of their candidates. As Justice Thomas put it: 'The very aim of a political party is to influence its candidate's stance on issues and, if the candidate takes office or is reelected, his votes.'[23] Somewhat in tension with this position, those four tend to support the idea that money passed through the party is cleansed of corrupting potential because parties sever the link between contributor and candidate[24]—that is, they dispute the idea of conduit corruption or corruption through the party. If officeholders look with favour on those who contribute to their party, they do so not for their own benefit but for the 'good of the team,' under this view. That variant on the traditional quid pro quo arrangement is sufficiently attenuated in the party context to fall beyond the notion of corruption, these Justices argue.

For Justices Stevens and Ginsburg, in contrast, the special nature of parties justifies greater regulation given the unique corruption risks the party-officeholder relationship poses. A contributor may more efficiently gain disproportionate influence over the policy-making process by giving a large contribution to a party at the behest of a party leader who can guarantee to whip groups of votes on the contributors' favourite bills. Indeed, under this view the party's financial clout—whatever the original source of its funds—poses a problem of undue influence of the party over its candidates: that is, corruption by the party. The awesome financial power of parties, under this view, threatens the independence of legislators and can tip the balance in favour or against a decision to take official action on legislation. With the power to pull the plug on a candidate's campaign by refusing to spend money in the race may come the power to induce an elected official to

[20] See *Colorado Republican I*, 518 US 604.

[21] See *Colorado Republican II*, 533 US 431.

[22] *Colorado Republican I*, 518 US at 630 (Kennedy, J, concurring in the judgment).

[23] *Colorado Republican I*, 518 US at 646 (Thomas, J, concurring in judgment and dissenting in part).

[24] See *ibid* ('American political parties, generally speaking, have numerous members with a wide variety of interests . . . Consequently, the influence of any one person or the importance of any single issue within a political party is significantly diffused. For this reason . . . campaign funds donated by parties are considered to be some of "the cleanest money in politics."' (quoting J Bibby, 'Campaign Finance Reform' (1983) 1 *Commonsense* 10)).

toe the party line when her conscience or constituents might lead to a different result.

Who and What is the Party

The American party finance 'problem' is as much a product of constitutional structure as it is constitutional doctrine. The party system mirrors the political system in its division among branches and levels of government. It also is archetypically American in the diffusion of power not only among the formal institutions but also among less formal groups in American civil society. Whereas in other countries one might more easily point to *the* party leader or even the party's headquarters, in the American system parties exist as networks of groups and institutions inside and outside of government. One of the goals of this discussion of party multidimensionality and campaign finance is to emphasise the often-made argument that entrepreneurial campaign contributors will always find some way to direct money into some part of the party system despite particular regulations. In listing the many dimensions and possible entities eligible to be called 'the party,' however, the discussion also draws attention to the possible tradeoffs of a campaign finance system that directs money toward one type or dimension of a party and away from others.[25] The multiple dimensions of parties are depicted in Table II.

VO Key's Three Dimensions of Party

Political scientists have often described American political parties as consisting of three parts: the party organisation, the party-in-government, and the party-in-the-electorate.[26] A party organisation, such as the Democratic National Committee, consists of professional political workers whose job is to build the party and further its interest both during and between elections. The party-in-government refers to elected or appointed officials at all levels of government, such as the members of the House Democratic Caucus and Republican Conference or even the President himself. Finally, the party-in-the-electorate refers to the party rank-and-file whose major activity in relation to the party is voting in primary elections, supporting the party's candidates in the general election, and maybe giving a contribution to the party every once in a while. As Key himself recognised, no subpart of the party is hermetically sealed from the other. All members of the party organisation and party-in government are also members of the party-in-the-electorate, for example.

Campaign finance reformers are principally concerned with restricting the influence of 'outsiders,' including members of the party-in-the-electorate, on the

[25] Much of the forgoing discussion is drawn from N Persily, 'Soft Parties and Strong Money' (2004) 3 *Election Law Journal* 315.

[26] See VO Key, *Politics, Parties, and Pressure Groups* (5th ed, New York TY Crowell, 1964) 163–5; N Persily and BE Cain, 'The Legal Status of Political Parties: A Reassessment of Competing Paradigms, (2000) 100 *Columbia Law Review* 775, 778–9.

party-in-government. The party-in-the-electorate or some subsection of it, under this view, can be a source of undue influence through excessive contributions. Those who fear corruption-of-the-party or corruption-by-the-party seek to limit the electorate's (and others') financial influence over the organisation or the organisation's influence over the party-in-government. What might be described as the purist reform position, tends to argue that the influence of any arm of the party over another should never be due to the exercise of financial clout. Votes, persuasion and mobilisation are the proper tools of intraparty influence; money is not.

The Federalism Dimension

The existence of different levels of government and corresponding elections presents formidable obstacles to the effective regulation of political party financing. Because federal election law regulates the financing of federal elections, the mere existence of state elections and parties creates inevitable difficulties for any federal regulatory regime. Parties in all three of VO Key's forms exist at the federal, state, and local level, and each level of the party can influence elections in another. The daunting challenge presented to any scheme of federal regulation is to regulate each level of the party, but only insofar as that level of the party participates or affects federal elections.[27]

Indeed, the 'federalism problem' helped puncture the soft money loophole into the pre-BCRA campaign finance regime. Several states allowed corporate and union contributions to state political parties, which federal law generally prohibited to candidates for federal office and which the national parties could use only for certain 'party building' activities. Thus, for state elections, permissive state laws applied, and for federal elections, the more restrictive federal law might apply. The question then arose how to classify state party expenditures that helped the party in all of its manifestations. Because state parties wear different hats depending on whether they are trying to influence a federal or state election, how does one know which hat they are wearing (and how they should be regulated) when their actions assist all components of the party at the same time? The existence of federal, state and local parties—each with a distinct claim to First Amendment protection[28]—necessarily leads to over and underinclusive regulation of each dimension of a political party. No law can be written with sufficient specificity such that it regulates parties in one electoral sphere without somehow impeding their activities in another one, or such that it captures the universe of

[27] See N Persily, 'Soft Money and Slippery Slopes' (2002) 1 *Election Law Journal* 401, 407 (describing the constraints on Congress' power to regulate state and federal elections).

[28] The procession downward from federal to state to local parties does not imply that a 'lower' level is subordinate to an upper level. In fact, each level of the party has First Amendment rights that can be asserted against the other. A local party that disagrees with a law sanctioned by the state party still could have a constitutional right to opt out. See *Eu v San Francisco County Democratic Comm*, 489 US 214 (1989). Conversely, state and local parties cannot force the national party to change its rules to accommodate them. See *Democratic Party of the United States v Wisconsin* 450 US 107 (1981); *Cousins v Wigoda* 419 US 477 (1975).

contributions and expenditures that a party can make even when it is acting within the relevant electoral context.

With respect to soft money and state parties, the most recent law (BCRA) errs on the side of overinclusion—meaning that in its attempt to regulate state parties in their federal capacity it necessarily regulates them in their state capacity. For example, a state party's voter registration and turnout efforts, as well as the salary of its employees that spend at least 25 per cent of their time on federal elections, must be paid for with money subject to federally imposed limits. For some state parties, such as those that have no competitive federal race on the ballot, all such activity will necessarily be exercised in the parties' state electoral capacity. Nevertheless, because such activities may generally affect the fates of federal candidates appearing on the ballot, the law regulates them or else all money banned to the federal parties would simply move toward the state parties.

The Separation of Powers Dimension

Just as parties can be conceptualised 'vertically' along the federalism dimension so too can they be conceptualised 'horisontally' along the dimension of separation of powers. At both the state and federal level and among the party as an organisation, in government and in the electorate,[29] the party adopts different personae depending on the branch of government in which it is operating or which it hopes to influence. We can therefore conceive of parties in the executive and in each house of a legislature.[30]

This feature of the American party system is probably so obvious that it does not warrant extensive elaboration. In each house of Congress, the parties organise themselves into respective caucuses, and those parties-in-the-legislature have corresponding campaign organisations, such as the Democratic Congressional Campaign Committee (DCCC) and Democratic Senatorial Campaign Committee (DSCC). Only the party with control of the Presidency can be said to have a party-in-the-executive, but once the presidential campaign begins, the separation of powers becomes relevant in distinguishing the party organisations dedicated to the presidential election from those committed to electing partisans to the House and Senate. Analogous institutions and organisations exist at the state level among governors, assemblies and state senates.

Just as they coordinate to pass legislation, so too the separate party organisations cooperate when it comes to campaigns. Each party organisation is aware of the activities of another and sometimes uses the same consultants, pollsters and

[29] Maybe less so with respect to the electorate. Separation of powers affects the party-in-the electorate insofar as the constituencies for elections to each branch of government are different. In other words, the party-in-the-electorate for a US Senate race are all the party members in a given state, while for a given House race the party-in-the-electorate is limited to the party members in the particular district.

[30] Perhaps one could conceive of parties in the judiciary as well, especially in states that elect judges. Even among appointed judges (at both the federal and state level) one might say that judges remain tied to a political party and could be influenced by the party. However, the 'party-in-the-judiciary' is probably not relevant to a discussion of campaign finance.

advertising agencies. However, their missions are distinct: to elect as many party members to their respective branches. Therefore, each campaign committee has its own accounts, websites, ad campaigns, etc, and each provides an opportunity for separate influence by the same pool of contributors.

To grapple with this multiplication of subparty institutions, the BCRA sets limits on an individual's total contributions to national party committees. An individual can give no more than $25,000 per year to national party committees and no more than a total of $57,500 over two years to all national party committees and other multicandidate political committees (including state party committees) combined. Were it not for the aggregate limit, individuals could evade the limits by contributing to each party committee in each branch and level of government throughout the 50 states.

The Formal/Functional Dimension

A tour through most college government textbooks would provide the information necessary to define the dimensions of party discussed thus far. In the context of campaign finance, however, unique party institutions have emerged with the specific goal of furthering a party's election-financing goals while not being recognised as the party itself. This dimension—which I am calling the formal/functional dimension—is the one that gives would-be reformers fits and that has spawned a cottage industry of campaign finance lawyers. It also has become increasingly relevant over the past year as the Federal Election Commission (FEC) has attempted to interpret what types of organisations are subject to the limits placed by the new law.

The formal/functional dimension arrays party institutions according to whether they take the form of a party, per se, or merely perform campaign-related functions that assist or advantage the party. This is the most difficult dimension to describe, but it is also the most important when it comes to assessing the effect of certain reform proposals. One of the principal criticisms of the BCRA is that it will move contributions away from the formal party apparatus and toward less accountable, less transparent, and less visible organisations. At least four types of organisations can serve the functions of the party without actually 'being' the party: multicandidate political committees (PACs), 501(c)(3) charitable organisations, 501(c)(4) lobbying organisations, and 527 political organisations. Merely listing the sections of the tax code associated with these organisations hints at the complexity of describing them and at their loophole-defining quality. Any number of what most observers would call 'interest groups' can reconfigure themselves to fit into one of these classifications. What makes them relevant for our purposes, however, is the opportunity they present to parties and their members to evade restrictions on the parties themselves while still achieving the parties' campaign objectives.

Multicandidate political committees (PACs) are the easiest to understand, in part because they are defined by the campaign finance laws as opposed to the tax code. Simply put, they are organisations that have registered with the FEC, have received contributions from more than 50 persons and have contributed to five or more candidates for federal office.[31] Corporations and unions can establish PACs, pay their overhead costs and then have a designated list of individuals contribute to them to constitute a separate, segregated fund, that is, distinct from the corporation or union's treasury money. In theory, PACs are the campaign arms of issue-specific interest groups seeking to elect candidates favourable to their cause. In reality, PACs can become extensions of the candidates and parties themselves. Elected officials, particularly party leaders and prospective presidential candidates, establish so called 'Leadership PACs' to make contributions and expenditures to benefit their preferred candidates, including their own candidacy.

Only some 501(c)(3) and 501(c)(4) organisations are relevant to elections and campaign finance, making regulation of those that are active in campaigns somewhat difficult. 501(c)(3) organisations are formed for religious, educational, charitable, or scientific purposes, donations to them are tax deductible, and the law prohibits them from supporting or opposing candidates in a campaign. 501(c)(4) organisations are different in that contributions to them are not tax deductible, they are generally formed to conduct lobbying activities, and they are allowed to participate in campaigns if they pay taxes on their campaign expenditures. Both types of organisations are allowed to receive unlimited contributions from individuals.

527 organisations differ from 501 organisations in that a 527 (sometimes called a 'Stealth PAC') is created specifically for the purpose of influencing elections. Most PACs are also 527 organisations. However, some 527 organisation do not register as a PAC, and therefore cannot support or oppose specific candidates. Like a 501(c)(4), contributions to a 527 are not tax deductible and they are potentially unlimited. Until recently, 527 organisations did not even need to disclose who gave them money.

Space considerations prevent a detailed analysis of the differences between these organisations.[32] However, the relevant similarity for purposes of campaign finance is the engagement of these organisations in advocacy—particularly television commercials, voter registration, and get out the vote efforts—that might affect the outcome of an election. Each organisation can perform some of the functions normally attributed to political parties. A PAC can collect contributions and redistribute them to a party's candidates. A 527 organisation can collect contributions and spend them to promote a political party—sometimes, as with Tom DeLay's 'Republican Majority Issues Committee,' not even feigning any distance between the organisation and the party. A 501(c)(4) organisation can run ads promoting the party, perhaps incurring taxes for its expenditures. And a 501(c)(3)

[31] 2 USC s 441a(a)(4) (2002).

[32] Two useful publications that analyse the differences are Common Cause, *Under the Radar: The Attack of the 'Stealth PACs' on our Nation's Elections* (2000), and JE Kindell and JF Reilly, *Election Year Issues* (2001) (available at http://www.irs.gov/pub/irs-utl/topici02.pdf). Readers eager to get a sense of the complexity of these organisations may want to take a look at DL Simmons, 'An Essay on Federal Income Taxation and Campaign Finance Reform' (2002) 54 *Florida Law Review* 1. Merely printing out the article proves the point: the 'essay' is 118 pages long with 774 footnotes.

organisation, as well as all of the organisations listed above, can run ads on issues and promote causes that might be salient to a given campaign and indirectly help a party.

Under current Supreme Court precedent, organisations other than unions or corporations have an unconditional right to make expenditures supporting the election of candidates.[33] To the degree the BCRA restricts electioneering by these independent groups—a somewhat open question—it comes very close, if not stepping over, the constitutional line. It is still too soon to tell whether the BCRA 527 loophole will merely replace the FECA soft money loophole as the way to evade the source and amount restrictions under the statute. The FEC has punted, for the moment, on an interpretation of BCRA that would settle this controversy.

Formal

		PARTY-IN-GOVERNMENT	*PARTY ORGANISATION*	*PARTY-IN-THE-ELECTORATE*
FEDERAL	Senate	Senate party caucuses	Party Senatorial Campaign Committees	Party members in each state
	House	House party caucuses	Party Congressional Campaign Committees	Party members in each congressional district
	Executive	President and cabinet	National Party Convention; National Party Committee (eg, DNC)	Party members throughout nation for presidential elections
STATE	Upper House	State senate (upper house) caucuses	State senate party campaign committee	Party members in each senate district
	Lower House	State assembly (lower house) caucuses	State assembly party campaign committee	Party members in each assembly district
	Executive	Governor and other elected and appointed members of executive branch	State party organisation	Party members in each state
LOCAL		Local elected officials	Local party organisation	Party members in each locality

[33] See *FEC v Massachusetts Citizens for Life* 479 US 238 (1986).

Functional

		PARTY-IN-GOVERNMENT	*PARTY ORGANISATION*	*PARTY-IN-THE-ELECTORATE*
FEDERAL	Senate	Leadership PACs led by individual senators	Interest groups organised to elect party members to Senate	State-based interest groups that could affect senate elections (not created by elected officials)
	House	Leadership PACs led by individual congressmen	Interest groups organised to elect party members to House	District-based interest groups that could affect House elections (not created by elected officials)
	Executive	PACs led by President	Interest groups organised for presidential election	National interest groups (not created by elected officials)
STATE	Upper House	Interest groups organisations organised by state senators	Interest groups created to promote party in state senate races	Interest groups that could affect state senate elections (not created by elected officials)
	Lower House	Interest groups created by state assemblymen	Interest groups created to promote party in state assembly races	Interest groups that could affect state assembly elections (not created by elected officials)
	Executive	Interest groups led by Governor	Interest groups created to promote party throughout state	State based interest groups (not created by elected officials)
LOCAL		Interest groups created by local officials	Interest groups created to promote party in locality	Locally created and based interest groups

TABLE II. *The Multiple Dimensions of Party in Campaign Finance*

Does Campaign Finance Reform Weaken American Political Parties and How Would We Know?[34]

In the recent debate over campaign finance reform culminating in the Supreme Court's decision in *McConnell v FEC*, everyone seemed to be a fan of strong political parties. Despite all the pyrotechnics launched by the various expert reports, a few fundamental points of agreement never seemed in dispute: strong political parties are desirable, rich parties are better than poor parties, and parties play a unique and important role in elections. Even in the 1,638 pages comprising the opinions of the district court judges and the more than 300 pages of opinions emerging from the Supreme Court, these maxims appeared uncontested. Of course, the agreement ended there, and the parties to the litigation, the district court judges and the Supreme Court Justices were bedeviled by the empirical details surrounding the BCRA's soft money ban: did soft money strengthen parties? Would the BCRA weaken parties? Were parties strong or weak before the passage of the BCRA?

Much of the subtextual battle concerning the effect of the soft money ban and the BCRA's threat to parties' freedom of expression and association grew out of contested definitions of party 'strength.' Needless to say, a lack of agreement as to whether the BCRA will weaken parties is unsurprising when no one can agree on what defines a strong party or how to measure a party's strength. I suggest here a few ways of defining party strength and evaluate the state of the parties before and after the BCRA according to these measures. Measuring party strength is difficult, however, not only because of the contested notion of 'strength,' but also because of the multiple incarnations of America's political parties, as noted above. BCRA may have weakened parties according to some measures while strengthening it according to others and, perhaps more accurately, has shifted power in the party system away from some incarnations of the party (such as the national party organisations) and toward others (such as the state parties and shadow interest groups). Finally, it may be the case that the soft money ban has had different effects on the two parties; contrary to the interests of its principal supporters and detractors, the ban may have made the Republican Party 'stronger' and the Democratic Party 'weaker.'

Despite the plaintiffs' hyperbolic claims in the litigation, no one can reasonably argue that the BCRA has or will silence political parties. Even those who forecasted doom and gloom need to admit that parties will remain the strongest non-candidate institutions in American politics for the foreseeable future. Moreover, despite the audacious predictions of the many experts on both sides of the case, neither before the case, nor after are we sure about the effect of the BCRA on party strength. Indeed, what do observers mean when they say that the BCRA will weaken or strengthen parties? It is not as if parties could lift x pounds before the BCRA

[34] Most of the discussion in this section is excerpted from N Persily, 'Soft Parties and Strong Money' (2004) 3 *Election Law Journal* 315.

and they now can lift *y* pounds, so if *x* is greater than *y* we can say parties have become weaker. We can begin to tackle this question by assessing the strength of each component of the party according to VO Key's distinctions: measuring the strength of the party-in-government by its ability to execute its programmatic agenda, the strength of the party in the electorate by rates of party identification among voters, and the strength of the party organisation by its ability to recruit, nominate and elect its candidates.

Parties' Ideological Coherence and the Frequency of Party-line Voting in the Legislature

In a historical and comparative sense, political scientists have considered the United States to have a weak party system.[35] This weakness was relative to the hierarchical and disciplined party systems in European parliaments. In particular, parties in those systems 'stood for something.' By that, observers meant the parties had recognizable and differentiated agendas with party platforms that sent a clear signal to the voters as to what they could expect from the party if elected. In contrast, America's 'umbrella-like' or 'big tent' political parties were considered comparatively weak, with watered-down platforms and electoral strategies that attempted to blur the differences rather than distinguish between the parties. Not only were 'strong' parties, under this view, ideologically coherent and defined, but they were also unified and hierarchical: once elected they could deliver on their promises. Individual defections from parties were relatively rare in 'strong' party systems, as compared to America's legislative party caucuses where the job of the whip was often analogised to herding cats.

Although historically American parties may have been weak according to this measure, in recent years they have become much stronger, even resembling their European counterparts. Whereas once it might have been difficult to say where the parties stood on civil rights, the environment, social issues, etc, now one can easily identify issues with one or the other major party. Of course, the parties blur or converge on certain topics (such as free trade, the war on terrorism, the pledge of allegiance, or for that matter, campaign finance reform), but on most issues where disagreement exists that disagreement usually falls along party lines. To be sure, there are some 'outliers,' but no longer are Rockefeller Republicans or Dixiecrats a significant bloc in their respective parties.

Perhaps it is fair to say that we have now achieved a 'more responsible two-party system.' One can easily see the evidence of the increased coherence and cohesiveness of the parties in the well-documented jump in party-line voting in recent years.[36] By

[35] See American Political Science Association Committee on Political Parties, 'Toward a More Responsible Two Party System' (1950) 44 *American Political Science Review* (Supplement).

[36] See R Fleisher and JR Bond, 'Partisanship and the President's Quest for Votes on the Floor of Congress' in *Polarized Politics: Congress and the President in a Partisan Era* (Washington, DC, Congressional Quarterly, 2000); M Collie and J Mason, 'The Electoral Connection Between Party and Constituency Considered' in D Brady, J Cogan and M Fiorina (eds), *Continuity and Change in House Elections* (Palo Alto, Stanford Press, 2000).

this measure, then, parties were arguably at their strongest level in recent American history before passage of the BCRA and have remained at that peak in the immediate aftermath of its passage. How might the new law affect this aspect of their strength? Perhaps campaign finance reform will have no effect, because other factors are primarily responsible for the remarkable levels of party cohesiveness and polarisation.[37] The rise of the Republican Party in the South, the creation of safe and ideologically pure congressional districts, and the centralisation of authority in the House of Representatives all contribute to highly disciplined and ideologically more cohesive parties. However, the campaign finance system and the rise of soft money, in particular, gave party leaders additional carrots and sticks to use to keep legislators from straying off the party's path. Rewards of party expenditures or threats of withholding funds in a particular race allowed party leaders to extort votes or to cajole members into toeing the party line. Indeed, this type of financial influence (or 'strength') of the party was part of the process of corruption-by-the-party the proponents of the BCRA alleged.

If, as the plaintiffs argued in *McConnell*, informal interest groups will become relatively more influential in elections as a result of the BCRA, perhaps the threats or rewards that come from party financing will have less force. If soft money flows to outside groups whose power and electoral influence rise at the party organisation's expense, the relative capacity of the party to whip its members into line could be undermined. As a result, the parties might become less cohesive and defined because their leaders may have less ability to aggregate the different interest groups together into the party.

Some might applaud such a development. To the degree the parties have polarised and become more cohesive they misrepresent the underlying American population, especially moderate voters who find the Republicans too conservative and the Democrats too liberal. If outside groups will fracture the party coalitions, perhaps members of Congress will be more 'free' to take positions not dictated by their party leaders. The opposite scenario is also possible, however. Perhaps these outside groups, which often come from the extreme ends of the political spectrum, will actually pull representatives and parties even farther apart. If interest group leaders replace (or at least undermine) party leaders as the principal legislative arm-twisters or cajolers, then the already unrepresentative Congress will become even more so.

The Strength of Party Identification in the Electorate

In describing American parties as weak, some point to the relatively low rate of party identification in the electorate. European parties are stronger in that voters are less likely to identify as independent, the argument goes, whereas about a third or more of the American population so identifies. Observers of American elections have pointed to split ticket voting and the dominant influence of incumbency and the 'personal vote' on voters' decisions, suggesting that party identification is less

[37] See R Fleisher and JR Bond, 'The Shrinking Middle in the US Congress' (2004) 34 *British Journal of Political Science* 429.

politically relevant in America than elsewhere. Indeed, even in the *McConnell* litigation, one expert report specifically referenced the low rate of strong party identification as an indication that soft money has not strengthened parties.[38]

This assessment of the state of the parties shares similar faults to the previous ones. Although Americans today may be less likely than those of previous generations to identify with a party, their voting behavior indicates strong party attachments. Most of those who identify themselves as independents are really closet partisans who vote similarly to those who proudly wear (or proclaim) the party label.[39] More importantly, party line voting has dramatically increased: if you know someone's partisanship or partisan preferences in the previous election, you can predict their vote quite reliably.[40] Although the 1970s and 1980s may represent periods of party weakness among the electorate, parties today have grown stronger.

If the parties in the electorate are relatively strong, what does campaign finance reform portend? To answer this question may require an exploration into the deep psychological roots of party attachment to investigate whether money, let alone the availability of soft money, might make a difference.[41] Voters often develop their party loyalties at a young age from their parents and as a product of voters' reference groups (such as race, religion, region).[42] Party identification is a social, as well as a political phenomenon; like allegiance to a sports team or a religion, for many these attachments, once formed, will be immune to the tactics money can buy. That being said, the effort and expense of party mobilisation efforts can pay off in the integration of interest groups into the party's coalition and the formation of lasting attachments among the group's members. As with any other association, attachments can form from outreach efforts by the organisation, even if in the case of parties political beliefs are deeply held.

The question then becomes: will the BCRA inhibit parties in their outreach efforts? Much ink was spilled in the expert reports in the *McConnell* litigation over the question whether party mobilisation efforts (to promote both the party and its candidates, as discussed in the next section) will decline as a result of the

[38] See JS Krasno and F Sorauf, 'Why Soft Money Has Not Strengthened Parties' in A Corrado *et al* (eds), *Inside the Campaign Finance Battle: Court Testimony on the New Reforms* (Washington, DC, Brookings, 2003) 51, ('In 1992, 29 percent of respondents identified themselves as strong Democrats or Republicans compared with 31 percent in 2000. These figures are near the historic low . . . whatever party building the $1.2 billion of soft money has funded over the past decade, it has done little or nothing to attract citizens to the party banners.').

[39] See BE Keith *et al*, *The Myth of the Independent Voter* (Berkeley, UC Press, 1992).

[40] See LM Bartels, 'Partisanship and Voting Behavior, 1952–1996' (2000) 44 *American Journal of Political Science* 35. Bartels explains:

> the impact of partisan loyalties on voting behavior has increased in each of the last six presidential elections, reaching a level in 1996 almost 80 percent higher than in 1972—and significantly higher than in any presidential election in at least 50 years. The impact of partisanship on voting behavior in congressional elections has also increased markedly, albeit more recently and to a level still well below that of the 1950s.

R Fleisher and JR Bond, 'The Shrinking Middle in the US Congress,' (2004) 34 *British Journal of Political Science* 429.

[41] See generally WE Miller and JM Shanks, *The New American Voter* (Cambridge, Harvard Press, 1996) 128–40.

[42] See generally, D Green *et al*, *Partisan Hearts and Minds* (New Haven, Yale Press, 2002).

disappearance of soft money.[43] Everyone seems to agree that if the BCRA made the parties poorer, then their mobilisation efforts might suffer, but experts could not agree on whether the parties could make up for the lost soft money in other ways (as it appears they currently have) or whether soft money (or much money at all) was being used for such mobilisation efforts to begin with.

At issue here, though, is the same question posed with respect to the parties in the legislature: will outside groups become more important than parties as sources of political identification and mobilisation? Partisan identification will likely remain the most electorally relevant political identity for most Americans for some time. However, if the party 'brand' becomes diluted as a result of the loss of power of parties in the legislature, and if parties choose to funnel their hard money toward electioneering ads rather than mobilisation, as many argue they will if forced to choose, and if outside groups become the primary face-to-face political contact for voters, then perhaps we can expect party identification in the electorate to weaken as well. The number of 'ifs' in that sentence should not be lost upon the reader; restrictions on party fundraising are only one component in the complicated parade of horribles that would produce wholesale weakening of the party in the electorate.

Power to Recruit, Nominate, and Elect Candidates

For many on the Court and in the litigation, the strength of parties can best be seen in their ability to recruit, nominate and elect candidates. Party organisations exist primarily to get their favoured candidates nominated and elected, and their strength can be measured according to their success. The story of party reform—in the realm of campaign finance and elsewhere—has been the transfer of this particular type of strength or power away from party organisations to the mass media, candidate organisations and interest groups.[44] According to this measure the parties are probably weaker today than they were during the good old days of urban machines and patronage politics. Some blame the rise of primary elections, the McGovern-Fraser reforms of the Democratic Party and the 1974 FECA Amendments for this transfer of power away from the parties.[45] Others point out that in recent years parties have resurged, perhaps because of the rise in soft money,[46] or perhaps because they have finally learned how to play the determinative role in candidate-centered campaigns.[47]

[43] For the position that such mobilisation efforts will decline, see SM Milkis, 'Parties versus Interest Groups,' and RJ La Raja, 'Why Soft Money Has Strengthened Parties' in Corrado *et al* (eds), n 38 above. For the position that soft money has not made any significant difference in parties' mobilisation effort and that parties will easily adapt to a world without soft money, see Krasno and Sorauf, n 38 above, and D Green, 'The Need for Federal Regulation of State Party Activity' in Corrado *et al* (eds), n 38 above.

[44] See generally N Polsby, *The Consequences of Party Reform* (Oxford, Oxford Press, 1983) (describing the effect of the McGovern-Fraser reforms on the Democratic Party).

[45] See SM Milkis, 'Parties versus Interest Groups' in Corrado *et al* (eds), n 38 above.

[46] See RJ La Raja, 'Why Soft Honey Has Strengthened Parties' in Corrado *et al* (eds), n 38 above.

[47] See J Aldrich, *Why Parties?: The Origin and Transformation of Political Parties in America* (Chicago, U Chicago Press, 1995) 273; VA Farrar-Myers and D Dwyre, 'Parties and Campaign Finance,' in JE Cohen *et al* (eds), *American Political Parties: Decline Or Resurgence* (Washington, DC, Congressional Quarterly, 2001).

In any case, party resources, both in absolute terms and relative to interest groups, candidate organisations, and the media, are a critical factor in assessing the strength of parties to conduct campaigns. On this measure the *McConnell* majority and dissenters disagreed as to the effect of the BCRA. Buying the argument of defendants' experts that parties will adapt to a changing financial environment, the majority implied that parties will not be weakened and might even be strengthened by the new reforms. According to the majority, 'the restriction here tends to increase the dissemination of information by forcing parties, candidates and officeholders to solicit from a wider array of potential donors.'[48] On this view, the soft money ban is bitter tasting but ultimately reinvigorating medicine. By starving the parties of large contributions it forces them to reach out to more people. As one of the defendants' experts explained this 'tough love' approach to campaign finance:

> Limiting soft money, far from weakening political parties, will make them stronger. Parties will be encouraged to reach out to their supporters for volunteer labor and small donations. To do so, parties will be encouraged to inspire their activists with a policy agenda. The free flow of soft money has meant that parties have little need to inspire support; they can simply purchase all of the labor they require to execute their campaign.[49]

According to its defenders, the BCRA might wean parties from their addiction to television advertisements and focus them on grass roots mobilisation.

According to the plaintiffs and the dissenters in *McConnell*, the disappearance of soft money will directly affect parties' ability to mobilise voters, coordinate with the various entities that comprise the party, and run effective campaigns on behalf of candidates. Justice Scalia's dissent went so far as to suggest that the majority's reasoning, if not the BCRA itself, 'threatens the existence of all political parties.'[50] Even under the most optimistic scenarios of party adaptation to the new reforms, it is difficult to make the argument that the parties will be better able to campaign. To do so requires an assumption of some form of false consciousness on the part of the parties pre-BCRA: It was always in the parties' interest to spend more time going for many small donations instead of a few big ones, but they did not know it. Even if available evidence since the passage of the BCRA indicates that the parties have raised more hard money (under the new, higher limits) than they previously did in hard money and soft money combined, it is difficult to understand how they are therefore stronger once one source of fundraising has been cut off. Unless parties have a limited appetite for cash that will be equally sated by many small donations as it would with a few large ones, then the absence of the soft money avenue leaves parties poorer than they otherwise would be. Maybe this is not such a bad thing if the parties have indeed misspent soft money, and

[48] 124 SCt at 658.
[49] D Green, 'The Need for Federal Regulation of State Party Activity' in Corrado *et al* (eds), n 38 above at 110.
[50] *McConnell*, 124 SCt at 725 (Scalia, J dissenting).

alternatively, maybe the state's anticorruption interests nevertheless justify weakening the party in this way. However, the BCRA, like any campaign finance restriction, prevents parties from using all possible tools that may advance the common interests of the party and candidates in a campaign.

Conclusion

Any assessment of the effect of campaign finance reform on America's political parties must examine party organisational strength *relative* to other groups or dimensions of the party, as well as the strength of the Democratic Party *relative* to the Republican Party. It may be too early to make such an assessment with respect to the effect of the BCRA. The early evidence in the post-BCRA period suggested that Democrats, despite their widespread support for the BCRA, were the early losers. With respect to their base of contributors, Republicans had always done better among individual donors, while Democrats had held their own in collecting money from corporations and, particularly, unions. The BCRA biases the system in favour of those individuals who can afford to give about $25,000 to a party, and Republicans are favourably represented in that pool. However, Democratic-leaning 527 organisations (interest groups serving as shadow parties for financing purposes) have fared better thus far than similar Republican organisations. Such an edge may be ephemeral though, as Republicans have only begun to explore this avenue of fundraising.

The story of the most recent reform efforts, judicial and administrative reactions, and subsequent responses by political entrepreneurs fits the pattern of party adaptation that has characterised regulation in this area. The ability of parties to morph along several dimensions and into and out of formal institutions leaves would-be reformers with the difficult choice of shifting power among different incarnations of the party or targeting the core First Amendment rights of a variety of associations. Because an individual's right to give money to an organisation and the right of organisations to express their members' political opinions exist at the core of First Amendment protections, corruption of the party or through the party may be the inevitable risk of a system that places such preeminent value on such rights. The alternative may be a system that aggressively regulates not just the formal party institutions that receive the greatest attention under the current law, but also any group of people that organises and raises money for political purposes.

To highlight the Hobson's choice between unconstitutional regulation and ineffective regulation is not to say that laws attempting to prevent corruption by way of party financing do nothing. Even when regulations only move money around the party system, the resultant transaction and opportunity costs change who exercises power in the financing of campaigns. Although observers lament the shift of money away from transparent and accountable formal party organisations and toward shadowy, unaccountable interest groups, the redirection of funds disperses and channels political power toward a broader range of people. Should Congress find that such a move threatens the party institutions in some tangible way, the party-in-government is hardly an impotent bystander: the next round of campaign finance legislation can then deal with this new set of problems.

The debate over party financing tends to vacillate between paranoia, irrational exuberance, and fatalism. Reformers paint a picture of corrupt parties beholden to moneyed interests and promise a future where politics is cleaner and more democratic. Detractors warn that reforms will decimate political parties, have perverse effects, or perhaps do nothing at all, so why bother? In truth, the history of regulation of party financing instructs us that the law is only one component of a complicated array of factors that affect the incentives and behaviors of the relevant political actors. The law can shape the relevant political environment but can also be overwhelmed by it. The most one can expect from any given reform is that it will address the problem of the day while fulfilling neither the most unrealistic expectations of its supporters nor the most apocalyptic projections of their opponents.

Part V

Regulation and Judical Review: Divergent Paths

12

The Supreme Court of Canada's Political Theory and the Constitutionality of the Political Finance Regime

COLIN FEASBY

Introduction

THE *CANADA ELECTIONS ACT* creates a comprehensive approach to political finance that consists of disclosure of financial information, limits on political contributions and expenditures, financial support for electoral participants, and the provision of discounted and free television and radio broadcasting.[1] The regime, taken as a whole, is an attempt to manage the flow of political money and, by extension, shape the contours of political discourse. Such an intervention into the democratic process necessarily raises constitutional questions. Foremost among the constitutional questions are: Do limits on citizens' ability to participate in the democratic process contravene the right to freedom of expression, the right to equal treatment under the law, and the democratic rights guaranteed by the *Charter of Rights and Freedoms*?[2] And, is the system of public support for electoral participants consistent with those same *Charter* rights?

Surprisingly, the constitutionality of the political finance regulation apparatus has only begun to be tested in Canadian courts. Indeed, after refusing to consider several important political finance cases in the 1990s, the Supreme Court of Canada has recently weighed into the debate. The Court's recent forays into the realm of political finance have seen the Court articulate a theory of democratic politics that may guide the resolution of future political finance cases.

The Court endorsed what it calls an 'egalitarian model of elections' in the context of upholding expenditure limits on third parties during election campaigns

[1] *Canada Elections Act*, SC 2000, c 9 ['*Canada Elections Act*' or '*CEA*'].

[2] Part I of the *Constitution Act 1982*, being sch B to the *Canada Act 1982* (UK), c 11 ['*Charter*'].

in *Harper v Canada.*[3] The egalitarian model, as I have argued previously, is rooted in the idea that citizens with equal abilities should have an equal ability to participate in the political process.[4] As such, the egalitarian model requires that the influence of private wealth be constrained.

Figueroa v Canada, another recent decision of the Supreme Court, considered several aspects of the *Canada Elections Act* including a restriction that prevented small political parties from issuing tax receipts to donors in the same fashion as large political parties.[5] The Court held that the restriction was unjustified and that Parliament has 'an obligation not to enhance the capacity of one citizen to participate in the electoral process in a manner that compromises another citizen's parallel right to meaningful participation in the electoral process.'[6] *Figueroa* indicates that the Court's political theory has application beyond the limited context of spending limits. Moreover, *Figueroa* provides important clues as to how the Court may deal with challenges to public funding and the regime governing the reservation and allocation of free and discounted broadcasting time for political campaigns.

This chapter begins by explaining relevant elements of the *Charter* and judicial review under the *Charter* so that the reader may understand the doctrinal context in which the cases to be discussed in the balance of the chapter were decided. The second part of this chapter discusses *Harper* and *Figueroa* and explains the political theory behind the egalitarian model endorsed by Parliament and the Court. Here it is argued that the egalitarian model and its animating concept—deliberative equality—is intended by the Court to guide the resolution of future political finance cases. The last part of this chapter reconsiders two important political finance cases decided by appellate courts in the 1990s: *Barrette v Canada*[7] and *Reform Party of Canada v Canada.*[8] *Barrette* and *Reform Party* respectively upheld the sections of the *Canada Elections Act* that pertain to public funding and the reservation and allocation of broadcasting time. The Court's adoption of the egalitarian model, it is argued, makes it likely that if heard today, *Barrette* and *Reform Party* would be decided differently. Indeed, it is argued that important elements of the public funding and broadcasting regime that exist today are unconstitutional. In conclusion, a subject conspicuously absent from both *Harper* and *Figueroa*—the impact of political competition on judicial review of the political finance regime—is raised.

[3] *Harper v Canada (Attorney General)* [2004] 1 SCR 827 at para 62 ['*Harper*'].

[4] C Feasby, '*Libman v Quebec (AG)* and the Administration of the Process of Democracy under the *Charter*: The Emerging Egalitarian Model' (1999) 44 *McGill Law Journal* 5. ['Egalitarian Model']; See also, H MacIvor, 'The Charter of Rights and Party Politics; The Impact of the Supreme Court Ruling in *Figueroa v Canada (Attorney General)*' (2004) 10 *Choices* (Montreal, Institute for Research on Public Policy) at 5.

[5] *Figueroa v Canada (Attorney General)* [2003] 1 SCR 912 ['*Figueroa*'].

[6] *Ibid* at para 50.

[7] *Barrette v Canada (Attorney General)* (1994) 113 DLR (4th) 623 (Que CA) ['*Barrette*'].

[8] *Reform Party of Canada v Canada (Attorney General)* (1995) 123 DLR (4th) 366 (Alta CA) ['*Reform Party*'].

A Primer on Charter Doctrine and its Application to the Democratic Process

The Canadian Constitution is comprised of various domestic and imperial statutes supplemented by unwritten constitutional principles. The most important constitutional acts are the *Constitution Act 1867*,[9] which sets out the division of powers between the federal government and the provincial governments, and the *Constitution Act 1982*, which contains the *Charter*. So far as judicial consideration of federal political finance regulation is concerned, the *Charter*—a constitutional Bill of Rights—is of greatest import. Courts may declare laws inconsistent with rights guaranteed by the *Charter* to be unconstitutional and of no force or effect.[10] A declaration of invalidity may be overridden by Parliament for a limited period of time under the *Charter*'s 'notwithstanding clause.'[11] The notwithstanding clause, however, has rarely been invoked.[12]

Judicial review under the *Charter* shares some characteristics with judicial review under the First Amendment and the *European Convention on Human Rights*.[13] *Charter* review is explicitly a balancing exercise where individual rights and state interests are weighed.[14] Under the *Charter*, the Court first determines whether a right has been infringed. Once an infringement is found, the Court then considers whether infringing law is a 'reasonable limit' that is 'demonstrably justified in a free and democratic society.'[15] The justification offered by the government is tested by first considering whether the objective of the infringing law is 'pressing and substantial.' If the objective is pressing and substantial, the Court determines whether there is a 'rational connection' between the law and the objective of the law and whether the law 'minimally impairs' the right in question. If the infringing law is rational and minimally impairing, then the Court weighs the 'salutary and deleterious effects' of the law to determine constitutionality.[16]

There are three *Charter* rights that have particular relevance to the law of the democratic process: (1) Section 2(b) which protects freedom of expression[17]; (2) Section 3 which provides that '[e]very citizen of Canada has the right to vote in an election of the members of the House of Commons . . . and to be qualified for membership therein;'[18] and (3) section 15 which guarantees to every individual 'the equal protection and benefit of the law without discrimination.'[19] Each of sections

[9] *Constitution Act 1867* (UK), 30 and 31 Vict, c 3.
[10] *Charter*, above n 2 at s 52.
[11] *Ibid* at s 33.
[12] See T Kahana, 'Understanding the Notwithstanding Mechanism' (2002) 52 *University of Toronto Law Journal* 221 at 223.
[13] *Convention for the Protection of Human Rights and Fundamental Freedoms* (4 November 1950) 213 UNTS 221.
[14] *R v Oakes* [1986] 1 SCR 153.
[15] *Charter*, above n 2 at s 1.
[16] *Dagenais v Canadian Broadcasting Corporation* [1994] 3 SCR 835 at 839.
[17] *Charter*, above n 2 at s 2(b).
[18] *Ibid* at s 3.
[19] *Ibid* at s 15(1).

2(b), 3 and 15(1) have developed unique doctrines and, as will become obvious in later sections of this chapter, the application of these doctrines to a common issue can lead to inconsistent or conflicting results. Not surprisingly, courts have struggled with how to resolve political finance issues when confronted with alleged violations of some or all of these *Charter* rights.

Expression protected by section 2(b) has been defined to include almost any human act short of violence.[20] Accordingly, impugned laws—almost all laws for that matter—invariably restrict an individual's freedom of expression. The result of this interpretation of expression is that in each case the Court is involved in balancing the objective and impact of laws in cases brought under section 2(b). This is in stark contrast to the interpretation of the scope of democratic rights under section 3. There have been relatively few section 3 cases heard by the Court since the adoption of the *Charter* in 1982. The cases fall into two identifiable categories. First, there are cases that deal with the denial of the right to vote to a whole class of individuals, the best example of which are the prisoner voting cases.[21] Second, there are cases, such as *Saskatchewan Electoral Boundaries*, which is a one person, one vote case, that deal with the qualitative aspects of the right to vote.[22] The approach to section 3 developed in the prisoner voting cases, stated definitively in the recent *Sauvé* case, is absolutist like the approach to expression in section 2(b) in the sense that the Court is hostile to any attempt by the state to abridge citizens' physical right to vote and any consideration of the merits of the restriction must take place in the context of section 1. The Court in *Sauvé* was deeply sceptical of the government's justification for limiting prisoner voting even in the face of popular support for the measure and a lengthy history of similar measures in Canada and other jurisdictions. The analysis in *Sauvé* suggests that where a violation of the physical right to vote is found, any justification offered by the state will be subjected to strict scrutiny.

Standing in seemingly stark contrast to *Sauvé* is the approach to defining the qualitative aspects of the right to vote in *Saskatchewan Electoral Boundaries*. The majority decision of the Supreme Court in *Saskatchewan Electoral Boundaries*—also written by McLachlin J—took an uncritical view of justifications offered for population deviations of up to 25 per cent from district averages. McLachlin J justified her deferential stance in *Saskatchewan Electoral Boundaries* by interpreting the right to vote as not guaranteeing the right to an equal vote, but a right to 'effective representation.' The concept of 'effective representation' is malleable—certainly more so than the idea of one person, one vote that predominates in the United States.[23] McLachlin J held that while '[r]espect for individual dignity and social equality mandate that citizens' votes not be unduly debased or diluted . . .', population deviations of up to plus or minus, 25 per cent do not violate section 3

[20] *Irwin Toy v Quebec* [1989] 1 SCR 927.

[21] *Sauvé v Canada (Attorney General)* [1993] 1 SCR 438; *Sauvé v Canada (Chief Electoral Officer)* [2002] 3 SCR 519 ['*Sauvé*'].

[22] *Reference re Provincial Electoral Boundaries (Sask)* [1991] 2 SCR 158 ['*Saskatchewan Electoral Boundaries*'].

[23] *Karcher v Daggett* 462 US 725 (1983) (no deviation tolerated in Congressional districting); *White v Regester* 412 US 755 (1973) (10 per cent deviation tolerated in state legislative districts).

and do not have to be justified under section 1. McLachlin J's rationale was that legislatures, frequently through the instrument of boundary commissions, must have sufficient flexibility to realise certain social objectives.

The effect of *Saskatchewan Electoral Boundaries* is that the primary consideration of questions relating to the quality of the right to vote—which arise in parallel with expression issues in the political finance context—will be in the context of the definition of the rights guaranteed by section 3 not in the evaluation of the government's justifications for limiting rights under section 1 as would be the case with section 2(b). A restriction on, for example, election day campaigning by candidates would be a violation of section 2(b) that the government would have to justify under section 1; whereas such a restriction may or may not constitute a violation of section 3 depending whether the Court determined that the concept of effective representation had been compromised. The incompatible analytical frameworks under sections 2(b) and 3 make it difficult as a practical matter for courts to consider section 2(b) and section 3 simultaneously.[24] As a result, there is a temptation for courts to identify one or the other section as the primary right engaged by a challenged law. The choice of section 2(b) or section 3 as the primary right engaged affects the structure of judicial reasoning and, one suspects, judicial psychology.

Section 15(1) and section 3 also overlap to some degree. Section 15(1) guarantees equality of all persons under the law whereas the equality of citizens, as seen in *Saskatchewan Electoral Boundaries*, informs the contours of the democratic rights protected by section 3. Whilst section 15(1) guarantees the equality of all persons under the law, it has been interpreted principally as an anti-discrimination measure that protects individuals who are members of historically disadvantaged groups. Section 15(1) protects individuals from discrimination based on certain specified characteristics such as race, age, sex and disability and unwritten, but analogous, grounds which have been found to include sexual orientation,[25] marital status,[26] citizenship,[27] and others. Moreover, discrimination on an enumerated or analogous ground only contravenes section 15(1) if it is also a 'violation of essential human dignity.'[28] The narrow interpretation of section 15(1) makes it of limited relevance to the resolution of election law disputes given that racial, linguistic, and religious limitations on the right to vote have been eliminated.[29] At the same time, the narrow interpretation of section 15(1) presents a difficulty for

[24] See, eg, *Harper*, above n 3 at para 66, finding that third party spending restrictions infringe the right to freedom of expression under s 2(b) and, at the same time, finding at para 74 that the same restrictions do not limit the 'informational component' of the s 3 right to vote. The Court concluded that the infringement of freedom of expression was constitutional under s 1.

[25] *Vriend v Alberta* [1998] 1 SCR 493.

[26] *Miron v Trudel* [1995] 2 SCR 418.

[27] *Lavoie v Canada* [2002] 1 SCR 769.

[28] *Law v Canada (Minister of Employment and Immigration)* [1999] 1 SCR 497 at 549–52.

[29] Section 3 has been interpreted to only apply to elections for provincial legislatures and for the federal Parliament. Accordingly s 15(1) is often the basis for challenges to referendum laws, municipal election laws, and other democratic processes outside the scope of s 3: See, eg, *Haig v Canada (Attorney General)* [1993] 2 SCR 995; *Borough of East York v Ontario (Attorney General)* (1997) 34 OR (3d) 789 (Gen Div) aff'd 36 OR (3d) 733 (CA). Indeed, the Court used s 15(1) in the context of Indian Band elections to remedy a restriction on voting by off reserve Band members: *Corbiere v Canada* [1999] 2 SCR 203.

Courts when presented with equality arguments advanced in the context of section 3. Should Courts, as was done in *Saskatchewan Electoral Boundaries*, read in to the democratic rights protected by section 3 a right to equality that is broader in scope than the explicit constitutional equality guarantee in section 15(1)? What is clear from the discussion of *Harper* and *Figueroa* that follows is that the Court is committed to the conclusion in *Saskatchewan Electoral Boundaries*; namely, that an implicit guarantee of equality exists within the democratic rights in section 3. The remaining question is: What are the contours of the equality guarantee in section 3? This question will be considered in the next section of this chapter.

The Supreme Court of Canada's Political Theory

Harper v Canada: The Endorsement of the Egalitarian Model

The right of third parties—individuals and interest groups who are neither candidates nor political parties—to make election expenditures has been the context within which much of debate over the place of political finance regulation in the democratic process has taken place.[30] *Harper* is the latest case to deal with the question of third party expenditures. Prior to *Harper*, two distinct lines of authority existed. First, in *National Citizens Coalition*[31] and *Somerville*[32] considering third party spending limits in the *Canada Elections Act* and in *Pacific Press*[33] considering similar restrictions in the British Columbia *Elections Act*, provincial trial and appellate courts adopted the simple view that the expression of political views was of paramount importance in a democratic society and could not be limited in the name of promoting a more fair political process. None of these cases concerning third party spending were heard by the Supreme Court. Second, in *Libman*, a case concerning provisions in Quebec's referendum legislation that limited expenditures by anyone who was not a member of the official 'Yes' or 'No' committees, the Court held that in pursuit of a fair political process the legislature may limit the ability of private wealth to dominate discourse.[34] In the wake of *Libman*, the federal Parliament enacted new third party expenditure restrictions which, in turn, were challenged in *Harper*.

Harper was a frontal assault on *Libman*. At trial and in the Alberta Court of Appeal, *Libman* was distinguished on the grounds that some aspects of an academic study relied upon by the Lortie Commission in recommending third party spending limits to Parliament which, in turn, was relied upon by the Supreme Court in coming to its decision, had been discredited.[35] *Harper* also concerned

[30] See A Geddis, 'Democratic Visions and Third-Party Expenditures: A Comparative View' (2001) 9 *Tulane Journal of International and Comparative Law* 5.

[31] *National Citizens Coalition v Canada (Attorney General)* (1984) 11 DLR (4th) 481 (Alta QB).

[32] *Somerville v Canada (Attorney General)* (1996) 136 DLR (4th) 205 (Alta CA).

[33] *Pacific Press v British Columbia (Attorney General)* [2000] 5 WWR 219 (BCSC).

[34] *Libman v Quebec (Attorney General)* [1997] 3 SCR 569.

[35] *Harper v Canada (Attorney General)* [2001] 9 WWR 650 (Alta QB); aff'd (2003) 23 DLR 275 (Alta CA) at 310–11.

issue advocacy and the delineation of the boundary between electoral expression and generic political expression.[36] The Court, however, focused on the first question and elided the second. The failure to address the issue advocacy problem is a fundamental flaw in the Court's reasoning in *Harper*, but it is not one that falls within the scope of this chapter.

Previously I have used the term 'egalitarian model' to describe the approach to election regulation recommended by the Lortie Commission, imperfectly embodied in the *Canada Elections Act*, and endorsed by the Court in *Libman*.[37] The egalitarian model as discerned from the entrails of *Libman* could only be described as an emerging model; the structure of which was as much hidden as it was exposed. The Court in *Harper* adopted the label 'egalitarian model' and emphatically endorsed the central premises of *Libman*:

> The Court's conception of electoral fairness as reflected in the foregoing principles is consistent with the egalitarian model of elections adopted by Parliament as an essential component of our democratic society. This model is premised on the notion that individuals should have an equal opportunity to participate in the electoral process. Under this model, wealth is the main obstacle to equal participation . . . Thus, the egalitarian model promotes an electoral process that requires the wealthy to be prevented from controlling the electoral process to the detriment of others with less economic power.[38]

The egalitarian model—as it relates to the justification of limits on election spending at least—is predicated on two themes that recur in liberal legal and political theory concerning the regulation of political finance over the last forty years. First, the egalitarian model is based on the idea that 'citizens similarly gifted and motivated [should] have roughly an equal chance of influencing the government's policy . . . irrespective of their economic and social class.'[39] The concept of equal opportunity of influence on public policy in practical terms means an equal opportunity to participate in political deliberation. 'Deliberative equality' is a useful term that I use to describe the equal opportunity to participate in political deliberation.[40] *Harper* notably highlights deliberative equality as normatively desirable.[41]

The greatest threat to deliberative equality is private wealth which, unlike other politically advantageous attributes such as charisma or eloquence, has an identifiable and self-serving interest. In other words, private wealth is a systemic challenge to public politics. While this idea is shared by many liberal theorists, it was expressed most clearly by John Rawls who wrote:

[36] See C Feasby, 'Issue Advocacy and Third Parties in the United Kingdom and Canada' (2003) 48 *McGill Law Journal* 11 ['Issue Advocacy'].
[37] Feasby, 'Egalitarian Model,' above n 4.
[38] *Harper*, above n 3 at para 62.
[39] J Rawls, 'The Basic Liberties and Their Priority' in S Darwall (ed) *Equal Freedom: Selected Tanner Lectures on Human Values* (Ann Arbor, Mich; University of Michigan Press, 1995) 105 at 175.
[40] Feasby, 'Issue Advocacy,' above n 36 at 16–21.
[41] *Harper*, above n 3 at paras 63 and 72.

> The liberties protected by the principle of participation [in the democratic process] lose much of their value whenever those who have greater private means are permitted to use their advantages to control the course of public debate. For eventually these inequalities will enable those better situated to exercise a larger influence over the development of legislation. In due time they are likely to acquire a preponderant weight in settling social questions, at least in regard to those matters upon which they normally agree, which is to say in regard to those things that support their favoured circumstances.[42]

Indeed, it is not a coincidence that the Lortie Commission which performed a comprehensive review of the regulation of Canada's democratic system quoted this passage from Rawls in its explanation of then current and recommended campaign finance regulations.[43]

Second, the egalitarian model is premised on an understanding that the state is not inevitably the enemy of freedom of expression. Indeed, the egalitarian model assumes that certain restrictions are necessary for the existence of an adequate public forum for political debate. To emphasise the point, the Court acknowledged Owen Fiss' argument that:

> [In some situations] the state may have to act to further the robustness of public debate in circumstances where powers outside the state are stifling speech. It may have to allocate public resources—hand out megaphones—to those whose voices would not otherwise be heard in the public square. It may even have to silence the voices of some in order to hear the voices of others. Sometimes there is simply no other way.[44]

Prominent in Fiss' view and that of the Court is that public funding is a necessary corollary to spending restrictions. The Court explicitly acknowledged this fact when it pointed out that,

> the State can provide a voice to those who might otherwise not be heard. The Act does so by reimbursing candidates and political parties and by providing broadcast time to political parties.[45]

Whereas the Court indicates that state support for political actors is permissible (even desirable), it is silent on the question of how such support may be allocated. Indeed, if anything, the implication is that such public support should be targeted at those whose voices would otherwise not be heard in the political debate. This latter view is consistent with the concept of deliberative equality, though not necessarily consistent with the current political finance regime.

[42] J Rawls, *Theory of Justice* (Oxford, Clarendon Press, 1972) at 225.

[43] Canada, *Royal Commission on Electoral and Party Financing, Final Report: Reforming Electoral Democracy*, vol 1 (Ottawa, Canada Communications Group, 1991) (Chair: Pierre Lortie) at 326 ['Lortie Commission'].

[44] O Fiss, *The Irony of Free Speech* (Cambridge, Mass; Harvard University Press, 1996) at 4; *Harper*, above n 3 at para 62.

[45] *Harper*, above n 3 at para 62.

Figueroa v Canada: Extension of the Egalitarian Model?

Whilst *Harper* is a restatement of the Court's egalitarian model, *Figueroa*, which preceded *Harper* in time, is in actual fact the next step in the evolution of the Court's articulation of its political theory. *Figueroa* demonstrates that the Supreme Court believes that deliberative equality is not merely a justification for spending limits, but also a principle that should generally inform the regulatory treatment of political parties and, presumably, candidates. Notably, in *Figueroa*, the Court prefers the objective of deliberative equality over a countervailing objection commonly raised against the equal treatment of candidates and political parties; namely, that only serious candidates and major parties deserve access to the full range of benefits because only they have a realistic chance of representing voters in Parliament.

Figueroa is the Supreme Court's first political finance case not to deal with third party election expenditures. Instead, *Figueroa* deals with the *Canada Elections Act* requirements to be registered as a political party. Whilst the registration of political parties may seem a mundane question, it has important implications for the political finance regime. Registered party status is the key to receiving many of the rights afforded to political parties under the *Canada Elections Act* and, in particular, benefits offered under the political finance regime. Among other things, status as a registered political party entitles a political party to ballot identification, the ability to issue tax receipts to donors between elections, and the ability to transfer unspent funds between candidates and the party after an election.[46]

Miguel Figueroa, the appellant and leader of the Canadian Communist Party, contended that the requirement that political parties field 50 candidates in an election to qualify as a registered party violated his democratic rights as a candidate, insofar as his party's inability to access financial incentives available to major parties undermined his ability to meaningfully participate in the electoral process. He further contended that the registration requirement undermined the democratic rights of voters by making it more difficult for small parties to publicise their views which, in turn, distorted the dissemination of political viewpoints in favour of the major parties. Figueroa's claims were based on the theory that section 3 and its animating principle, 'effective representation,' require all political parties to be treated fairly and equally. Figueroa's submission was essentially that section 3 guarantees deliberative equality in the democratic process.

Figueroa was successful at trial, but was rebuffed in the main by the Ontario Court of Appeal. To the Court of Appeal 'effective representation' described the end product of the democratic process. If 'effective representation' is viewed as an end rather than a means, then it makes sense for section 3 to be engaged only by those electoral participants who stand a reasonable chance of election. The Court of Appeal held that:

[46] *Figueroa*, above n 5 at para 18.

> [T]he purpose of section 3 is engaged only by those political parties that possess the capacity to aggregate interests on a national level and participate in the governance of the country subsequent to an election. A party that does not participate in an election with a view to forming a government, or at least winning a substantial number of seats in Parliament, is not a party that possesses the capacity to advance the objective of effective representation. Thus, it is not improper to withhold benefits from political parties whose level of participation is so minimal as to be incapable of serving that goal.[47]

The Court of Appeal's approach is consistent with the view, and indeed it was argued before the Supreme Court, that the political finance system should promote majority governments. Majority governments, it was argued, are normatively desirable because they tend to be more stable and 'provide more effective governance than governments that consist of coalitions between or among various political parties.'[48]

The majority of the Supreme Court rejected the government's position and held that the quality of the electoral process is more important than the outcome of the process. The Court explained the inherent importance of participation in the electoral process in the following terms:

> [P]articipation in the electoral process has an intrinsic value independent of its impact upon the actual outcome of elections. To be certain, the electoral process is the means by which elected representatives are selected and governments formed, but it is also the primary means by which the average citizen participates in the open debate that animates the determination of social policy.[49]

The Court further elaborated that section 3 guarantees the right of each citizen to play a meaningful role in the electoral process.[50] The Court's elevation of the value of meaningful participation over an orderly outcome (*ie* effective governance) leads ineluctably to the conclusion that electoral participants—candidates and political parties—must be treated equally irrespective of their likelihood of success. Essentially, if a candidate or political party is to meaningfully participate in the electoral process, there must be a level playing field or, to put it differently, deliberative equality.

The right to meaningfully participate in the electoral process seems, in some respects, to be based upon an expressive theory of law.[51] Laws that foster equal participation in political discourse contribute to citizens' dignity and self-worth and thereby enhance the legitimacy of the political process. Deliberative equality, in

[47] *Figueroa*, above n 5 at para 22.
[48] *Ibid* at para 79.
[49] *Ibid* at para 29.
[50] *Ibid* at para 30.
[51] E Anderson & R Pildes, 'Expressive Theories of Law: A General Restatement' (2000) 148 *University of Pennsylvania Law Review* 1503; C Sunstein, 'On the Expressive Function of Law' (1996) *University of Pennsylvania Law Review* 2021; R Levy, 'Expressive Harms and the Strands of *Charter* Equality: Drawing Out Parallel Coherent Approaches to Discrimination' (2002) 40 *Alberta Law Review* 393.

this respect at least, is analogous to the right to an equal vote.[52] The Supreme Court, however, also offered an instrumental reason for protecting the right of citizens to meaningfully participate in the electoral process:

> Large or small, all political parties are capable of introducing unique interests and concerns into the political discourse. Consequently, all political parties, whether large or small, are capable of acting as a vehicle for the participation of individual citizens in the public discourse that animates the determination of social policy.[53]

In other words, small parties with their unique perspectives add a dimension to the process of public deliberation that may indirectly result in better governance. Levelling the playing field for small parties, then, may contribute as much to the good governance of the country as measures that enhance the prospects of majority government.

Section 3 jurisprudence, as is clear from the preceding discussion, is replete with concepts and principles, but precious few rules. Nevertheless, what emerges from *Figueroa* comes close to being a rule. The Court held that 'legislation that exacerbates a pre-existing disparity in the capacity of the various political parties to communicate their positions to the general public is inconsistent with section 3.'[54] This statement indicates that the Court intends to provide guidance to lower courts in resolving section 3 cases that has hitherto been lacking. With this in mind, Part IV of this chapter revisits two prominent provincial appellate cases concerning public funding and allocation of discounted and free broadcasting time.

The Egalitarian Model and the Constitutionality of Public Funding and the Political Broadcasting Regime

Revisiting *Barrette v Canada* and the Constitutionality of Candidate Funding Thresholds

The Structure of Public Funding of Candidates

The *Canada Elections Act* provides that a percentage of candidate election expenses and registered political party election expenses will be reimbursed from the public purse if certain thresholds are met.[55] The provisions governing the

[52] See R Dworkin, 'What is Equality? Part 4: Political Equality' (1987) 22 *University of San Francisco Law Review* 1 at 9, distinguishing between equality of impact (*ie* voting) and equality of influence (deliberative equality).

[53] *Figueroa*, above n 5 at para 41.

[54] *Ibid* at para 54.

[55] Political parties must receive five per cent of the vote in the electoral districts in which they endorse candidates or two per cent of the national popular vote in order to qualify for reimbursement of expenses: *CEA*, above n 1 s 435. The level of reimbursement was raised from 22.5 per cent to 50 per cent in connection with the enactment of contribution limits in 2003. The level of reimbursement for the 2004 election was set at 60 per cent because political parties had little time to adjust to the changes

reimbursement of candidate expenditures provided that all candidates receiving at least 15 per cent of the popular vote in their district were entitled to reimbursement of 50 per cent of their election expenditures.[56] These thresholds for reimbursement may at first glance appear to be a small obstacle for candidates. The results of the 2000 general election, however, showed that the thresholds were, in fact, a significant barrier. Indeed, a majority of candidates failed to achieve the threshold of support required to qualify for reimbursement of election expenses.

In 2002, the Chief Electoral Officer ('CEO') released a report entitled *Modernizing the Electoral Process.*[57] The CEO recommended that the 15 per cent popular vote threshold for candidates to qualify for reimbursement of election expenses be lowered to 5 per cent. The CEO recognised that the 15 per cent threshold is intrinsically flawed and stated that, '[t]he existing qualification level for candidates places more emphasis on public support and less emphasis on enhancing access to the system.'[58] The obvious question that arises upon recommending a reduction in the qualifying threshold from 15 per cent to 5 per cent is: Why stop there? Why not reduce the threshold to zero? For the CEO, reason for limiting the availability of reimbursement is the potential burden on public finances.[59] The question is whether this is a reasonable fear.

The information presented in Table 1 suggests that lowering the threshold for reimbursement to zero would not unduly burden the treasury. Of course, a change to a zero threshold might alter the spending behaviour of marginal candidates and political parties. Even recognising this possibility, it is hard to see how

to the financing regime: *An Act to amend the Canada Elections Act and the Income Tax Act (political financing)* SC 2003, c 19, s 72 *('CEA 2003')*. The reimbursement of political party expenses during the 2000 election are shown in the table below.

Political Party	Number of Candidates	Total Election Expenses	Limit of Election Expenses	Reimbursement
Bloc Quebecois	75	1,968,693	3,383,175	404,402
Canadian Alliance	298	9,669,648	12,638,257	2,167,520
Canadian Action	70	392,108	3,097,545	0
Christian Heritage	*	35,126	*	0
Communist	52	13,563	2,264,407	0
Green	111	17,747	4,888,177	0
Liberal	301	12,525,174	12,710,074	2,809,219
Marijuana	73	9,724	3,284,537	0
Marxist-Leninist	84	2,088	3,817,444	0
Natural Law	69	38,304	3,096,518	0
NDP	298	6,334,585	12,584,911	1,423,516
PC	291	3,983,301	12,352,405	875,701
Total	**1722**	**34,990,661**	**74,117,450**	**7,680,358**

[56] *CEA*, above n 1 ss 464 and 465. The reimbursement amount for candidates was raised to 60% in 2003: *CEA 2003* s 49.

[57] J-P Kingsley, *Modernizing the Electoral Process: Recommendations from the Chief Electoral Officer of Canada Following the 37th General Election* (Ottawa, Elections Canada, 2001) ['*Modernizing the Electoral Process*'].

[58] *Ibid* at s 3.1.1.1.

[59] *Ibid* at s 3.1.1.1.

Political Party	Number of Candidates	Total Candidate Expenses ($)	Authorised Limit of Election Expenses ($)	Actual Refund (15% threshold)		Projected Refund (0% threshold)
				Number of Candidates	Amount ($)	
Bloc Quebecois	75	4,254,434	5,173,089	69	2,150,314	2,150,314
Canadian Action	70	313,024	4,765,655	0	0	156,512
Canadian Alliance	298	9,514,889	20,288,121	182	4,216,160	4,757,445
Communist	52	14,760	3,442,556	0	0	7,380
Green	111	201,801	7,622,028	0	0	100,901
Indep/Unaffiliated	86	358,486	5,935,689	2	42,581	179,243
Liberal	301	14,633,510	20,473,830	288	7,036,924	7,316,755
Marijuana	73	6,992	4,966,992	0	0	3,496
Marxist-Leninist	84	7,916	5,735,466	0	0	3,958
Natural Law	69	4,463	4,692,900	0	0	2,232
New Democratic	298	3,954,481	20,279,509	57	1,187,063	1,977,241
Progressive Conservative	291	4,572,457	19,839,223	87	1,617,459	2,286,229
Total	**1,808**	**37,837,213**	**123,215,028**	**685**	**16,250,501**	**18,918,606**

TABLE 1: *Reimbursement of Candidate Expenses—2000 General Election*[60]

extending the reimbursement program to all candidates would unduly burden the public treasury. First of all, Canadian elections are inexpensive as a result of spending and contribution limits. Second, candidates are only reimbursed 60 per cent of their expenses. Reimbursement would no doubt be an incentive to increased expenses, but it would be a limited incentive—especially for candidates funding their own campaigns—because candidates would remain responsible for covering 40 per cent of their expenses. Third, political parties allocate their resources rationally. Political parties will continue to focus spending on races that are competitive. Candidates of major political parties in electoral districts where

[60] All data except projected refunds at zero per cent threshold taken from <www.elections.ca>. Not all actual refund figures provided by Elections Canada equal 50 per cent. The projected refund at zero per cent was estimated using the higher of: (a) the actual refund figure for those parties that qualified for reimbursement; or (b) 50 per cent of total candidate expenditures.

the party has dim prospects are unlikely to attract the same kind of financial support from the national party organisation as candidates in districts where the party is competitive. Fourth, most marginal candidates are unlikely to attract substantial donations for the same reasons that they are unable to attract substantial support at the polls. As a result, it will likely be only the exceptional case where an individual receiving between zero per cent and five per cent or even 10 per cent of the vote in a constituency would be reimbursed more than a token amount.

Prior to the 2004 general election, Parliament introduced reforms based on the Chief Electoral Officer's recommendations. The amendments to the *Canada Elections Act* deviated from the Chief Electoral Officer's recommendations in one important respect; the threshold for reimbursement of candidates was only lowered from 15 per cent to 10 per cent. The apparent reason for setting the threshold at 10 per cent was that in the five party system that prevailed in 2003 when the amendments were adopted, the government believed that at that level most major party candidates would stand a good chance of qualifying for reimbursement.[61]

Reconsidering Barrette v Canada

The threshold for reimbursement of candidate election expenses was challenged following the 1988 election by a failed New Democratic Party candidate in Quebec. The action was brought in the name of M Barrette, the failed candidate's official agent. The candidate, M Payette, received only 11.89 per cent of the vote in his constituency; short of the 15 per cent of the popular vote required to qualify for partial reimbursement of election expenditures. Payette testified that he never expected to win the election, but that he ran because he believed that his party's point of view should be put before the electorate for discussion. He went on to explain that in order to disseminate his message he had to incur costs that, whilst moderate, were beyond the funds available from the constituency association. In order to make the payments necessary to publicise his platform, he borrowed funds anticipating that the reimbursement after the election would be enough to satisfy this debt. The trial judge accepted that the expectation of reimbursement affected Payette's decision to become a candidate as well as the conduct of his campaign. More importantly, the trial judge found that the partial reimbursement threshold might affect the decisions of other potential candidates in the future.[62]

Payette complained that making reimbursement conditional on obtaining a percentage of the popular vote violated the right to freedom of expression in section 2(b) of the *Charter*, the right to vote in section 3 of the *Charter*, and the equality rights in section 15(1) of the *Charter*. The trial judge found that the purpose of the 15 per cent reimbursement threshold was 'to discourage the proliferation of parties and candidates unable to attract an important following' and parties and candidates that are 'ephemeral, marginal, frivolous or insignificant.'[63] He went on to observe that:

[61] 37th Parliament, 2nd Session, Standing Committee on Procedure and House Affairs, (3 April 2003) at 1210.

[62] *Barrette v Canada* (Attorney General) (1992) 14 CRR (2d) 166 (Que Sup Ct) at 178.

[63] *Ibid* at 181.

> In theory, each candidate should be afforded an equal opportunity to communicate his views to the electorate; otherwise there is a danger that the latter will be given a distorted or incomplete view of the issues. Of course, perfect equality is impossible. Much will depend upon the capacity of each candidate to use effectively and persuasively the opportunities afforded to him, but *the law should not contribute to or aggravate inequalities.*[64]

The trial judge held that the reimbursement threshold 'tends to discourage some serious candidates for election from conducting an effective campaign, for fear of incurring costs that may or may not be subsidised by the government.'[65] The trial judge went on to find that the preferential reimbursement scheme was contrary to section 3 of the *Charter* because it denied candidates 'equal opportunity' which the trial judge noted is 'essential to fairness in elections.'[66]

The trial decision in *Barrette* in some respects anticipates the reasoning adopted by the majority of the Supreme Court in *Figueroa*. The idea that 'the law should not contribute to or aggravate inequalities' is simply a different way of expressing the rule in *Figueroa* that 'legislation that exacerbates a pre-existing disparity in the capacity of the various political parties to communicate their positions to the general public is inconsistent with section 3.' Similarly, the idea that candidates have a right to 'equal opportunity' which includes equal access to public funds is consistent with the egalitarian model explained in *Harper*. The *Barrette* trial judge anticipated the Supreme Court's approach to section 3 challenges by considering equality arguments relevant to the right to vote and, indeed, the Court's egalitarian political theory.

McCarthy JA, writing the primary judgment of the Court of Appeal, accepted the trial judge's characterisation of the purpose of the reimbursement threshold; namely, to discourage the proliferation of parties and candidates. And without any sense of irony, McCarthy JA went on to claim: 'No one suggests that that purpose as such interferes with the rights guaranteed by section 3.'[67] In other words, the law is designed to discourage participation in elections, but it does not infringe upon the right to vote or the right to stand for election guaranteed by section 3. McCarthy JA was able to take this seemingly absurd position because of his view on the appropriate constitutional standard for adjudicating equality issues. McCarthy JA held that if equality arguments are to be considered, the standard must not differ from that embodied in section 15(1). Essentially, McCarthy JA held that section 3 does not create a different approach for equality issues that are peculiar to the democratic process. McCarthy JA opined:

> [N]othing in the *Charter* . . . support[s] the supposition that there are two kinds of prohibited discrimination, one explicitly prohibited and one implicitly prohibited.

[64] *Ibid* at 181 (emphasis added). A similar view was expressed in the context of a challenge to an up front funding scheme for Quebec provincial elections that provided funds on a preferential basis to incumbents: *Hébert v Quebec (Procurer Général)* [1998] AQ No 3675 (Que Sup Ct) at para 96.

[65] *Ibid* at 182.

[66] *Ibid* at 182.

[67] *Barrette*, above n 7 at 625.

> In other words, if the portions of the Act here in question are unconstitutional it must be because they infringe not on section 3 or section 2(b) but section 15. They do not impede the right to vote or to express oneself freely; the question is whether they encourage with discriminatory purpose or effect the exercise of any of those rights.[68]

McCarthy JA went on to hold that:

> I am unable to see in the 15 per cent threshold for partial reimbursement of election expenses any discriminatory purpose or effect within the meaning of section 15 of the *Charter*. Unsuccessful candidates who do not obtain at least 15 per cent of the valid votes cast are not, in my view, a "discrete and insular minority." Nor are they a "disadvantaged group in Canadian society." If the 15 per cent threshold discriminates against them, such discrimination is not based on any analogous ground. For the same reasons, the 15 per cent threshold involves no prohibited discrimination against voters who, if they are more fully informed, might vote differently.[69]

Having found that no *Charter* rights were violated by the 15 per cent popular vote threshold for reimbursement of candidate election expenses, McCarthy JA declined to undertake section 1 analysis weighing the merit of the state's objective. Mailhot JA in a concurring decision considered on a hypothetical basis whether the law could be upheld under section 1 if it contravened section 3. Mailhot JA concluded that given the 'government's limited financial resources . . . [it] is justified in limiting the access to a reimbursement to candidates who receive a certain amount of support from the voters . . .'[70]

The Court of Appeal's decision in *Barrette* is predicated entirely on the understanding that section 3 does not provide any substantive protection for equality interests or, if it does, those interests mirror the protections afforded by section 15(1). In light of *Figueroa*, the Court of Appeal in *Barrette* is plainly wrong. *Figueroa*, like *Barrette*, was framed as a constitutional challenge under sections 2(b), 3 and 15(1) of the *Charter*. The Supreme Court, however, 'determined that this matter can be disposed of solely with reference to section 3 of the *Charter*.'[71] As such, *Figueroa* confirms that section 3 is the proper venue for the consideration of equality issues—such as those in *Barrette*—pertinent to the democratic process. The assumption that informed the Court of Appeal's decision in *Barrette* is, therefore, incorrect.

Given the Court of Appeal's decision in *Barrette* was based on a now discredited doctrinal approach and acceptance of an anti-democratic and anti-egalitarian legislative purpose, the only remaining question is whether the threshold could be upheld under section 1 if a different state objective was asserted. The most logical alternative justification for the popular vote threshold is that identified by the CEO and Mailhot JA—cost. The question of cost has the potential to

[68] *Ibid* at 627.
[69] *Ibid* at 628.
[70] *Ibid* at 632.
[71] *Figueroa*, above n 5 at para 17.

chill judicial fervour. Courts may be unwilling to override Parliament's judgment when cost is the basis for limiting access to social programs.[72] Courts have recognised that Parliament must make choices between competing social objectives when allocating finite financial resources. Whilst cost might be a persuasive objection to judicial activism in some circumstances, the discussion in the preceding section of this chapter suggests the cost of extending funding at current levels to all candidates would not result in a significant increase in the total cost of reimbursements. The safeguards against runaway costs—for example, spending limits—that are already built into the public political finance regime make cost containment a state objective unworthy of overriding citizens' democratic rights.

Revisiting *Reform Party v Canada*—the Constitutionality of the Reservation and Allocation of Discounted and Free Broadcast Time

The Structure of the Political Broadcast Regime

Television is one of the most expensive means of communicating political messages, but it is nevertheless widely thought to be an effective way of reaching large numbers of electors. The irregular timing of elections in Canada's Westminster-style political system creates the possibility that political parties—except for the governing party that usually controls the timing of the election—will, as a practical matter, have difficulty in purchasing television advertising in advance of the election.[73] The *Canada Elections Act* remedies this perceived problem by requiring national television and radio networks to provide 390 minutes of radio and television time during an election period at their lowest commercial rate to political parties for election advertising. In addition to the discounted advertising time reserved, the *Canada Elections Act* in tandem with the *Broadcasting Act*[74] reserves free television and radio time that may be used for advertisements or lengthier political programming by the political parties. The political broadcasting regime provides that the television and radio networks must reserve an amount of free time at least equivalent to the amount provided in the previous election. During the last three elections, the amount of free television broadcast time provided by the networks has been 214 minutes. Of particular significance, the free time provided to political parties does not count as an 'election expense' and is not included when calculating political party spending limits.[75] Prior to the *Reform Party* case discussed below, the reservation and allocation provisions were complemented by a prohibition on political parties purchasing broadcast time outside the statutory framework.

[72] *Ibid* at para 66. See also, *Nova Scotia (Workers' Compensation Board) v Martin* [2003] 2 SCR 504 at para 109: 'Budgetary considerations in and of themselves cannot normally be invoked as a free standing pressing and substantial objective for the purposes of s 1 of the Charter.'

[73] *Reform Party*, above n 8 at 386.

[74] *Broadcasting Act*, SC 1991, c 11, as amended.

[75] *CEA*, above n 1 s 339.

An independent Broadcast Arbitrator allocates the paid and free advertising time among the registered parties. The Broadcast Arbitrator is guided in his allocation by the statutory formula set out in section 338. The formula instructs the Broadcast Arbitrator to give equal weight to

(a) the percentage of seats in the House of Commons held by each of the registered parties at the previous general election, and
(b) the percentage of the popular vote at the previous general election of each registered party.

The Broadcast Arbitrator is also to give,

> half the weight given to each of the factors referred to in each of paragraphs (a) and (b) to the number of candidates endorsed by each of the registered parties at the previous general election expressed as a percentage of all candidates endorsed by all registered parties at that election.[76]

New political parties are entitled to the lesser of the smallest amount of time allotted to a registered political party or six minutes. Subsection 5 provides that the Broadcast Arbitrator may 'modify the allocation in any manner he deems fit' if he considers the allocation dictated by the formula to be 'unfair to any of the registered parties or contrary to the public interest.' Section 345(2) provides that the statutory allocation formula applies to the allocation of free television and radio broadcast time as well.

The allocation system embodied in section 338 has its origins in the informal system used by the CBC to allocate free time among parties.[77] The allocation system was codified in the 1958 *Broadcasting Act* and in 1974 migrated to the *Elections Act* where it was applied to the allocation of paid advertising time as well.[78] From 1974 to 1991 the Broadcast Arbitrator allocated paid and free advertising time according to the statutory formula with discretionary deviations from the formula's allocation being made on an ad hoc basis. With a legal challenge to the allocation system pending, in 1992 the newly appointed Broadcast Arbitrator invited all political parties to offer suggestions as to how he might exercise his discretion in a systematic fashion to address the inequities of the statutory allocation formula. All of the political parties except the governing Progressive Conservative Party rejected strict adherence to the statutory formula. For their part, the Progressive Conservatives contended that they 'more than any other group or individual, are entitled to use the public airwaves.' This windy pronouncement was justified in the following way:

> [I]t is reasonable that the party in government should be provided with ample opportunity to defend its record in government and to outline its plans to build on

[76] *CEA* above n 1 s 338.
[77] J LaCalamita, 'The Equitable Campaign: Party Political Broadcasting Regulation in Canada' (1984) 22 *Osgoode Hall Law Journal* 543 at 553.
[78] *Ibid* at 553.

> that record. It is equally reasonable then, to expect that the party in official opposition, the party charged with the parliamentary responsibility for challenging the record and the plans of the governing party to be provided with the second largest opportunity to summarise its criticisms and offer alternatives. Lastly, other opposition and non-parliamentary parties could then reasonably expect to be allocated sufficient but less time to outline their platforms and policies.[79]

The Broadcast Arbitrator then considered three alternatives to the statutory formula. The first alternative suggested dividing the available time allotment equally among all of the registered parties. Equal allocation approach was rejected because it was fundamentally inconsistent with the statutory formula. Moreover, the Broadcast Arbitrator observed that allocation of significant amounts of paid time to the smaller parties would result in that time going unused. The second alternative, proposed by the Reform Party, is really a variant of the equal allocation approach. The maximum approach, as the Broadcast Arbitrator termed it, would have allowed any party to purchase up to 110 minutes of time at the discounted rate. The problem with the maximum approach was that it was not only inconsistent with the statutory formula, it would require the reservation of more than the 390 minutes reserved by the *Canada Elections Act*. The alternative adopted by the Broadcast Arbitrator is the formula promoted by the Liberal and New Democratic Parties. This approach, called the one-third minimum approach, allocates 130 of the 390 reserved minutes equally among all parties. The remaining 260 minutes are then allocated according to the statutory formula. The Broadcast Arbitrator has employed the one-third minimum approach for every allocation since 1992. The Broadcast Arbitrator's allocation of paid time in election years for the 1993, 1997, 2000, and 2004 federal general elections is set out in Table 3.

Reconsidering Reform Party of Canada v Canada

The reservation and allocation of paid and free broadcast time was challenged by the Reform Party prior to the 1993 federal general election. At the time of the legal challenge, the Reform Party only had one member of Parliament who had been elected during a by-election. Despite being a relatively new party, prior to the 1993 federal general election the Reform Party was running a major party-type campaign with substantial funding and candidates in all of the electoral districts in Manitoba, Saskatchewan, Alberta and British Columbia. The Reform Party, however, was only given the right to purchase 17 minutes of discounted television and radio advertising and a corresponding amount of free time by the Broadcast Arbitrator using his one-third minimum approach.

The Reform Party challenge was principally to the allocation of discounted and free broadcast time and the prohibition on purchase of broadcast time outside the statutory framework. The Reform Party contended that the allocation formula, even as amended by the Broadcast Arbitrator, unjustifiably gave weight to

[79] Broadcasting Arbitrator, *Reasons for Decision: 1992 Allocation of Paid Time* (31 December 1992) at 8. Available at <www.elections.ca>.

Party	1993	1997	2000	2004	TOTAL
Liberal	78:00	118:00	113:00	122:30	431.30
Progressive Conservative	116:00	34:00	48:00	–	198.00
New Democrat	55:00	26:00	40:30	39:00	160.30
Bloc Quebecois	5:00	43:00	40:30	41:00	129.30
Conservative	–	–	–	88:30	88.30
Reform	17:00	51:00	–	–	68.00
Green	15:00	13:00	15:30	20:30	64.00
Canadian Alliance	–	59:30	–	–	59.30
Marxist-Leninist	5:00	12:00	14:30	18:30	50.00
Christian Heritage	16:00	13:00	14:30	6:00	49.30
Communist	14:00	6:00	6:00	17:30	43.30
Natural Law	5:00	17:00	17:00	–	39.00
Canadian Action	–	6:00	14:30	18:00	38.30
Libertarian	16:00	13:00	–	–	29.00
Party for the Commonwealth of Canada	14:00	13:00	–	–	27.00
Marijuana	–	–	6:00	18:30	24.30
Option Canada	14:00	–	–	–	14.00
Canada Party	–	13:00	–	–	13.00
Collective Group	–	6:00	–	–	6.00
Rainbow Coalition	–	6:00	–	–	6.00
Canadian Party for Renewal	5:00	–	–	–	5.00
Confederation of Regions Western	5:00	–	–	–	5.00
National Party of Canada	5:00	–	–	–	5.00
Nationalist Party of Quebec	5:00	–	–	–	5.00
Total	**390:00**	**390:00**	**390:00**	**390:00**	

TABLE 3: *Allocation of Paid Television and Radio Broadcast Time for Purchase—1993–2004 Federal General Elections*[80]

political parties' performance in the last election with no regard to changes in popular support since the last election The allocation formula, therefore, discriminated against emerging parties such as the Reform Party. The impact of the allocation formula was crystallised by the prohibition on purchase of time outside the statutory framework. Essentially, the discounted and free political broadcasting

[80] Broadcasting Arbitrator, *Reasons for Decision: 1993 Allocation of Paid Time* (3 August 1993); *Reasons for Decision: 1997 Allocation of Paid Time* (21 April 1997); *Reasons for Decision: 2000 Allocation of Paid Time* (20 October 2000); *Reasons for Decision: 2004 Reallocation of Paid Time* (16 April 2004). All available at <www.elections.ca>.

regime discriminated against emerging parties and prevented them from mitigating the impact of the discrimination.

The government responded to the Reform Party's position by asserting that: (1) broadcasting is an important means of political communication; (2) broadcast time is limited and sometimes unavailable; (3) broadcasters might favour the messages of certain parties over others; (4) broadcasting is expensive and it is in the public interest that costs be controlled so that one party does not out bid others; and (5) providing discounted and free broadcast time contributes to the overall control of election expenditures.[81] The essence of the government's submission was that the discounted and free political broadcasting regime was designed to mitigate the distorting effects of wealth on the political process. In other words, the provision of discounted and free broadcasting time to political parties was part and parcel of what is now called the egalitarian model. The government also contended that the unequal allocation was necessary to prevent the allocation of precious broadcasting time to 'single issue' or 'regional' political parties.[82] Broadcast time must be allocated principally to the political parties with a reasonable chance of forming the next government so that voters can inform themselves of the policies of, and decide among, the major contenders.

McFadyen JA, writing for the majority of the Alberta Court of Appeal, held that the prohibition on the purchase of broadcast time outside the statutory framework infringed the right to freedom of expression and was not justified because it was not integral to political broadcasting regime. With respect to the reservation and allocation of discounted and free broadcasting time, however, McFadyen JA accepted the government's position. She found that the paid and free political broadcasting regime addressed a pressing and substantial objective; namely, ensuring 'the availability of broadcast time to political parties during federal election campaigns and the control of costs . . . .'[83] She went on to find that the unequal allocation of reserved time was not only reasonable, but necessary, holding that:

> [E]qual allocation of these limited resources is not feasible and is not in the public interest which requires that the public be informed of the major issues in an election and the position being taken by political parties which stand a realistic chance of forming a government. While other voices and interests have the right to be heard, lesser access to the free and purchasable time, which broadcasters are required by legislation to provide, is a reasonable and proportionate response to the problem.[84]

McFadyen JA's conclusions can be assailed on several fronts. To begin with, she followed the logic of the Quebec Court of Appeal in *Barrette*. To the extent that the claim by the Reform Party was an equality claim—essentially a claim for equal treatment in the allocation of discounted and free broadcast time—she held that

[81] *Reform Party*, above n 8 at 386.
[82] *Ibid* at 387.
[83] *Ibid* at 386.
[84] *Ibid* at 387.

the threshold to be met was that prescribed by section 15(1) of the *Charter*, not section 3. As discussed previously in the context of *Barrette*, this doctrinal approach is a fundamental error in light of *Figueroa*. McFadyen JA found that the Reform Party did not enjoy protection under section 15(1) and that the individual members of the Reform Party were not discriminated against by the unequal allotment of discounted and free time under the broadcasting regime. McFadyen JA opined that:

> I do not accept that there is unfairness to or discrimination against individual members of political parties by unequal access by political parties to broadcast time. I do not accept that a political party, which enjoys limited support of a small number of individuals who wish to promote a specific interest or to ridicule the process, is the equal of a political party which has the support of a far greater number of voters and genuinely strives to provide information about its program for governing the country.[85]

McFadyen JA went on to note that any unfairness to emerging political parties could be addressed by the Broadcast Arbitrator who maintains discretion to deviate from the statutory formula.

McFadyen JA also refused to accept that the reservation and allocation provisions—once freed from the prohibition on purchase of additional time outside the statutory framework—violated either section 2(b) or section 3 of the *Charter*. Nevertheless, McFadyen JA went on to consider hypothetically whether the reservation and allocation provisions could be saved under section 1 if she was incorrect and they did, in fact, violate section 2(b) or section 3. McFadyen JA first considered the purpose of the broadcast regime. She adopted the trial judge's conclusion that the allocation provisions 'assured that the limited time available would not be unduly occupied by groups who had no interest in or chance of succeeding in the election.'[86] This is the same rationale that was behind the provision limiting the ability to issue tax receipts to registered parties that was discredited in *Figueroa*.

Madam Justice Conrad, writing for the minority of the Court in *Reform Party*, offered a criticism of the majority's position from an egalitarian perspective. Unlike McFadyen JA who accepted the Government's characterisation of the purpose of the legislation, Conrad JA questioned whether, in fact, the political broadcasting regime was truly motivated by a desire to mitigate the influence of wealth on the political process:

> [T]he challenged scheme creates . . . the very inequity which it is feared wealth would create; favouritism and free time to the established parties. Moreover, the free time does not need to be accounted for in election expenses. Thus it cannot be a lack of equality, or fairness, created by wealth that is the objective of this particular legislation, because the allocation formula is inconsistent with such a goal.[87]

[85] *Ibid* at 390.
[86] *Ibid* at 378.
[87] *Ibid* at 409.

Conrad JA's point is powerful, but she overreaches. The allocation formula does not show that the political broadcasting regime lacks an egalitarian purpose. Instead, the allocation formula is an example of how high-minded interventions in the democratic process can be distorted by Parliamentary perceptions of the public interest. Without going so far as to attribute self-serving motives to elected representatives, it is reasonable to suppose that Parliamentarians may unjustifiably conflate their self-interest and the public interest. Indeed, Conrad JA later observed that legislative history showed that, 'Parliament wanted to ensure there would be free time and that all broadcast time would be controlled by a reservation and allocation system favouring the incumbents.'[88] Conrad JA likened the impact of the broadcasting regime on political discourse to the impact of a gerrymander on the right to vote.[89]

Undoubtedly, the Parliamentary self-interest that Conrad JA identified as being behind the broadcast regime's allocation formula also informed the statutory requirement that political parties have 50 candidates to be 'registered' and to issue tax receipts that was considered in *Figueroa*. The rule that emerged from *Figueroa*—that legislation may not exacerbate a pre-existing disparity in the capacity of political parties to communicate with the public—will address the problem of legislative self-interest in many circumstances. Remarkably, the broadcast time allocation formula, despite its obvious flaws, does not necessarily contravene the rule in *Figueroa*. The allocation formula replicates, not exacerbates, pre-existing disparities between political parties. Giving McFadyen JA the benefit of the doubt, this may be what she meant when she found that the allocation formula did not discriminate against small political parties.

One of the problems that emerges from the majority and minority reasons in *Reform Party* is that the Westminster Parliamentary system together with the difficulty in obtaining prime broadcasting time on short notice at a reasonable price makes it difficult to create an effective and fair means of allocating discounted and free broadcasting time. If there is no reservation and allocation of broadcast time, there is the risk that only the party in government, which usually controls the timing of an election, will be able to obtain prime broadcasting time. Accordingly, the absence of some form of political broadcasting regime may be worse than the imperfect one that exists. There are only two real alternatives to the current allocation formula. First, broadcasting time could be allocated quarterly or even monthly based on an opinion poll conducted for that purpose. This approach would not address Conrad JA's concern about replicating disparities in wealth, but it would substantially address the concern about discrimination against emerging political parties. Second, broadcasting time could be allocated equally to all political parties irrespective of their past performance or current prospects. This approach would address Conrad JA's concern that an allocation formula not echo the disparities in wealth between the parties, but might invite pragmatic objections.

88 *Ibid* at 418.
89 *Ibid* at 424.

Conclusion: The Egalitarian Model and Competition

The Supreme Court is clearly committed to ensuring that the egalitarian model of election regulation enacted by Parliament is true to the political theory that inspired it. The egalitarian model as presently conceived, however, is impoverished by a lack of attention to the role of competition in the political process. Competition is normatively desirable in the political process because when challengers are competitive they either bring renewal by defeating incumbents or, when they fail, incumbents are pushed to be better candidates and representatives.[90] Moreover, competition raises the level and intensity of political discourse and cannot help but enhance citizens' participation in the political process. By way of contrast, lack of political competition breeds complacency and contempt for the democratic process. As a result, regulations of the political process should promote, not inhibit, competition. Too often, however, competitive pressures can distort the regulation of the political process. As Conrad JA pointed out in her dissent in *Reform Party*, regulations adopted by Parliament can favour incumbents and operate as entry barriers to the political process.

One of the central tenets of the political theory that underpins the egalitarian model is that the state is not to be inherently distrusted. Indeed, the state has a role in facilitating the equal participation of all citizens in the political process. The Court is right to accept as a matter of theory that the state can act to promote egalitarian objectives; however, there are clear warning signs that the Court should not turn a blind eye to the possibility that political finance regulations can reflect the self-interest of parliamentarians in being re-elected. Indeed, the idea that some participants in the electoral process are more legitimate than others is a recurring example in the cases discussed in this chapter of Parliament's perspective as a participant in the electoral process rather than an impartial rule-maker. Moreover, important parts of the political finance regime have anti-competitive aspects. Public funding by way of reimbursement, for example, favours those candidates and parties who can finance election campaigns up front. Anti-competitive effects can also be identified in the political broadcasting regime and political party expenditure limits which are determined with reference to the previous election. These measures institutionalise historic advantages and help to perpetuate the status quo. Not surprisingly, some scholars who argue for increased awareness of the impact of political competition on the regulation of the democratic process contend that political finance regulations must be subjected to strict scrutiny.[91]

The question going forward, then, is whether the egalitarian model is inconsistent in that it appears to require both a deferential approach and strict scrutiny. Whilst it is a subject that deserves its own chapter, it can be posited that an

[90] R Briffault, 'Public Funding and Democratic Elections' (1999) 148 *University of Pennsylvania Law Review* 563 at 569.

[91] S Issacharoff & R Pildes, 'Politics as Markets: Partisan Lockups of the Democratic Process' (1998) 50 *Stanford Law Review* 643 at 688–90.

approach to judicial review may be developed that is not intrinsically hostile to political finance regulation, but, at the same time, is capable of subjecting Parliament's motives to close examination. The egalitarian justification for such an approach can be found in the dissenting reasons of Conrad JA in *Reform Party*—the advantages of incumbency overlap to a significant degree with the advantages of wealth. In other words, regulations that favour incumbents will in many cases favour the candidate or party with the most financial resources. Conrad JA's view is much the same as that of John Rawls who wrote that,

> Political power rapidly accumulates and becomes unequal; and making use of the coercive apparatus of the state and its law, those who gain the advantage can often assure themselves of a favored position.[92]

Conrad JA's and Rawls' approach is consistent with the Court's political theory and provides a foundation for the Court to adapt its approach to judicial review without undermining the egalitarian model.

[92] J Rawls, *A Theory of Justice, Revised Edition* (Cambridge, Mass; Belknap Press, 1999) at 199.

13

Elections, Democracy and Free Speech: More at Stake than an Unfettered Right to Advertise

JANET L HIEBERT

ALL DEMOCRATIC POLITICAL communities must establish fair election rules to ensure that the electoral processes and the outcomes generated are legitimate. Unlike the obvious requirement of ensuring that all adult citizens are entitled to vote,[1] that the vote is free from intimidation and violence and that turnout is robust, the criteria for fair elections raises a number of philosophical quandaries. Amongst the most important of these is what role should money play in elections? Specifically, what balance should be struck between (i) the ability of individuals and groups to spend money on election advertising to promote issues or to spend money on advertisements that support or oppose particular candidates and parties, and (ii) the opportunity of citizens to participate in the election process on equal terms, given unequal access to the monetary resources required for political advertisements?

Canada has regulated the federal election spending of candidates and parties since 1974 in an effort to promote equality in citizen participation. But the sustainability of this regulatory framework has been in jeopardy almost since its inception because of a number of successful constitutional challenges to one essential element of the electoral regime: restrictions on 'third party' or what will be referred to in this chapter as 'independent expenditures' (the election spending of individuals or groups other than registered candidates and parties).[2] Trial and provincial appeal court judges have repeatedly ruled that limits on independent expenditures are unconstitutional. In so doing, they have adopted a narrow view of the relationship between democratic principles and election rules, focusing on whether the state can demonstrate that actual harm would arise if independent

[1] This claim may be contested because many believe that it is legitimate to ban prisoners from voting. However, the Supreme Court of Canada has ruled that such prohibitions are unconstitutional. See *Sauvé v Canada (Chief Electoral Officer)* [2002] 3 SCR 519.

[2] I prefer the term 'independent expenditures' because the term 'third party spending' is confusing in Canada's multi-party political system.

expenditures were not subject to spending limits. But in reaching this conclusion, the relevant judges have not only mischaracterised the purpose of the impugned legislation, they have also failed to acknowledge a rival and, arguably, more robust model of democracy that emphasises equality of citizens: a goal that depends upon regulating the amount of all forms of election spending.

Although limits on independent expenditures have had a 'high mortality rate'[3] at the trial and provincial court of appeal levels, the Supreme Court of Canada in 2004 upheld their legitimacy in *Harper v Canada (Attorney General)*.[4] If there is now any lingering doubt about the stability of this regulatory regime, the reason for this is entirely political. At the time of writing, the Official Opposition in the federal Parliament is headed by Stephen Harper, the very individual who launched the latest constitutional challenge to limits on independent expenditures while serving as president of the National Citizens' Coalition (NCC). The NCC, a right-wing group that advocates 'freedom through less government', has a history of challenging the constitutional validity of limitations on independent expenditures, and has characterised the Supreme Court decision as 'a tragic day in Canadian democracy.'[5] Harper, now resigned from the NCC and leader of the Conservative Party stated publicly that the Supreme Court had made a 'terrible mistake' in upholding limits on independent expenditures,[6] and while campaigning in the 2004 federal election promised that if elected his government would allow Canadians to disseminate their views during elections—a decision that would require repealing the legislation.[7] His criticism of this Supreme Court decision, which is characterised by considerable deference to Parliament (discussed below), appears extremely hypocritical in light of Harper's public denouncement of the Supreme Court for being generally too activist in its interpretation of the *Canadian Charter of Rights and Freedoms* (from herein Charter) and his campaign promise to reduce judicial activism by appointing judges who are more deferential to Parliament.[8] In the 2004 federal election that was held shortly after the Supreme Court verdict, the incumbent Liberal government was reduced to minor status, suggesting that the future of the regulatory framework for election expenses cannot be taken for granted.

This chapter will discuss the judicial treatment of this issue and assess the implications of judicial review for the normative objectives of the election regulatory framework. This analysis is important both to understand the role of the courts in

[3] This characterisation is borrowed from the majority Alberta Court of Appeal ruling in *Harper v Canada (Attorney General)* (2002) 14 Alta LR (4th) 4 at para 4.

[4] *Harper v Canada (Attorney General)* [2004] SCC 33.

[5] National Citizens Coalition, 'NCC Battles Gag Laws'; <http://www.morefreedom.org/NCCLive/campaigns/campaignsArticle.jsp?PageID=4&ArticleID=130>, (21 July 2004).

[6] The Conservative Party of Canada was officially formed on 8 Dec 2003, after the merger of the Alliance and Progressive Conservative parties.

[7] 'The Conservatives and the Judges' *The Globe and Mail* (Toronto), 21 June 2004, <http://www.globeandmail.com/servlet/ArticleNews/TPPrint/LAC/20040621/EJUDGE21/TPComment/>(21 July 2004).

[8] This campaign promise was reported in the above story, and prompted considerable election commentary on what the election of a Conservative government would mean for the evolution of the Charter.

resolving this issue and to assess critics' opposition to limits on independent expenditures during federal elections.

Regulating Election Costs

The central purpose of limiting independent expenditures is pursuit of equality amongst citizens in their election participation. This normative goal is sought, primarily, by regulating the amount of money that candidates and parties can spend during the election campaign, in conjunction with a system of partial public funding of candidate and party election costs.[9] Limiting independent expenditures is an essential but ancillary element of this regulatory framework.

In restricting the amount of money that can be spent in elections, the regulatory framework is premised on the assumption that disparity in resources affects citizens' capacity to participate in a fair and equitable manner. Limits on campaign spending, along with partial reimbursements for election costs, promote equality in citizen election participation by preventing elections from becoming so exorbitantly expensive that only those who are wealthy, or have support from wealthy donors, can contest office in a meaningful way. By restricting the cost of elections, candidate and party spending limits also release elected officials from their dependency on wealthy donors and, with that, liberate them from having to cater to the demands of organised interests that may conflict with constituents' or public interests. These spending limits promote equality in citizen participation in another way as well, by preventing those who are wealthy from dominating electoral discourse. They prevent wealthy individuals or groups from purchasing large quantities of commercial advertising to promote the issues they consider important, or draw attention to the candidates they support or oppose, while the majority of citizens remain silent because of their inability to *purchase* comparable opportunities for *speech*.

The central element of this regulatory framework, spending limits for candidates and parties, has never been constitutionally challenged. Nevertheless, the difficulty of successfully defending limits on independent expenditures in lower and provincial appeal courts had cast serious doubt on the continued viability of the entire regulatory framework. Why the issue of regulating independent expenditures was so important is because their fate would almost certainly have determined the viability of the broader goal of promoting equality by controlling candidate and party election spending. It is highly unlikely that the objective of controlling the election expenses of candidates and parties could be sustained indefinitely, if independent expenditures continued to be unregulated. Candidates were particularly vulnerable to unregulated independent expenditures. What made them so vulnerable was the potential for their modest levels of permitted spending to be matched or exceeded by independent expenditures. For example, candidates in the Canadian general election of 2004 were legally entitled to spend

[9] The public funding dimension has recently been changed, as will be discussed below.

between $51,854.63 and $83,471.30 depending on the size of their electoral districts.[10] If independent expenditures were to target candidates in a negative manner, candidates would be placed in an unfair position because their own spending limits would constrain their ability to purchase advertising to reply. Alternatively, independent expenditures could be used for supportive parallel campaigns to augment what a candidate was legally entitled to spend. Thus, if this gap in the regulatory framework were to persist, the likely result would be unenforceable spending limits.

Quite apart from the issue of whether candidate or party spending limits would be enforceable if independent expenditures were not also regulated, was the question of whether they could be legally sustained. It is highly unlikely that candidates or parties would have continued to accept the constitutional validity of their own spending limits, particularly if they believed that their election chances were being hurt by this incongruity in the regulatory rules for election spending. If candidate or party spending limits were themselves challenged as an unconstitutional violation of freedom of expression, it is difficult to imagine that the judiciary would have looked favourably upon a regulatory arrangement that was so incoherent as to be manifestly unfair. The illogical asymmetry that would exist from restricting candidate or party spending but not restricting independent expenditures, would have rendered the entire electoral regulatory regime extremely vulnerable from a constitutional perspective.

Constitutional Challenges to Regulating Independent Expenditures

The Canadian Parliament has on four different occasions passed legislation that regulated independent expenditures during federal election campaigns; each of the last three initiatives was motivated by the need to respond to a judicial decision that either negated the effect of the restriction or, after the Charter was adopted in 1982, rendered it unconstitutional for violating freedom of expression.

Limits on candidate and party spending passed in 1974 were accompanied by a prohibition on other individuals or groups from spending money to promote or oppose a candidate or party. The only exception to this prohibition was if these independent expenditures were incurred 'in good faith' for the purpose of gaining support for an individual's views on an issue of public policy, or to advance the aims of a nonpartisan organisation. But within a few years it became apparent that this 'good faith' defence was not enforceable because it could be invoked for ostensibly partisan purposes.[11] In 1983 the federal Parliament passed legislation to

[10] Elections Canada, General Election 2004, 'Final Candidate Election Expenses Limits', <www.elections.ca>. (21 July 2004).

[11] The ineffective nature of this defence became clear after an individual was acquitted of violating the law despite not having any articulated policy position, and advocating a direct partisan message not to vote 'Liberal'. *R v Roach*, unreported, (Judicial District of York, Ont Prov Ct (Crim Div) 24 Oct 1977)), aff'd (1978), 25 O (2d) 767 (Co Ct).

redress this situation and banned all forms of independent expenditures. This legislation was soon subject to litigation, was declared unconstitutional in Alberta, and was not enforced anywhere else in the country.[12] The third legislative attempt to control independent expenditures, in 1993, introduced a $1,000 spending limit for partisan advocacy, while imposing no restriction on issue advocacy. Like the earlier ban on independent expenditures, this legislation was soon declared unconstitutional at trial,[13] a decision that was upheld by the Alberta Court of Appeal[14] and was not appealed further. However, in an unrelated decision, the Supreme Court of Canada specifically disapproved of the Alberta Court of Appeal's ruling.[15] The fourth federal attempt to regulate independent expenditures, (the current legislation passed in 2000), was declared unconstitutional at the trial level,[16] a decision upheld by the Court of Appeal,[17] but reversed on appeal by the Supreme Court.[18] These restrictions on independent expenditures, which have now been declared constitutional by the Supreme Court, establish strict spending limits for individuals and groups but also for the first time impose a requirement that groups register and, depending on the level of their spending, submit audited accounts of their expenditures. The legislation limits independent expenditures, by either individuals or groups, to a maximum of $150,000 nationally, in which no more than $3,000 can be spent in any electoral district, to promote or oppose the election of candidates by naming them, showing their likenesses, identifying them by their respective political affiliations or taking a position on an issue with which candidates are particularly associated.[19]

Canada has held six federal elections (1984, 1988, 1993, 1997, 2000 and 2004) in which independent expenditures have been regulated only twice (during the last two elections).[20] With the exception of the 1988 election, the other elections where independent expenditures were not regulated did not result in substantial levels of individual or interest group election spending. Many believe the 1988 election, which had unprecedented levels of independent expenditures, was an aberration. What distinguished this election from others was both the prominence of a single issue—Canada's Free Trade Agreement (FTA) with the United

[12] *National Citizens' Coalition v Canada (Attorney General)* [1984] 5 WWR 436 (Alta QB).
[13] *Somerville v Canada (Attorney General)* (1993) Oral judgment (Alta QB 25 June) J McLeod.
[14] *Somerville v Canada (Attorney General)* (1996) 136 DLR (4th) 205 (Alta CA).
[15] *Libman v Quebec (Attorney General)* [1997] 3 SCR 569 at 619.
[16] *Harper v Canada (Attorney General)* (2001) 93 Alta LR (3d) 281.
[17] *Harper v Canada (Attorney General)* (2002) 14 Alta LR (4th) 4.
[18] *Harper v Canada (Attorney General)* [2004] SCC 33.
[19] The legislation uses the term 'third party' spending and defines a third party as an individual, corporation or a group. A group is defined as an unincorporated trade union, trade association or other group of persons acting together by mutual consent for a common purpose.
[20] Independent expenditures were regulated only during the last three weeks of the 2000 election. On 22 Oct 2000, an election writ was issued for an election date of 27 Nov 2000. Stephen Harper applied to the same trial judge who had earlier declared the legislation unconstitutional, to seek an injunction that would restrain the Chief Electoral Officer of Canada and the Commissioner of Canada Elections from enforcing limits on independent expenditures. This injunction was granted [2000] AJ No 1226 (QL), and was upheld by the Alberta Court of Appeal [2000] AJ No 1240 (QL). On 10 Nov, the Supreme Court granted a stay of the injunction [2000] 2 SCR 764. Spending limits were in force for the remainder of the election.

States—and the fact that the two leading political parties could be distinguished according to whether they supported or opposed the FTA. Only one political party, the governing Progressive Conservative Party (PC), supported the FTA. Consequently, it was possible to infer from issue-oriented advertisements that promoted free trade, that the message conveyed support for the PC party.[21] But while the amount of money spent by independent expenditures favoured one side of the FTA issue, no empirical evidence suggests that this spending had an effect on the election outcome.

Few scholarly studies have been undertaken to monitor independent expenditures in elections or to assess how they influence voters' behaviour. The most systematic attempt was conducted in relation to the 1988 election. The author of this study, political scientist Richard Johnston, sought to measure the effects of independent expenditures (in newspaper advertising) on voters' intent. For this assessment he used data provided by the Royal Commission on Electoral Reform and Party Financing (Lortie Commission, which was established in November 1989). Johnston initially concluded that independent expenditures might have helped increase intentions to vote for the PC party late in the 1988 campaign, although not enough to explain the entire gap in the popular vote between the PC and Liberal parties.[22] But upon subsequent review, Johnston revised his opinion, concluding that the net impact of independent expenditures related to the FTA was null.[23] In his revised opinion, 'third-party advertising coefficients defy substantive interpretation: some are large and significant but the pattern is offsetting and the total coefficient effectively zero.'[24] A study was also done that recorded independent expenditures in the 1993 election. But unlike the 1988 election, no attempt was made to evaluate the effects of this spending on election behaviour. The study of 1993 election expenses, which

[21] In that election, the estimated amount of advertising in the form of independent expenditures was $4,729,104. The overwhelming majority ($3,638,904) was spent promoting free trade. In comparison, the amount of political advertising by the PC party was $4,716,737, combined with $7,462,877 by PC candidates, which meant that for every advertising dollar the party and candidates spent, 30 cents of independent expenditures were also spent on the most important issue to that party and its candidates. This estimation understates the actual amount of spending and was based on interest group advertising for the entire election period in 14 newspapers, supplemented by information provided by some of the interest groups involved. See J Hiebert, 'Interest Groups and Canadian Federal Elections' in FL Seidle (ed), *Interest Groups and Elections in Canada*, Research Studies, (Toronto, Dundurn Press, 1991) 20–23.

[22] R Johnston 'The Volume and Impact of "Third-Party" Advertising in the 1988 Election' Memo to the Royal Commission on Electoral Reform and Party Financing (unpublished, 1990).

[23] N Nevitte has interpreted Johnston's revised opinion as meaning that independent expenditures had no effect on the 1988 election. But Bakvis and Smith disagree, and draw upon Johnston's original study that suggested 'while it is true that the data disclose nothing firm about the effects of third party advertising, still from a social science perspective it would be unwise to reject altogether the possibility of such effects': Bakvis H and J Smith, 'Third-Party Advertising and Electoral Democracy: The Political Theory of the Alberta Court of Appeal in *Somerville v Canada (Attorney General)* [1996]' (1997) 23 *Canadian Public Policy* 164 at 171.

[24] R Johnston *et al*, *Letting the People Decide: Dynamics of a Canadian Election* (Montreal, McGill-Queen's University Press, 1992) 163.

focused principally on newspaper advertisements, revealed independent expenditures of $235,000.[25]

The validity of restricting independent expenditures has been subject to debate almost from the time such measures were first implemented three decades ago. Critics argue that restrictions on independent expenditures stymie the articulation of ideas at the most important time in a political cycle, the election contest, and believe that the governmental and parliamentary support for them has been based entirely on self-interest: to insulate established parties from public scrutiny and criticism. Many who are critical of limits on independent expenditures reject the premise that they are necessary to protect the integrity of candidate and party spending limits. They consider the only compelling reason to restrict independent expenditures is if these expenditures would otherwise harm the political process, but argue no evidence of this problem exists. For example, Brian Tanguay and Barry Kay conclude that not only is there no substantive evidence to justify severe restrictions of independent expenditures, but that institutional differences between Canada and the United States make it unlikely that interest groups will present the same kind of threat to electoral democracy in Canada as they produce in the United States.[26] Alternatively, some argue that if the integrity of candidate and party spending limits is dependent upon restricting independent expenditures, all spending constraints should be removed. Independent expenditures force candidates and parties to address issues that may otherwise be neglected or to respond to criticism of their positions or records. Thus protecting independent expenditures is important for citizens' right to freedom of expression and to provide society with a more informed citizenry.[27]

But critics of limits on independent expenditures cannot possibly anticipate how their removal would affect election behaviour. As suggested above, it is unlikely that candidates or political parties would continue to accept the legitimacy of their own spending limits, particularly if these left them unable to fully respond to negative advertisements or if they perceived that their partisan rivals were being advantaged by favourable advertisements paid for by independent expenditures. Moreover, if elections were to become laissez faire contests in terms of how much money candidates and parties could spend, this would require

[25] The low level may be explained, in part, by uncertainty about the legality of independent expenditures. At the time of the election, legislation was in place that restricted independent expenditures to $1,000. But the status of this legislation was uncertain because it was subject to constitutional challenge. A ruling that the legislation was unconstitutional was being appealed to the Alberta Court of Appeal during the election campaign. This uncertainty about the status of the legislation led to the decision by Elections Canada not to enforce the spending regulations. J Hiebert, 'Money and Elections: Can Citizens Participate on Fair Terms amidst Unrestricted Spending?' (1998) 31 *Canadian Journal of Political Science* 91 at p 96.

[26] B Tanguay and B Kay, 'Third-Party Advertising and the Threat to Electoral Democracy in Canada: The Mouse that Roared' (1998) 17 *International Journal of Canadian Studies* 57.

[27] See, eg, F Palda, *Election Finance Regulation in Canada. A Critical Review* (Vancouver, Fraser Institute, 1991); J Cameron, 'Participation and Democratic Process: Do Third-Party Spending Limits Protect or Threaten Democratic Values?' *Canada Watch*, July/August 1993, pp 7–8; D Francis, 'A New Attack on Freedom of Speech' *Maclean's*, 31 May 1993; B Tyler, 'Third-Party Limits Hurt Public's Right-to-Know' *The Gazette* (Montreal), 31 July 1997.

reassessing uses of public monies and tax credits, particularly in light of legislation passed in 2003 (An Act to Amend the Canada Elections Act and the Income Tax Act (Political Financing)), which bans corporate and union contributions to candidates and parties, restricts the amount that individuals can contribute to candidates and parties, and introduces a scheme of public financing related to the level of support a party receives in federal elections. This legislation was motivated by an attempt to create more public confidence in the political and electoral process by enhancing the fairness and transparency of candidates' and parties' election finances.[28] It represents the most significant development in terms of election finance since the 1974 legislative amendments were passed.

Judicial Treatment of Restrictions on Independent Expenditures

Before addressing the judicial treatment of this issue, it is helpful to first explain the structure for reviewing claims that rights have been infringed under the Charter. The Charter envisages a two-stage process for evaluating the constitutionality of legislative actions. In the first stage, courts address the issue of whether a right has been infringed. Only upon finding that there has been an infringement do judges proceed to the second stage, which is to determine whether the restriction is justified and reasonable.[29] The government has consistently conceded that limits on independent expenditures violate freedom of expression. Consequently, the focus in judicial review has been on whether restrictions on independent expenditures are justified. When determining the validity of these, the essential criteria boil down to the following: does the legislative objective represent a sufficiently important public purpose to justify restricting a right and, if so, has it been

[28] Bill C-24, An Act to Amend the Canada Elections Act and the Income Tax Act (Political Financing) introduced a new requirement that only citizens and permanent residents can make financial contributions to registered parties, candidates, constituency associations, and leadership and nomination contestants. These contributions by individuals are subject to an annual limit of $5,000 for each party, including amounts given to electoral district associations, candidates and nomination contestants. The legislation prohibits corporations, trade unions and associations from making contributions to any registered political party or to any leadership contestants. However, they are allowed to contribute small amounts, a maximum of $1,000 collectively, toward a party's candidates, nomination contestants and electoral district associations or to a candidate who is not associated with a registered party. The legislation was controversial and was passed by vote of 172 to 62. The government bill was supported by the New Democratic Party and the Bloc Québécois, and was opposed by the Canadian Alliance and the Conservatives (which have since merged to create the Conservative Party). For more information about this legislation, see Legislative Summary, 'Bill C-24: An Act to Amend the Canada Elections Act and the Income Tax Act (Political Financing), <http://www.parl.gc.ca/common/Bills_ls.asp?Parl=37&Ses=2&ls=C24> (21 July 2004), and 'Campaign financing: Chrétien's plan for reform' CBC News <http://www.cbc.ca/news/> (21 July 2004).

[29] The relevant provision is s 1, which provides: 'The *Canadian Charter of Rights and Freedoms* guarantees the rights and freedoms set out in it subject only to such reasonable limits prescribed by law as can be demonstrably justified in a free and democratic society.'

developed in a way that is rational, minimally intrusive, and are the effects of the impairment proportional to the importance of the legislative objective?[30]

Trial and provincial court of appeal decisions reveal considerable scepticism about the merits of regulating independent expenditures. This scepticism has been influenced by the following three judicially-held assumptions. First, legislation that intentionally restricts independent expenditures is inherently suspect because limiting free speech is inconsistent with democratic principles. Second, the only possible justification for restricting independent expenditures is to prevent corruption to the political process. Third, demonstrating this harm exists requires empirical evidence that if independent expenditures were not regulated, they would result in actual harm, such as evidence that money 'buys' elections. Each of these assumptions is problematic on their own. Together, they operate so as to make it virtually impossible for a government to satisfy judges that limits on independent expenditures are a reasonable and justifiable restriction of freedom of expression under the Charter.

Assumption One: Limits on Independent Expenditures Contradict Democratic Principles

Until the 2004 Supreme Court ruling in *Harper*, Canadian courts showed little sympathy for arguments that the purpose of regulating independent expenditures is sufficiently important that it justifies restricting expression.[31] The highest degree of scepticism came from Justice Conrad of the Alberta Court of Appeal who, while reviewing the 1993 limits on independent expenditures, characterised as contradictory the claim that such restrictions are a justifiable limit on speech because the legislation 'purports to protect the democratic process, by means of infringing the very rights which are fundamental to a democracy.'[32]

Judicial treatment of this issue prior to the Supreme Court's 2004 *Harper* decision reflected a narrow conception of democracy, focusing entirely on the negative dimension of the speech claim, freedom from state interference, rather than on what effects unregulated spending could have on election participation. By conceiving of this constitutional conflict exclusively in terms of an assault on free speech, the judiciary turned a blind eye to the argument that an unrestricted opportunity to engage in advertising is not the only, or even best, measure of a healthy democratic polity. Yet an alternative perspective is that restricting the amount of election spending (including that by candidates and parties as well as other individuals and groups) is vital to the health of a liberal democratic community. [33] Indeed, concerns about the negative ways that money affects the

[30] The judicial approach to this inquiry is set out in *R v Oakes* [1986] 1 SCR 103.

[31] The one exception was a 1988 Supreme Court judgment that did not address the specific issue of regulating independent expenditures, but in dicta, characterised the objective of controlling referendum costs as laudable. *Libman v Quebec (Attorney General)* [1997] 3 SCR 569.

[32] *Somerville v Canada (Attorney General)* (1996) 136 DLR (4th) 205 (Alta CA) at para 66.

[33] Smith and Bakvis make this argument particularly forcefully when suggesting that the 'manner in which election campaigns are conducted and financed is a significant factor in the health of liberal democracies.' J Smith and H Bakvis, 'Changing Dynamics in Election Campaign Finance: Critical Issues in Canada and the US' (2000) 1:4 *Policy Matters (*Montreal, IRPP) 4.

political process explain why so many democratic communities have deemed it necessary to regulate election spending.[34] Translated into the language of rights, controlling election costs protects the equal right of citizens to contribute to self-governing. Restricting independent expenditures is an ancillary dimension of the larger normative project of attempting to control the costs of elections to ensure meaningful citizen involvement in all aspects of elections—both in public debate about the importance of issues and in the right to seek public office.

Experience has shown that many candidates raise more money than they are legally entitled to spend[35] and would almost certainly spend more money if they were not prohibited from doing so and if they presumed that increased spending would enhance their prospect for election. Yet costly elections undermine citizens' right to be treated equally when participating in one dimension of self-government—seeking public office. Regardless of personal skills or merit, those with modest means would have extreme difficulty mounting an effective campaign if election spending were extremely costly, unless capable of raising large amounts of money. Candidates' dependency on wealthy donors could lead to the very 'harm' the judiciary seems willing to contemplate as a justification for restricting election spending (discussed below): that money will have a corrupting influence on the political process. If contesting elections becomes so exorbitantly costly that candidates become dependent on donors with deep pockets, citizens will have an obvious concern about whose interests are being given consideration in the development and passage of public policy.

There is a second way in which a citizen's right to be treated equally is undermined by costly elections. All citizens may have an equal right to vote. But money is the currency that controls access to the principal venue for election debate; specifically, paid advertising in the commercial media. Citizens are simply not equal in their capacity to 'command the attention of others for their own candidates, interests, and convictions.'[36] Most citizens cannot afford any significant opportunity to participate in this venue. Only a very small minority of citizens can afford to purchase commercial advertising to promote issues that are important to them, or to draw attention to the candidates they support or oppose. Thus, unregulated election spending could lead to such serious discrepancies in citizen participation as to normatively cast doubt on the primacy of an unrestricted ability to 'purchase' speech. As Ronald Dworkin argues:

> No citizen is entitled to demand that others find his [or her] opinions persuasive or even worthy of attention. But each citizen is entitled to compete for that attention, and to have a chance at persuasion, on fair terms, a chance that is now denied [in the US] to everyone without great wealth or access to it.[37]

[34] H Alexander and R Shiratori (eds), *Comparative Political Finance among the Democracies* (Boulder, Westview Press, 1994).

[35] W T Stanbury, *Money in Politics: Financing Federal Parties and Candidates in Canada* (Toronto, Dundurn Press, 1991), 361.

[36] R Dworkin, 'The Curse of American Politics', *The New York Review of Books*, 17 Oct 1996, 19 at 23.

[37] *Ibid.*

The concern is not simply how citizens' different levels of wealth afford some citizens more opportunity to exert influence on the election. In an unregulated election environment, many of the key election participants will not be citizens at all—but corporations, often internationally controlled. But it is important to remember that elections are for citizens to participate in the act of self-governing. For the very reason that citizens alone are given the right to vote, a political community should be worried about corporations or foreign residents being able to use their financial resources to help frame national electoral debates and, through large political donations, determine which candidates can afford to be competitive.

Far from concluding that democratic principles cast suspicion on the goal of regulating independent expenditures, these spending limits, when part of a coherent and comprehensive attempt to control all election costs, actually enhance democratic values. To refer again to Dworkin, one of the most passionate advocates of rights-based principles, defending spending limits does not mean abandoning a commitment to rights (or, in the context of his intellectual contributions, turning one's back on the argument that rights should 'trump' social policy objectives that would threaten these). On the contrary, Dworkin believes that the amount of money raised and spent impacts in a negative way on citizens' equal right to influence the democratic outcome.[38] Dworkin is writing of American politics but his concerns about unregulated election spending have universal resonance.

Supporters of an unregulated election environment claim that the best remedy for distortion or a lack of truth in election advertising is more advertising. But it is simply not the case that more election advertising ensures that manipulative advertisements will be clarified or that all important issues will be debated. The classic portrayal of the unregulated exchange of ideas and opinions draws upon the analogy of the marketplace. Defenders claim that the marketplace of ideas provides the best opportunity for free and open debate, because ideas must stand up to broad scrutiny and only the most meritorious of these will emerge triumphant. The unstated assumption about how this marketplace works is the pluralist expectation that all ideas, or different perspectives on issues, will be aired and citizens, once armed with full and complete information, will be able to reach prudent judgments. Proponents of this 'romantic' conception of the exchange of ideas do not adequately acknowledge what effect money has on the functioning of this marketplace.[39] In contemporary elections, it is not the power of ideas but money that is the most important commodity for political debate. The ability to purchase advertising determines how much attention will be drawn to particular issues, and how these will be portrayed. Only those whose desire to participate in election debate is matched by the financial resources they need to 'speak' can participate in this marketplace. The majority of voices must remain silent, resulting in attention given to only some issues and only partial perspectives on these. Far from encouraging a free exchange of all ideas, the commercial marketplace for election advertising is more aptly characterised as an

[38] *Ibid.*
[39] Long ago Zechariah Chaffee criticised this romanticised version of the marketplace of ideas. Z Chaffee Jr, *Free Speech in the United States* (Cambridge, Harvard University Press, 1941) 137.

exclusive club where membership is restricted to the extremely wealthy or to those with access to others' wealth.[40]

Some also lament the nature of the debate that costly elections produce, suggesting a relationship between expensive elections and a diminution of the quality of electoral debate. When regulations do not restrict the cost of seeking election or trying to influence the vote, television advertising becomes an extremely important venue for electoral debate. Although this venue has broad exposure, it also takes on a character that is the antithesis of meaningful debate. Costs dictate the format for the majority of political advertisements. This format, often 30-second and even shorter commercials, denies the opportunity to develop arguments and counter-arguments. Driven by the constraints of time, designers of these advertisements turn these into memorable television moments by relying on sensational claims that voters can remember, but which are often couched as negative advertisements and even manipulative and misleading messages.[41]

Assumption Two: The Only Justification is to Prevent Corruption to the Political Process

One measure of the level of judicial scepticism about regulating independent expenditures was the extent to which some judges have downplayed arguments that spending restrictions were necessary to promote equality, and their determination instead to characterise their central purpose as to prevent mischief or harm to the political process[42] or to minimise corruption in elections.[43]

The purpose of regulating independent expenditures has frequently been mischaracterised by the judiciary, which has linked these spending limits to concerns about corruption. Although an historical impetus for controlling election costs was fear of corruption, the trading of votes for money and the exchange of policy consideration for financial support,[44] this concern has been mitigated significantly by the establishment in 1974 of spending limitations for candidates and parties, which have reduced candidate and party dependency on a small number of large contributors.[45] Nevertheless, the judiciary has frequently assessed the limits on independent expenditures in terms of their purported connection to redressing fears of corruption. But as argued above, this is not the purpose of these spending limits. Limits on independent expenditures are an ancillary element of the normative project of promoting equality in citizen participation in elections.

[40] This argument draws from J Hiebert, 'Money and Elections: Can Citizens participate on Fair Terms amidst Unrestricted Spending?' (1998) 31 *Canadian Journal of Political Science* 91 at 102–3.

[41] For discussion of the effects of television advertisement on the election process see, S Ansolabehere and S Iyengar, *Going Negative: How Political Advertisements Shrink and Polarize the Electorate* (New York, The Free Press, 1995).

[42] *National Citizens' Coalition v Canada (Attorney General)* [1984] 5 WWR 436 (Alta QB) at 453.

[43] *Somerville v Canada (Attorney General)* (1996) 136 DLR (4th) 205 (Alta CA) at para 81.

[44] WT Stanbury, *Money in Politics: Financing Federal Parties and Candidates in Canada* (Toronto, Dundurn press, 1991) 52.

[45] *Ibid* at 411.

The judicial treatment of this issue prior to the Supreme Court's ruling in *Harper* provides strong support for those who accept the importance of rights yet are sceptical about the benefits of judicial review of a bill of rights. If a benefit of a bill of rights is that it requires governments to explain and justify decisions that unduly infringe upon rights, a shortcoming is that judicial review assess the legitimacy of governmental decisions based on classical liberal assumptions that assume (a) the state is the enemy of freedom and that (b) freedom is realised by the absence of constraints. Thus, a bill of rights can complicate the assessment of what comprises an appropriate relationship between the opportunity to purchase advertising and the normative objective that citizens participate in the election process as equal members of the political community. It is not that a bill of rights forbids consideration of state actions that may be necessary to promote equality, as distinct from action to prevent actual harm or inaction to protect freedom. But the hegemonic assumptions associated with legal liberalism, upon which the Charter like most bills of rights depend, influence judicial assumptions that the essential purpose of judicial review is to protect citizens from the state, that freedom is engendered principally through limiting the state, and that unless proof of harm is established, state actions that appear to limit a right are inherently suspect. Thus, the argument that legislation that deliberately seeks to restrict a form of speech is nevertheless justified, particularly in the absence of concrete proof of actual harms that have or would arise, has received a rocky judicial reception.

That trial and provincial appeal courts have been wholly reluctant to give serious consideration to the argument that spending constraints enhance democratic values, suggests one of two explanations, both equally troubling. One possible explanation is that the courts involved subscribed to a thin understanding of democracy; one that assumes the only relative consideration is the negative dimension—the ability to be free from state constraints. This view may be consistent with a libertarian approach to freedom. But democracy is seldom defended entirely on the basis of libertarian principles. Only an extremely narrow definition of democracy, one that is intentionally oblivious to the power and influence that accrue from money, would assume that an unfettered ability to engage in election advertising is the obvious or only compelling interpretation of democratic values. An alternative possibility, no less troubling, was that judges (below the Supreme Court level) were intellectually arrogant by portraying the resolution of this complex and contested issue as amenable to a singular answer—theirs. But far from giving rise to a singular response to the question of whether election advertising can or should be regulated, the relevant issues are complex, philosophical and subject to considerable contestation.

Assumption Three: Justification for Limits Requires Proof that Money 'Buys' Elections

A consequence of the trial and provincial appeal courts' determination to assess the legitimacy of limits on independent expenditures in terms of whether they were required to prevent harm was judicial demand for empirical proof of their necessity. Judges queried how restricting independent expenditures could possibly be considered legitimate in the absence of proof that if not regulated these expenditures would have resulted in harm or corruption. Moreover, judges implied that this proof would have to be extremely compelling. For example, in *Pacific Press v British Columbia (Attorney General)*, which looked at the validity of this issue at the provincial level, the Court characterised the 'presumed link' between candidate and party spending and independent expenditures as 'theoretical abstractions' and 'unproved hypotheses' that were not empirically verified.[46] In the absence of empirical evidence showing what problems might occur if independent expenditures were unregulated, the Court concluded there is 'no authority for the proposition that claims of common sense justification are to be preferred over scientific evidence or that claims of common sense justification can rebut scientific evidence.'[47] Also insisting upon demonstration of harm was the Alberta Court of Appeal in *Somerville v Canada*. Justice Conrad acknowledged the difficulty of measuring the effects of money in terms of quantitative analysis. Nevertheless, her characterisation of the issue revealed the expectation that the government must demonstrate a causal relationship between money and harm, as evident in the question: 'Is there a danger that someone could "buy" an election?'[48]

Even when judges indicated that scientific proof of the financial link between independent expenditures and harm was not required, they still demanded empirical evidence to satisfy a less burdensome standard—such as apprehension of harm.[49] But even if this evidence could have been amassed (the implications of having to do so are discussed below) it is still not clear whether the trial or provincial appeal court judges would have accepted the legitimacy of restrictions on independent expenditures, as suggested in the startling statement by Justice Conrad, that even had the government demonstrated that independent expenditures have had an effect on an election outcome, she would 'have great difficulty accepting' that their limitation is constitutionally justified.[50]

Canadian trial and provincial appeal court judges have drawn considerable support for their conclusion that there is no justification for restricting independent expenditures from the fact that the author of the only empirical attempt to assess the effects of independent expenditures on voters' intentions (the Johnston study discussed above) subsequently revised his assessment. Judicial insistence on evidence of harm led some judges to conclude that this revised opinion has repudiated the justification for limiting independent expenditures.[51] But this

46 *Pacific Press v British Columbia (Attorney General)* [2000] BCSC 248 at paras 77–9.

47 *Ibid* at para 79.

48 *Somerville v Canada (Attorney General)* (1996) 136 DLR (4th) 205 (AltaCA) at para 66.

49 *Harper v Canada (Attorney General)* (2001) 93 Alta LR (3d) 281 at para 275.

50 *Somerville v Canada (Attorney General)* (1996) 136 DLR (4th) 205 (AltaCA) at para 69.

51 Thus in the *Pacific Press* case the Court concluded that since Professor Johnston no longer stands by his original findings, the conclusions of the Lortie Common on this issue 'can no longer be said to be based on empirical findings.' Similarly, in the *Harper* decision the Court states that since the Hiebert study was 'materially dependent' on the initial study by Johnston, this leaves the Hiebert study 'bereft of the only scientific analysis of the effects of third party election expenses in a Canadian federal election.' *Pacific Press v British Columbia (Attorney General)* [2000] BCSC 248 para 105, *Harper v Canada (Attorney General)* (2001) 93 Alta LR (3d) 281 at paras 67–8.

assumption was problematic for two reasons. First, the judiciary has been under the mistaken impression that the principal sources that influenced legislation (the Lortie Commission's Final Report, and a study on independent expenditures conducted on its behalf) were aware of Johnston's reversal before they were completed.[52] Second, and more significant, the judiciary failed to acknowledge that the argument made by the Lortie Commission was a normative one—that principles of fairness and equity underlie the Canadian regulatory regime and that these are dependent upon regulating all election expenses, including independent expenditures. Although empirical evidence demonstrating a link between advertising and voters' intentions would certainly lend force to this normative argument, and support the recommendation to regulate independent expenditures,[53] the Lortie Commission would have argued in favour of regulating all election expenses, including independent expenditures, even in the absence of empirical evidence demonstrating any linkage between voter intentions and election advertising.[54]

Quite separate from the problem of this judicial misunderstanding about the reasons that motivated a Royal Commission to recommend limits on independent expenditures, a serious concern with the lower and appeal courts' insistence on proof, or empirical justification for an apprehension of harm, was that it established a standard that simply could not be satisfied, especially within a political regime that seeks to control election costs. Until a political community is either required by the judiciary, or chooses voluntarily, to conduct elections that are not subject to spending limits, how can it demonstrate what consequences will arise from unregulated spending? How can anyone prove something that has not yet happened? Yet the implication of the judiciary's treatment of this issue was that not until Canadian regulatory attempts were so paralysed that the state was no longer able to restrict campaign spending, would it be in a position to gather information to support the apprehension that costly elections have a negative impact on democratic values. And after this occurs, the community would have to watch and chronicle signs that campaign donations had been traded for influence, or that elections had become too costly for many would-be-candidates to seek public office. But would a political community ever have confidence that it had a constitutional green light to proceed with spending restrictions, no matter how

[52] The Johnston memo was submitted December 1990. The original Hiebert study was completed 29 April 1991 (the completion date of the study is published on p 64). Neither Johnston nor myself, author of the study, can pinpoint the precise date in which he advised me, by telephone, of his revised opinion, but we agree it was sometime between Feb and March 1992, by which time the Commission had finished its work and the Hiebert study was very likely published (although the release of this volume was delayed to coincide with the published release of most of the other 23 volumes of studies). The Lortie Commission signed off on its four volume report Nov 1991.

[53] J Hiebert, 'Interest Groups and Federal Elections', above n 21 at 3–76.

[54] I make this argument as the author of the principal study of independent expenditures conducted on behalf of the Lortie Commission. Moreover, in court testimony, Research Director Peter Aucoin testified that Johnston's preliminary findings regarding the effect of third party spending on the 1988 federal election were not determinative of the position taken by the Lortie Commission on third party spending, and that even if aware that Johnston would later revise his assessment, he would still have recommended third party spending limits to preserve the fairness of the electoral system. *Harper v Canada (Attorney General)* (2001) 93 Alta LR (3d) 281 at para 77.

important these seemed, given the inherent difficulty of satisfying the judiciary's insistence on empirical proof of the harmful effects of money or demonstrating the causal relationship between money and harm?

Courts are understandably reluctant to entertain restrictions on freedom of expression. But it is disheartening to have a court pose the question of whether regulating independent expenditures is justified in such crude terms as requiring proof that a person can somehow 'buy' an election. This characterisation of the role of money in elections reveals judges' failure to comprehend the complex ways that money affects other values that are integral to democracy. Critics of spending regulations predictably point to examples of candidates having spent large amounts of money, and yet failing to win a plurality of the vote. Ross Perot may have spent a large personal fortune while failing in his 1992 bid for the presidency of the United States. But all this proves is that money may not actually save a failed candidacy. A better lesson to be drawn from the Perot experience is how an extremely rich person was able to exercise far more influence on the campaign agenda for the presidential race than the majority of his fellow citizens with ordinary financial means. Whatever the power of ideas that Perot held, these would not have swayed anywhere near the vote they did had Perot not been able to saturate the media through paid political advertisements.[55]

The role of money in elections is far more nuanced than the judiciary and many critics of campaign spending limits seem willing to acknowledge. Social scientists have not yet determined predictable and acceptable methods to determine how expensive elections must become before they discourage candidates from contending for public office; how money affects the competitiveness of a candidate; and how the volume, nature and timing of election advertising influences the way voters determine which issues are important. But the inability to demonstrate how money affects voting behaviour, or to establish empirical verification of the precise relationship between dependency on large political donations and political conduct once in office, does not mean that money has a benign influence on the election process, particularly when the amounts spent are large and inevitable discrepancies exist between how much citizens can afford to spend.

In addition to the judiciary's naïve assumptions about the role of money in the election process, its treatment of independent expenditures revealed a poor understanding of the different functions that political parties and independent expenditures serve. For example, in *Somerville v Canada* the Alberta Court of Appeal rejected the validity of regulating independent expenditures because the legislation gives 'preferential protection' to political parties. In the court's view, not only did this aspect of the legislation conflict with the Charter, it was so directly contrary to the purpose of the Charter that it could never be constitutionally justified.[56] This conclusion revealed the court's failure to comprehend the different role political parties play in an election from that of interest groups. The centrality of political parties in the Canadian political system distinguishes them

[55] C Sunstein, *Democracy and the Problem of Free Speech* (New York, The Free Press 1999) 99.
[56] *Somerville v Canada (Attorney General)* (1996) 136 DLR (4th) 205 (Alta CA) at para 78.

from other organisations or groups. Parties organise the political processes of democratic parliamentary government. Their role is integrally connected to Canada's constitutional system, based on the Westminster model of parliamentary government and the principle of responsible government. Canadians do not elect the Prime Minister. It is through parties that the positions of executive authority in the government are filled. Political parties also organise the competition for elected office. Parties are the primary institutions for recruiting and selecting candidates for elections to the House of Commons.

The lower and appeal courts also revealed poor understanding of how spending limits would have a differential impact on candidates and interest groups. In *Somerville v Canada* the Alberta Court of Appeal concluded that the contrast between what individuals or groups are allowed to spend and what candidates are entitled to spend was so disproportionate that it was 'arbitrary and unfair' (the legislation at issue imposed a $1,000 spending limit on independent expenditures, while candidates were permitted to spend approximately $55,000).[57] But spending limits affect candidates differently than they do independent groups. Candidates are subject to a finite spending limit. Yet a plurality of interest groups can organise around an infinite number of issues and, by coordinating their efforts or by coincidence in their spending patterns, can augment the amount of money used to engage in partisan advocacy for or against a candidate. Thus, establishing comparable levels of spending for candidates and any single individual or group would not only undermine the integrity of spending limits for candidates but would be manifestly unfair, particularly for those candidates who were targeted by multiple, negative advertisements.

The Supreme Court in *Harper v Canada (Attorney General)*

The Supreme Court of Canada handed down its judgment in May 2004, in which a 6–3 majority held that the limits on independent expenditures were constitutionally valid. A majority of the Supreme Court explicitly repudiated the approach to this issue taken by lower courts. Unlike the earlier courts' focus on whether the legislation was necessary to prevent corruption, the majority recognised the intent of the legislation as promoting equality in citizen participation. Justice Bastarache, writing on behalf of the majority, characterised Parliament's legislative objective as the promotion of 'electoral fairness' by 'creating equality' in political discourse.

> The overarching objective of the [independent expenditure] limits is electoral fairness. Equality in the political discourse promotes electoral fairness and is achieved, in part, by restricting the participation of those who have access to significant financial resources. The more voices that have access to the political discourse, the more voters will be empowered to exercise their right in a meaningful and informed manner. Canadians understandably have greater confidence in an electoral system which ultimately encourages increased participation.[58]

[57] *Ibid* at para 80.
[58] *Harper v Canada (Attorney General)* [2004] SCC 33 at para 91.

In defending the legislation, the Attorney General had expressed concern that lower courts had inappropriately required scientific proof that harm had actually occurred or, alternatively, proof that independent expenditures had influenced voters' intentions and election outcomes to the point of unfairness. The majority agreed with this characterisation, concluding that the requirement that the Attorney General produce definitive social science evidence 'establishing the causes of every area of social concern' represented an unreasonably high onus.[59] The majority ruled that the Attorney General need not demonstrate evidence of actual harm to demonstrate that the legislation represents a pressing and substantial objective, ruling that what was required was 'sufficient informed evidence of the importance of electoral regulation in our free and democratic society.' From the majority's perspective, the Lortie Report was the central piece of this evidentiary record.[60]

But unlike the trial judge and a majority of the Court of Appeal, which discounted the Lortie Report because of its use of the controversial Johnston study, the Supreme Court did not accept that this reliance lessens the persuasiveness of the Royal Commission's recommendation to restrict independent expenditures or the reasonableness of the legislation that followed. From its perspective, this judicial finding was wrong, as were those in earlier cases that had ruled that independent expenditures were invalid because of a lack of actual evidence that this advertising influences the electorate. The majority held that the fact that the Johnston opinion was revised does not negate the persuasiveness of the argument for regulating independent expenditures.[61] Moreover, the majority was highly sceptical about the appropriateness of requiring awareness of 'evidence of the actual pernicious effect of the lack of spending limits in past elections' in order to justify that limits on independent expenditures are warranted, stating, '[s]urely, Parliament does not have to wait for the feared harm to occur before it can enact measures to prevent the possibility of the harm occurring or to remedy the harm, should it occur.'[62]

In explaining its disagreement with lower courts, the majority stated that the lower courts had shown insufficient deference to Parliament's normative objectives and had placed too much emphasis on the lack of empirical evidence demonstrating a link between independent expenditures and voters' intentions.[63]

> Under the egalitarian model of elections, Parliament must balance the rights and privileges of the participants in the electoral process: candidates, political parties, third parties and voters. Advertising expense limits may restrict free expression to ensure that participants are able to meaningfully participate in the electoral process. For candidates, political parties and third parties, meaningful participation means

[59] *Ibid* at para 93.
[60] *Ibid* at paras 93–4.
[61] *Ibid* at paras 94–9.
[62] *Ibid* at para 98.
[63] *Ibid* at para 64.

> the ability to inform voters of their position. For voters, meaningful participation means the ability to hear and weigh many points of view. The difficulties of striking this balance are evident. Given the right of Parliament to choose Canada's electoral model and the nuances inherent in implementing this model, the Court must approach the justification analysis with deference. The lowers courts erred in failing to do so . . . In the end, the electoral system, which regulates many aspects of an election, including its duration and the control and reimbursement of expenses, reflects a political choice, the details of which are better left to Parliament.[64]

A central issue in the litigation was whether the spending restrictions were too low to allow for meaningful participation. The majority recognised that spending limits must be carefully tailored to ensure that they do not unduly restrict the informational component of the right to vote. Yet, from the majority's perspective, the trial judge had not given sufficient attention to the potential number of independent expenditures or the abilities of individuals or groups to coordinate their activities to augment the influence of their advertisements. In its view,

> meaningful participation in elections is not synonymous with the ability to mount a media campaign capable of determining the outcome. In fact, such an understanding of 'meaningful participation' would leave little room in the political discourse for the individual citizen and would be inimical to the right to vote.[65]

The dissenting judges differed sharply in their characterisation of the effects of the legislation, indicating they thought that the low level of allowable spending was 'draconian', particularly in the absence of any demonstration that such low spending limits were required to meet the perceived dangers of inequality, an uninformed electorate and the public perception that the system is unfair. As the minority stated, the legislation itself may exacerbate the dangers it was intended to address:

> Citizens who cannot effectively communicate with others on electoral issues may feel they are being treated unequally compared to citizens who speak through political parties. The absence of their messages may result in the public being less well informed than it would otherwise be. And a process that bans citizens from effective participation in the electoral debate during an election campaign may well be perceived as unfair. These fears may be hypothetical, but no more so than the fears conjured by the Attorney General in support of the infringement.[66]

Conclusion

Until the majority Supreme Court ruling in *Harper* Canadian judges had become alarmingly close to the position taken by the US Supreme Court ruling in *Buckley*

[64] *Ibid* at para 87.
[65] *Ibid* at para 74.
[66] *Ibid* at para 38.

v Valeo,[67] which held the notion of fairness in elections as foreign to the constitutional values that underlie the political community. Whether Canadian judges rejected fairness explicitly, or implicitly, by demanding unrealistic proof that money 'buys' elections, the result was the same. Trial and provincial court judges gave primacy to negative liberty—the ability to advertise without being subject to strict spending limits—without considering the effects this has on citizens' equality.

The Supreme Court's approach differs from the earlier judicial treatment of this issue in a number of ways, the three most significant being: its recognition that the objective of the legislation was to promote equality in citizen participation, and not to address corruption; that this was an objective that was valid and consistent with democratic values; and its willingness to defer to Parliament when defining the exact balance that should be struck between opportunities to spend money on political advertising and the attempt to limit election spending.

Not everyone will accept that judicial deference is appropriate, particularly when the parties in Parliament are affected by the rules they adopt for electoral contests. It makes no sense denying that the political parties that supported the legislation have self-interest in the rules for election conduct. This self-interest explains why decisions about other aspects of the electoral process, such as establishing federal electoral boundaries, have been taken out of Parliament's hands and the responsibilities given to independent boundary commissions. Whether or not an independent body should also make decisions about what rules should govern election finance, the levels of allowable election spending, the decisions about who can contribute to candidates or parties, or whether and how much public funding should be available, will be the subject of much debate. But whatever the arguments made to defend such an idea, there are serious concerns about assuming the judiciary is the appropriate body for making such decisions. Judicial review may serve an important role in assessing the rules of election engagement, to ensure that they are not manifestly unfair, privilege specific parties or candidates or obviously disadvantage specific groups or particular individuals. But this oversight role is not the same as actually determining the substantive content of the rules themselves, decisions that require choices between competing normative values, a task that, arguably, does not comfortably fit with the role of judicial review or the method associated with judicial interpretation. As the Alberta Court of Appeal stated in *Harper*, a difficulty it perceived when assessing arguments that restrictions on independent expenditures were necessary to foster egalitarian principles was the requirement of 'balancing the competing normative values' involved.[68]

Determining the appropriate resolution of the different normative values associated with the question of what role money should play in elections is not amenable to an obviously correct or singularly more persuasive answer, even when reviewed under a bill of rights. The questions that arise in constitutional

[67] *Buckley v Valeo*, 424 US 1 (1976) 48–9, 56–7.
[68] *Harper v Canada (Attorney General)* (2002) 14 Alta LR (4th) 4 at para 126.

challenges, such as the ones discussed in this chapter, speak to important philosophical quandaries about what priorities and values should be protected and promoted in the electoral process. And like many other philosophical debates, reasonable citizens will have differences on the resolution of this conflict.

If citizens believe that an inappropriate balance has been struck under the current regulatory regime, which clearly emphasises the primacy of political parties and candidates over non-registered individuals or groups during elections, they should argue for continued deliberation—a robust public debate—about what values should be protected in election law: whether, for instance, more libertarian interpretations of the election process should prevail over more egalitarian concerns of equality. Some will argue that because the election period in Canada is both finite and short, this is too crucial a period to silence diverse opinions. If it is a choice between equality, on the one hand, and unrestricted opportunities to engage in paid debate, on the other hand, then the choice is the latter. Others will counter that equality is too important to be adversely affected by laissez faire spending. Some might, nevertheless, concede that more imagination is required to allow for interest group participation in election debate in ways that do not undermine equality. Apart from these basic philosophical disagreements on first principles, some of the questions that might arise are: Should commercial media time be set aside for independent expenditures and, if so, should the state pay some or all of these costs? How would eligibility to participate be determined? What alternative venues can be provided for individual or interest group participation? Should the incumbent government be precluded from spending public monies to publicise that government's record, particularly in the period immediately before the election campaign?

But substituting judicial opinion for these debates is not the answer. Although some may worry about whether the deference extended by a majority of the Supreme Court in *Harper* was appropriate, others are every bit as troubled by the trial and provincial court treatment of this issue. Whatever the appropriate answer(s) to this quandary about which normative values election rules should promote, the trial and appeal courts' insistence that the validity of regulating independent expenditures be treated as an empirical and not normative issue, and their imposition of a standard of justification (proof of harm) that is extremely difficult, if not impossible, to satisfy, introduced a chilling quality to this debate. These assumptions frustrate meaningful debate by portraying critics of spending limits as the only defenders of democracy and casting doubt on the motives and merits of alternative views, even when these reflect a compelling interpretation of democratic values. The issues at stake are too serious and too philosophically contested for the judiciary, singularly, to define the bounds and parameters of what constitutes a free and democratic society. For this reason, the Supreme Court's deference may not be misplaced.

Part VI

Starting from Scratch

14

Developing Political Parties in the European Union: Towards a European Party Statute?

STEPHEN DAY AND JO SHAW[1]

Introduction

This chapter redirects the inquiry a bit. Instead of looking at the funding of political parties in the context of established democratic political orders, our attention turns to the development of political parties in the context of creation of a Europe-wide political arena—in this case the European Union. Hence our focus is on the recent institutional development of the so called European political parties ('euro-parties'), an indispensable feature of which is the manner in which these emergent political parties are to be funded. As this chapter will seek to show, the constitutional framework within which this has developed is a central aspect of the evolution of transnational parties in the European Union context. One of the key reference points is Article 191 of the EC Treaty (formerly Article 138a EC) which provides that:

> Political parties at European level are important as a factor for integration within the Union. They contribute to forming a European awareness and to expressing the political will of the citizens of the Union.

This provision was originally introduced by the Treaty of Maastricht in 1993. Ten years later, the Treaty of Nice added an important second paragraph allowing for legislative measures to be adopted to give more than mere rhetorical force to these principles:

[1] The chapter draws upon joint research by Stephen Day and Jo Shaw on *The Constitutionalisation of Transnational Political Parties* (ESRC Grant Number: R000223449). It draws on an earlier publication in *Election Law Journal*, vol 3, no 2(2004) at 259–64. The funding of the ESRC is acknowledged with thanks.

> The Council, acting in accordance with the procedure referred to in Article 251, shall lay down the regulations governing political parties at European level and in particular the rules governing their funding.

The procedure in Article 251 EC to which the provision refers is Council-Parliament co-decision. Legislative measures about the institutional framework for the future development of European political parties can now be adopted as the culmination of an interactive legislative process involving all three political institutions. The Council decides by a qualified majority vote, and in addition the measure must be approved by the European Parliament. The Commission provides vital input into the legislative process through its power to make legislative proposals and its ability to change the proposal to reflect both European Parliament amendments and the Council's initial 'Common Position'. In sum, each institution has a form of veto power over legislation, and some capacity to shape the form and content of legislative measures. On the other hand, no single Member State has a veto over the adoption of legislation, given that the Council must act by a qualified majority.

The chapter concentrates only on the most recent efforts made by euro-parties to increase their significance within the institutional architecture of the European Union by pressing for the practical legislative tools now offered by Article 191 to be put to use. Only a brief presentation is made of earlier efforts which focused primarily on emphasising the normative force of the first paragraph of Article 191, given the absence of a credible legal basis. However, some background is presented in the second section given there remain profound doubts in both the academic literature and within the realm of politics as to the real value of euro-parties.[2] As *European* parties, do these federations of national parties have some real 'value-added' as meta-networks for transnational party cooperation? In so far as they are European *parties*, what is their relationship to other vehicles for citizen interest representation at the EU level, notably (transnational) civil society?

The central narrative of the chapter is concerned with institutional developments. In the third section we review briefly the history and general approach of the proposals made by the European Commission in 2000 and 2001 to establish a legal framework for European Party Statutes. This was intended to increase the visibility (and legitimacy) of the euro-parties and to operationalise Article 191 by means of measures adopted on the basis of Article 308 EC. Thereafter, we discuss the subsequent adoption in 2003 of a more limited Regulation based on the second, new, paragraph of Article 191 setting down outline rules governing European political parties, including rules on funding.[3] This measure defines 'political parties at European level' (Article 2). These are parties or 'alliances of parties', with legal personality under national law in the Member State in which they have their seat, which must satisfy certain conditions relating to

[2] L Bardi, 'Transnational Party Federations, European Parliamentary Groups and the Building of Europarties' in R Katz and P Mair (eds), *How Parties Organise* (London, Sage, 1994).

[3] Regulation 2004/2003 of the European Parliament and of the Council of 4 November 2003 on the regulations governing political parties at European level and the rules regarding their funding, [2003] OJ L297/1.

representativity, the observance of fundamental principles upon which the EU is founded (eg liberty, democracy, rule of law, human rights), and the intention to participate in elections for the European Parliament (Article 3). Parties which satisfy these conditions may apply for funding from the European Parliament, under conditions managed by the European Parliament (Article 4). To obtain funding, they must provide a series of documents to back up the application such as a programme and a statute. The European Parliament is in charge of verifying compliance with the conditions, as well as disbursing the funds (Article 5). It must also therefore verify compliance with conditions and obligations relating to the disbursement of funds, such as what types of funding and donations are permissible for euro-parties, and what activities it may apply these funds to (Articles 6–8). The Parliament is required to put in place mechanisms to control implementation, including seeking reimbursement of funds improperly received or applied by euro-parties (Article 9). To understand better what difference in practice the measure will make, we also look at some of the immediate effects of this measure, including the implementing measures within the European Parliament and in particular its Bureau, and the initial implications for euro-parties in terms of compliance with the Regulation in order to make successful applications for funding.

In brief, the new Regulation finally brings to EU law an institutionally focused definition of the general characteristics that are required for a body to be classified as a 'political party at European level', in terms of its legal basis, representativity, and basic adherence to political values. By bringing a sense of order and regularising some aspects of behaviour, the process of institutionalising the euro-parties within the EU constitutional architecture can be seen to be taking place. This has long been the goal of many actors operating within and around European political parties.[4]

The narrative is brought to a conclusion in the fifth section with a review of measures taken to implement Regulation 2004/2003. The conclusion offers some brief thoughts regarding the significance of the new institutional arrangements for euro-parties for the future of euro-parties more generally.

The Evolution of the Euro-Parties in the Post-Maastricht Era

There have been, up to mid-2004, five main euro-parties:[5] the European People's Party;[6] the Party of European Socialists (PES);[7] the European Liberal, Democrat

[4] See the narrative set out in KM Johansson and PA Zervakis, 'Historical Institutional Framework' in KM Johansson and P Zervakis (eds), *European Political Parties between Cooperation and Integration* (Baden-Baden, Nomos, 2002). For a critique of the new party financing regulation, see HH von Arnim and M Schurig, *The European Party Financing Regulation*, (Munster, Lit Verlag, 2004).

[5] For a brief discussion of other initiatives to establish euro-parties see below text accompanying n 95.

[6] Usually referred to as the EPP. Website: <http://www.eppe.org/>.

[7] Usually referred to as the PES. Website: <http://www.pes.org/>.

and Reform Party;[8] the European Green Party/European Federation of Green Parties;[9] and the Democratic Party of the Peoples of Europe-European Free Alliance (nationalists and ethno-regionalists of a broadly progressive hue).[10] They are composed of parties from each of the EU Member States (sometimes more than one per state) and in some cases from countries outside of the EU (especially in the case of the European Green Party which is more pan-European in nature with 33 full member parties). As the EU has enlarged, so new national parties have been received into membership, in many cases after a period of associate membership during the accession process. Each euro-party has some form of relationship with a European Parliamentary Group,[11] but in essence they are distinct and exist to fulfil a different agenda. As a 1996 Report to the European Parliament (the 'Tsatsos Report') put it:

> The party and the body representing it in Parliament, the political group, are naturally closely linked. The party and political group must, however, each have their own institutional and political role. The political groups' arena is parliament. The party cooperates with the political group in this context, but it must also perform its tasks in the run-up to elections and—unlike the political group—seek to inform and engage in public debate and political education in society between elections.[12]

In practice, until 2004, (with the exception of the EPP which had already earlier developed a separate legal existence and presence outside the European Parliament) the euro-parties were based in the European Parliament, and largely staffed and funded out of the budgets of the European Parliament party groups.

The formal constitutional legitimacy of the euro-parties stems from Article 191(1) EC. This is very much a framework provision, which is widely regarded as having an 'influential' effect rather than a direct 'hard' legal effect, although it has only been substantially subjected to analysis in the context of German legal science.[13] Curiously, while referring to the relevance of parties to 'integration', Article

[8] Usually referred to as the ELDR. Website: <http://www.eldr.org/index.php>.

[9] Usually referred to as the Greens. Websites: <http://www.europeangreens.org/> or <http://www.eurogreens.org/>.

[10] Usually referred to as the EFA, or sometimes the DPPE-EFA. Website: <http://www.efa-dppe.org/>.

[11] In some cases, there is a direct relationship between the European Parliamentary Group and the transnational party, eg PES—Socialist Group in the European Parliament (<http://www.socialistgroup.org/>). In the case of the EPP, the European Parliamentary Group is somewhat wider, and incorporates conservative political forces which are not in full membership of the party: Group of the European People's Party and European Democrats in the European Parliament (<http://www.epp-ed.org/>). In the 2004–2009 European Parliament, the situation of the ELDR has changed, as it no longer has its 'own' group, but participates in a somewhat broader centrist group entitled the Alliance of Liberals and Democrats for Europe (ALDE) (<http://eld.europarl.eu.int/>). The case of the Greens and the European Free Alliance is different, as these two transnational parties work within the same Parliamentary Group so as to increase their significance (<http://www.greens-efa.org/>). The Protocol of Understanding between the members of the Green Group and the EFA Group states:

> This group is the expression of the political will of two separate and progressive European political families to co-operate in order to strengthen their mutual political interests in the European Parliament. The visibility of the component parts will be guaranteed.

[12] *Report on the constitutional status of the European political parties* (A4-0342/96), Committee on Institutional Affairs, Rapporteur: Dimitris Tsatsos, at p 9.

[13] See eg M Morlok, 'Constitutional Framework' in Johansson and Zervakis, above n 4.

191 does not refer directly to democracy or other political values of a legitimate polity. Furthermore, it does not as such give a constitutional definition of what a party actually is—whether, for example, they are fundamentally 'private' or 'public' entities. It does mention the 'political will' of the citizens, a reference point which recalls the strong influence of the German Constitution on this particular European provision, especially Article 21 on political parties which is phrased in not dissimilar terms. However, despite the reference to citizens, Article 191 is not individual rights oriented, but is concerned, like Article 21 of the German Constitution, with a structural guarantee of the system of party-based democracy.[14]

In the text of the Constitutional Treaty ('CT') negotiated on the basis of the draft prepared by the Convention on the Future of Europe, and agreed by the Intergovernmental Conference of Heads of State and Government in June 2004,[15] the euro-party provision has found a new home. This text sets out for the EU, for the first time, certain key principles of democracy. The provision on political parties is housed in a chapter on 'the democratic life of the Union' (Article I–45(4) CT). Article III-331 CT allows for regulations governing such parties to be established by European laws, including rules governing their funding, replicating Article 191(2) EC.

We would argue for a many-stranded approach to understanding what euro-parties are and how they work, which allows space not only to include the existing variety of euro-parties, but also allows for the possible intensification of their role in the future.[16] Thus we adopt a three-fold typology of euro-parties. One vision sees the euro-parties merely as facilitating bodies for national party leaders. Those who view the EU primarily as an intergovernmental project with only relatively weak and dependent supranational elements see euro-parties not as autonomous transnational actors but as arenas for bi- and multi-lateral relations. Alternatively, euro-parties can be seen as 'value added' meta networks with a political and organisational reach (dependent on resources). Such entities can reduce transaction costs of cooperation, which is particularly important for the smaller parties. That cooperation might include, where appropriate, seeking to influence the policy direction taken by the EU's legislative institutions through transnational party coalition-building, or seeking to influence the constitutional direction taken by the EU in the context of intergovernmental conferences and, more recently, Conventions. The euro-parties should only exist to fulfil those tasks which the national parties cannot. This means that they should not be seen as a competitor

[14] See generally, T Papadopoulou, *Politische Parteien auf europäischer Ebene. Auslegung und Ausgestaltung von Article 191 (ex 138a) EGV* (Baden-Baden, Nomos, 1999); R Stentzel, 'Der normative Gehalt des Art. 138a EGV—Rechtlicher Grundstein eines europäischen Parteiensystems?' (1997) *Europarecht* 174.

[15] See the draft Treaty establishing a Constitution for the European Union, elaborated by the Convention on the Future of Europe during 2002 and 2003 ([2003] OJ C169/01), and the consolidated text of the Treaty establishing a Constitution for Europe agreed by the IGC on 18 June 2004 ([2004] OJ C310/1).

[16] This is developed in more detail in S Day and J Shaw, *Transnational Parties and the European Constitution* (Oxford, Hart Publishing, 2006) forthcoming.

to the national party. The contestation between different actors and interests involved in euro-parties resolves very much around these two alternative visions of euro-parties. Finally, it is possible to see euro-parties as representative vehicles for an emerging European demos built upon mass-type party qualities including individual party membership, localised branches, the privilege and indeed duty to present candidates for election, and internal democratic procedures including the election of delegates to Party Congresses with responsibility for formulating party policies and positions. This remains very much the minority (and idealistic) position.

Each of these visions of the euro-party can be seen as valid projections of the hopes, aspirations and indeed intentions of some of those working within the framework of euro-parties at present. European parties are currently in a state of flux, responding to and at the same time impacting upon evolving institutional and constitutional environments. In order best to demonstrate these tensions, the remainder of this chapter will address the adoption of measures regulating European Parties as a case study of the institutional development of political parties 'at European level', in the terms initially given voice by Article 191 EC.[17]

The Initiative to Develop the Legal Basis for a European Party Statute

There have been a number of attempts to develop and promulgate a legal basis for European political parties and even a formal framework for the recognition of party statutes. This has followed two pathways. The first involved amendments to the EC Treaty first to establish constitutional recognition of political parties and subsequently to provide for a specific legal basis for the adoption of measures regulating political parties. The latter was eventually adopted in the Treaty of Nice. The second involved the use of the EC Treaty as it stood to bring about the early adoption of a measure, even in advance of amendment of the Treaty.

Although the introduction in 1993 of a provision such as Article 138a (now 191) could be seen as a limited success for the three largest euro-parties (EPP, PES, ELDR) which supported the initiative at the time, in particular through pressure from their Presidents (all Belgian at the time) and from their Secretary Generals (all German at the time), the euro-parties failed in their second objective to secure a clause in the provision which would allow for the operationalisation of the rhetorical force of promoting 'political parties at European level'. Some years later,

[17] In this chapter, we do not discuss in detail other possible initiatives to formalise or strengthen the role of the euro-parties in the European political system, such as the suggestion that at every European Parliament election there should be a set of reserved seats in the Parliament for which the members are elected off common European-wide party lists of candidates chosen by the euro-parties, or the possible enhanced role in the future of the euro-parties in the selection of the President of the Commission. On some of these questions, see the contribution of S Hix, 'Possibilities for European Parties: 2004 and Beyond', 27 February 2003, <http://www.theepc.net>. See also Day and Shaw, above n 16 for further details.

the point was taken up again in a 1997 European Parliament Resolution, based on the 1996 Tsatsos Report. The Resolution argued that:

> European political parties organized and acting on a transnational basis are necessary so that a genuine European citizenship may emerge which monitors, discusses and influences the expression of political will at European level.[18]

Although unsure of what the exact parameters of their organisational nature ought to be, Tsatsos foresaw how 'various features [could be] derived from the image of the political parties in the Union's Member States and transferred—mutatis mutandis—to the level of the European Union.'[19] However, he was clear that such parties had to be 'more in terms of goals and organization than a mere electioneering organization or an organization that merely supports a political group and parliamentary work.'[20] It was the supranational bias of these comments—which also raised the prospect of individual membership and the spectre of increased use of majority-based decision-making in the future—which rendered the report unacceptable for many of the national delegations in the Council of Ministers and resulted in it being sidelined and not taken forward as the basis for action. However, the significance of this episode, and of a subsequent unsuccessful initiative on the part of the Greek Government to seek an amendment to Article 191 in the context of the Treaty of Amsterdam, was that it was laying down markers which could be picked up again at a later date and creating a set of assumptions about 'what is' a transnational party which would influence subsequent initiatives.

The pressure for reform picked up again once more in February 2000 when a joint letter was sent to the European Commission by the leaders of the five europarties, in combination with a letter and draft proposal from the leaders of the four Parliamentary Groups to which these parties were linked, claiming that,

> strong European parties, complementing the European Parliament and its political groupings, can become a vital element of democratic life and political debate in the Union.[21]

Their call for action was bolstered by the role which the parties had taken in democracy promotion in central and eastern Europe, and the associated costs which had arisen as a consequence of this.[22] At that stage the proposal was in a

[18] Resolution on the constitutional status of European political parties, [1997] OJ C 020/29, at point C, A4-0342/96, Rapporteur: Dimitris Tsatsos (PES).

[19] Tsatsos Report, above n 12 at para 8

[20] Tsatsos Report, above n 12 at para 9.

[21] See letter headed 'The Importance and further development of European political parties', from the leaders of the four Parliamentary Groups to Commission President Romano Prodi, 21 February 2000; document held on file by authors.

[22] See Day and Shaw, above n 16, esp Chp 5 on enlargement. See also G Mangott, H Waldrauch and S Day (eds), *Democratic Consolidation: International Influences in Hungary, Poland and Spain* (Baden-Baden, Nomos, 2000).

very rudimentary form. It contained five general areas that dealt with the issues of definition, organisational provisions, tasks, funding and recognition.[23]

Additional pressure to clarify the financial arrangements for euro-parties also came from the Court of Auditors' yearly financial reports, which one former leader of a European Parliament political group has claimed were 'awaited with dread'.[24] The Court's Special Report (2000) on *The expenditure of the European Parliament's political groups* concluded that the present financial set-up whereby funds were being siphoned off from the party groups in the EP to support the party federations was illegal under EU law.[25] These developments culminated, in October 2000, in a European Parliament Bureau decision on 'European Parliament support for European Political Parties' which sought in the very short term to lay down stricter guidelines and enhance the transparency under the present rules, but which was coupled also with a recognition that,

> the existing system of support for European political parties must be replaced, at the latest by the end of 2004, by a definitive, permanent Community regulation defining and giving substance to the concept of 'European political party'.[26]

Historically, the funding of the euro-parties remained dependent upon subsidies from the European parliamentary groups. Staff, logistical costs and funds for conferences, workshops and so on all came from the budget of the European Parliament. One insider suggested that 'an analysis of the books would be an eye-opening experience.'[27] It came to be widely recognised in political circles that only specific parliamentary work (eg the work of the political groups) should be eligible for funds from the Parliament's budget. The broader-based tasks of a European political party, which took it beyond the Parliament, should be financed by other means. Promulgation of the measure allowing for the recognition of party statutes would enable a percentage of future funding to come from the general budget of the EC by creating objective conditions for the allocation of funds.

It was left to the Commission to draw up a draft proposal—on the legal basis of Article 308 EC and thus requiring only one-time consultation of the European Parliament and a unanimous vote in the Council. However, some of those involved in discussions remained unsure of the appropriateness of using Article 308 since it could easily be claimed that such a measure was an example of the alleged 'competence creep' which contributes so much to making the European Union appear much more omnipotent than it really is. The House of Commons Select Committee on European Scrutiny in the United Kingdom, while not proposing to withhold clearance and to apply the scrutiny reserve, nevertheless remained 'doubtful about the adequacy of the legal base.' These doubts arose despite the assurances of the minister who argued that 'Article 308 is justified

[23] *European Party Statute: Working document of European Political Parties*, Brussels, 15 February 2000, held on file.

[24] Interview with former EP Group Leader, April 2002.

[25] See Court of Auditors Special Report No 13/2000, [2000] OJ C181/1, 28 June 2000.

[26] See Bureau Decision on European Parliament Support for European Political Parties (adopted at the Bureau meeting of 2 October 2000) DV\424902EN.doc.

[27] Interview, December 2001.

legally. Provided we get the details right, I am content that Article 308 be used, not least to ensure full transparency of funding for [euro-parties] as soon as possible.'[28] During the European Parliamentary debate, the legality of the proposal was questioned by MEPs from various euro-sceptic and/or rightwing groups in particular such as EDD,[29] UEN[30] and TGI,[31] with one MEP even threatening court action in the event that the measure was adopted.[32]

The publication of the Commission's proposal[33] was accompanied by all the expected rhetoric on enhancing the connectedness of the EU to its citizens. The Commission's press release commented that:

> This legislative initiative represents major political progress. It helps to create the right conditions for forging the much needed link between the institutions—the European Parliament in particular—and the citizens of the Union.[34]

Alongside the rhetoric of democratising the EU, the draft dealt in practice with the more banal aspects of the functional criteria necessary for an organisation to be constituted as a European political party, including the requirement that a European party have a formal statute in the sense of formal establishment in the European Union, and that it have appropriate levels of representation across the EU and its Member States. The measure would also have regulated the nature and extent of funding that could be expected and how that should be spent and accounted for. The proposal comprised a number of central principles which have continued to dominate debate about institutional forms for euro-parties, notwithstanding the eventual failure of this first formal proposal:

- The requirement that parties must address issues relating to European integration in their political work, but with no stipulation that they must adopt pro-European standpoints;
- The principle that any parties which are recognised must apply democratic party procedures;
- The principle that *European* political parties must necessarily be representative beyond national borders (although the precise degree of that transnational representativeness always remained highly contested); and

[28] Select Committee on European Scrutiny First Report,' Statute and Financing of European Political Parties,'<http://www.publications.parliament.uk/pa/cm200102/cmselect/cmeuleg/152-i/15260.htm> (14 April 2005).

[29] Europe of Democracies and Diversities: a euro-sceptic group with a broad political base, superseded in the 2004–2009 European Parliament by the Independence/Democracy group.

[30] Union for a Europe of the Nations: a rightwing euro-sceptic group.

[31] Technical Group of Independents, mainly composed of rightwing MEPs not affiliated to any other group; this group no longer exists in the European Parliament.

[32] See 'Report on the proposal for a Council regulation on the statute and financing of European political parties', Debate May 16 2001, verbatim report available on the EP website <http://www.europarl.eu.int>.

[33] Commission Proposal for a Council Regulation on the statute and financing of European political parties, COM(2000) 898, [2001] OJ C 154 E/283.

[34] *Commission proposes statute for European political parties* Press Release IP/01/106, Brussels, (25 January 2001).

- The application of transparent procedures for the disbursement of funds from the EU budget and the expenditure of the euro-parties.

During 2001, the European Parliament's Constitutional Affairs Committee worked on the proposal, and Ursula Schleicher (EPP-ED—rapporteur) drafted a report proposing a series of 25 amendments to the Commission draft which were adopted in Committee in May 2001,[35] perhaps the most significant of which concerned the threshold for what constitutes *European* party entitled to financial support. With enlargement in view (and consequently what was then an uncertain number of future members), the Committee adopted an amendment requiring any putative euro-parties seeking financing under the budget to be present in *one third* of the Member States. In the event, the parliamentary plenary in its vote on 17 May 2001 opted for a threshold of *one quarter* of the Member States.[36]

Many of the amendments were concerned with issues of democracy and transparency, in particular the requirement that not only should a party's statute proclaim the organisation's adherence to democracy and rule of law but also that these commitments should appear in the party programme. The Committee also sought to ensure that, once recognised, the European political parties would have legal personality which would enable them to 'purchase and dispose of movable and immovable assets and bring legal actions.'[37] In addition, the Committee wanted to see the scope of certain budgetary aspects extended, including the requirement to publish a list of donors and the prohibition on all anonymous donations.[38]

The report was eventually forwarded to the plenary session by the Constitutional Affairs Committee after a vote of twenty members in favour, four against and five abstentions. A minority opinion was presented by José Ribeiro e Castro (UEN) who argued strongly against the proposal:

> I consider the adoption of this report to be premature and the approval of any regulation intended to finance European political parties to be inappropriate.[39]

The motion supporting the proposal was passed in the plenary session of the European Parliament, but not without doubts being expressed in some quarters. Speaking on behalf of the Greens/EFA group, Professor Sir Neil MacCormick said:

> Any proposal for public funding of political parties is open to serious risks, and may add to the suspicion many people feel towards politicians. Above all, this must not become a device whereby big or established parties use tax payers' money to protect

[35] See also *Report on the proposal for a Council regulation on the statute and financing of European political parties* (A5-0167/2001), Committee on Constitutional Affairs, Rapporteur: Ursula Schleicher, 3 May 2001.

[36] Texts adopted by Parliament, Thursday 17 May 2001, Statute and financing of European political parties, P5_TA(2001)0272.

[37] Above n 35, Amendment 12, Article 1a (new).

[38] Above n 35, Amendment 15, Article 3 para 2.

[39] See Report, *Minority Position* by José Ribeiro e Castro, included in the Report above n 35 at 22.

> their near monopoly of Parliamentary representation. A democratic system must always be open to new voices, and new entrants. The tendency of the Schleicher report to revise thresholds for recognition of European Parties discriminates actively against new voices. It also discriminates against parties which are by their nature based in small regions and countries of the EU that are part of large member states.[40]

After approval by the European Parliament, the Commission reconsidered its proposal and adopted the majority of the Parliament's amendments.[41] The amended draft went before the General Affairs Council at the end of October 2001. Three main areas of concern had emerged by this stage concerning representational criteria, democratic criteria and financial criteria. Moreover, it was becoming apparent by this stage that there was a significant danger that the draft as approved by the Parliament and amended by the Commission was going to be substantially watered down during its passage through the Council legislative machinery. A number of significant reservations about what was happening to the draft were expressed by the heads of the five transnational parties in a letter addressed to Belgian Presidency in October 2001.[42] These concerns coalesced around the criteria to qualify for funding, the timetable associated with the implementation of any measure adopted which appeared to require a complete separation of the euro-party from the Party Group within 20 days of the publication of the Regulation in the Official Journal of the European Communities, and the levels of funding particularly in relation to initial start-up costs. Even so, the existing euro-parties did not waver in their general support for the measure.

Despite this consensus of the actors affected, the requirement of unanimity in Article 308 saw the proposal fall in particular as a result of two key disagreements. The Austrian and Italian governments found themselves under pressure from smaller coalition partners over the question of what, in representational terms, constitutes a euro-party. They argued for very low thresholds. France and Germany (then two PES governments) disagreed between themselves sharply over the question of allowing or prohibiting sponsorship and donations. The proposal went back to the Committee of Permanent Representatives (COREPER) after preliminary discussion in Council on 29 October 2001,[43] but in COREPER the problems concerning the definition of a European political party and issues relating to funding failed to be resolved by the Belgium Presidency at the end of 2001. The proposal was therefore shelved, and it would appear that by this stage some of the euro-parties may have been content that the proposal was lost because the effect of unanimous voting under the pre-Nice arrangements had resulted in an unacceptable watering down of the proposals. They preferred to wait for the

[40] Press Corner Greens-EFA, *Calls for Openness, inclusiveness and transparency on financing of European Political Parties* Press Release Strasbourg (16 May 2001).

[41] COM(2001) 343, 2001 OJ C 270 E/103.

[42] See letter of 10 October 2001, sent to the Belgian Presidency (Council Document 12738/01, PE-L 100 INST 86, 26 October 2001); document held on file by authors.

[43] See Presidency press release PRES/01/390 (29 October 2001).

maturing of the EU political system in the sense that qualified majority voting would be available for the party statute initiative once Nice was ratified.[44]

Thus the failure to secure the adoption of the proposal was even turned into a positive. PES Secretary General Ton Beumer took the line that,

> the Presidency proposals, in particular the threshold for recognition and funding, had been watered down so much, that the non-decision gives a chance for an agreement on a better basis in the near future . . . This is against the spirit of Article 191 of the Treaty and would have led to a total between 15 to 20 'European Parties'. The majority of these parties would be constructed for financial reasons and would have no representative character at EU level.[45]

Once the Treaty of Nice had been finally ratified by Ireland after its second referendum in late 2002, and had entered into force on 1 February 2003, this changed the terrain. It enabled the issue to be dealt with on the basis of co-decision procedures between the Council and the European Parliament and qualified majority voting (QMV) within the Council.

However, one final piece in the political jigsaw needs to be considered before the focus is placed on the 2003 proposal, and that concerns the Declaration on Article 191 EC issued by the Member States at the same time as they agreed the amendment to Article 191 EC through the Treaty of Nice. This Declaration provides:

> The Conference recalls that the provisions of Article 191 do not imply any transfer of powers to the European Community and do not affect the application of the relevant national constitutional rules.
>
> The funding for political parties at the European level provided out of the budget of the European Communities may not be used to fund, either directly or indirectly, political parties at national level.
>
> The provisions on the funding for political parties shall apply, on the same basis, to all the political forces represented in the European Parliament.

In other words, notwithstanding the strengthening of the terms of Article 191, through the addition of a operational clause, the Member States still wanted to signal their concern to protect the autonomy and interests of national constitutions and their fear that subventions through the EU budget might be re-directed towards *national* political forces, thus giving rise to the accusations of interference. Paradoxically, it is hard to see how the further institutional and political development of the euro-parties inevitably can avoid the outcome where euro-parties gradual develop their *sovereignty vis-à-vis* their member parties.

[44] The proposal was only finally withdrawn on 31 December 2003, after the subsequent proposal had been adopted in accordance with the revised post-Nice legislative process.

[45] See Ton Beumer, *The European Party Statute: how to proceed after the Council's failure to decide*, 13 December 2001, p1; document on file with authors.

The 2003 Regulation on European Political Parties: Negotiation, Adoption and Implementation[46]

The Commission wasted little time after the coming into force of the Treaty of Nice on 1 February 2003 before introducing a new proposal for a Regulation. From certain political perspectives there was only a short and a restricted window of opportunity to finalise the Regulation. The EU Presidency in the first half of 2003 was held by Greece. Greece had a history of giving support to supranational political initiatives such as the development of Article 191. Greece's Presidency was to be followed by that of Italy in the second half of 2003, and Italy was known already to be a sceptic, if not an opponent of regulating political parties at European level, having opposed the 2001 proposal. It could hardly have been expected to be an enthusiastic broker of an agreement between a majority of Member States during its Presidency. Thereafter the Presidency passed to Ireland in early 2004, and Ireland likewise had never been a driving force in the matter of euro-parties. Consequently, if developments were not to be furthered delayed until well into 2004, there remained only a short five month window of opportunity between the coming into force of the Treaty of Nice and the end of the Greek Presidency. Matters were further complicated by other developments expected and unexpected which occurred to crowd the agenda the Greek Presidency, such as the completion of the work of the Convention on the Future of Europe in June/July 2003 and the war in Iraq from March 2003 onwards.

Officially, the co-decision procedure between the European Parliament involves a Commission proposal, a European Parliament first reading, and then a Council common position. At that point, if the three institutions are agreed on the text, the measure can be already adopted at that point in the procedure, but if not—as normally happens—a second European Parliament reading will follow. There may also be a period of conciliation between the Parliament and the Council to reach a final agreed text. All this takes more time than was available. Some liberties had to be taken with the process. Consequently, once the Commission's proposal was published in March 2003,[47] both the European Parliament *and* the Council, in the form of Working Groups, immediately started work on the text, both separately and in close collaboration. The process was actively facilitated both by the Greek Presidency, and also by the Commission. The task of preparing the crucial Report for the European Parliament was given to PES member Jo Leinen, a German MEP. His report to the Constitutional Affairs

[46] Much of the data which is used to inform the analysis in this Section is derived from presentations and interventions made by key practitioner informants from the EPP, the PES, the ELDR and the Greens at a European Science Foundation funded workshop on the future of Transnational Parties organised by Stephen Day, and held at Goodenough College, London, 17–18 December 2003. We are grateful to these practitioners for sharing their views about the 2003 Regulation and the task of implementing it so frankly. For the final workshop report see <http://www.esf.org/generic/1654/EW02163 Report.pdf>.

[47] Proposal for a Regulation of the European Parliament and of the Council on the statute and financing of European political parties, COM(2003) 77 final.

Committee was accepted on 20 May 2003,[48] suggesting 24 amendments to the original Commission proposal. As a result of the regular contacts with Council and national officials, the MEPs were by then already sanguine about what could be achieved in this phase of the legislative evolution of the system of European political parties, and much of the emphasis of the amendments was upon scaling down expectations which the wording of the Commission proposal might have given rise to, as well as trying to secure the Parliament's position on what it saw as some of the crucial questions. In particular, the Parliament wished to see the Commission take responsibility for disbursing the funds available for euro-parties, rather than this being the responsibility of the Parliament.

At this point, the Council took the relatively unusual step of engaging in a detailed political procedure leading to a specific political agreement *before* the formal first reading in the European Parliament (scheduled for 19 June 2003). Alongside the regular contacts that took place with key MEPs involved in the Parliament's work, at the initiative of the Greek Presidency the Working Party on General Affairs had discussions on the proposed Regulation at 10 meetings between 7 March 2003 and 10 June 2003, which produced a compromise agreed text[49] and identified five issues which could only be resolved at ministerial level. These did not include the European Parliament's wish to be relieved of responsibility for the disbursement of funds. That point was lost even below the ministerial level. After a final meeting of COREPER on 11 June 2003, just below the level of the ministers, which likewise failed to find a consensus, the Greek Presidency put forward a number of proposals to the meeting of the General Affairs Council on 16 June 2003 specifically on the disputed points.[50]

These concerned the level of representativity of a *European* political party, the threshold for declaring the sources of donations, the maximum limits on donations from individual donors, the maximum level of contributions from national political parties to euro-parties as a proportion of the euro-party's budget, and question of a reference to the financing of (European Parliamentary) election campaigns in the list of permissible or impermissible activities for euro-parties. In contrast to 2001, with the shadow of qualified majority voting and of the impact of Council-European Parliament co-decision hanging over the legislative process, agreement could be reached at the political level[51] on a text based closely on the Presidency compromise.[52] This in turn was forwarded to the Parliament as the hoped for basis for the Parliament plenary first reading of the proposed Regulation on 19 June 2003.

The Council's political agreement was then converted into a series of compromise amendments to the text approved by the Constitutional Affairs Committee, put forward in the name of Jo Leinen, the Rapporteur, to the plenary. This allowed

[48] *Report of the Committee on Constitutional Affairs on the proposal for a European Parliament and Council regulation on the statute and financing of European political parties* (A5-0170/2003), Rapporteur: Jo Leinen, 21 May 2003.
[49] Council Document 10296/1/03 REV 1, 10 June 2003.
[50] Council Documents 10451/03, 12 June 2003 and Council Document 10530/03, 16 June 2003.
[51] General Affairs Council, Council Press Release 10370.03 (Presse 167) 16 June 2003.
[52] Council Document 10601/03, 16 June 2003.

the Parliament to avoid endangering the effective conclusion of the legislative process before the end of June 2003, although possibly at the expense of failing to exercise the full extent of its political powers under the co-decision procedure. Certainly, the co-decision process was peculiarly truncated on this occasion. On the other hand, as there had been regular contacts all along between Council and Presidency officials and MEPs, it can be assumed that the Presidency text itself was designed to meet the minimum expectations of MEPs. There were certainly some key areas of difference between the original Leinen Report and the agreed Council text. For example, the latter contained references to 'alliances of political parties', which means 'structured cooperation between at least two political parties', which had been in original Commission proposal. Many MEPs had earlier expressed objections to the idea that a euro-party could be formed through an 'alliance' of political parties, which they felt opened the way for too much opportunism through parties coming together for the precise objective of securing EU level funding, rather than because of some shared ideological objectives. However, this Council-inspired wording survived into the final Regulation (Article 2(2) and (3)) because it was adopted—albeit a little reluctantly—by the European Parliament in its first reading.

Furthermore, the Council text was structured in a rather simpler way distinguishing the 'essence' of a political party at European level (Article 3), from the question of application for funding, which in turn required the applicant to satisfy the conditions in Article 3 (Article 4). Crucially, however, the European Parliament majority view on the representativity of euro-parties largely carried the day, with the following key thresholds being eventually adopted:

- representation in the European Parliament, or national or regional legislative assemblies in at least one quarter of the Member States; or
- receipt of at least three per cent of the votes cast in one quarter of Member States at the most recent European Parliament elections.[53]

In respect of the latter condition, the Leinen Report indicated that the majority of MEPs would probably have preferred a five per cent threshold.[54] The reduction to three per cent was undoubtedly intended to be a gesture towards the situation of the regionalist party-based European Free Alliance, which would not be contesting elections on a nationwide basis.

On the fraught question of donations, positions very close to the Leinen Report were adopted in the Presidency compromise and the eventual Regulation. Thus euro-parties are prohibited from receiving any anonymous donations, any donations from the budgets of the political groups of the European Parliament, donations from state-controlled public bodies, and donations exceeding €12,000 per annum from any one donor.[55] Euro-parties must declare all sources of income,

[53] Article 3 of Regulation 2004/2003, above n 3.
[54] Leinen Report, above n 48 at 12.
[55] Article 6(c) of Regulation 2004/2003, above n 3; the Leinen Report had suggested capping individual donations at €15,000, above n 48 at 14.

with the exception of donations under €500.[56] The compromise text introduced one limitation not included in the Leinen Report, namely a capping of the ceiling of the possible contributions of national member parties to euro-parties at 40 per cent of the annual budget of the euro-party. It is worth noting that the proportion of the funding charged to the general budget of the EU must not exceed 75 per cent of the budget of any given euro-party, so that in practice national party funding cannot fall below 25 per cent of the annual budget (Article 10(2)).[57] This is because the likelihood of any euro-parties receiving donations or payments other than national party membership subscriptions remains, in almost all cases, rather remote. This means that membership subscriptions are likely to be important sources of revenue in the medium term. Article 10(1) of the Regulation also maintained the longstanding compromise between the parties that the distribution of the budget for euro-parties should be based on equal shares for each eligible euro-party of the first 15 per cent of funding, plus distribution in proportion to the number of MEPs for the residual 85 per cent.

One final controversy divided the parties involved in the legislative procedure, namely the question of what purposes the funding of euro-parties could be devoted to. In accordance with the requirements of the Declaration appended to Article 191, the parties were all agreed from the beginning that the contributions to euro-parties should not be used to finance, directly or indirectly, national parties.[58] There was no such agreement on whether there should be any reference to election campaigns, notably European Parliament election campaigns, in the list of permissible activities. The Leinen Report had inserted a specific reference to financing European Parliamentary election campaigns,[59] but the compromise text and the eventual Regulation opted for a vaguer formulation, referring to appropriations being used for the purposes of the political programme which each euro-party must put forward as part of its funding application package, and referring to an non-exclusive list of possible activities which euro-parties might pursue such as meetings, research, cross-border events, studies information and publications.[60] This formula did not opt for any of the contradictory alternatives put forward by various parties which included explicitly including EP election campaigns, and explicitly excluding any election campaigns. Presumably EP election campaigns are included so long as the proviso in Article 7 on national parties is observed. In other words, they must be genuinely *European* campaigning activities.

One element which was no longer a matter of controversy and dispute between the majority of parliamentarians, the Commission and the overwhelming majority of Member States was the inclusion in the Regulation of an explicit statement

[56] The Leinen Report, above n 48 at 14 had suggested €1000, while the original Commission proposal suggested a rather unrealistic €100 (see above n 47, Article 5(3)(b)). The Presidency text was a true compromise between the two!

[57] Euro-party insiders had long—and ultimately unsuccessfully—argued for this figure to be 85%, requiring them only to raise 15% of their revenue from other means.

[58] Article 6 of the proposal, above n 47; Article 7 of Regulation 2004/2003, above n 3.

[59] Leinen Report, above n 48 at p 16.

[60] Article 8 of Regulation 2004/2003, above n 3.

requiring euro-parties to respect the fundamental principles on which the European Union is founded (ie liberty, democracy, respect for human rights and fundamental freedoms, and the rule of law[61]) in both their programmes and activities. This is to be found in Article 3(c) of the new Regulation, and verification of compliance with this condition is passed under Article 5(2) to the European Parliament. If the issue is raised by one quarter of the MEPs, then successful verification that the condition continues to be met requires an absolute majority of MEPs (ie 50% + 1). Before carrying out such a verification, natural justice must be observed, with the Parliament giving hearing rights to any euro-party affected. Furthermore, it also must ask for the opinion of a committee of independent eminent persons.[62] However, there is no reference in the body of the Regulation to the Charter of Rights, although it is referred to in paragraph 4 of the Preamble.

The approach to the legislative process taken to secure this rather hasty agreement upon a compromise text unsurprisingly perturbed opponents of the Regulation on euro-parties in the European Parliament. At the beginning of the Parliament's first reading debate on 18 June 2003, objections were raised to the presentation of more than 50 additional amendments just one day before the plenary session, which arguably challenged the Parliament's capacity to act democratically and openly. Some therefore called for the text to be referred back to the Committee—a tactic which would obviously have had the effect wrecking the delicate political compromise.[63] Although the compromise text was passed by an overwhelming majority (when only a simple majority was required),[64] the results of the roll call vote recorded on the Parliament's website show that a number of Party Groups were split by the proposal. This was the case in particular for the composite Green/EFA Group, with the Greens being largely in favour, and the EFA MEPs being overwhelmingly against. The reason for this lay for the most part in the 'statist' nature of the criteria of representativity (Article 3), even though they included representation in regional parliaments and legislative assemblies. Professor Sir Neil MacCormick (Greens/EFA) referred during the debate to the nine stateless nations from just *three* Member States from which members of the EFA in the European Parliament were drawn. He went on to argue for rejection of the compromise on the grounds that:

[61] This list is drawn from Article 6 of the Treaty of European Union.

[62] This echoes the informal procedure used to settle the dispute within the EU under which 14 of the Member States purported to apply 'sanctions' at a political level against Austria, when the Austrian conservative People's Party entered into a coalition with the far-right Freedom Party (FPÖ) at the end of 1999. Three 'wise men' (Martti Ahtisaari, former President of Finland, Jochen Frowein, eminent international lawyer, and Marcelino Oreja, former Spanish Foreign Minister, European Commissioner and Secretary General of the Council of Europe) were given a mandate by the President of the European Court of Human Rights to examine a number of key questions about the nature of the FPÖ. They reported at the end of September 2000, giving Austrian politics a broadly 'clean' bill of health and allowing the lifting of the 'sanctions'.

[63] See contribution of Ribeiro e Castro (UEN) at the Plenary Debate, supported by Berthu (NI), verbatim report available on <http://www.europarl.eu.int>.

[64] 354 MEPs voted in favour; 102 against; and 34 abstained. See European Parliament legislative resolution, P5_TA-PROV (2003) 0289 of 19 June 2003.

> The European Free Alliance has been recognised for a long time as one of the original Europe-wide political families, and yet we stand on the margins of being excluded and de-recognised under these proposals.[65]

The formal first reading of the measure by the Council did not come until after the summer, in September 2003, and although this was under the Italian Presidency there were no further political compromises to make and consequently no political role for the Presidency to adopt. Even so, it is worthy of note that the decision in the Council was indeed taken by a qualified majority, with the Danish, Italian and Austrian delegations voting against.[66] The text was signed off by both the Parliament and the Council on 4 November, and the Regulation was published in the Official Journal in mid November 2003, to come into force three months after its publication with the exception of Articles 4–10 (on funding), which applied only as of the date of the opening of the first session after the European Parliament elections in June 2004 (ie 20 July 2004).[67]

It is worth noting the key differences in Regulation 2004/2003, compared to both the proposal made by the Commission and—especially—the predecessor proposals of 2001. In the first instance, the scope of the proposal is much narrower. All references to the term 'statute' have been dropped, except as something which a party must provide as part of its application for funding, rather than something which EU legislation is offering to euro-parties. It follows from this that legal personality is required under the law of the Member States in which the seat of the party is located (Article 3(a)). This means, in practice, Brussels, although it is true that the European Green Party has only just relocated its seat from Vienna to Brussels as part of its latest round of reorganisation and restructuring with a view to benefitting from the Regulation. In practice, this also means that the legal personality framework for euro-parties must be organised around the rather constraining possibilities provided under Belgian law on non-profit making bodies corporate, especially the ASBL (*association sans but lucratif*) and the AISBL (*association internationale sans but lucratif*). The constraints of the ASBL, which is the chosen legal form of the EPP under the title 'Concordia', which is a legal person which holds the physical assets and issues the employment contracts of the EPP, is that it requires a high percentage of the board members to be Belgian. The ELDR and the Greens formed new AISBLs in the first months of 2004 in preparation for the rules coming into force,

The eventual compromise view was that since it was clear that the Regulation was not going to provide a 'real' statute, in the sense inspired, for example, by the model of the European Company Statute or *societas europaea*, then all references to the term 'Statute' should disappear from the text of the Regulation. The Regulation is a limited, baseline, mechanism for regulating *some* rules relating to political parties at European level and the rules regarding their funding (Article

[65] See the verbatim report of the debate available on <http://www.europarl.eu.int>.
[66] *Formal Council First Reading* Press Release PRES/03/251, (29 September 2003).
[67] Regulation 2004/2003, above n 3.

1). Equally it does not provide an exhaustive or complete set of rules, and many MEPs wish there to be further developments in the context of a review and report in 2006 (Article 12).[68] Certainly, it would be true that a *genuine* European Party Statute would provide as a minimum a common legal personality valid across all Member States, rather than requiring reliance upon the vagaries of national law, and the mutual recognition of legal forms across the EU. On the other hand, this has not prevented euro-parties themselves and other political actors consistently referring to the Regulation—in shorthand—as the 'European Party Statute'.

Second, the measure is more tightly drafted, especially in so far as it refers to terminology drawn from Article 191 such as 'political party at European level', rather than 'European political party'. On the other hand, it is interesting to see that it uses a fiction relating to the euro-party in the text of the Regulation as well as in the implementing rules which are discussed further below. The Regulation requires, as noted already, that 'it' (ie the euro-party) must be represented in at least one quarter of the Member States. The Regulation does not say 'must be represented by its constituent members.' The same applies in respect of the phrase 'must have received at least three per cent of the vote in EP elections' (Article 3). This clearly articulates a fiction of citizen linkage between euro-party and citizen, since it is clear that in almost all cases the citizens will have thought they were voting for a constituent national member party, and not a euro-party. On the whole, however, the final Regulation resembles quite strongly the recommendations of the Tsatsos Report and the 2001 proposal, and it avoided much of the watering down which the 2001 proposal faced once it entered the negotiating phase within the Council of Ministers.

Four of the five main euro-parties (EPP, PES, ELDR and Greens) warmly welcomed the adoption of the Regulation, issuing positive press releases. For the Greens, for example, the adoption of the Regulation opened the way for the co-ordination of 'substantive and meaningful European election campaigns.'[69] The EPP went perhaps furthest in talking of the contribution of the Regulation to the creation of 'a European polity'.[70]

However, in addition to fervent support from some quarters, Regulation 2004/2003 also attracted fervent opposition from elsewhere in the European Parliament. The European Free Alliance condemned the Regulation as 'unfair and discriminatory' against small and regionally-based parties.[71] Jens Peter Bonde (EDD) had referred regularly to his wish to see a challenge to the legality of the Regulation on the grounds that it breached, in particular, the principle of equality, arguing that it was a system structurally biased against euro-sceptic parties. Indeed a coalition of MEPs from a number of euro-sceptic groups and national

[68] See, eg, the contributions from Leinen (Rapporteur, PES) and Marinho (PES) in the Plenary Debate on 18 June 2003 (<http://www.europarl.eu.int>).

[69] 'European Political Parties', Press Corner, 18 June 2003 <http://www.greensefa.org/en/press/detail.php?id=1448&1g=en> (14 April 2005).

[70] *Towards a European Polity* EPP Press Release, Brussels, (19 June 2003).

[71] European Free Alliance in the European Parliament, 'Proposed Statute for European Political Parties "unfair and discriminatory"', 18 June 2003, Brussels.

parties, including not only Bonde, but also a number of members of the UK Conservative group in the European Parliament,[72] have mounted an action for annulment of Regulation 2004/2003 on the basis of Article 230 EC.[73] In breach of the common convention of the confidentiality of legal proceedings, Bonde is also pursuing a policy of revealing all the key documents from the case on his website.[74]

However, it seems unlikely in view of the Court of Justice's refusal of standing under Article 230 EC to a group of MEPs seeking to challenge a measure of the Parliament concerning the terms and conditions governing internal investigations in relation to the prevention of fraud,[75] that the case will pass an initial scrutiny of admissibility raised by the defendants—the Council and the Parliament. In the *Rothley* case, the Court indicated that the requirement of effective judicial protection—including the possibility to challenge *general* measures (such as the measure on fraud prevention at issue, and doubtless also the Regulation on europarties in the *Bonde* case)—can be ensured under the legal order of the EU by means of an indirect challenge to such a measure in the event of judicial proceedings arising under an individual implementing act. Consequently, it can be anticipated that at a later stage a more fruitful line of legal challenge may lie in actions against individual disbursement decisions, or refusals.

The Implementation of Regulation 2004/2003

Veteran EPP MEP Giorgos Dimitrakopoulos was entrusted on behalf of the Committee on Constitutional Affairs with drawing up a report on the necessary amendments to the Parliament's Rules of Procedure in order to give effect to the Parliament's obligations under the Regulation.[76] These were substantially accepted by the European Parliament, meeting in Plenary on 9 March 2004.[77] The

[72] See eg, D Hannan, 'Why I am Going to the European Court', EClub/Campaign for the Truth About Europe, <http://www.campaignfortruth.com/Eclub/210404/>.

[73] Case T-13/04 *Bonde et al v Parliament and Council*, [2004] OJ C71/34 pending.

[74] See <http://www.bonde.com>, specifically the section devoted to SOS Democracy. This is an official 'intergroup' in the European Parliament, which works for openness, decentralisation and democracy in the EU. Article 4(2) of Regulation 1049/2001 regarding public access to European Parliament, Council and Commission documents, [1991] OJ L 145/43 provides that:

The institutions shall refuse access to a document where disclosure would undermine the protection of . . . court proceedings and legal advice . . . unless there is an overriding public interest in disclosure.

This provision has been interpreted by the Court of First Instance in T-105/95 *WWF UK v Commission* [1997] ECR II–313 and Case T–191/99 *Petrie et al v Commission* [2001] ECR II–3677.

[75] See Case C–167/02 P *Rothley et al v Parliament*, judgment of 30 March 2004.

[76] Report on the amendments to the European Parliament's Rules of Procedure following the adoption of the Regulation governing the statute and the financing of political parties at European level, A5–0071/2004, 19 February 2004. This was a typical example of European Parliament bipartisanship and 'balance'. Note that it was a joint Dimitrakopoulos/Leinen Report on proposals for the Nice IGC which firmly placed the issue of operationalising Article 191 EC on the agenda (A5–0058/1999, PE 231.873/fin, 10 November 1999).

[77] European Parliament Decision on the amendments to the European Parliament's Rules of Procedure following the adoption of the Regulation governing the status and the financing of political parties at European level, P5_TA–PROV(2004)0144.

changes to the Rules of Procedure,[78] in accordance with a wide consensus within the European Parliament, passed the role of implementing the Regulation in large measure to the Bureau of the European Parliament. The Bureau consists of the President of the Parliament, and the 14 Vice-Presidents, the role of which—in essence—is to 'take financial, organisational and administrative decisions on matters concerning Members and the internal organisation of Parliament, its Secretariat and its bodies' (Rule 22(2) of the Rules of Procedure). However, applications for funding are made—nominally—to the President of the Parliament who is now officially entrusted with the Parliament's relations with euro-parties and thus will sign contracts disbursing funds. The next and final stage of general implementing rules required a Decision of the Bureau of the Parliament, laying down the procedures on calls for proposals and funding applications, as well as grant award agreements.[79] Simultaneous calls for proposals to access the budgets for 2004 (€6.5 m) and 2005 (€8.4 m) were issued on 18 June 2004, with an initial deadline for the 2004 call for proposals of 23 July 2004.[80] By that time, each party would know what its likely share of the pot would be. This is a calculation to be made on the basis of how many euro-parties were formally in existence and able to apply for funding on 23 July 2004, combined with the results of the European Parliament elections of June 2004, and the consequential formation of political groups within the European Parliament themselves allied to one or more euro-parties.[81]

Before dwelling in more detail on these rules, it is first worth noting that back in 1996, the Tsatsos Report helpfully articulated the basic principles under which it would be acceptable and legitimate to use public funds to finance the euro-parties[82]:

> The contributions must
>
> (a) be based on explicit authorization granted by a Community legal act passed specifically for this purpose and be shown separately in the Community budget;
>
> (b) be distributed in accordance with the principle of equality of opportunity, with newly established parties given a fair chance, with account being taken of the number of Member States in which the parties are represented;

[78] The 16th Edition of the Rules of Procedure (July 2004 edition) is available from the European Parliament's website (<http://www.europarl.eu.int>).

[79] See Decision of the Bureau of the European Parliament laying down the procedures for implementing Regulation 2004/2003 governing political parties at European level, etc [2004] OJ L155/1.

[80] See Call for Proposals, Budget Line 3710, Contributions to European Political Parties, [2004] OJ L161/2 and L161/5.

[81] It is interesting to note that since the basis of the distribution of amounts is already predetermined by legislation, those parties passing the basic thresholds for funding will not as such be competing for funds. The difficulty will be in working out in advance what a party's putative share would be (based on the number of eligible parties, and the number of MEPs assigned to each party), and then planning the budget around that, bearing in mind the residue must come from other sources such as donations (limited both by legislation and also in practice) and fees from member parties. As the budget for 2005 is €8.4 m and there are expected to be seven parties eligible to apply (rather than the current five) then each party would get just €180k basic as their equal share of the first 15%.

[82] See Tsatsos Report, above n 12 at para 16.

(c) be tied to the fulfilment of the mission at European Union level resulting from Article [191] of the EC Treaty;

(d) be linked to the requirement that the recipients disclose their financial circumstances; such mandatory disclosure includes all other revenue (Members' contributions, donations, etc);

(e) give the recipients a financial incentive to strengthen their roots in society and seek greater financial autonomy.

These constitute a useful reference point against which to judge the composite system comprising Regulation 2004/2003 itself, the amendments to the European Parliament's Rules of Procedure, and the Decision of the Bureau. It is worth noting that there is a potential 'bad press' for the euro-parties associated with the receipt of 'taxpayers' money', not only in Member States where parties are not so funded (eg the United Kingdom), but even in Member States where they actually are (eg Germany). Consequently, every element of the rules is focused on financial probity and transparency—doubtless to some extent at the expense of simplicity, with heavy bureaucratic requirements now placed on euro-parties wishing to apply for funding. At the same time, euro-parties themselves have many more practical tasks associated with 'cutting the umbilical cord' linking them to the European Parliament Groups, in particular tasks associated with the running of separate premises and the employment of staff under contracts governed by Belgian law. This is problematic for euro-parties, whose staff were previously predominantly employed on contracts as *fonctionnaires* within the European Parliament. Contracts governed by Belgian law mean employment subject to Belgian law, with all the taxation, social security and employment law consequences which follow from that. In practice, employees employed under Belgian law require gross pay which is double that of *fonctionnaires* to receive the same net pay, because of the level of mandatory deductions.

Budgetary autonomy brings responsibility. Not only must euro-parties apply for funding, they must also report before they receive a final tranche of their funding (20 per cent)—normally in arrears after the end of the financial year. That suggests they must have reserves to bridge them from one financial year to the next. They must produce financial statements for the previous year verified by an external auditor in order to qualify for funding for the following year, and yet the deadline for funding for each year falls before the end of the calendar year. Although Regulation 2004/2003 refers to certain documents being produced for the first application only (eg statute and political programme), in practice the Calls for Proposals appear to require these documents on each and every occasion an application is made.[83] The approach of the Regulation and the implementing rules seems to constrain the freedom of manoeuvre of the euro-parties which must notify changes in their political programmes to the European Parliament. Furthermore the Bureau Decision[84] refers to a 'programme of activities' (Article

[83] See above n 80 at point 2.5.
[84] See above n 79.

6(3)), which is a much more specific and constraining concept than a 'political programme' and seems calculated to prevent euro-parties responding in a flexible way to political developments by planning new activities. To obtain all the funding it is awarded, the euro-party will be required to demonstrate that the programme of activities promised in the application for funding has actually been carried out.

The requirements associated with applying for funding and then reporting to secure the full payment of budgetary appropriations together mean that verification of euro-parties' compliance with the conditions in Article 3 of the Regulation on what constitutes a 'political party at European level' will in practice and at a basic level be constant and ongoing, rather than 'regular', as is proposed by Article 5(1) for Article 3(a) and (b) (legal personality and representativity), and episodic on request of one quarter of MEPs, as is proposed by Article 5(2) for Article 3(c). Rather the obligations imposed—largely for reasons of budgetary propriety—on the Bureau under its own Decision require constant checking of the compliance of the euro-parties with every element of the conditions. In addition, the Article 3(d) condition will have to be verified (intention to participate in European Parliament elections), even though somewhat strangely no verification mechanism is provided in respect of this condition in the Regulation.[85]

The condition relating to legal personality was introduced to ensure the permanence and formal legal status of all euro-parties; the condition on representativity was introduced to secure a minimum concept of what constitutes a euro-party; the condition on EU principles was introduced to ensure that anti-democratic parties could not secure funding as euro-parties; the condition relating to participation in the European Parliament elections was introduced to ensure that euro-parties would address European integration issues—in whatever way—in their political activities. In practice, compliance with two of the conditions can be demonstrated as a simple matter of fact (legal personality and representativity); regarding participation in the European Parliament election, this is also either a matter of fact (in the event of a party that has existed during a time period when such an election has been held) or alternatively, for a new euro-party, must be a matter for self-certification regarding a future intention. Only the application of the fourth condition regarding liberty, democracy, human rights and the rule of law will involve political judgment, and it is likely to be hugely controversial in practice to apply. Thus it is rather hard to see the Bureau actually applying that condition to deny funding at the application stage—since it would prefer presumably that formal verification should take place under the provisions of Article 5(2) of the Regulation. Even so formal compliance with the condition, in the sense of production of relevant documents and statements will nonetheless constitute a continuing burden on all parties which must prove their democratic credentials every time they apply for funding. However, in all cases, all these

[85] Richard Corbett (PES) drew attention to what he assumed to be an oversight in his contribution to the Plenary First Reading debate in the European Parliament on 18 June 2003, verbatim report on <http://www.europarl.eu.int>.

burdens will fall disproportionately and more heavily upon the smaller parties, where administrative back-up will be much more limited than it is for either the EPP or the PES, or even for the ELDR.

The requirements on the parties comprise, in sum, a combination of one-off set-up costs, and ongoing bureaucratic constraints and frameworks, which will imply higher operating costs for the euro-parties, and may make their operation less efficient in the future. On the other hand, they will operate on a substantially more transparent and open basis, and their activities will be more immediately visible as autonomous and separate activities of 'political parties at European level'. The question is: with the level of funding available, and the requirements which they must satisfy, what level of activities will they be able, in practice, to undertake? Moreover, with such bureaucratic and budgetary constraints, it is hard to see in practice how and why the availability of funding will be an overwhelming incentive for national parties to set up a political party or alliance of parties at the European level, absent other strong reasons for creating such an arrangement.

This would seem to suggest that there is some risk that EU budgetary funding for euro-parties will indeed increase the risk of the emergence of the so called 'cartel party' in the EU context. Katz and Mair argue that

> by operating as a cartel, by attempting to ensure that there are no clear 'winners' and 'losers' among the established alternatives, and by exploiting their control of the state to generate resources which can be shared out among themselves, the cartel parties are often unwittingly providing precisely the ammunition with which the new protesters of the right can more effectively wage their wars.[86]

One of the amendments to the 2001 proposal brought before the European Parliament Constitutional Affairs Committee by Olivier Dupuis (TGI) highlighted those fears. The amendment, which was rejected, suggested that

> it is necessary to stress the perverse effects which the public funding of political parties has had in a number of countries of the European Union, notably Italy, both from the point of view of corruption and from the point of view of the functioning of the institutions.[87]

Funding was also an issue picked up by members of the British Conservative Party, who would find themselves unlikely to be able to benefit from the EU funding of political parties as the Party is not a member of the EPP.[88] Frances Maude claimed that:

[86] R Katz and P Mair, 'Changing Models of Party Organisation: The Emergence of the Cartel Party' (1995) 1 *Party Politics* 5–28 at 24.

[87] See 'Amendment 21' in Amendments 11–78 Draft Report by Ursula Schleicher on the proposal for a Council regulation on the statute and financing of European political parties, PE 294.765/11–78.

[88] British Conservative MEPs do, however, sit with the broader EPP-ED group in the European Parliament, although their generally euro-sceptic tinge contrasts strongly with the federalist heritage of the Christian Democrat core of the EPP-ED.

> People will be highly suspicious of this attempt to increase the European Union's control of political parties. This cannot be good for freedom of speech or democracy . . . It will increase the pressure on all EU political parties to dance to the tune of EU bureaucrats rather than voters.[89]

Whether, on the contrary, as Tsatsos earlier suggested they should, the new rules will 'give the recipients a financial incentive to strengthen their roots in society and seek greater financial autonomy'[90] seems more doubtful. In many respects, Tsatsos' contribution must be seen as prescient in respect of the types of constraints which the receipt of public funding would be likely to result in bringing about for euro-parties.

Conclusions: Pathways and Crossroads

These reflections lead neatly into an attempt to draw together some of the threads of this chapter into a concluding section. There are, of course, clear advantages for the euro-parties and for the probity of EU budgetary affairs overall stemming from the conclusion and implementation of Regulation 2004/2003. The adoption of this measure, albeit limited and indeed limiting in its effects, did at least bring to an end a period of considerable legal and budgetary uncertainty. There will be no more criticisms, it is to be hoped, from the Court of Auditors, on the budgetary front.

It is commendable—if politically disappointing for strong partisans of the idea of supranational European parties placed on a common legal basis—that the misleading language of the 'Statute' has effectively been eradicated from the Regulation, if not from political discourse. Urged in this respect by the Leinen Report,[91] the final Regulation declared its modest scope in Article 1 to be that of establishing 'rules on the regulations governing political parties at European level and rules regarding their funding.' It is hardly surprising, given that it took more than thirty years to agree a common framework for incorporation of the so called European Company or *societas europaea*, that no political agreement could be reached on rules which might provide even the embryo of a genuine 'party statute' in the very limited time available. On the contrary, a party statute is something provided under the Regulation and the implementing rules *by the euro-party* itself in the course of applying for funding, and it must define,

> in particular the bodies responsible for political and financial management as well as the bodies or natural persons holding, in each of the Member States concerned, the power of legal representation, in particular for the purposes of the acquisition or disposal of movable and immovable property and of being a party to legal proceedings' (Article 4(1)(c)).

[89] 'Tory furore over EU party funds' BBC News, 17 January 2001, <http://news.bbc.co.uk/1/hi/uk_politics/1121785.stm>(16 May 2005).
[90] See above n 82.
[91] Above n 48.

Legal personality is to be obtained under *national law* alone.

The swiftness with which agreement was reached on the Regulation between the three key parties—European Parliament, Council and Commission—showed the overwhelming value and flexibility of the co-decision procedure in facilitating decision-making at the EU level. Without co-decision, it is hard to imagine that any type of agreement would have been reached, and consequently the legally uncertain situation pertaining hitherto would inevitably have continued, with all the attendant difficulties that it raised in budgetary terms.

On the other hand, as the previous section highlighted, there are clear disadvantages for the euro-parties. One of the ironies of the change in the funding arrangements is that there will doubtless be a need—so far as possible—to increase funding from membership fees received from the member parties. This means that during the transitional phase and the process of breaking the umbilical linkage with the European Parliamentary Groups there is likely to be increased financial reliance on the national member parties.

Furthermore, the changes have introduced considerable upheaval. Only the EPP had premises outside the European Parliament buildings before July 2004. The other parties—with the exception of the Greens—made their moves to temporary or permanent premises in July 2004. Several of the parties changed their legal status in the run up to the coming into force of the Regulation both in terms of the adoption of forms of legal personality which would satisfy the requirements under Article 3 of the Regulation, and in terms of moves toward less confederal[92] and perhaps rather tighter frameworks as 'Parties' rather than 'Confederations' or 'Alliances'. This was the case with both the Greens (Rome, February 2004)[93] and the EFA (Barcelona, March 2004),[94] and both parties each acquired new statutes. A party of the far left was founded in Rome in May 2004,[95] and in July 2004, shortly after the European Elections, much was made in the press of the announcement of a new party of the Centre, in which both Commission President Romano Prodi and François Bayrou, leader of the French centrist UDF were said to be involved.[96] This party then immediately entered into a new alliance to form a joint Group within the European Parliament in the 2004–2009 term around an explicitly pro-European platform, the Alliance of Liberals and Democrats for Europe (ALDE). The UEN Parliamentary Group (Europe of Nations) is said to have drawn up a set of provisional party statutes so as to be eligible for funding and the former leader of the Austrian Freedom Party, Jörg Haider has also continued to pursue the goal of some form of far-right transnational entity,[97]

[92] See T Dietz, 'European Federation of Green Parties' in Johansson and Zervakis, above n 4 at 125.

[93] 'Greens meet to start up a Europe-wide party' *International Herald Tribune*, 21 February 2004; 'Green launch "first real European party"', *EU Observer*, 23 February 2004, <www.euobserver.com>.

[94] *New European Political Party to be founded in Barcelona* EFA Press Release (17 March 2004); 'Regional parties to form a European Party' *EU Observer*, 10 March 2004, <http://www.euobserver.com>.

[95] 'Communists found EU-wide party' *EU Observer*, 10 May 2004 <http://www.euobserver.com>. See its embryonic websites at <http://euroleft.org and http://sozialisten.de/sozialisten/el/index.htm>.

[96] 'Prodi to help create centrist party' *Financial Times*, 10 May 2004; R Heuzé, 'Avec le PDE, Bayrou veut faire échec au PPE' *Le Figaro*, 17 July 2004. Details of the new party can be found on the website of a national member party, the UDF, at < http://www.udf-europe.net/ >

[97] 'Haider plant EU-Liste der "populistischen parteien"' *Kurier online*, 19 May 2002.

although other evidence points in the direction of a rightwing party not emerging before 2009.[98] All this certainly appears to suggest a changing in the party landscape within the EU as a whole, including perhaps most significantly the creation of the strongest centrist Party Group in the history of the European Parliament with nearly 90 MEPs at the outset of the new Parliamentary term. It could therefore be suggested that some of the most significant developments, including the strengthening of euro-sceptic forces within the European Parliament and thus the enhancement of their already vociferous opposition to the idea of euro-party funding (although not necessar-ily the reality . . .), not to mention the increased press attention that has been given to the spectre of parties of the far right including transnational cooperation amongst them, are all products of political realignments of one type or another within both the nascent European political sphere and the national political spheres. These include, of course, EU enlargement itself. Certainly in the new landscape of potentially more diverse euro-parties, it is interesting to question what might become in the future of the dominant shadow of positive 'visions of Europe' as important catalysts for change often mentioned in earlier studies of the euro-parties. Such a vision was, for example, one of the raison d'êtres of the EPP as an explicitly federalist party, although according to critics it has found it increasingly difficult to sustain a common political platform as more traditionally conservative, rather than Christian Democratic, parties have joined its ranks. In recent years it has found that it has increasingly had to share the middle 'pro-European' ground with forces such as the ELDR and more recently the ALDE.[99]

In sum, it is clear that the effects of cutting the umbilical cord to the party groups are that the euro-parties must 'sink or swim' and they must work to prove their value-added. It is ironic that the moment of greatest opportunity for the euro-parties is simultaneously the moment of greatest risk. This is in part because of the bureaucratic constraints outlined in particular in Section V. It is also because, with the completion on 1 May 2004 of the first and largest round of post-Cold War EU Enlargements, one of the most important catalysts for the political significance of the euro-parties, namely the project of democracy promotion in the accession states has largely come to an end. The disagreements between national governments over the war in Iraq, moreover, also increased the stresses and strains on the euro-parties, as they struggled to find common ground and useful frameworks for discussion for their traditional pre-European Council party leader summits during 2003 and 2004. Other strains included the effective dismantling of the stability and growth pact, as a result of an alliance between France and Germany at the end of 2003 to evade effective sanctions for their budgetary

[98] 'European rightwing party perhaps in 2009' *EU Observer*, 31 July 2002, <http://www.euobserver.com>.

[99] 'Les partis manœuvrent pour construire une majorité au Parlement européen' *Le Monde*, 15 June 2004; 'European federalists try to regroup' *EU Observer*, 8 March 2004, <http://www.euobserver.com>; 'EPP is not swinging towards the right' Letter from EPP President Wilfried Martens to *European Voice*, 11–17 March 2004; 'Political groups in European Parliament exchange fire' *EU Observer*, 7 April 2004, <http://www.euobserver.com>; 'EPP risks split over fate of UK Conservatives', <http://www.euractiv.com>, 13 February 2004.

indiscipline.[100] Moreover, the euro-parties remained almost entirely invisible in the European Parliament elections of 2004, with the exception of the Green Party, which pushed hard its case that unity as a party also boosted election hopes[101] based on something approaching a common electoral platform. Its campaign attracted praise from the *Financial Times*.[102] After the elections, however, prospects for effective transnational parties improved again, as the party groups in the Parliament combined with euro-party interests to block the Italian government nominee to the Barroso Commission, Rocco Buttiglione, on the grounds of his highly traditionalist views on women, the family and lesbians and gays. Europarty cooperation also offered itself as one constructive way out of the crisis which arose for the EU as a result of the French and Dutch no-votes in referendums on the Constitutional Treaty in May/June 2005, and the failure of the government leaders at the European Council meeting in June 2005 to agree a budget for the EU for the financial perspective 2007–2013.

Overall, therefore, the outlook for euro-parties in the mid-2000s did not appear particularly positive, despite the tremendous optimism, at least for insiders, associated with securing agreement on Regulation 2004/2003, just a few years earlier. It is clear that Regulation 2004/2003 did provide some important concrete steps towards the institutionalisation of the normative content of Article 191 in relation to the role of political parties at the European level. There is no necessary assurance that this will have strengthened the hand of those arguing for a more supranational vision of euro-parties as genuinely autonomous political actors within an emergent European public sphere, as portrayed in the three fold typology of euro-parties outlined in Section II of this chapter. On the contrary, just as the messages regarding the future of EU integration in 2003 and 2004 were highly ambiguous, so the future of euro-parties remains uncertain for the foreseeable future.

[100] Eg 'France, Germany have "killed" stability pact: EU's Monti' *EU Business*, 3 December 2003, <http://www.eubusiness.com/afp/031203080655.gjxog0cz>.

[101] 'European Greens unite to boost election hopes' *Reuters*, 21 February 2004.

[102] See *Update*, Newsletter of the European Green Party, June 2004, <http://www.europeangreens.org/news/update/june2004.pdf>.

Index

www.ingramcontent.com/pod-product-compliance
Ingram Content Group UK Ltd.
Pitfield, Milton Keynes, MK11 3LW, UK
UKHW020831290926
15470UKWH00009B/1849/J

9 781841 135700